M000078609

KARELIA

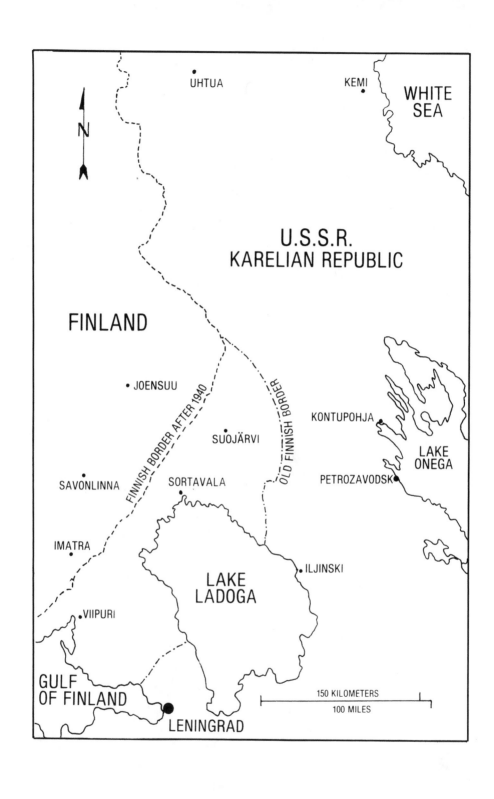

Karelia

A Finnish-American Couple in Stalin's Russia

Lawrence and Sylvia Hokkanen
with Anita Middleton

North Star Press of St. Cloud, Inc.

Library of Congress Cataloging-in-Publication Data

Hokkanen, Lawrence, 1909-
    Karelia : A Finnish-American couple in Stalin's Russia / Lawrence
and Sylvia Hokkanen with Anita Middleton.
    160 p. 23 cm.
    Includes bibliographical references.
    ISBN 0-87839-065-0 : $12.95
    1. Karel 'skaîâ A.S.S.R. (R.S.F.S.R.) — History. 2. Hokkanen,
Lawrence, 1909- . 3. Hokkanen, Sylvia, 1913- . 4. Finnish-Amer-
icans — Russian S.F.S.R. — Karel 'skaîâ A.S.S.R. — Biography. 5.
Soviet Union — History — 1925-1953. I. Hokkanen, Sylvia, 1913- .
II. Middleton, Anita, 1942 . III. Title
DK511.K18H65   1991   91-32977
947'.25—dc20   CIP

Pen and Ink Drawings: Anita Middleton

Design: Corinne A. Dwyer

Copyright: © 1991 Lawrence & Sylvia Hokkanen

All rights reserved. No part of this book may be reproduced in any form
without prior written permission from the publisher.

Published by North Star Press of St. Cloud, Inc., P.O. Box 451, St. Cloud,
Minnesota 56302. Printed in the United States of America.

ISBN: 0-87839-065-0

Foreword

This story has not been easy to write. The events took place almost sixty years ago, and much of what happened then has faded from memory—some was deliberately blocked out—and can no longer be retrieved. Recollection has been emotionally draining. Tears come easily, for what has not faded with the years, what still remains to haunt and torture us, is the fear—the stark panic of the times—the times of the Stalinist purges through which we lived. The memory of relatives and friends disappearing into the night has stayed with us through all these years.

Occasionally since that time, our daughter, Anita, and her husband, Len, would remind us that we ought to write the story of our life in Russia, but we did nothing. It was too painful to think about all that we and our friends had been through. Then too, we doubted that anyone would be interested. Finally we decided to try to recall as much as we could. Anita and Len, and even our grandchildren, have been very helpful. If it weren't for Anita, the story would even now remain unwritten; she has done a tremendous job of editing and arranging and typing—in addition to breathing down our necks. We especially appreciate the scholarly work done by Alexis Pogorelskin in providing an historical perspective to our story. Help has also come from several friends who have taken the time to read the story and have graciously submitted many helpful suggestions. We thank each one of them: particularly Flora Laun; also Hal Seppala, Bill and Nancy Saunders.

Now our story is complete, and we hope that you will find it interesting and thought-provoking.

Lawrence & Sylvia Hokkanen
Sugar Island, Michigan
September 1991

Lawrence and Sylvia Hokkanen in 1985. (Photo credit: Vivi Wiitala.)

Contents

Historical Preface

The memoir before you, while engaging in its own right, contributes to the understanding of a phenomenon of no small importance to both American social history and the history of the Soviet Union. That phenomenon is the "Karelian Fever" of the 1930s, when North American Finns, largely from the Upper Midwest and Canada, were lured to settle in Soviet Karelia to contribute to the building of communism. This subject, despite its significance, has received far too little scholarly attention and is little known, at least in this country, outside Finnish communities. For that reason alone, the labor that Lauri and Sylvi have performed, painful for them, deserves to be known.

As a professional historian I am not supposed to intrude into what I write, but in this instance the temptation is too great. Although possessing a doctorate in Russian history from Yale and having conducted research in numerous Soviet and European archives, I had never encountered a reference to Karelian Fever until coming to Duluth to teach at the University of Minnesota. I was stunned to discover neighbors and acquaintances who have relatives in the Soviet Union or who knew of those who had gone there and returned in the 1930s. Untapped sources of information about Stalin's Russia resided at my very doorstep.

I have twice been to Petrozavodsk and conducted research on Karelian Fever. The questions that formed in my mind were those of a Russian historian. Who decided to recruit American Finns to the Soviet Union and for what reason? Why Finns in particular? And finally, the question that seemed most important of all and yet whose answer might be most elusive: what impact would those foreigners have had on a closed society whose inhabitants had virtually no direct contact with the West?

After reading Lauri and Sylvi's story, I met with them, and our conversation provided an added dimension to their memoir. Lauri emphasized how distinctive were the Americans from the Soviets. Sylvi recounted that as she began to write each chapter she cried out of guilt over surviving what had destroyed so many others. A wonderfully cultured and informed person, she said she reads to understand the why of things. Their statements returned me to the questions that had already formed in my own mind. I will now attempt to address the why of Karelian Fever in my introduction to Sylvi and Lauri's memoir.

To understand Karelian Fever, one must begin with Edvard Gylling. Before becoming a Soviet citizen Gylling, as a Finn, had been a citizen of the Tsarist Empire. Russia had conquered the Grand Duchy of Finland from Sweden in 1809. The Finns retained a measure of administrative autonomy and appeared to prosper quietly under Russian control.

The apparent contentment of the Grand Duchy in fact hid a bitterly divisive issue that pitted the dominant Swedish minority against an exploited peasantry whose language was Finnish. Starting in the 1840s, a small group of Swedish intellectuals, calling themselves Fennomen, took up the cause of Finnish language and culture in opposition to their upper class brethren. Gylling joined the Fennomen early in his career but with the emergence of a Marxist party in the late 1890s he, along with "an important sector of Finnish-speaking intellectuals" abandoned the moderate Fennomen approach and joined the Marxist Social Democrats.[1]

As someone of uncommon abilities and a born politician, he played an important role in that particularly traumatic period of Finnish history, 1917-1918. Finland no sooner proclaimed its independence from Russia in December 1917, than the new nation was plunged into civil war. The landless Finnish peasantry and their Red Guards confronted the White forces representing the Swedish establishment. Gylling served as Minister of Finance in the revolutionary government that represented the cause of Finnish peasants and workers.[2]

By the spring of 1918 the Finnish radicals were clearly nearing defeat at the hands of Mannerheim and his troops. The new state of Soviet Russia offered Finnish Communists sanctuary there rather than see them massacred by Mannerheim's forces. Many, though not all, of the radicals were Communists. Gylling at that critical moment proposed to the Soviets that the Finns should settle in a seemingly obscure place of refuge, Soviet Karelia.[3] Gylling had several reasons for that suggestion. He wanted to develop the economic potential of a previously neglected region; he also saw Karelia as the base of a future Scandinavian Soviet Republic.[4] Gylling hoped that revolution would spread from Karelia to Finland and from there to the rest of Scandinavia. By monopolizing the forest wealth of Northern Europe, the Scandinavian Republic could subsidize revolution elsewhere and exert leverage on capitalist countries.[5] There is some confusion in the sources, but it seems that Lenin's government did not at first support Gylling's scheme, or at least its starting point, namely investment in the development of Soviet Karelia. Disappointed, Gylling, though a Communist, went into exile in Sweden rather than the Soviet Union. There he might have remained had not Finland and Soviet Russia begun an armed struggle for control of Karelia that raged well into 1919.[6] Finland agreed to negotiate that dispute and other outstanding issues at a conference to be convened in Dorpat, Estonia, in the fall of 1920. Lenin was determined to commence negotiations with the issue of Karelia already settled.

Gylling's previously eccentric interest in Karelia now became of prime importance. Lenin sent for him to come to Moscow and discuss the possibility of forming "an autonomous Karelian state in the Russian Socialist Republic."[7] Gylling could not help but heed Lenin's call because he was to be the "chief organizer" of the new state.[8] He placed certain conditions, however, on his cooperation. Those conditions grew out of his experience in the politico-linguistic conflicts of pre-war Finland. They were also supposed to forge Karelia as the starting point for the future Scandinavian Republic. That Lenin agreed to Gylling's conditions was a measure of his anxiety so close to negotiations with the Finns over the status of Karelia. He also recognized the merit of Gylling's argument that a stable, prosperous Karelia on the Finnish border held potential for the revolutionary cause throughout Northern Europe. No Karelian possessed the organizational abilities of Gylling. Lenin had to rely on him.

Gylling insisted that the region in population and language be Karelo-Finnish. Neither the Russian language nor a Russian population were to be allowed to dilute the ethnic homogeneity of the new state. Finally, at least a quarter of the profits from exploiting Karelian forests were to remain in Karelia.[9]

For Gylling the ethnic question was critical. As Kustaa Rovio, the first Secretary of the Karelian Communist Party and Gylling's closest associate observed, "If Russian *had* been made the language for the Karelians, the formation of an autonomous republic would have been nonsensical."[10] Gylling moved quickly to make Finnish the primary language of Karelia. He convinced Lenin that Karelian, without a written language of its own, was simply a Finnish dialect.[11] Therefore, Finnish along with Russian should be the state language of Karelia. In the absence of significant Russian immigration to Karelia, Finnish would remain the dominant language. Gylling very nearly refused to allow Petrozavodsk (the obvious choice because of its size and location) to serve as the capital of the new Karelian Workers' Commune on the grounds that it was already too Russian.

As long as Lenin lived, Gylling had his support for the existence of Karelia as a Karelo-Finnish enclave that would ignite revolution in Scandinavia. With the failure of Lenin's health in 1922, a tug of war for ethnic, (i.e. political), control of Karelia ensued. Hopelessly outnumbered, Gylling was bound to lose and be swallowed by Karelia's "host state," the greater Russian Soviet Republic.

Language, at first, constituted his primary weapon. In the early 1920s the Karelian Congress of Soviets cut the budget for Russian schools and extended financing to expand the network of Finnish schools. By 1931 "all schools in Karelian areas were operating in Finnish."[12] But Gylling could not stem the tide of Russian migration. At his insistence certain population ratios for Karelia had been established when the Treaty of Dorpat was signed.[13] By 1923 those ratios were a farce. In that year the Karelian Workers' Commune acquired new status as the Karelian Autonomous Republic. At the same time its territory was expanded, and 65,000 new inhabitants, mainly Russian, were added to its population.[14] Through the 1920s as many as four to five thousand Russians moved annually to Karelia, and Gylling frequently expressed concern over that fact.[15]

The situation became critical at the time that the first Five-Year Plan was launched in 1928. The imposition of a massive program of industrialization would provide an excuse for more intense immigration to Karelia. Party Secretary Rovio complained that Karelia's industrial work force was already "almost exclusively Russian." A new wave of Russian workers would overwhelm the more backward, agrarian Karelians whose Finnish identity Gylling had carefully nurtured through his language policy.[16]

Gylling now saw the economic potential of Karelia in direct conflict with the policy of Finnish ethnic identity which he had fostered in Karelia and supported throughout his career. The first Five-Year Plan put the issue in stark terms: how to reconcile the industrialization of Karelia and the Karelo-Finnish character of the region.

Through the course of 1929 and 1930 Gylling, Rovio and others spoke of the necessity of creating a "national proletariat" in Karelia.[17] In March 1931 Gylling began to implement a means to that end. He ordered the establishment of an Immigration Bureau to recruit labor for Karelia from elsewhere in the Soviet Union but also, the innovative addition, to recruit it from Canada and the United States.[18] Gylling's novel, yet seemingly obvious, solution to his ongoing struggle with Moscow for ethnic control of Karelia by 1931 had launched the phenomenon known as Karelian Fever.

There is an uncanny parallel between Gylling's political solution to his dilemma of the early 1930s and the central legend of the Finnish national epic, *The Kalevala*. Elias Lönnrot compiled the work in the 1840s from songs and folk tales in northern Karelia. More than a work of folklore, *The Kalevala* established a Finnish literary tradition and became the bible of the Fennomen movement. Gylling, as a committed Fennomen in his youth, would have been steeped in *The Kalevala*. There, the hero Ilmarinen, renowned for his mechanical skill and inventiveness, forges in a place called North Farm a wondrous device or miraculous mill called the Sampo, which churns out untold wealth and creates leisure. The Finns of North America, latter day Ilmarinens, traveled to the land of Kalevala and forged the "Sampo" of modern industrialization.

The Finnish communists of North America had a long record of support for Karelia and were known for their radical politics. A vehicle for recruitment among them had existed almost since the Russian Revolution. Gylling's Immigration Bureau worked through an organization called the Soviet-Karelian Technical Aid, an outgrowth of an earlier Society for Technical Aid to Soviet Russia, which began operation in New York in 1919. Its Karelian office (Karjalan Toimisto), through the 1920s had channeled assistance, mostly financial, to Karelia.[19] In fact, the Finnish communities of North America had organized "festivals, balls, theatrical performances, rallies and drives the proceeds from which were sent to the Karelian commune."[20] A few workers were recruited, but their numbers were negligible by comparison to what was to occur in the early 1930s.

Most sources maintain that as many as 10,000 people left North America for Karelia in the early 1930s, although one, probably erroneously, puts the figure at 5,000.[21] Kaarlo Tuomi, who went as a young boy with his family to Karelia, describes the mood of those people: "Group after group, in about two to three week intervals, left the shores of America full of dreams and determination to find what they considered a new and better world."[22]

Tuomi also describes the recruitment process in the Finnish communities. Enthusiastic speakers who had visited the Soviet Union on tours subsidized by the Communist Party gave glowing accounts of the character of life there with its unparalleled opportunities. Such accounts stood in stark contrast to the uncertainties of Depression-ridden America. A speaker would end his spiel with a screening of the Soviet propaganda film "The Old and the New" to dispel any doubts that might remain.[23]

The experience of Lauri's mother is probably typical for a whole generation of Finnish immigrants in North America. She was a regular reader of the Finnish-American radical newspaper *Työmies* (Workingman) which painted a serene picture of equity and fairness in the Soviet Union. "In the *Työmies* it all sounded great."[24] Kaarlo Tuomi has explained that, on the pages of that newspaper, Finns were treated to a regular dose of items from the British communist newspaper *The Daily Worker*, which, in turn, received much of its material from *Pravda*.[25] In the early 1920s, moreover, *Työmies* was filled with articles by Finnish communists who had fled to the Soviet Union and used it to proselytize for their cause.[26] Linguistically isolated and knowing little if any English, many immigrants relied on *Työmies* for their information which, it is now clear, was hopelessly skewed and inaccurate.

Other less obvious factors existed to encourage North American Finns to immigrate to Karelia. The appeals were made directly to them. The ads in *Työmies* in the early 1930s informed applicants that they must submit to Karelian Technical Aid "a recommendation from a Finnish Workers' Association or from two association officials."[27] There were certainly other immigrant groups known for skills in forestry and construction to which Gylling and Rovio could have appealed. They did not. It was important that they recruit not only a competent work force (which the Finns certainly were) but also an ethnically Finnish and Finnish-speaking one as well.

Finns responded to a cause that was clearly their own. Simply put, recruitment to Karelia engendered Finnish national pride. The issue of pride was an important one for Finnish immigrants who felt isolated and even scorned. In Sinclair Lewis' novel *Cass Timberlane*, set in the Minnesota of the 1930s, he refers to a pecking order among Scandinavian immigrants. The Finns were at the bottom of it. This unfortunate situation had grown out of the intense animosities between Finnish and Swedish speakers in Finland. The language conflict, in fact, dominated Finnish politics from the 1860s onward. Encouraged by the extreme Swedish nationalist A. O. Freudenthal, Swedish militants had "adopted the racist doctrines of the time to brand Finns as racially inferior."[28]

Such doctrines encouraged Finnish migration to America. Transported here, they discouraged Finnish assimilation in the new world. One appeal of Karelian recruitment, and hence its transformation into a "fever," lay in its endowing Finnish immigrants with significance and a special purpose. Some went to Karelia to find a self-esteem that had eluded them in America. Some went, like Lauri and Sylvi, because they were intelligent and hard working. They saw opportunity elsewhere at a time when the American dream seemed further than ever from realization. Some went to fulfill a commitment to the ideal of Communism. Some went to escape a business failure or the grief of a death in the family. Karelian Fever gave one particular ethnic group in America a unique opportunity to undergo a total change in their lives in what was a decade of uprootings. As Woodie Guthrie's songs of wanderlust from the 1930s reveal, Americans, out of necessity, were on the move.

Gylling's very policy of recruiting North American Finns proved his undoing. To begin with, even 10,000 immigrant Finns did not suffice as a counterweight to Russian immigration into Karelia.[29] Even before such recruitment began. Moscow had deplored the "Finnicization" of Karelia, and the early 1930s saw increasingly adverse attention given to policies in Karelia which allegedly "fostered withdrawal into a national shell."[30]

By the spring of 1935 the leaders of the Leningrad party organization, which had jurisdiction over the Karelian party apparatus, were openly attacking "local nationalism" in Karelia.[31] The policy of recruiting North American Finns was clearly over. Sylvi mentions that already by 1934 the fever had begun to subside.[32] She and Lauri left with only eight others and there was no celebration at their departure from New York as had occurred with groups that left earlier. Gylling's policy was already in trouble.

In addition to the ethnic question, Stalin had other reasons for eliminating Gylling and his programs. In late 1933, only months before Lauri and Sylvi's departure, the Soviet Union had obtained long-coveted diplomatic recognition by the United States. Stalin wanted the Americans to join him in curbing Japanese expansion in the Pacific. Vigorous recruitment of American workers to a better life in Soviet Union could not help but antagonize his new-found ally. Gylling's efforts were undermining Stalin's diplomacy. Gylling himself constituted a phenomenon also anathema to Stalin: he was a popular figure who dominated the local administrative apparatus that he himself had created. Gylling had run Karelia since 1920. He would have to go. In the fall of 1935 both Rovio and Gylling were removed from their positions in Karelia.

With Gylling's departure and the discrediting of his policies, the North American Finns became isolated. They remained a minority within a minority as no new waves of immigrants arrived. The special INSNAB stores which had catered only to the newcomers were closed, and the kind of personal contact with Rovio and Gylling which Lauri and Sylvi describe was no longer possible with the new leadership.

What had begun to appear ominous in 1935 turned into a nightmare by 1937 and 1938. In 1937 Gylling and Rovio were executed. They were destroyed in a holocaust that victimized much of the command structure of the Soviet Union. In Karelia the victims were those communists who had fled Finland in 1918 and those North American Finns who had joined the communist party, that is, those who had administered the region.

The regime held back at first from touching those Finns who had never joined the communist party or who had not renewed their North American party membership in Karelia as was required. It was possible that Stalin regarded such people as genuine foreigners. He was courting Western aid against Hitler. Executing westerners could antagonize the very governments whose assistance he sought.

But in July 1938 the turn came for non-party members among the Finnish immigrants. Lauri's account of the "*suuri kauhu*" or "great terror" is chilling. The Finnish language was banned. Those events coincided with the initiation of Soviet pressure on Finland to cede it certain strategic territory. Soviet demands culminated in the Winter War with Finland in 1939. Stalin's regime could regard its Finnish minority as a potentially disloyal element in the event of war with Finland. In the summer of 1938 it had begun brutally to prepare for that eventuality. Only a few such as Lauri and Sylvi miraculously survived along with the younger generation of Finns that had barely reached adulthood by 1938.

By way of epilogue, I will turn to the question: did nothing good come of the high hopes and enthusiasm among Finns infected with Karelian Fever? An answer emerges from this memoir. Repeatedly one is struck with how distinctive were the North American Finns in Karelia. Almost inadvertently Lauri and Sylvi describe a competence, mechanical training, technical inventiveness, over-all quality of work, standard of cleanliness and generosity of spirit which set the foreigners apart. Soviets who would otherwise never see the West for themselves were exposed to Western standards and mores simply by living in Karelia starting in the 1930s.

One such individual was Yuri Andropov, later head of the secret police and party General Secretary. He ruled the Soviet Union along with Brezhnev from 1967 and then singly from 1982 to 1984. He mentored Gorbachev and advanced him as his successor. Observers have long wondered at Andropov's awareness of Western standards. He introduced computers to the KGB, made its agents study foreign languages, and encouraged Gorbachev's early travels abroad.

The solution to the Andropov puzzle overwhelmed me on my first visit to Petrozavodsk. I encountered survivors and descendents of the North American migration all over town. Some remembered Andropov. To honor him, a local museum devoted an exhibition to the period of his life spent in Karelia, from the late 1930s to the early 1950s. There was his foreign language dictionary. He had worked with those who, in the late 1930s, belonged to the younger generation of North American Finns. Too young to be party members, they had escaped the holocaust that destroyed their parents. They had exposed him to the West; and they were the source of his hitherto unexplained knowledge of English.

Finally, I will describe an evening in the summer of 1991 in the home of Sylvi and Lauri's daughter. The occasion was a party in honor of visiting dignitaries from Petrozavodsk. Sylvi and I sat in a corner while she told me how emotionally traumatic it was for her to remember her Karelian experiences. She cried quietly. I thought, if she and Lauri and others like them had not gone to Russia, Gorbachev might never have come to rule the Soviet Union or at least not have initiated the policies of openness and modernization his exposure to the West encouraged. Andropov had initiated Gorbachev to the West. Something positive had come of Karelian Fever after all.

Alexis Pogorelskin, Ph.D.
University of Minnesota
Duluth

Notes

1 Gylling had traded liberalism for radicalism. Nonetheless, he had been formed in a society where Finnish language and culture had had to fight for their right to exist against the dominant Swedish culture and the overlordship of Russia. Gylling never forgot those early experiences. Peter Kivisto, "Pre-Migration Factors Contibuting to the Development of Finnish-American Socialism," *Finnish Americana*, 1982-83, p. 26.

2 John H. Hodgson, *Communism in Finland: A History and Interpretation*, Princeton University Press, 1967, p. 147; Arvo Tuominen, *The Bells of the Kremlin*, University Press of New England (Hanover, New Hampshire), 1983, p. 282.

3 Ibid, Hodgson.

4 Z. Strogal'shchikova, "S uchetom proshlogo," recent Karelian newspaper unattributed; Tuominen, p. 45, 46.

5 Ibid.

6 Hodgson, p. 152.

7 Tuominen, p. 282.

8 Ibid.

9 Tuominen, p. 282.

10 Hodgson, p. 156.

11 Tuominen, p. 285-285.

12 Hodgson, 156-158.

13 Tuominen, p. 284.

14 Ibid.

15 In *Punainen Karjala*: 8 Oct. 1927; 28 July 1929; 31 March 1931; as cited in Hodgson, p. 161.

16 Ibid.

17 Hodgson, p. 161.

18 Ibid.

19 Auvo Kostiainen, "The Forging of Finnish-American Communism, 1917-1924," *Turun Yliopiston Julkaisuja*, Ser. B., Vol. 147, 1978, p. 164.

20 Ibid.

21 Piltti Heiskanen. Editor's note in *Bells of the Kremlin* by Arvo Tuominen.

22 Kaarlo Tuomi, "The Karelian Fever of the Early 1930s," *Finnish Americana*, Vol III (1980), p. 63.

23 Ibid, p. 62-63.
24 Text, p. 2.
25 Tuomi, p. 63.
26 Kostiainen, p. 160.
27 *Työ*mies, undated.
28 Kivisto, p. 24.
29 Hodgson, p. 164.
30 Ibid, p. 165.
31 Ibid, p. 167.
32 Text, p. 14.

References

Heiskanen, Piltti. Editor's note in *Bells of the Kremlin* by Arvo Tuominen.

Hodgson, John H. *Communism in Finland: A History and Interpretation.* Princeton University Press, 1967.

Kivisto, Peter. "Pre-Migration Factors Contributing to the Development of Finnish-American Socialism." *Finnish Americana* 1982-83.

Kostiainen, Auvo. "The Forging of Finnish-American Communism 1917-24." *Turun Yliopiston Julkaisuja* Ser. B., Vol. 147, 1978.

Rovio, Kustaa. "*Kielikysymys Neuvosto-Karjalan Kansallisuus-politiikassa.*" *Kommunisti* No. 8 (80) August 1931, p. 385, as quoted in Hodgson, p. 156.

Strogal'shchikova, Z. "S *uchetom proshlogo.*" Recent Karelian newspaper unattributed.

Tuomi, Kaarlo. "The Karelian Fever of the Early 1930s." *Finnish Americana.* Vol. III (1980).

Tuominen, Arvo. *The Bells of the Kremlin.* University Press of New England. Hanover, N.H., 1983.

Sylvi and Lauri Hokkanen.

It Couldn't Have Happened

L: "That couldn't have happened," my mother said, and she turned away. A quick-tempered, strong-willed little woman, she made it very clear that she did not want to hear any more.

I had been trying to tell her what our lives had been like in the Soviet Union where my wife, Sylvi, and I had spent the last seven years. We had just returned to the United States, that spring of 1941, with almost nothing but the clothes on our backs and feeling lucky to have gotten out safely. I wanted to tell my mother what we had gone through in Russia, and I tried, but what she said was, "That couldn't have happened." "Couldn't have," when I had just told her it did. Why didn't she believe me? What reason could she have had to doubt her own son's story about things that he had seen and heard and actually experienced?

Lauri Hokkanen (L)

1

I think the problem was that what happened to us, and to so many others in Soviet Karelia, went against the political beliefs that she had held very strongly for most of her life. Her view of the world had been shaped by the Finnish-American radical newspaper, *Työmies* (*The Worker*), that she read every week. She was a kind-hearted woman, and she really believed that in the communist "workers' paradise" every man would have a chance to make a good life for himself. That was the plan: "From each according to his ability; to each according to his need." There wouldn't be a ruling class that had all the money and a working class that had a hard time finding jobs to pay enough to feed a family. Everyone would be a worker, and everyone would share alike.

This "workers' paradise," my mother also knew from her newspaper, was being created and lived out in the Soviet Union, a glorious country where no one went hungry and where the communist party, a group of loyal, dedicated and unpaid workers with the highest of ideals, saw to it that everything was done right. In *Työmies* it all sounded great.

Now here we were, just returned from that wonderful place, scared half to death and telling her about arrests, disappearances, beatings, escapes. The dream that she had believed in and worked for ever since she was a girl was sounding like a nightmare.

Sylvi was angry with mother for refusing to believe me, but I felt that she really was not *able* to believe it. Many things that happened over there had been hard for *us* to believe, even while they were happening to us! So many innocent people arrested—people we knew, good friends—and never heard from again. It didn't make any sense. We gave up trying to tell my mother about it. She was very sick with arthritis at that time, so we felt it best to treat her the way we always had and not aggravate her.

Mother wasn't the only one who didn't want to hear what we had to say about Russia. There were others back home in Michigan who had their own ideas about what was going on in the Soviet Union and didn't want them disturbed. There was one man from Sault Ste. Marie, for instance, who had been to Karelia himself for a very short time and returned to the states because he could not live on the Soviet diet. He came to see us after we returned and told us right out that no one had been arrested in the Soviet Union who was not guilty. Of course he didn't know anything about it; he had returned before the purges. But there was no changing his mind.

There were also people who were suspicious of us. Why were we allowed to come back when others couldn't? Some people thought they had it all figured out. Behind our backs, they said we had to be spies for the Soviet Union or we never would have gotten permission to return. I suppose it made a good story. And we certainly couldn't explain, and can't to this day, why we were among the very few who were allowed to come back from Soviet Karelia.

So, after we returned to the United States, we didn't talk much about the experiences we had had. We never knew whether other people wanted to hear our story, and, many times, other people weren't sure whether we would want to talk about it and hesitated to ask. If someone who knew where we had been asked a question, we would answer, but we never told any new friends or acquaintances where we had lived between 1934 and 1941. We just never mentioned it. We didn't even tell our daughter, born the year after we returned, the whole story. We had a few items, just trinkets really, from Russia and Japan. When she asked how we had gotten these things, we told her we had been around the world on our honeymoon. It was stretching the truth a little—seven years is a long honeymoon!

In the fifties, when Senator Joe McCarthy was hunting down communists and communist sympathizers and anyone who had ever had anything to do with communists, some FBI agents asked some of our neighbors in Detroit about us. Our good friend Mary, next door, came and told us about it. It scared us. It was too much like being back in Russia. But nothing ever happened to us. We had never been party members anyway.

In 1984, fifty years after we left for the Soviet Union, we decided to tell our story. We decided, before Mikhail Gorbachev had even been elected General Secretary, that it was time for our own "glasnost." Stalin's crimes were pretty well known by then, and many of the families of those who had been arrested had received word that their relatives had been cleared of any crime—posthumously.

Sylvi and I have spent many hours trying to remember all the things that happened to us so many years ago when we set off on what we thought was going to be an exciting adventure. There are probably still some people who will not want to believe this story. We don't blame them. It is hard to believe that men can do the things that we have seen. It is also hard to understand how a system that was intended to benefit the working man could turn out so differently. But we have tried to be scrupulously honest and tell everything just as we remember it.

To Build a Workers' Paradise

S. Lauri and I grew up on Sugar Island which is located in the St. Mary's River below Sault Ste. Marie, Michigan. The island was originally inhabited by Indians; then French and Irish moved in. In the early nineteen hundreds a Finnish land agent persuaded many Finns from Michigan's Upper Peninsula and Canadian mining communities to move to Sugar Island to try their hand at farming. Our parents were among them.

These first generation American-Finns were literate and culture-conscious people. Although most of them spoke only Finnish, they kept up with world events by means of Finnish language newspapers. Their children, including Lauri and me, spoke only Finnish when they entered school but learned English very quickly. A few discarded their mother tongue in em-

Sylvi Hokkanen (S)

5

barrassment. In a reverse situation, when Lauri entered kindergarten, all except two of the children were Finnish. The teacher was English, and classes were conducted in English, but at recess, of course, the Finnish language held sway. By the end of the year, all of the children spoke Finnish, including the two non-Finns, who then retained it for the rest of their lives.

Many of the Finns who settled on Sugar Island were politically oriented towards the left and joined the workers' movements: first the Socialists, and later the Communist Party. My father, Frank Kuusisto, donated a corner of his farm land for the construction of a hall where political meetings and social events could be held. There were dances, box socials, sporting events and plays—some comedies and some with a political message, always leftist. Even those Finns who were not interested in politics joined in all the other activities for they constituted the social life at the time. And, in those pre-babysitter days, when the parents went out, the children did too. It was also our social life. We learned to dance and do athletics soon after learning to walk. We had opportunities to perform in plays, and many Finns became very able actors and actresses. Lauri and I appeared in a few plays at our Sugar Island Hall, though neither of us really got into acting.

The depth of commitment to the workers' movement seems to have varied from generation to generation. As far as our families were concerned, I am not sure how our grandparents in Finland felt. They were poor, hard-working people with deep religious faith. They probably bore their hardships quietly, believing that the hereafter would bring a better life for them. But our parents, both Lauri's and mine, had begun to look at conditions from a workers' viewpoint. They saw the unjust way the state church of Finland treated the poor. The tithing system was in full force; the church had to have its full share regardless of whether or not there was anything left for the family. The landowner also had to have his share, leaving the poor tenant farmer with very little on which to survive. Our parents and many others came to America hoping for a better, easier life away from the oppression of state church and landed gentry. But here, too, they saw oppression and exploitation of the worker, especially the immigrant worker who, partly because of the language barrier, was unable to fight for his rights. And so they joined the American socialist movement, which at that time was quite strong.*

---

*It is estimated that twenty-five to forty percent of the Finnish immigrant population participated in radical political groups. (Kivisto 16).

After the revolution in Russia there came a turning point in the social-ist movement: those who felt that revolution was the best solution to the problems of the working class turned to communism; those who thought that improvements should come through peaceful means followed socialist tactics. This division caused much bitterness among the Amer-ican Finns. Our parents, at this point, joined the communists. They be-lieved that the Soviet Union had done the right thing in revolting, and they were willing to follow Russia's lead. They were sure the Soviet Union would truly become a workers' paradise.

Some of the Finns of our generation, the second generation, became interested in politics and carried on the beliefs of our elders. My oldest brother, for one, became a communist party youth organizer, but he died of tuberculosis at the age of twenty-one, so I cannot say how deeply committed he would have been when older. Some few from Sugar Island rose in the ranks of the communist party; others joined the union move-ment.

But many of us who left home at an early age to work (like Lauri) or to go to school (as I did) grew away from the political activism of our parents. We hadn't, as yet, fully understood what they were striving for, or what the true meaning of communism was. The slogans were great, the workers' anthem was inspiring, but there were so many other things that occupied our minds. Lauri was working on the lake freighters, in lumber camps and sawmills. I finished my schooling and began to teach in the fall of 1931, and it was that same fall that Lauri and I started "going together."

Lauri was a very handsome, personable young man, clearly the type who could sweep a young woman off her feet. He was ambitious, eager to work at most any kind of job to make a good living. I was irresistibly drawn to him, although he was considered by some of the older genera-tion to be a bit on the wild side. An elderly lady, a dear and close friend of ours, even went so far as to warn me against marrying "that wild one"—a warning that (fortunately for me) I decided to ignore. My fa-ther approved of Lauri whole-heartedly. And so, in December of 1932, the day after Christmas, we were married.

Our decision to go to the Soviet Union was made not long after our marriage. Since the 1920s there had been a great need in Soviet Karelia for technical aid and for skilled lumber workers with tools and machines. They were needed to harvest the vast forests of Karelia for export in ex-change for *valuutta* (foreign currency) which was sorely needed by the Soviet government for trading with other countries. The Finnish workers' organizations in Canada and the United States, in cooperation with Moscow, had begun to recruit workers with this in mind. Then in 1931 the Soviet government set up the Karelian Technical Aid organization to manage the recruitment process.

Headquartered in the Harlem area of New York City, Karelian Technical Aid employed several recruiters who traveled around to Finnish communities in the United States and Canada making speeches about the wonderful opportunities for workers in Soviet Karelia. Those who signed up were organized into groups, and Karelian Technical Aid arranged for their transportation to Russia from New York. The recruiters were quite successful. It has been estimated that as many as ten thousand Finns from the United States and Canada emigrated to Karelia in the thirties. The passion to go and build a workers' paradise became so strong and so prevalent that it was known as "Karelian Fever."

The fact that the United States was in the grip of the Great Depression naturally made the communist experiment in Russia look more attractive. We had read in the paper about the stock market collapse (known as "Black Friday"), on October 28, 1929, and we heard about people who had committed suicide after losing all their money. This made us wonder what the future would hold for us on Sugar Island. At the same time, we read in the *Työmies* about the many job opportunities and freedom from exploitation in the Soviet Union.

Some of our relatives answered the recruiters' call early in the thirties. Lauri's cousin Lily, her husband Dave Metsälä and their two children, Viola and Hugo, from Ontonagon, Michigan, went to Karelia before we did. Dave went first and, we learned later, did not like what he found. He wrote to Lily not to come, and that he would return as soon as he could. But she had progressed too far with her preparations to leave—the house was sold, the farewell parties were over—and so she followed him anyway. Among my relatives, my mother's brother Frank Pihlava went with his wife and their son, Arvo. An older girl, Eva, had elected to stay in the States.

Few people went from Sugar Island. There was a family named Soini, whom we never heard of again, and three single fellows: John Boman, Victor Viiki and our friend, Albin Heino. Heino was the only one we had heard from; he had written, urging us to come too. There would be work for Lauri, he said, and for me a chance to continue my schooling and teaching. I had taught school for two years, from the fall of 1931 to the summer of 1933, but at that time people looked askance at married women who held jobs that could have gone to single people, and so I had given it up.

It was difficult, though. Teaching had been my dream since I was a little girl. I had completed the eight grades in a Sugar Island school, then high school in Sault Ste. Marie, and I had even had two years of college with great financial sacrifice on the part of my father and brothers.* (My mother had died when I was thirteen.) So the two years I was able to teach on Sugar Island were indeed a dream come true. I taught in the same one-room school I had attended as a child, and my pupils were Finnish and Indian children of neighboring families. I enjoyed it very much and giving it up was not easy, but I did have hopes of continuing my education in the Soviet Union—if indeed we did go there.

Although Lauri was doing well at that time running the sawmill that he had purchased from Heino, he was worried about the future. Those of us living in the country had not been hit as hard by the Depression as city dwellers. We had our vegetables, our milk, fish and venison. But even for us, money was hard to come by, and we would resort to bartering. Lauri often had to take lumber for pay when sawing logs for neighbors. Then he would try to sell the lumber for cash in order to buy fuel. White pine was twenty-five dollars for one-thousand board feet delivered—certainly a bargain if you had the cash. At the suggestion of a neighbor, Lauri purchased a grain grinder which he set on a trailer so he could move it around. With it, he ground wheat, barley and oats for the neighboring farmers, and they would give him flour in return. So we were getting along all right, but the future did not look promising in the United States at that time. Of course we didn't expect to find wealth and material comforts in the Soviet Union, but we did feel that there would be an opportunity to work for a better life with a good chance of success.

We decided to apply. Immigrants to Soviet Karelia had to be cleared by the Karelian Technical Aid organization and also by the American Communist Party. Although the party was, of course, in favor of helping Karelia and all of Russia improve their economic status, it did not want to lose its best political workers and comrades in the United States. So the preferred recruits were middle-aged to elderly people who spoke only Finnish and would therefore be less able to help with the class struggle here. Although we were young and spoke English, we were not party members and were more or less apolitical. So the party probably felt that we could best serve their purposes in Karelia, especially with our

*In 1928, at the age of fifteen, Sylvia Kuusisto was the youngest person ever to graduate from the Sault high school.

lumbering and teaching skills. At any rate, we received permission to go.

Most of the immigrants took with them all they could afford of clothing, food and tools. Many used all their savings to buy whatever could be used in Karelia: cars, trucks, farm machinery. Some sold their homes and farms, getting very low prices for them because of the Depression. They were urged to make donations, if they could, to the "machine fund" of either money or tools and machines, and many did.

We had no savings to donate. In the spring of 1933, when I was still teaching, money was so scarce in the Sault that the banks issued scrip instead of money. This was fine as long as we were using it locally, but when we decided to go to Karelia we had to have cash for our fares. So we hoarded all the coins we got in change, and Lauri was fortunate enough to find a buyer for the sawmill who had real cash, a man on Drummond Island who had kept his money under his mattress.

In order to deliver the mill, Lauri hired a trucker friend to drive it across the ice. The ice was thick, but the mill was a heavy load; they kept the cab doors open all the way, ready to jump out if the ice gave way. The St. Mary's River ice was tricky due to the strong current and to springs in the river bottom. We knew of several cars and teams of horses that had broken through and been lost over the years, but it was the only way to get across to the mainland in winter, and folks often took chances. Fortunately, Lauri and his friend had no trouble. The mill was delivered, and we had the cash for our transportation to Russia.

Our preparations to leave were quite simple. Compared to others, we took little. We had no savings to spend. As for clothing, we just took what we had, feeling that we should make do with whatever was available in the Workers' Paradise. Surely we could manage where others did. We took one pound of A & P Bokar, our favorite brand of coffee at the time. Lauri took what tools he had; they were mostly for auto repair. We also had our friend Albin Heino's tools with us. He had left them behind and now wanted us to bring them. We did take one big piece of furniture, a Simmons hide-a-bed sofa. We knew furniture was scarce over there, and, a good bed being essential to one's physical well-being, we made this one exception. One of our pieces of luggage was unusual: an old wooden box the size of a large trunk that had been used by my father in the barn for storing oats. We emptied and cleaned it as best we could. Much later I wondered where my poor father stored his oats after we took his box to the ends of the earth.

Before we left, our friends gave us a going-away party. It was held at the Hall. We danced and enjoyed the usual cakes and coffee. A collection had been taken earlier, and at the party we were presented with a "going-away" gift: a genuine Hudson's Bay blanket. It was a wonderful gift. We took it with us and made good use of it.

On a sad day in May 1934, I bade good-bye to my father and brothers. This parting was most heartbreaking for me, for I had a very close relationship, especially with my father and my brother Andrew, who was only a year and a half younger than I. Brother Arvo was six years younger and did not feel as close. Although I had been away at school since I was eleven years old, this parting was different. I would be very far away . . . in another world, so to speak. As hard as this parting was for me, parting with my wonderful young husband would have been unbearable. My place was with him, and so I followed him gladly, though tearfully. As I said good-bye to my father and brothers, I wondered when, if ever, I would see them again. It was to be my last good-bye to Andrew and my father.

I have often wondered how our folks, my father and Lauri's mother and father, felt about our going to Karelia. As I recall, they neither urged us to go nor did they advise us against it. Stoic Finns that they were, they did not speak much of their feelings. My father must have felt his loss deeply; I was the only girl in the family, and we were very close. Furthermore, after years of struggling to help me get an education, he was now on the point of getting some return for his investment. I doubt that this was on his mind, but I myself have often regretted leaving him at this point. I wonder if perhaps our parents thought of our going as a gift from them to the Soviet Union; since they could not go, the next best thing was to send us instead. I may be wrong; I may be right.

The first leg of our journey took us as far as Detroit, where we spent a few days with our friends Paul and Ingrid Middleton. They were a Finnish couple; their name had been Muttilainen originally. Paul's sister Martha, her husband, Dave Nieminen, and their daughter, Ella, had gone to Karelia in 1931.

We continued by bus to New York City. There, too, we remained for a few days in a hotel near the Karelian Technical Aid headquarters in Harlem until the rest of our group arrived. Then, at last, we boarded the ship *Majestic*, headed for England.

Ours was a small group compared to those that had gone before us. By 1934 the "Karelian Fever," which had peaked during the first years of the decade, had died down. There were only about ten people in our group, and we held no political meetings, no programs, no flag waving or hurrahs as the earlier, larger groups had been in the habit of doing. These earlier groups were well organized with elected officials, entertainment committees, and rules of conduct. They held meetings and social events, and in this way kept up their spirits and their sense of camaraderie. Red flags were everywhere and were waved at farewells and also for greetings when stopping at foreign ports. Although we did none of these things, we were also a dedicated group and on the way to help as best we could in building a workers' land.

The ocean trip was most unpleasant for me since I suffered with seasickness much of the way. On our first morning, as we set out for a walk on deck, Lauri suddenly grabbed me and turned me around saying, "Don't look that way!" All around us, people were vomiting over the side of the ship. Soon, unfortunately, I was one of them, but Lauri never felt sick at all and enjoyed the meals all the way across. Later, on the North Sea, seasickness again hit me, to the point where I fainted dead away and thought I was dying.

Early in June we landed in Southampton, England, and continued from there by train to London, where we stayed for three or four days in modest accommodations arranged for us by Karelian Technical Aid. This short stay convinced me that I did not care for English cuisine; to me, it seemed heavy and indigestible. However, had my taste of English food followed our stay in Karelia, the verdict might have been different.

It had been said that more older people came back in short order because they could not cope with the realities of life in Karelia. Many of them had lived through a harsh childhood in Finland, had immigrated to the United States or Canada and, with hard work and many deprivations, had managed to attain a fairly good life. Now they had given this up and once again faced hard work and primitive conditions. Poor diet, especially the sour black bread so common in Russia, brought on health problems, and it was too much for many of them. But coming back did not necessarily mean that they disapproved of the concept of a workers' paradise, nor did they withdraw their support of the Soviet Union. Young people, on the other hand, were more often able to adapt to life in Russia. They were full of strength and vitality and imbued with the idea of a classless society, although perhaps not so class conscious as their elders. They took the hardships in stride, believing that everything would improve in time.

We were part of this latter group. We expected life in Karelia to be difficult, especially at first. But we were sure that with hard work and the support of so many comrades with the same vision, things would soon change for the better. We had a dream.

Bedbugs, Bricks and Big Trees

L: I had worked in lumber camps, on lake freighters and in saw mills ever since I had finished the eighth grade and had learned quite a bit about mechanics from running the mills and from repairing boats and automobiles. It was the kind of work I liked to do. After Heino left I became curious about the opportunities in Karelia. It sounded like everyone who went there was doing all right. Sylvi and I were both healthy and just wanted a chance to use our skills and make a living. We never ruled out the idea that we might want to come back to the United States some day.

I was also fascinated with the idea of seeing other countries and peoples. It was exciting to go overseas. My first taste of being a foreigner came in London when I went to buy some ink. The clerk had no problem understanding me but when she said, "That'll be tuppence," I had no idea what she meant.

"Tuppence . . . tuppence," she repeated.

By this time I felt really foolish and extended a handful of change from which she, laughing merrily, extracted two pennies. With a sheepish grin, I left in a hurry.

A few days later, we boarded the Russian ship *Smolny* that took us, via the North Sea and the Kiel Canal, through Germany to the Gulf of

The Ship *Smolny*.

Sylvi (left) with a Mr. Koivu and a woman on her way to get married.

Finland and on to Leningrad. As I watched the cargo being loaded on the *Smolny* by derrick, our old oat box appeared, swinging crazily in the air for a few seconds before hitting the hold with a thud that caused a whole cloud of oat dust to rise from its cracks. If anyone had asked, I would have said I didn't know whose it was.

Our first meal on the Russian ship was a big surprise. The table was loaded with cold cuts, herring, canned fish, cheese and lots of good bread. We were all hungry, so we cleaned the table pretty well, thinking that was it. Then they proceeded to bring on the main course: chicken with many side dishes and all kinds of goodies. We stuffed ourselves but made a very poor showing, unfortunately, as this was the last good meal we were to see for quite a few years.

Customs inspection in Leningrad took one whole day. We didn't lose anything, but had to open all our luggage, even the oat box which was roped every twelve inches and knotted at every joint. It proved impossible to untie the ropes so I had to cut them all with a knife, and I threw them into a corner in disgust while the indifferent inspector pawed through the contents. Irked as I was, I couldn't help but notice one fellow who breezed through the line without having to open anything. When I got a chance, I asked him what sort of magic he possessed.

"I shook hands with a five dollar bill," he explained.

It seemed that even Marxists were not immune to a little capitalist graft, especially, we discovered, when the bribe was in American dollars. It was a little disappointing to see that this was going on, but of course it wasn't Russia's fault if a few unscrupulous and materialistic workers had gotten in.

We were met in Leningrad by a guide from the Karelian Technical Aid organization whose job it was to take care of us while we were in Leningrad and then send us on to our government-assigned work locations. As we waited to complete customs, we watched some stevedores loading a ship in the harbor, and I commented to the guide that they seemed to be barely moving.

"If you had to do that kind of work with the food they're getting, I doubt you'd do any better," was his terse reply. This made me wonder if the food shortages in Karelia were worse than we expected. We would soon find out.

After customs our guide took us to a hotel where I had my first whiff of a really rank odor that was to become very familiar.

"What the hell smells so bad?" I asked.

It was homemade cigarettes. Although good, factory-made cigarettes were available, they were very expensive, and most people made their own from a tobacco called mahorka which they rolled up in newsprint. The accepted method was to roll a small piece of newspaper into a cone, bend the wide end up forming what looked a little like the bowl of a pipe, and fill that with tobacco. I eventually learned to make them but I never did like mahorka.

The Karelian government was eager to utilize new American techniques of lumbering to harvest the "green gold" of Karelia. Given my experience in lumber camps and in running a saw mill, it was perhaps inevitable that we would be sent to a lumber camp. Sure enough, a few days after arriving in Leningrad, we received a "command" to go north to Uhtua, a town about one hundred miles south of the Arctic Circle.

On the train we became acquainted with the director of a paper mill, the Kontupohja Paperi Tehdäs. He suggested that we get off the train at Kontupohja and come to work for him, but since we had been assigned by the government to work in Uhtua, I didn't see how we could change the plan.

"Are we allowed to come and work for you?" I asked.

"It's a free country," he said. "You can go wherever you want."

We were hesitant. At any rate, our baggage was on its way to Uhtua and we decided we had better go there too. Now, looking back, I am sure that it is a good thing we went where we had been told to go. It wasn't a "free country" over there as we knew the term, and we think it strange now that this factory director would have said it was.

At Kemi, on the western shore of the White Sea, we left the train and rode in the open box of a Ford Model A pick-up truck the 180 kilometers west to Uhtua. One other family from the United States was with us. It was very cold for mid-June with even a little snow that made it feel colder.

Uhtua was a small town on the shore of Lake Keskikuitti (the town has since been renamed Kalevala). It was the commercial center for that part of Karelia. There was no railroad, only a poor gravel road from the Kemi station. The town did have a clinic and hospital, grocery store, schools and the usual government offices. A liquor store was a recent addition; for years Uhtua had been a "dry" town where the state sent drunks to work. There were also docks along the shore for the small ships and tugs that were used for transportation to lumber camps and villages in the summers. Recruits like ourselves came first to Uhtua and then were sent out to the different lumber camps in the area wherever they were needed. We were just a few days in Uhtua before we were taken across the lake about thirty kilometers in a cute little wood-fired steamboat to the Vonganperä Lumber Camp. I enjoyed that trip. I was reminded of the boat later when I saw the movie "African Queen."

Vonganperä had several large barracks and a horse barn that had been built for the time when the timber was being harvested. Now it looked quite deserted as the place was pretty well logged out. All the lumbering and transporting had been done with horses and men; it was hard to believe how much they had accomplished in the three years or so that the camp had been in operation.

The blacksmith shop and blacksmith were still there when we came; he was hammering scythe blades out of steel bars—very thin, narrow and light weight—which were attached to straight wooden handles. The smith was from Finland, and I was told that he was very good at his trade. He also liked his drink, and, when there was no vodka to be had, which was often, he would drink aftershave lotion with a high alcohol content. (Oddly enough, that was usually available.) This brand of lotion had a picture of a reindeer on the bottle so the blacksmith called it *poro rommi* (reindeer rum).

We slept in a log barracks. Each couple had a room to themselves, and they were nice enough but quite full of bed bugs. We had been warned about these back in New York and told to bring some "twenty mule team Borax," a white cleaning powder. I first tried putting some Borax around each leg of the bed* to discourage them but that didn't help at all—we just had white bugs. So next I put water into tin cans and set each leg of the bed into a can. That did help for a while—the bugs were poor swimmers—but pretty soon they got smarter and climbed to the ceiling from which they dive-bombed the bed by air. At least there were less of them. Bedbugs were a constant problem all the time we were in Karelia.

The cooks at Vonganperä were Finnish women so the food was better than average. They baked their own bread, a mixture of wheat and rye that was very good. "This bread is what keeps us on the trail," the men used to say, but after hiking a few kilometers single file the men in the rear would complain about being gassed.

Many trees had been cut down and hauled out the previous winter, and the tops of these had been left lying on the ground. I was given the job of trimming them in order to get all the branches close to the ground

---

*Our hide-a-bed was not shipped up to the lumber camps. We used it later, when we settled in Petrozavodsk.

where they would decay instead of drying out and becoming fuel for forest fires. It also allowed new growth to start sooner. It was a sensible practice, and one I had never heard of before. The accepted method in the United States was to leave the branches and tops where they fell, (except in hardwood forests where the tops were later trimmed and used for firewood, charcoal and chemicals). Perhaps the millions of trees and hundreds of lives lost in the forest fires of Michigan and Minnesota could have been saved had this trimming been done. My pay for this work was ten *kopecks* per tree top. I kept count, and had a hard time making any money. Of course, our room and board were provided so I didn't need much either.

After a couple of weeks of trimming trees at Vonganperä, my hands were full of blisters, and I was glad when we were sent to a new camp called Kannussuo, which was being built about ten kilometers further inland from the lake. Here everybody, men and women, slept together on a raised shelf in a big loft. Sylvi was uncomfortable with the lack of privacy and the crude jokes that were passed around.

My first job there was making shingles with a machine run by man power. It consisted of a large wooden frame from which hung a wooden box filled with sand weighing six to eight hundred pounds. Above the box, the wooden poles suspending it were attached to a steel blade so that swinging the box back and forth also caused the blade to move back and forth horizontally. Each forward motion of the blade sliced a shingle from an eight-by-eight-by-twelve-inch block of pine. Four men stood on the ground swinging the sand box back and forth; a fifth man fed the blocks of wood to the blade. The shingles were about three-eighth-inch thick, cut with the grain. I was told that shingles made this way were superior to those that had been sawed because the saw cut leaves a rougher surface that would not shed water as well as a shaved shingle.

In a few more weeks, some of us were sent out to a grassy area around some small lakes about five miles from Kannussuo to make hay for the horses. We cut the grass with scythes and coiled it onto poles to dry as they did in Finland. The hay was left like that until it was needed in the winter months. There was a small shack at this location in which we kept supplies, but we slept outside on pine boughs with our feet toward the fire. It was quite comfortable after a long day of hard work.

Again we worked as a five-man team. The lead man would be a few feet ahead of the second, who was a bit ahead of the third and so on so we formed a diagonal row (just as the big harvesting machines do in the fields today). In this way, we all had to keep up with the leader and everyone would cut the same amount.

There was also a woman in the camp who did all the cooking on an open fire. One evening she dipped into her personal supply of coffee and made a pot for all of us. It was a real treat. We had all been sitting quietly around the fire but when the coffee came, everyone began to talk. What a difference coffee can make, especially to people who haven't had any for a long time.

I have always enjoyed fishing, so after the evening meal I would venture out to a small lake to fish for perch. I found a log raft someone had made, big enough to hold two or three people, and soon I had an older fellow coming to fish with me. We would pole it out on the quiet lake and fish until it got dark. He had a funny habit of spitting on the fish hook after he baited it and then he would twitch the pole on the surface to attract the fish. I'm not sure if any of this made any difference but we got plenty of very good fish.

We had been there about a week when I told the others that I would like to go back to Vonganperä to see Sylvi. I knew she must be lonesome and I was lonesome for her too. The others said it was okay with them; some even encouraged me to go. One man told me to follow some ridges through the woods until I came to a logging trail that would take me to the camp. About nine at night I took off for the ten kilometer hike. So far up north there was ample light on the trails, although it was difficult to see in the heavy timber. I watched the stars to keep my direction. In about two hours I was at Vonganperä, and Sylvi and I were happy to be together for a little while. The time went so fast. I left early in the morning in order to be back to work, and on the way I met one of the camp bosses. He had come out from Kannussuo to see how our work was progressing and discovered that I had gone to see my wife. He really chewed me out and told me never again to leave work without permission. "It is not done," he insisted. "When you're on a job, you stay there."

The job was more important than family! I kept my cool but I sure felt like telling him off. What an attitude! But this, I thought at the time, was only one man. For the most part, the camp bosses were fair, and morale was high among the workers. Anything you did was noticed and appreciated, and we were all proud of what we had been able to accomplish.

My next job was floating logs to the sawmills down the river at a place called Sakura Järvi. Happily, Sylvi was sent along as cook. We left Vonganperä in a motorboat, eighteen men and Sylvi. All we could do by motor was cross the lake to where the river started; then we had to portage about a quarter mile and put our things into two large rowboats for the rest of the trip. We ate our lunch sitting there on the river bank—some good herring and rye bread—a real treat for me.

The rowboats were about twenty feet long with three pair of oars and a steering paddle in back. After rowing a short distance we stopped at a small village to pick up a young Karelian girl to be a helper to Sylvi. It was probably the first time she had been with Americans and Finns. When she came into the boat she took a rower's seat but the men chased her into the bow with Sylvi. At first she couldn't understand what they meant. When she realized they didn't want her to row she was really surprised.

The camp at Sakura Järvi was another log building with a cook shack attached. Sylvi and I slept in the cook shack the first night and suffered from bed bugs. From then on we retired to the pantry floor where they were less plentiful. The Karelian girl made her bed outside in a large oat box; it was a good choice—no bed bugs.

The weather being very hot, we decided to work at night. It was light enough to see, even at midnight; the only problem was the little black flies or no-see-ums. We used string to tie our pants shut at the ankles and our sleeves tight at the wrists and put scarves around our necks, but the flies still got through somehow, and we were bitten all over our bodies. The bugs were so thick they even got in our eyes and mouths.

The work was very hard there. The logging crews had left fourteen- to twenty-foot pine logs scattered all over as they had had no means to stack them. We ourselves had only axes to work with, and we cut long poles with which to pry the logs and built skids to help us roll them over stumps in order to get them down to the river.

This job had been contracted for a lump sum with Karelles, the largest of three lumber trusts in Karelia. The man in charge of our group, a communist party member named Seppala, had negotiated the price. The eighteen of us had been divided into three work gangs. After a few days work Seppala called us all to a meeting. The purpose of the meeting, he said, was to evaluate each man's worth and decide how much each one would be paid. He would call out each man's name and someone from his gang was supposed to say whether he was one hundred percent productive (did as much work as anyone) or ninety percent, eighty percent or whatever. Those who were more productive would then be paid proportionately more.

Some of the men in our group were older men, and not as strong. There was clearly a difference in what each man was able to do, but who was going to volunteer to make that evaluation when it would result in someone getting less pay? This deal went against the grain with me, and I think with the others too. We had been taught that even though some people weren't physically able to do as much as the others, they deserved full pay if they were doing their best. I believe all of us—Americans and Canadians felt this way. It probably went against party instructions, but we finally decided that every man was one hundred percent productive. Our pay was divided equally.* What happened then was that after a week or so, three of the older men, trying hard to keep up with the rest for their pride's sake, became too sick to work and were taken back to Vonganperä.

My most pleasant memory of the whole job was getting to go for a swim and wash in the river morning and evening.

From Sakura Järvi we went back to Kannussuo and were then sent to a brick factory a short distance away. Here we made use of horse power. Sylvi got the job of driving the horse in a circle to turn the mixer, a rotating paddle inside a large wooden barrel. Meanwhile I shoveled sand and clay into the barrel with just enough water to make a thick mortar. When the mix was ready, I opened a door at the bottom of the barrel and it flowed out. I then carried it in buckets to the brick makers who worked it into molds. It was interesting to watch them. They would shake the mold and tamp it to get the mixture into the corners, then turn it upside down to slip the brick out. It was important that the mixture was the right consistency or they would have trouble getting the brick to slide out of the mold. After the bricks dried they were stacked into a huge circular mound with a hole in it. The others told me that wood would be placed in the hole and set on fire to cure the bricks. In other words, the bricks themselves formed the kiln. Unfortunately, we left before they were fired so I didn't get to see how it worked.

The completed bricks were sent out by truck, but they didn't always make it to their destination. Some of the truck drivers were Karelians, and the trucks that foreigners had brought over were something new to them. They were very proud and excited about how fast they could drive their trucks. With the roads being dirt or gravel, the bricks bounced around in the back and many cracked or crumbled.

After we got back to Kannussuo I had orders to go to Uhtua to dismantle a sawmill and get it ready to be moved to Kannussuo. I made

---

*During the second five year plan, 1933-1937, Stalin decided that equalization of pay was a "petty, bourgeois" practice. Hosking (156) and Kort (187).

sketches of all the wooden parts while my three helpers unbolted them. Then we loaded them onto skids and hitched horses to drag them through woods and swamps the thirty or so kilometers to Kannussuo. The power plant for the mill was the toughest job; a semi-diesel weighing about two tons, it took a whole week to transport. Meanwhile, the sawyers were cutting the necessary timbers and planks for reassembly of the mill according to my sketches. This two-man team of sawyers, who were from Finland, was fast and skillful. They evidently had worked at the trade a long time. They would roll a log onto supports about seven feet off the ground. Then, with one man on top of the log and the other underneath, they cut with a long saw along a chalkline. With each downstroke they cut about one inch into the log. The method is called "whip-sawing." I was surprised how accurate the lumber was. They usually made one-inch boards but they could even do half-inch boards.

All the time we were in the lumber camps we had been trying to arrange to move to the town of Petrozavodsk (Petroskoi in Finnish), the capital of the Karelian Republic. Sylvi wanted to go back to school, and I wanted to do mechanical and metal work. We had written to Heino and asked him what to do to get ourselves transferred. Heino worked at the ski factory in Petrozavodsk, and he had gotten some people there interested in me. The factory director was interested because I had considerable experience in auto mechanics and also because of my sawmill work; there was a sawmill connected to the ski factory. Another man who was interested in me was Laine, a musician in the ski factory band, who knew I played the trumpet. Near the end of the summer, Heino wrote to us in Kannussuo suggesting that Sylvi come down and enroll at the Teacher's College. His idea was that if she were already in Petrozavodsk, I would have a better chance of getting sent there. We decided to try it.

I went with her by boat as far as Uhtua (with permission from the boss—they weren't all sticklers to the rules) and there we met two American boys who were truck drivers between Uhtua and Kemi. One of them agreed to let Sylvi ride in his cab. I was glad about that because the weather was cool and sitting in an open truck box for hours could get miserable.

After Sylvi left on the truck, I decided to look for a dentist while I was in town. I had been bothered with a toothache for some time. So I checked in at the local clinic. The nurse there was a big woman who looked like a prize fighter. Her shoulders were wider than mine. She took one look at my tooth and said it had to come out, but the dentist, unfortunately, would not be there that day or the next. I told her my boat would be leaving that evening and asked if she could call the dentist and explain my predicament. She thought about it for a moment and told me to sit in a high back chair. Then she called in another powerful-looking woman and announced that she was going to pull my tooth and the other one should stand by and help. The helper right away got behind me and put a hammer lock on my head while the first one told me to open wide. When I did, she latched on to my tooth with forceps and started pulling. Even though I had decided I was not going to yell, I did, and tried my best to squirm free. I know my hind end came up from the chair but Katinka behind me held on tight, and the nurse kept pulling. I could feel the pain all the way down from my tooth to my seat.

Finally it came out. What a relief! I walked out in a daze, spitting blood, and headed for the liquor store where I bought a half liter of vodka which I took down to the water front. Sitting on a piling I took a couple of pulls out of the bottle and gingerly felt my gum where the tooth had been. It didn't hurt at all anymore and wasn't numb, just a little tender. By evening when the boat left my jaw was back to normal, a result, I believe, of the fact that it wasn't "frozen" and had a good chance to heal. All the vodka did was to relax me. I don't recommend this method of tooth extraction, but if you can stand the pain, it will heal faster.

Later on, in Petrozavodsk, I had to have a tooth capped. Silver was in very short supply at that time; patients provided their own. I gave the dentist an American dime which he sent to Leningrad to process the silver. I then had a silver cap covered with steel on my tooth which I didn't much like because it was so shiny.*

I went back to Kannussuo and continued with the sawmill. When we first tried it out, the power plant was not running right. We tore it apart and found the gaskets leaking. There were no spare gaskets to be had. I remembered having learned in the United States that several layers of newspaper would work in a pinch, so I suggested that we try it, but the young man in charge of the power plant gave me an argument. Machines were expensive and very hard to come by, and he felt responsible for it. He had gone to school to be a diesel operator. He would not help with anything else at the mill, just sat by the engine. If it had been my mill I would have booted him out, but no one there had

---

*After our return to the States, a dentist in Detroit found this tooth an object of great interest. Later, when it had to be extracted, I asked to keep it as a souvenir, but the dentist claimed he had already thrown it away.

authority to fire him, and anyone who had a little knowledge about machinery was looked upon as someone special. Eventually I convinced him to try the newspaper gaskets, and he even helped me make them. They worked.

I enjoyed running the sawmill but I was worried about how Sylvi was managing. Then came the day that the director called me to his office to tell me there was a command from Petrozavodsk for me to report there to work at the ski factory. "But you don't have to go," he said. He wanted to keep me in Kannussuo and could have arranged it, but I refused to stay. I wanted to be with my wife.*

I learned later that Laine, the fellow from the ski factory band, had approached Kustaa Rovio, secretary of the Karelian Communist Party, and asked to have me transferred to the ski factory. Hearing that I had already been sent up north to the lumber camps, Rovio had first said it was too late and why hadn't I been sent to Petrozavodsk in the first place. But later he relented and went along with the plan.

---

*Early Communist doctrine included intentional weakening of family ties; marriage and divorce (even bigamy) was easy. Abortion was readily available. Children were encouraged in school to disobey parents who went against communist ideology, and husbands and wives were often assigned to work in different places. However, this family disintegration policy had undesirable side effects: low birth rate and high juvenile delinquency. By 1935, the party was swinging back toward upholding family values. This would turn out to be very helpful to Lauri and Sylvi in the end, as well as at this time (Rostow 110, Timasheff 195).

Reading, Writing and Shooting

S: The summer of 1934 is a blur of conflicting emotions and impressions to me now. We were still newlyweds; this was, in a way, our honeymoon, but in no way could it be compared to a traditional honeymoon. I was very happy to be with my wonderful husband but terribly homesick and lonesome for my father and brothers. It seemed hard to believe that we were even on the same planet, so distant did they seem to be. The world is much smaller today, and people think nothing of hopping from one continent to another. Not so, at that time. Then too, going to the Soviet Union was a very serious step to take, and, in most cases, the immigrant considered it final. We did not think of ourselves as emigres in the true sense of the word as we had left with the idea that this was not necessarily a final commitment; we assumed that a return was possible.

During the two months or so of summer 1934 that I spent in the north of Karelia, I held several odd jobs. Having never done anything but attend school and then teach, I was ill-prepared for any of the work that needed doing at the lumber camps.

While in Vonganperä, I had no work, and since Lauri had been sent to Kannussuo to make hay, I had a very lonely time of it. A Canadian woman was in the room next to mine. She had a lovely voice, and the

25

old Finnish songs she sang increased my feelings of homesickness and nostalgia, for they reminded me of home and dances at the old Finn hall on Sugar Island.

There was another woman at Vonganperä, a crabby, fault-finding Finnish woman of about sixty who didn't help matters any. One day I happened to be wearing my "beach pajamas," a favorite outfit I'd brought from the States. It consisted of a blouse with pants that were tight-fitting at the waist but flared out to about a yard wide at the ankles. When old Crabby saw me, she proclaimed for all to hear that in all her life she had never seen such ugly clothes! Even then we had a generation gap, old and young criticizing each other.

However, after his hay-making stint, Lauri became one of a group of men that was sent to float logs down a river. Seppala, the man in charge, took pity on me and arranged for me to go along with the group as cook. He also found a Karelian girl, Katja, to work as my helper, but the titles could very well have been reversed as far as I was concerned since it wasn't always clear just who was helping whom! Katja was a gentle soul, always willing to do her share and more. She was accustomed to doing men's work as is generally true in societies not as far developed as ours, so she was very much surprised when she stepped into our boat and took her place at the oars, to find that she was not required to row. Our men told her to sit in the bow while they did the rowing. She was thrilled to find that now she could watch the scenery, and many were her exclamations of surprise as we passed scenes she had often passed before but had not had time to see. Katja and I worked well together, and I liked her. Before we parted, I gave her a purse that she had admired. It was a two way purse, white on one side and blue on the other. She had never seen anything like it, although the women in Karelia did use purses at that time.

We cooked in a huge kettle over an open fire. The hardest part of the job was building the fire each morning. Lauri would help me with it. The menu was simple and monotonous: porridge in the morning, usually cream of wheat or millet, soup at noon made of dried potatoes, canned meat and a lot of river water, and the same in the evening. It hurt to see that often the men would have eaten more had we had more to offer, for there were times when the food ran out. We had a certain amount to be used for each meal and occasionally it just was not enough. This would anger the men, but I don't think their anger was in any way directed against the system in general. It was just a more localized reaction to the place and conditions at hand.

Morale was high. The men worked hard and they also enjoyed themselves, as men are apt to do, with small talk and lumberjack humor. This down-to-earth humor was a cause of great embarrassment to me. I had not been accustomed to rough jokes and was often reduced to tears on hearing them. The little schoolmarm had much to learn about the real world out there!

When we returned to Kannussuo I was given a job gathering moss to be used in caulking. I was paid by the weight of the moss. I never did figure out what was more advantageous: to fill the bag with dry moss, which was faster but did not weigh as much, or to pick wet moss in which case it took longer to fill the sack but then it weighed more when full.

Then of course there was the time when Lauri worked at the brick factory, and I was given the job of driving the horse around in a circle. He was hitched to a long pole that turned the mixer that stirred the mortar. The little horse and I went round and round by the hour. The men told me I was foolish to walk behind the horse. "Just stand off to the side and every time he comes around yell at him or give him the switch," they suggested. But I couldn't do that; I wouldn't have been doing my part of the job.

None of these jobs made me feel very important, but at least I was doing something. Evidently I had written to my father about my feelings of inadequacy concerning the work at the lumber camps. Later, my friend Impi wrote me that others had read my letter and concluded that I was dissatisfied and homesick and unhappy. In my answer to Impi I admitted that I was homesick, at times terribly so, but, to quote from my letter, "that doesn't mean that I don't like it here." As with other difficulties and disappointments, we took everything in stride; we had great hopes for the future.

Late that summer, I received permission to enter the Pedagogical Institute (or Teachers' College) in Petrozavodsk, the capital of the Autonomous Republic of Karelia. I was happy about that because it meant going to school again and teaching, but Lauri had no permit to leave the lumber camps so I had to take off by myself. Naturally I was not at all happy about leaving him, but my great love for study and my interest in becoming a teacher again helped us decide. It did not seem fair to separate husband and wife, and this would not have happened back in the States, but we knew when we came that there would be difficulties of all kinds, and we were prepared to do our bit for the country. Then too, we were quite sure that Lauri would be able to follow me soon, for Heino and a friend of his were working together to get him a command to come to the ski factory where they worked.

The trip from Uhtua to Petrozavodsk was a harrowing experience. Lauri had arranged for me to ride with an American truck driver from Uhtua to Kemi, a distance of 110 miles. Although it was only the first of September, it was very cold and windy so I was glad to be sitting in the warm truck cab. But my joy was short-lived. A few miles down the road an Army officer hailed the truck. He motioned for me to get out of the cab and into the truck box. For the rest of the journey, I sat in the box, cold and miserable, while the officer shared the warm cab with the driver. I know the driver, being an American, would not have had it so, but there was nothing he could do about it. The officer had rank and he pulled it; chivalry did not enter into the case.

At Kemi I sat in the railroad station for hours waiting for a train to Petrozavodsk. I had much more baggage than I could handle because I had with me the tools we had brought for our friend Heino. I knew I could not get them into the train by myself so I spoke to a nice-looking young Karelian lad; I gave him three rubles and asked him to help me whenever the train came in. He took my three rubles, and that was the last I ever saw of him. Somehow I managed. I sat for hours on my pile of luggage, fighting sleep. The train came in, and someone helped me on.

Heino met me at the station in Petrozavodsk and took me to my future home. I was to live with Ilmi and Keijo Frilund and their little girl, Irma, who was about four. They had a two-room apartment which was a luxury in Karelia at that time. We had known Ilmi slightly back home; she often spent summers on Sugar Island with friends, whom we also knew. She and Keijo had lived in Chicago; they'd been married in the States but Irma had been born in Karelia.

Back in the United States, Keijo and his mother had been deeply dedicated to the workers' cause, and she was very active among the Finnish radicals in Chicago. But she elected to stay in the States while Keijo and Ilmi took off for the Soviet Union. Keijo was an electrician at the ski factory, and his wife worked there too. He had become a party member soon after arriving in Karelia. It was not easy to join the party, and they weren't recruiting members. A person had to take the initiative to apply and just having been a party member in the United States didn't guarantee acceptance in Karelia.

If an application was accepted, one first became a candidate for membership and attended classes on political theory. Later, if approved, one became a member. There seemed to be no discrimination against women. We knew only a few party members, and a few more who were candidates, but it was something that was not much discussed. Political matters in general were not discussed as freely over there as in the United States. Perhaps it was because there was only one party, and they made all the decisions. We had no choice.

I was very depressed and poor company at that time. There I was, all alone in an alien land, missing Lauri and homesick for my father and brothers. Heino was determined to raise my spirits and made every effort to get me to smile. One evening he took me to an amusement park and stood me in front of the crazy fun house mirror; he was sure I would smile at my silly reflection. I did smile, but mostly for his sake.

The Frilunds lived in ski factory barracks, a complex of half a dozen or so two-story wooden buildings. They were divided into one or two room apartments, to use the word loosely. Almost all of the residents were Finns from the United States, Canada or Finland. Finnish was one of the official languages of the Karelian Republic, along with Russian, so the language barrier was not too solid although most stores and businesses used only Russian.

Ilmi and Keijo treated me well although they had to give up a lot of their precious privacy on my account. I enjoyed school. However, I was unhappy because my husband was not with me. Then, on the eighteenth of October, Ilmi answered a knock on the door and was handed a telegram. She opened it, read it, looked at me and grinned. For some time she just stood there and grinned. Finally she told me what was in the telegram: Lauri was arriving that very day! I was overjoyed. Heino and I met him at the station, and from then on I was much happier.

I had arrived in Petrozavodsk in the beginning of September, in time for the start of the school year. The Karelian Pedagogical Institute was a two-year school that prepared teachers for the secondary or middle school. Although I had taught school back in the States, I did not have the political knowledge required of a Soviet teacher. Then too, I wanted to speak Finnish correctly and fluently, and I wanted to know something of Finnish literature. For these reasons, the Institute was the place for me. It was located across a large field from the ski factory, and I would usually take a path through the field to get to my classes. Most of the students lived in a dormitory called the Internat. It amused those of us who came from further away in town that these dormitory residents were generally the last ones to get to class. All students received a monthly stipend. The students at the Institute were Finns from Finland, Karelians, and those of us from the United States or Canada. We all got along very well; there was no antagonism among us.

I majored in Finnish language and literature. The curriculum also included Russian language and literature, Russian history, pedagogy (the art or science of teaching), philosophy and war study. All the students on this curriculum spoke Finnish, and some knew Russian or Karelian as well. Karelian seemed to be a mixture of the two languages but more closely related to Finnish. A Russian class for those of us who knew no Russian at all was held after school. The German language was on the curriculum when we started classes at the Institute, but, for some strange reason, which we were not told, it was discontinued after only one session.

Since I was on a Finnish language-literature curriculum, my professors were mostly Finns who presumably had come from Finland at some earlier time. Russian literature and history, however, were taught by a Russian and pedagogy by a Karelian.

Finnish language was taught by Professor Salo who was the very picture of an absent-minded professor, with glasses continually slipping down his nose. He had a habit of calling on me to compare Finnish and English grammar and to translate words from one language to another. This was often difficult for me since I knew nothing of Finnish grammar. I had grown up speaking the dialect of the Varsinais-Suomi region of Finland where my parents had been born and raised. Like most dialects, it was far from book language. During the course of my studies I was often amazed to learn how the correct way to speak or write Finnish differed from what I had known at home. To this day I feel grateful to Professor Salo for what he taught me of my mother tongue.

Professor Ruhanen taught us Finnish literature. He was a handsome young man, well-liked by all the class for his easy-going, good-natured personality. Preparations for this class were difficult since few books were available to us. I would often stay up most of the night to finish a novel in order to have it back at school in the morning for someone else to read.

I had never read Finnish literature and found it very interesting. We also read many Finnish translations of English books. All these novels were studied with the class struggle in mind. This was new to me since of course it had not been so in the United States. A story by the nineteenth-century Finnish author Juhani Aho has stayed in my mind. It was called "Train" and told about the reactions of the residents of a small town to the arrival of the first train in their area. I think I remember this story well because I happened to be the only one in class to see the symbolism of the train. It represented the industrial revolution, and the villagers were unhappy and frightened at the prospect of its coming. I was continually amazed to see how the class struggle and the ideology of the working class were brought into each story we studied.

Professor Bazanov taught us Russian literature and history. I did not learn very much in his class because of the language barrier—he knew only Russian. I had to rely on notes taken by some of my classmates who knew some Russian. Professor Bazanov was a dour young man who seldom smiled or joked. He had a crush on Aini, a young Karelian girl in the class, and we teased her about him.

Our pedagogy teacher, whose name I do not recall, was a Karelian who spoke with a heavy accent and seemed to be a beginner in the field of teaching. He had one peculiarity that aggravated many of us; he would mention a particular topic briefly and then say that we would delve into it more fully later on. But the next time he brought it up, he would simply remind us that we had already dealt with the subject! Consequently, we acquired a rather superficial knowledge of pedagogy as practiced at that time in the Soviet Union. One story the teacher told us has stayed with me.

After the revolution much experimentation went on in Soviet teaching. At one point they tried a method in which the children would study one subject from every possible angle. For instance, they studied chickens: their biology, then their history, then the economics of raising them, and literature about them. It didn't go over well. The children grew weary of it and would plead with the teacher to make an end of the chicken.

Our philosophy class was taught in Finnish by Professor Jaakkola, but, since philosophy is not an easy subject in any language, I found it difficult. I understood it at the time but at this late date, I cannot recall much of it. It was, of course, dialectical materialism, which is the philosophy of communism. It was based on Karl Marx's theory, which had the class struggle as its main doctrine. Marx believed that, since the economic forces in the modern world were in constant conflict, the working class needed to unite and bring about social and political changes that would then result in the dictatorship of the proletariat, which would work for and finally achieve communism, a social system based on common ownership of the means of production and equal distribution of the products of industry. (What we had in the Soviet Union at the time was supposed to be the dictatorship of the proletariat.)

One of our classes, "Sotilas Oppi" (War Study), was something new to most of us. It entailed a study of the rifle and its parts and also shooting practice. Our teacher was the typical, tough sergeant type so often portrayed in war movies. One afternoon when we were out for rifle practice, lying on the ground and shooting at paper targets, a breeze came up and caused the targets to move about. My friend Flossie complained about this, to which the old sergeant replied, "The Capitalist Exploiter won't hold his head still either." This was a startling thought; we were preparing for the final conflict!

Although I had heard the words "final conflict" all through childhood, it was a shock to have it brought to my attention in such a realistic way. Were we really preparing to go out into the battlefield and do actual combat with the enemy (the enemy being the capitalist exploiter)? Was I ready for that? It had never occurred to me so vividly before. But, if this was what was needed, then so be it. We had our warfare classes and our target practice. Luckily I never had to make use of it.

The two smartest pupils in our class were a Finnish man named Sampsa Pulkkinen (for fun we would call him Pumpsa Salkkinen but he didn't mind) and a Finnsh girl named Maiju Gylling. Maiju's father was the Chairman of the Executive Committee of the Karelian Republic (the top man in Karelia) when we first went there. Maiju was a little older than most of us, and very intelligent.

A young Karelian lad whose name I do not recall was a constant source of amusement to us. He had witty sayings that he would always quote at opportune moments. Whenever someone became excited, he would caution them, "*Rauhallisuus ennen kaikkea*," (Above all, keep calm). When something needed straightening out, he would say, "*Huonokin järjestys on parempi kuin epäjärjestys*," (Even poor order is better than disorder). We always enjoyed his comments; they are funnier in Finnish. As is true in all languages, something is lost in the translation of proverbs, axioms, etc.

The little group with which I often studied was comprised of Selma Anderson and Flossie Merilä from the States; Inkeri Letonmäki and Lempi, originally from Finland; Aino from Karelia; and Katri Muukkonen, a Russian who had lived in the United States for a few years. Katri had been born in Russia, but in the twenties she had met and married an American Finn who had come to the Soviet Union to work in an automobile factory. When he returned to the States, he took Katri with him, and they lived there for some years, lastly in Detroit, before coming back to the Soviet Union in 1933. Katri was always in our small study group

Class from the Karelian Pedagogical Institute. Inkeri Letonmäki is on the left in the front row. In the middle row, Professor Bazanov is third from the left, followed by Professor Salo. Sylvi is second from the right with Maiju Gylling at the far right. Flossie is in the back row directly behind Sylvi, with Sampsa Pulkkinen next to her.

and did her best to translate Russian into Finnish or English.

None of us in this group lived at the dormitory, and we would get together in each other's "homes" (rooms, actually) to study. Of course, we did a lot of visiting too, and drank coffee if it was available, which was seldom. *Chai* (tea) or *mocha* (coffee made from wheat, rye or other grains) was the common fare. It was a wonderful treat to get real coffee.

At one such gathering I got in trouble with the rest of the group. I have always enjoyed making rhymes and quoting from poets and rhymesters. This time I began to recite what I thought was a cute little rhyme that went thus: "There's nothing new under the sun, nor poem nor pun. . . ." I got no further when the other girls informed me, in no uncertain terms, that this was a decadent, bourgeois way of thinking, and not at all in line with Soviet philosophy. I took heed.

This made me realize how easy it was to think and voice opinions that could be construed to be bourgeois and against Soviet philosophy. According to the Soviet line of thought, they were constantly coming up with new ideas and new inventions, progress in every field, and to say there was nothing new under the sun was indeed wrong. I would do well to think twice before reciting even humorous bits of verse or prose

learned earlier in our capitalist environment. They might be miscon-
strued.

As I have mentioned before, we did not, as a rule, talk politics with
our friends. All power came from above, and we soon realized that even
constructive criticism was not welcomed and could be misunderstood
or deliberately twisted. Politics entered every phase of our lives and, in
that respect, life differed greatly from what we had lived back in the
States. Of course, our parents had been involved in politics and discussed
it among themselves, but Lauri and I had not paid much attention. I, for
one, was concerned only with school and the social life connected with
it. But in Karelia, each school, each factory, every workplace had its
political organizer or teacher. They held meetings regularly at which
the workers and students were taught the tenets of communism. They
would also hold meetings at the various barracks, and, although attend-
ance was not required, it was what we called "voluntary compulsion";
it was best to go.

Two very important celebrations took place during the school year.
One was in honor of the October Revolution of 1917, and the other was
May Day, the first of May. Big parades were held on these occasions
with the whole town taking part. Students from the Institute met at a
predetermined street corner very early in the morning to await our turn
in the parade. Much talking and joshing took up our time while we
waited. These parades and the speeches we heard were stirring experiences as, of course, they were meant to be. High officials of the Karelian
Autonomous Republic, such as Maiju's father, Edvard Gylling, were in
the reviewing stand with perhaps one or two from Leningrad or Moscow. They made speeches praising the Communist Party, the workers'
government and, above all, Stalin. Stalin was the mightiest of the mighty,
a demigod, from whom all blessings flowed, to whom we gave thanks
for any and every good we received.*

Stalin had been in power for ten years by this time, and his personality cult had already become very strong. It was cultivated in every possible way. Among ordinary people there was already a feeling that perhaps it was a little bit exaggerated, but we still felt that Stalin was the true
ruler of the people and had only our welfare in mind. He was a father
figure to all of us. And so we listened to the speeches and hurrahed and
applauded at the right times.

---

*A typical song about Stalin went: "We give thee our thanks for the sun thou has lit" (Kort 198). An-
other was called, "Glory to the Great Name of Stalin" (Randall 118).

In December of 1934, Kirov, a prominent member of the Soviet government, was assassinated in Leningrad. The day of his funeral was a public day of mourning. Zinoviev and Kamenev, also government officials, were arrested and charged with the crime. According to the newspapers, they pleaded guilty. They did not, however, have a public trial at this time.

In 1935 we began to read in the papers about other arrests of government officials. They were accused of being "counter revolutionary" which meant they were against what the Communist Party wanted. The Party was in charge. What the Party said was right, was right. You didn't argue with the Party. That was the system. Party members were thought of as being representatives of the people. They were from the working class (we were *all* working class), and they weren't making any money for their work in the Party—why shouldn't they look after the interests of the people? There seemed to be no reason not to trust the Party to do the right thing. And so it seemed to be a good idea to get these "counter revolutionaries" out of positions of authority, "purging" the Party, as it later came to be known. Of course we had no inkling, at that time, what these "purges" would turn into.

Boats, Trumpets and Piston Rings

L: I stayed at Kannussuo long enough to train an American Finn to operate and take care of the sawmill. Then I too caught a ride in the cab of a truck to Kemi. (Luckily, no officers needed a ride that day.) Arriving in Kemi, I was left at the railroad station with my suitcases and trunks, which included that heavy oat box. I was worried that I didn't have enough money for my ticket plus all the baggage so I asked, in Finnish, at the ticket window how much it would be.

The ticket seller was a young Karelian girl who spoke some Finnish—reluctantly. From what I understood, she told me to purchase a ticket, and then she would tell me what the baggage cost. I tried to explain that I needed to know the full price before I bought the ticket but she slammed the window shut and refused to open it for me. This kind of behavior was typical of many little bureaucrats we were to see later.

I left, looking for help, and met a friendly Karelian woman who understood my Finnish and also spoke Russian. She seemed to be a smart and capable person, and I explained my predicament. With a twinkle in her eye she agreed to translate for me, so back we went to the ticket window where she knocked, producing the same ticket seller. An exchange of Russian followed, of which I understood nothing except the ticket seller's firm *"nyet."*

My translator wouldn't take that and began to yell, even to spit, at our adversary. Of course, that didn't help, but my Karelian friend was not one to give up easily. With me in tow she scouted around for a policeman, and the three of us returned to face the mistress of the ticket window. There was more heated Russian, but this time the little bureaucrat, red faced and angry, had to come around. I had enough money to buy my ticket and ship all the baggage.

Of course there are petty bureaucrats everywhere who seem to like to hassle people, but it was disappointing to find them over there, because it wasn't supposed to be that way. In a socialist society all workers were supposed to be equal. That was part of the dream.

The train I was to take didn't leave until the following day, so I had to find a place for the night. As it happened, a young Russian army officer came to talk to me. He spoke very good Finnish; I later learned he was a Finn. I asked him about hotels in Kemi, and he invited me to go along with him, and we would get a room together. We sloshed through the muddy streets, he cursing that the place was always muddy whenever he came. He was very interested in the United States and asked a lot of questions. He also wondered how I got stuck in such an awful place as Kemi.

He was in the army, he said, because it was a better life than civilian work and, with his experience, suited him better. I learned later that army food and clothing were much better than what the average worker could get. The next morning after breakfast we returned to the station and sat and talked some more. He was one of the nicest people I met over there—very intelligent and helpful.

When my train came, I got into a compartment with a Russian fellow. Finding my Russian poor, he began with sign language, inviting me to join him for a drink. I was afraid to leave my suitcases but he assured me they were safe. So we drank together and talked, or mimed, in our own way and it was surprising how well we could understand each other.

Across the aisle from me and my friend were about ten men dressed just in rags with birch bark shoes. They were not prisoners but displaced persons, called "*usloni*" in Russian.* They looked pitiful. At that time almost everyone carried their lunch along with them—if they had nothing else they usually had bread. When I finished my lunch of bread and a small tin of fish, one of these ragamuffins pointed to the can. He wanted

---

*These were probably kulaks; Russian peasants who were torn from their homesteads after the Revolution and told to go and join collective farms. Many starved.

it. There was a little bit of oil left in it. I handed it over and when he was through wiping it with his bread it was completely clean. He thanked me over and over. My Russian friend didn't seem at all concerned at their plight, and that was the general attitude we saw over there toward those people. Those who were better off seemed to think, "Whatever they've done, they probably deserved it. It's not my responsibility." This attitude bothered me.

When I arrived in Petrozavodsk, Sylvi was still living with Ilmi and Keijo Frilund. I moved in, too, for a few months until we got to move into another ski factory barracks a stone's throw away.

The Gylling Ski Factory, named for Edvard Gylling, leader of the Karelian Republic, employed about 250 workers. It was the second largest factory in town, the biggest being Onegzavod, where cast iron and steel castings were made. Located on the shore of Lake Ääninen (Onega in Russian), the ski factory had a wood-fueled power house, a lumber yard to store the bolts* that the skis were made from, a heated kiln for drying, and a sawmill to cut the bolts and material for the wood-working shop. There was also a small machine shop where cutters were made and machines repaired. The whole area (except for the lake side) was surrounded with a wire fence about ten feet high, and there were watch dogs on long wire ropes patrolling inside the fence. The one entrance was guarded day and night. You couldn't just walk in; if the guard didn't know you, you had to show your pass.

The director of the ski factory, Elias Tuomainen, was from the Savo region of Finland. He had been in Karelia for years, since shortly after the Revolution. He wanted to know if I had any experience on auto and marine engines which, of course, I had, having operated and repaired marine engines on the St. Mary's River since I was twelve years old. He was having a boat built for the ski factory by an American boat builder from Oregon, another immigrant to Karelia, who had been a commercial fisherman on the Columbia River. (I think his name was Kari.) The craft he was building was about twenty-eight feet long and modeled like the Columbia River boats were at that time. To me it was just beautiful, and subsequently proved to be seaworthy as well.

The ski factory had an old six-cylinder automobile engine that they hoped to repair and use in the boat. It was an Oakland engine just like

---

*A bolt of wood is a one-quarter lengthwise section of a log. Skis were made from the outside of the log, always with the bark side down because that side had a tendency to form a natural arch which is good on the bottom of a ski.

one I had had in 1928 on an old Oakland four door. They told me to check it out and give them a list of parts to be replaced. I did and it was a long one, including pistons, piston rings, valves, plugs, springs, gaskets, and more, none of which were ever procured. "Do the best you can," I was told.

The director's brother, Arne Tuomainen, was shop foreman. "We can make the piston rings and valves in the shop," he told me. I gave the lathe hand the size for the rings; he turned them; we peened the inside for tension, cut and fitted them in place. It was quite an experience for me. We decided to use the old pistons, but we even made a new propeller, welded construction. It worked very well.

The propeller shaft extended from the stern to the engine, which was mid-ship, and was uncovered—at first. One day while I worked on the boat with the engine running (and the shaft turning), I stepped quickly over it and one leg of my pants caught on a set screw and immediately started to wrap around the shaft. I grabbed the cabin wall and hung on for all I was worth. There was a ripping sound, and I found myself standing there with only one leg on my pants. The other one was torn off at the waist and wrapped around the propeller shaft. My leg was okay—just scratched a bit—but I had to go home for another pair of pants. After that I built a box around the prop shaft.

I worked off and on between the boat and machine repair all winter. Then in the spring when the ice went out we put the boat in Lake Ääninen, a fairly large body of water.

It took me a couple of days to get the motor started and then it was running on only four or five cylinders. All the spark plugs were old, and I kept changing them around. One day the director came out to the boat to ask how I was doing. I told him it wasn't running well, and we needed better plugs. He listened to the motor but, undaunted, said we would take the boat to a neighboring village about twenty-five miles away and get some fish for the ski factory cafeteria from the kolkhoz° there. "We'll leave tomorrow afternoon," he said, "and stay overnight."

We had only tried the boat a couple of times, and the motor was still very tight. I worked on it late that night and early the next morning. It was still not right when we started out on the open lake, but after about two hours of coaxing the engine finally took off on all six. What a difference! Now we were doing fourteen to fifteen miles an hour, and soon were at the village where we were invited in to eat at the home of the

° A collective farm.

kolkhoz director. I felt bad because my clothes were oily and dirty, but I needn't have worried; they draped a white sheet over each of us before serving. (Of course then I worried about getting the sheet dirty!) The first course consisted of water that fish had been boiled in. Next we had the boiled fish with sour bread and tea.

Meanwhile the wind had picked up and was blowing quite a gale. We went to bed hoping the storm would let up during the night. It didn't look too bad in the morning, so we shoved off. We had a head wind and ran at half speed. I was afraid to pound the boat any harder. The weather kept getting worse, and we were making very little headway.

Tuomainen asked me if I thought the engine would keep running, and I told him that at the rate we were going we wouldn't have enough fuel to make it. So we turned back to the village, and he telephoned back to Petrozavodsk to send us some fuel as soon as the weather permitted. A small diesel tug arrived that afternoon but had no fuel for us. Instead, they started to tow us back, which made Tuomainen very unhappy. He asked me to let him know when we were close enough to make it with the fuel we had. As soon as I gave the word, we were off, leaving the tug behind and beating them in by half an hour. Tuomainen was really pleased, and I felt better too.

The ski factory had a restaurant located outside the fence, with two eating areas, one for technical personnel and the other for workers. I never had the pleasure of eating with the technical people, but I was told by some that they had better food. In our area, the mainstay of the meals was sour bread, and we often had cabbage soup and very little else. Sometimes there was a bit of meat in the soup. I was lucky because I like cabbage soup. I used to keep ladling it away, telling the others how good it was for them, but nobody would buy that. I just got dirty looks.

There was a little beer kiosk about a quarter mile from our barracks. The place was so small that only five or six people could stand inside; some got their drink and went outside to drink it. I would take a bucket there, get it filled, and drink it at home. One time I remember when I was having my bucket filled that there was a man inside with his eight- or nine-year-old son; they were drinking beer together. The son looked like quite a little man as he raised his mug and said, "*Davai Papa vypim*" ("Come on Papa, let's drink"). Somehow it struck me so funny that I remember it to this day.

Life went along smoothly. Sylvi went to school and I continued to work in the ski factory machine shop where I was soon made foreman of machine repair. I liked it, although I was on call day and night if there was any problem the shift workers couldn't handle. Of course this was overtime, which meant more money; sometimes I would more than double my salary. I also got bonus checks for improvements in the machines. If the improvement eliminated one worker, they would pay a certain percent of the savings.

The ski factory also had a section where they built furniture—tables, chairs, cabinets, and other pieces—mostly of birch with some poplar and pine. The machines—planers, saws, and trimmers—were primarily Swedish made, some Finnish and some American. (I seem to remember one saw that was stamped Three Rivers, Michigan.) Many of these things had probably been brought to Karelia by recruits like us, but the Russian government did send buyers to the United States and possibly to other countries as well.

The skis, mostly for cross country, were birch and very well made under the direction of Snellman, a Finnish engineer who had been with the factory from its very beginning, some time in the early twenties. The ski machinery was all of his design, made in Sweden, and very efficient.

After I had worked there awhile, I was sent to Moscow along with some of the engineers and foremen to look over another ski factory. As I wrote in a letter to my sister back in Michigan:

It's a bigger outfit than ours, but the quality of their skis was poorer than ours. We make good skis. Wanna buy a pair?

There were some apprentices at the factory learning to do the handwork on the skis. At first I thought they were only about twelve or thirteen years old, but I was told that none of them were under sixteen. They were small because they had been born during really hard times and hadn't gotten enough food for growth.

One morning the head engineer at the ski factory, a Russian, came to me wanting to know if I knew anything about diesel engines. He had gotten a call from a school that their power plant was out of order. I thought maybe I could help, so we went to take a look at it.

The power plant had a big single-cylinder semi-diesel for generating enough energy to light up the school dormitory and several buildings around. The operator was a Finnish lady; her husband had died, and she had inherited his job. After talking to her I realized she was well qualified. She told me the rod bearing had burned out. We tore down the engine, took the bearing back to the ski factory and poured a new one out of babbit. After we fitted it in and started up the engine I was satisfied that the job was done, but the operator kept checking the oil and saying it just didn't act the way it used to. We waited a couple of hours, then left telling her to call if she had any trouble. The following morning she did, telling us that the engine was knocking loudly and the bearing was burned out. We went back and did the job over again, fitting the new bearing as perfectly as we knew how. She was still skeptical, saying the foam on the oil didn't look right, but I assured her it was a good bearing and she shouldn't worry.

The same thing happened again: there was the phone call and the plant was down again with no electricity. This time we tore that engine down so we could inspect every moving part. Finally one of the men asked me why a certain copper tube was bent. There was the problem. The tube was the source of oil for the crank; because of the bend in it, the rod bearing wasn't getting the full amount of oil. We corrected it and this time when we started the engine up again the operator was happy. The foam on the oil was the way it should be.

I got extra pay for that job, and the engineer got a new bicycle that he had wanted from the school management. I like to think we saved the lady's job.

There was always need for machine repair at small woodworking shops in town, so I decided to do repair work evenings and weekends along with Keijo Frilund who was an electrician. I knew this kind of thing was frowned upon, but Keijo was a Party member so I figured it was probably okay.* At first we found it difficult to get a decent price; the people just loved to haggle, and we would end up cutting our price and making very little. After we got onto their ways, we started making our first bid about forty percent higher than what we wanted and then we did quite well. We allowed our customers to chew us down quite a bit, which made them happy, but we still had a comfortable fee for our services.

One of the things I liked most about the ski factory was their brass band. As I mentioned, one of the reasons I got to go to the ski factory was because I played the trumpet. I started right in practicing with the group.

Laine, a baritone player, was the best musician in our band. He had learned to play in the Russian army. Before the Russian revolution when Finland was under Russian rule, Finns were conscripted into the Russian army. They also took young boys with musical talent and taught them to

---

*It was *not* okay—officially. Private enterprise employing hired labor was considered a crime with which there could be no compromise. (Dallin 8).

The ski factory band. Lauri is second from the right in the back. Laine is on his right.

Lauri, honored as a *Stakhanovist*.

play. They had to learn to march and play under all kinds of conditions, even on horseback. Finns called them "battalion players." They had to be good in order to graduate. Laine was one of these.

I started out playing the trumpet and later switched to baritone, which suited me better. There were about twenty-five of us in the band, and we practiced every week. Occasionally we even played in a combined group of bands from all over the territory with about a hundred and fifty musicians. The director of this large group, Teplitsky, was an amazing man. There was talk that he had been a prisoner building the White Sea canal.* He could pick out individual players if they sounded a sour note and make them play a part over again. I had a hard time hearing my own horn.

Elis Ranta was the leader of our ski factory band. We were called upon to play at dances, parades, an occasional concert, and various affairs at the ski factory club. We received no pay for this; it was a civic duty, and one we enjoyed. But we did get paid for playing at funerals. Often, when people had a death in the family, they would hire a band to play the funeral march while the body was being taken to the grave. We would walk directly behind the pallbearers playing slowly in time with our walking. When we got to the grave we would usually go to one side and wait to see if we were needed. There would be a lot of wailing and crying; the women would throw themselves on the grave and carry on for some time. Then they would ask everyone to come to their home for food and drinks, usually plenty of both. I was always amazed at how much food they were able to serve since everything was in short supply.

Once when we were taking a Jewish man to his grave I noticed that his head was rocking from side to side in time with the music. I nudged the guy next to me and pointed it out, and we both grinned. The Jewish grave was different from most. There was a narrow trench dug at the bottom just big enough for the body with a ledge on each side. After the body was put in they laid boards on top so the earth was not thrown directly on the body. They never buried the coffin so they could use it again.

Often we were asked to play at doings some distance from town.

---

*The 142-mile White Sea to Baltic canal project was assigned in 1930 to Henry Yagoda, notorious head of the secret police. Between 1931 and 1934 the canal was built at the ridiculously low cost of 95,000,000 rubles using 300,000 prisoners from labor camps who worked eleven-hour days on twenty-nine ounces of bread, watery soup and salt fish (Dallin 198). According to Michael Kort (179) it was a "tragic fiasco" costing at least 250,000 lives and then "too shallow to serve its strategic objectives."

We would ride on trucks with some benches in the back so the older folks could sit while the younger ones stood. On rough roads standing was sometimes easier. There was no place to put the instruments so everyone took care of his own. What with hanging on to your instrument and keeping your balance in the truck it was not the most pleasant ride, but we had fun just the same.

Once we went to a Karelian village about a two-hour ride from Petrozavodsk for a young man's funeral. This time we were taken directly to the large old house where he had died. The body was in a coffin to one side for viewing, and a large table was in the middle of the room just loaded with food and glasses of vodka. There weren't enough chairs so we all stood up to eat and drink. The glasses of vodka must have contained about six ounces. I took one and drank it right down, Russian style, and immediately took some sour Russian bread, as was the custom, and sniffed it before eating it. I was talking to someone on my right and didn't notice when my glass was filled up again. When I saw another six ounces of vodka, I asked the fellow what I should do.

"As long as you drink it," he said, "they will fill it up again."

I just left it full.

On this occasion, the funeral procession came after the food was served. I think it was better to have it the other way, because some of the boys drank too much, and we didn't sound as good as usual. Besides that, the road we had to walk was full of ruts and holes. It was a good thing we all knew our notes; it would have been impossible to follow music. Our director was not very happy with us. (He didn't drink.) We did not go back to the house after the burial—it was straight home for us.

One night after the ski factory band had played at some doings, we stopped at a beer garden that was housed in an old church in Petrozavodsk that the state had taken over. We had a hard time talking to each other as we sat with our drinks, because the sound of our voices would go high up in the tower and then bounce back. With forty or fifty people all talking at the same time it was really weird. It did not help to talk louder, in fact, the louder the talk, the more confusing it became.

There were no rest rooms in this place, only outhouses. When I ventured out I heard loud swearing coming from the toilet. Curious, I opened the door. What a sight that was. The toilet was filthy, as they usually were over there, and a drunk had been sliding and falling all over the place. He was a real mess, and he kept swearing in Finnish about how bad it smelled. I just went back to the beer garden, but somehow the beer did not interest me anymore, and I soon left.

One day at band practice Laine asked me if I would like a job repairing some instruments for a lumber camp band. I was agreeable; a little extra money was always nice. He said he knew how, and we would work together on them in the evenings. We sat for many an evening straightening, cleaning and repairing horns. It was interesting work. I had to scrounge around for different-sized ball bearings, used ones. We would break the rings and salvage the round balls which would be pushed through the various tubes on a horn until all the kinks were out. Sometimes the valves would have to be hammered out, they were so corroded, and then soaked in kerosene, sanded, polished and buffed until they looked like new.

We were almost finished when the expeditor from the lumber camp came to see them. He was so pleased, he said, and wanted to take them back with him except for the few that weren't finished yet. He would pay for the whole job when he returned to get the rest. He had been drinking, so we didn't trust him. Laine said no, but after some argument he let the fellow take a couple to show to the camp director. Some weeks later he stopped by again and asked us to deliver the horns to a certain house, and he would pay then.

"Nothing doing," said Laine. "You deliver the cash, and *then* we will deliver the horns."

He did finally come up with the cash, and we brought the horns to a house where he was staying. The lady of the house let us in, and we found him sitting at the table chewing away on a chicken with several children watching. I could see the kids were hungry and undernourished, but the fat slob ignored them and continued to crunch away, grease dripping down his chin. It was a depressing sight, and we were glad to get out of there.

I was earning more than twice the average income. It all went for food and drink and an occasional ticket to a theater or show. I could just imagine how difficult it was for a family with a few kids to get along. I remember a time when the lady who did our wash came over for coffee. We had cookies, and when we put butter on them, she was horrified at our extravagance. She was a good worker and so was her husband, but they had four or five children, and it was tough going.

We had shop meetings at the factory where we would discuss various projects and plans. Shortly after I went to work there, we learned that the factory fire department had decided to cover all the steam heating pipes with metal to make them safer. I thought that was unnecessary and a stupid idea and said as much at one of the meetings. Nobody said anything in reply, either to agree or disagree, and I wondered why. Later Heino told me that he had heard about my remarks from someone in the Party. I had criticized someone in authority. "Don't do that," he warned me, "It isn't healthy."

That scared me. They claimed that they had freedom of speech in the Soviet Union. It was in their constitution. But going against the Party was something different. If you said anything against the Communist Party, you didn't deserve to be protected by the constitution. You had to go along with the Party, and it just seemed to follow that you weren't supposed to criticize anyone in authority. This was hard to take.

Everything came from the top down, even more so than in the United States. This wasn't at all what we had expected. We knew the revolution was built on the idea of a dictatorship, but it was supposed to be a dictatorship of the proletariat. The workers. Us! We were supposed to be running the show. But I guess we hadn't really thought it through, because a dictatorship couldn't possibly be run by everybody. Some small group had to have the real power, and over there it was the Communist Party. So I began to learn to keep some of my opinions to myself.

At Home on Swamp Street

S: We lived with the Frilunds through the winter of 1934-35 and then, early in the spring, were able to get a room for ourselves in another ski factory barracks, on *Bolotnaya Ulitsa* (Swamp Street). It was a very small room (having originally been intended for a toilet) but we were overjoyed to be by ourselves—I even enjoyed keeping house.

The barracks had no running water. A barrel of water was hauled to the back yard every day in a horse drawn wagon. When it arrived, the driver would come into the barracks, yelling, *"vodi, vodi;"* everyone would then rush out with a bucket and get his share. We did not have to pay for it. Slop water went into a bucket in the room and was carried out and dumped into a pit in the back yard.

Our first place was a little corner room and very difficult to heat; many nights the water would freeze in our buckets right in the room. Our stove, which we used for heating as well as cooking, was made of brick with a metal plate on top and used wood for fuel. The fire would go out during the day and have to be lit when we got home at night. Then it would go out at night and have to be lit in the morning. We were on our own as far as getting wood, sometimes using slabs from sawmills or trimmings from the ski factory, which we had to collect and carry up to the room. With time we learned how much wood to use and how to operate the draft to keep the fire going all night. Our Hudson Bay blanket came in handy at this time, as well as a lamb's wool comforter that had been made by Mrs. Lahti, a neighbor of ours in Michigan, and was very warm but lightweight. We lived in this small room for only a few months and then succeeded in getting a bigger, sunnier one on the second floor of the barracks.

Besides our hide-a-bed, we had plain but adequate furniture made at the ski factory. The walls of the room were papered. At that time green was my favorite color, and I managed to have so much of it in the room that it evoked comments from friends who came over. Hanging above our bed we had a picture of a baby. Lauri's sister Irja had drawn it for us—to serve as a sample, she said. We also had a lovely snow scene taken at a friend's home on Sugar Island. It hung on another wall. Above the dresser we had pictures of my friend Impi, my brother Andrew, and Ingrid Middleton, our friend in Detroit. On the dresser were more pictures from America. I made curtains of cheesecloth (brought from the United States) with green trim for the one window in the room. This window was in the only outside wall we had. It was of good size, made up of many small panes, one of which opened on hinges to form what was called a *fortochka* in Russian, used for ventilation.

Our privies were outdoors, five of them for the whole barracks, in a row over a huge box. Occasionally, this box would be emptied. A stout-hearted man would come along with a sturdy little horse pulling a large wagon, which some of us dubbed the "gold wagon." He had a bucket attached to the end of a long pole with which he would empty the contents of the privies into the wagon. Then he would sit on his wagon with a hunk of black bread and a bottle of vodka beside him on the seat and cart his load out of town to some predetermined spot. His way out of town led him right by the Pedagogical Institute, and one warm, sunny day in early summer, when we had all our classroom windows opened to let in the fresh air, his wagon overturned just below us—an event which was immediately and sickeningly evident to all. We closed the windows as quickly as possible. It took days for the aroma to vanish from the vicinity during which time we bravely endured the closeness of the classroom rather than let in the tainted springtime air.

L: At Barracks 50 there was originally a toilet planned for each end of both hallways, but when the Finns and Americans moved in they used these rooms for people to live in. One reason they weren't left as toilets was that they would have smelled (the building had no running water); another was to make more room for occupants. They then built the five outside toilets and assigned each one to a group of four families. We would wash them down every day with each family taking their turn at this chore for a week at a time. It happened that it was our turn at latrine duty when a Russian family moved into the barracks and became a part of our "group." When I went to clean I could see that someone had been standing on the seat and missed the hole. I decided I'd better have a talk with them. I explained that we cleaned carefully every day and wanted it kept that way. Apparently the Soviet government had recently had a campaign in which they warned people not to sit on toilet seats for fear of catching infectious diseases. I don't know why they didn't think of telling them to wash the seats and keep them clean. Anyway the Russian family caught on right away; there was no more crap on the seat and they took their turn washing and cleaning. A few months later, another Russian family moved in and the same thing happened, but this time the first Russian came to me cussing the "dirty Russians" who soiled our toilet. Then he added, "I'll take care of it." And he did.

Some time later, a lady health inspector came to our building. She was seen walking the halls with her nose in the air, sniffing, and asking, "*Gdye ubornaya?*" (where is the toilet?). When she was shown, she couldn't seem to understand why they didn't smell, but she was satisfied that there was no health hazard.

There was (and I gather there still is) a chronic shortage of toilet paper in the Soviet Union. We usually carried paper, mostly newsprint (there were no Sears catalogs of course). Once when I had to go to the outhouse from the ski factory yard and was without a supply, I asked the Chief Engineer for some. He took out his notebook and tore out one sheet, about two inches by five. I held my hand out for more and he gave me one more sheet. I had to make that do. Of course people often got caught without and so you saw brown streaks on the walls inside the toilets—they had done the best they could without equipment.

Many of the rooms we lived in also had brown streaks on the walls; these came from killing bedbugs, a constant pastime. I remember a newly arrived young fellow from Chicago, familiar with the bedbug problem, was amazed when he first saw the streaks in the outhouse.

"*Voi saatana, onko täälläkin luteita?*" ("What the devil, are there bed-bugs in here too?") he asked. We repeated the remark often, whenever we needed a good laugh.

S. The room at 50 Swamp Street was our home for the next six years. We were comfortable there. We had privacy of a sort, but the walls were thin and family secrets hard to keep. The other residents in the building were, for the most part, a friendly and well-meaning group.

Our closest friends were Eino and Sylvia Dahlstrom who lived in the room right below us. Lauri became acquainted with Eino at the Ski Factory garage where Eino worked as a mechanic. I didn't get to know Sylvia well until after I had graduated from the Institute and was at home more, but, after that, we were often together. Many were the evenings when we would signal each other with a thump of the broom handle on the floor or the ceiling and get together. Their beautiful baby had died in infancy from some digestive disorder, so they were childless just as we were at this time.

Miriam and Benny Laine were also very close friends, although we did not see as much of them as we did of the Dahlstroms. For one thing, they did not live at the Ski Factory Barracks. Like many others, they had come to Karelia with their parents. They had a baby born to them who almost died before the doctor discovered that she was unable to get nourishment from her mother.

Irma and Urho Hill were often in our group. Urho was a Canadian, an electrician. Irma was an American and had a job tarring skis at the ski factory. They married in Karelia and had a baby girl born in the fall of 1937. Before the baby's birth, a group of us decided to help Urho and Irma select a name for it. Each of us put a name into a hat. When the winning slip was pulled, it turned out to be the one Lauri had put in. . . . "Nelda." He had used the first names of both grandmas, Ida and Helen, to form it. The girl is Nelda to this day.

Lauri's cousin Lily and her husband, Dave, were also with us often. They lived on the other side of Petrozavodsk where Dave worked in a blacksmith shop. They were a few years older than we were, but we had fun together.

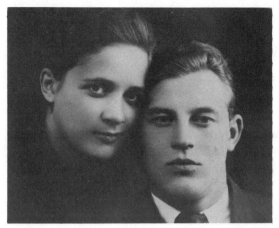

Miriam and Benny Laine.

Then there were Mary and Eino next door. Mary and her first husband had come to Petrozavodsk several years earlier. Her husband had been killed in an accident, and she then married Eino. Mary was one of the best-natured women I have ever met, with never a harsh word about anyone. Even when she gossiped, it was never malicious.

Next to Mary and Eino lived John and Inkri Saari. They were already middle-aged. Inkri was a small, cheerful lady who always had a witty story to tell. Her husband John was more staid but yet a likeable sort. John Kulmala, an American Finn married to a Karelian, was also in the building. Many American and Canadian men married Karelian girls; the girls obtained better food norms as wives of recruited workers, and the men were proud of their young brides. Viktor Viiki, whom we had known on Sugar Island, married a young Karelian girl in Petrozavodsk and was very proud of the fact.

Across the hall from us lived Aili Salo with her daughter Lillian and son Richie. Lillian was a few years younger than we were, and we did not get to know her very well. Richie was even younger, but since he played cornet in the ski factory band, we knew him well, and he was with us a lot. Whenever his money ran short, he would come to us. Lauri was apt to refuse him, so Richie would come to me, knowing I would help him out.

The librarian from the ski factory also lived in our barracks. He had come from Finland several years earlier and already knew Russian quite well. His wife was a haughty, supercilious Russian who not only ironed her pillowcases both inside and out but also pressed her husband's socks. Since we were not supposed to use electricity except for lights, she was certainly going out of her way to disobey orders. When I rather proudly told her of the progress I had made with my new Russian-Finnish dictionary, she pooh-poohed my accomplishment and said her husband knew every word in the book. This woman probably resented foreigners, for she seemed to enjoy putting me down. I had had two sweaters knit by a Finnish woman out of yarns we brought from America. The sweaters were well made and very nice looking, but this woman took time to tell me one day that while they did look rather nice from a distance, a closer view showed how cheap looking they actually were. However, she could not stop me from enjoying the sweaters, which I brought back with me and wore for some time here in the States.

The ski factory had several barracks forming a complex. Our barracks had twenty rooms with a family in each one. It was a two-story building with a door and stairway near each end and a hallway running the length of each floor. Some of the people kept goats, and in the summer when the outer doors were open, it was not uncommon to meet a goat or two on the stairs. When this happened to me, I would backtrack and take the other stairway.

The goats were stubborn, obstinate animals. In the ski factory area we had wooden sidewalks, raised about six inches or so from the ground. The goats would often be seen walking along these. Meeting one head-on, most people would give way and step off the sidewalk. I, for one, would go far out of my way to avoid the critters. Lauri, however, would stand his ground until they got off the sidewalk. Once he even booted one down the stairs at the barracks. It looked back up at him reproach-fully as if to say, "Why did you do that?"

Gypsies were another annoyance that occasionally descended upon us at the barracks. They reminded me of a big flock of black birds. If we saw them first, we would lock our doors. If not, they would push their way in and, in return for money, food or most anything, tell our fortunes. They were very aggressive and would not take no for an answer. I once had an elderly gypsy woman come in; she came right up to me and, as I backed away, she followed me, poking her bony finger into my chest as she foretold my future: I would live to be eighty years old, and I would have two husbands in my lifetime.

The gypsies were very quick to steal if you did not watch them closely. The women wore long black dresses and shawls under which they could hide pilfered items. I do not recall ever seeing men in their groups, and I think gypsies in general had women do this part of the "work."

With housekeeping a difficult chore at best, most of us were not sticklers. One of the worst chores, if not the worst, was trying to keep the cockroaches at bay. Since they moved with ease from room to room, it was a never-ending task. Bedbugs were slightly more controllable. The memory of one woman who lived in the complex has stayed with me. She was a Mrs. Mattson who had emigrated from the United States and brought with her the one-day-a-week cleaning habit. Her room was always spic and span. She even changed the towels each week on that day. I also remember her for this quote: "If a man drinks, it is because of the woman's laxity." Since drinking was common among us at that time, it put the burden of the problem on the women.

I did my own cleaning and cooking which was very simple, but an elderly Finnish woman living in the barracks did our washing. She had four children whose names all began with "T": Tarmo, Taisto, Toivo and Taimi. She would stop in for tea, or coffee if we had it, when she came for our clothes. She was the lady who was so horrified to see us put butter on our cookies—how extravagant! This was during our first year when we were still able to buy from a store called "INSNAB"* which sold only to foreigners and had a bigger selection than was available elsewhere. Later on, when this store was closed, we no longer put butter on cookies.

We usually bought our evening meal at the Ski Factory cafeteria until it burned down. Meals were very simple and varied little from day to day, but we had enough to eat, and it was surprising how eagerly we looked forward to them.

Coffee was a wonderful treat for us all, since it was so seldom available. When we did get some it was in the bean and, often as not, raw. We would then roast it in a pan on the stove, stirring it constantly as it had a tendency to burn easily. In those days we liked our coffee very strong so we felt the lack of it deeply but also found it a great pleasure when we did have some.

We had an electric hotplate but we were forbidden to use it in the barracks; we could use electricity only for lights. To get around this, I had placed our suitcase on the big trunk we had in our room and kept the electric plate in the suitcase. If someone came around while I was making coffee, I would remove the pot from the plate and quickly close the suitcase. Some of our friends found this amusing. We could hide the plate but no one could make coffee in secret: whenever anyone was lucky

---

*INSNAB was an acronym for *inostrannyy snabzheniye* which means "provisions for foreigners."

enough to have coffee to make she would soon find unexpected company at her door, coaxed there by the tantalizing smell of the freshly-made brew.

Shopping for food in Soviet Karelia at this time differed greatly from what we'd known back home. Aside from the fact that very little was available in the stores and we stood in queues for hours to get whatever was for sale, there was the matter of packaging. This was entirely up to the customer. The stores had no wrapping paper, no bags, no boxes. If we expected to get flour or cereal or sugar, we would take our home-sewn cloth bags in which to carry it home. For meat, the daily newspaper would do. Empty vodka bottles were fine for oil (sunflower seed) or milk. For beer (*piva*) or *kvass* (a Russian malt drink) a bucket was best. Loaves of bread came unwrapped and you did what you could. I once saw a woman pull off her slip right in downtown Petrozavodsk and wrap a loaf of bread in it. But packaging was not important. The main thing was to get something, anything.

We had very little room to store our groceries either. Lauri built a small storage cupboard on the wall in the hallway next to our door. Several people had cupboards in the hallway; they all had locks on them but things did disappear. Lauri made a strong door on ours and then drilled a hole in the wall from the inside of our cupboard into our room. Then he put a heavy leather thong on the cupboard door, put it through the hole and hooked it to a stout spike in our room. We always had to unhook the cord in the room before opening the cupboard door, but we never lost anything from that cupboard.

During part of our stay in Karelia we were buying milk from an elderly Russian lady. She was a lovely person, stately and very lady-like; I felt she must have been an aristocrat before the revolution. At times she would bring the milk to us; sometimes I would go for it. She lived in a small house with gingerbread trim on the eaves. It was always neat, and I remember the bed had several pillows piled high. She had a cow but goat's milk was also much used. We paid a ruble for half a liter of milk and brought it home in empty vodka bottles. We did not squander it. One morning at breakfast we had a shot glass full of milk between the two of us. I had made porridge and we made do.

Since our diet was so very simple, anything extra was apt to be of great importance. A simple cake was cause for great joy. One incident has stayed in my mind. It happened while we were living with the Frilunds. When I came home from school one day, I found no one there but saw that a cake baked by Ilmi before leaving was on the table. I

Keijo and Ilmi Frilund with little Irma.

helped myself to a piece of it, and it was wonderful. Little Irma arrived soon after, but I knew that Keijo would be home at any moment, and I felt that, since the cake had so much meaning for all of us, he would prefer to serve it to Irma himself. Alas, I was wrong. He was quite provoked with me for not having served Irma already. I never did explain to him just how I had felt and why I did as I did.

Another treat in our diet was whipped pudding made of lingonberry juice and cream of wheat. We would cook the juice, sweeten it with sugar (if we had it) or with hard candy (if we had it) and thicken it with cream of wheat. To whip it, we would use a homemade whisk of small twigs. The juice had to cool fast so we would take the bowl into a snowbank, meanwhile whipping vigorously. Potato flour could also be used to thicken the pudding. On a few occasions we made our own by grating the potato, letting it settle and then pouring off the liquid and letting the remaining flour dry.

The lingonberries were picked in the fall—a chore which Lauri took care of each year—and kept in barrels in an outside shed. They would freeze in winter and sweeten a bit. I loved eating the frozen berries although they were still quite tart if no sugar was available. Sugar, when we did get it, came in large chunks of odd sizes and shapes. We had small scissors specially made for cutting sugar.

Our clothes were far from fancy, but they were serviceable. It was amazing how little would satisfy us when we saw that our neighbor had no more than we had. Some Americans and Finns brought more in the way of clothes than others, but no one was richly dressed. I think it would have been, and sometimes was, resented by some of the natives. I had brought with me a cloth coat with a mink collar which I had purchased when I was teaching school. One day I was standing in a queue, wearing this coat, when I noticed a Karelian man eyeing me. I thought no more about him until a Karelian woman spoke up and began to berate him. She told him he had no business giving me such dirty looks; I had come by my clothes honestly and was entitled to them!

I also remember a good looking Finnish girl at school who appeared one day in a full-length muskrat coat. She had an aunt in America who had sent the money with which Maire had bought the coat. No one seemed to envy her her good fortune.

Through the Institute one winter I was able to buy what we then called a snowsuit. It was brown suede-type material: the pants were form-fitting, up to the armpits and had shoulder straps and elastic at the ankles. The jacket was short and also form-fitting. The style was popular with sportsmen over there. I also had felt boots with leather soles and heels. It was my favorite winter outfit.

The students at the school wore skirts and blouses or sweaters. The clothes worn by women in outside jobs were especially ugly. Mary, our next door neighbor, worked at the ski factory and wore black quilted pants and coat. I had forgotten how pretty clothes could be until later when we made a trip to Moscow to the American Embassy. Several young American girls worked there, and to me they looked like angels in their pretty, colorful clothes. But clothes were not as important to us over there as they had been in the States. Among our friends, clothes had nothing to do with the true worth of a person. To this day I find myself giving less and less importance to clothes. I do remember being able to buy some corduroy which I made into a straight skirt and wore with sweaters. I had brought a white silk dress from home which did not seem to be appropriate wear in our surroundings so Lauri's cousin Lily, who was a seamstress, took it apart and made it into collars for me to wear with my sweaters.

In connection with sewing, I had a most embarrassing experience. I had taken sewing back in high school but never had sewn anything for a man. We'd been able once again to buy some rather heavy material out of which I decided to make a pair of workpants for Lauri. I doubt that I had a pattern but probably opened an old worn-out pair to use in cutting. I then proceeded to sew up all the long seams which were the easiest to start with. At that point, however, I was at an impasse: how to put in the pockets, the fly, etc. Finally, I asked my friend Edla, who was a tailor, to finish them. She took one look and exclaimed in disgust, "What lame brain would start a pair of pants by first sewing up the sideseams?" She might have guessed who had done it, but I don't recall confessing to it.

We had movies in Petrozavodsk—we called them the *kinos*. One evening during the summer of 1935 we saw *Les Misérables* with my schoolmate Inkeri. The film was supposedly American-made but it did not strike us as such. It was shown in a "summer theater"—a wooden hall built in a park. All that day we'd had sudden downpours of rain every hour or so. We got to the theater during one of the dry periods but it soon began to rain again and, we discovered, the roof leaked copiously. Several umbrellas went up. We hadn't brought one, but stayed to see the movie even though soggy wet from head to bottom.

Although in the States we had lived a simple country life, in Karelia we found conditions even more primitive with hard work and only the bare necessities, so to speak. But being young and imbued with the idea of building a workers' paradise, as it was called, we took all the difficulties in stride, more or less. And we had fun, real fun. We saw humor in situations that at other times in other places might have offended us. We had good friends with whom we were compatible, who felt and thought as we did. So, although I was homesick . . . desperately homesick for my father and my two brothers . . . it was a thing apart from my daily life. I was quite content with never a thought of going back: I only wished my father and brothers could have been there with me.

Youth is resilient—hopeful—optimistic. And we were young.

Dave and Lily Metsälä, and their children, Viola and Hugo, taken in Michigan before they went to Karelia.

Ducks and Dachas

L: Hunting has always been my favorite sport and so I asked around the ski factory and found several hunters. They were mostly Finns from Finland, though, and they did not seem to think that an American could be any good as a hunter. Finally one foreman decided that I could go along on the next duck hunt. I was thrilled. Having hunted ducks ever since I was big enough to hold a shotgun, I felt I could handle my end.

So one weekend five of us, (three Finns, a Karelian and I), took the ski factory motor boat, towing two small rowboats, and arrived in the late afternoon at a bay on Lake Onega where we camped overnight. In the morning we split up and took off in the row boats: three in one boat and two of us in the other. I was with a guy who was supposed to be a real hot shot so I started poling the boat. There were plenty of birds. After my hot shot missed some easy shots, I decided to be ready for the next one. When it flew up we both shot, and he picked up the bird satisfied that he now had the range. The next bird he missed and began cussing his gun. I asked if I could try so we changed places. A pair of mallards got up and I got them both. In about an hour I'd shot three more and it was time for lunch. The other three hunters were back in camp without a single bird. My partner was all smiles as he showed our birds and kidded them about their lousy shooting. He never mentioned how he had done! In fairness I must say that I had the best gun in the gang. It was a Remington pump, twelve-gauge, that I had brought from the states, one of the best duck guns I have ever owned. I was glad to have it.

We knew of others who had been recuited in the States to work in the mines in Siberia and been urged to bring guns for hunting with them. The area, they were told, teemed with game. When they got to Leningrad customs officials took their guns, promising to send them on later. "Later" never came. I was lucky; I got to keep my gun. Perhaps it depended on the individual customs official.

After lunch I decided to walk the shoreline and jump shoot. After I had seven or eight birds my ammo got low. Back in camp one of the men, Vilho Saarinen, started reloading shells for me. I kept hunting, and by evening we had twenty-five ducks, I got credit for all but one. From then on I was never left out when there was a hunt planned.

We did quite a bit of hunting, mostly for sport, but, with meat so scarce, it sure was a big help to our diet. We would usually hunt in pairs and divide our catch fifty-fifty no matter who shot them. In the fall it was mostly partridge and rabbit. The rabbits were actually European hares much larger than our Michigan snowshoes. When we got only one I would split it down the middle. There was always more meat in half a rabbit than Sylvi and I could eat for one meal. The partridge were like ours—if anything, smaller. Squirrels were like our grey squirrels. We did eat a couple but somehow we didn't like the idea, and I usually gave them to my partner.

There was also a bird about the size of a pheasant called *tetyorka* in Russian and *teeri* in Finnish.* It was very good eating, and we were allowed to shoot them spring and fall. In the spring they would gather in certain little openings or fields and perform their mating dances. We would post ourselves in blinds before daybreak and wait for them. In March it was often very cold. We had to sit perfectly still; they were wary birds. A scout would come first and check the area. If he was satisfied, the rest would follow. On one occasion a bird settled right on top of my blind about three feet above my head. I didn't dare move a muscle. When it finally flew to the ground to join the others, I was so cramped I could hardly raise my gun but I got him: a nice big rooster with beautiful, colorful feathers.

The *metso* or capercaillie was the king of birds. It was a large grouse

---

*According to the Finnish-English dictionary by Aino Wuolle it is a black grouse.

about the size of a wild turkey. They were not very plentiful, and we had to travel quite deep into the woods to find them. The spring hunt was the most fun.

It would be some time in April when snow was still on the ground that we would venture into the deep woods after work. By 11:00 P.M. we would get to a likely area, build a fire and relax until 2:00 A.M. Then we would start out walking silently and listening for the male metso's song. It was just a light tapping, as if you were tapping a matchbox with your fingernail. "Tap, tap." Then he would listen a minute or so. Then there would be three or four taps. Pause. Five or six taps. Pause.Then, as he grew more confident, he would increase the pace to maybe three seconds of very fast taps followed by a short rubbing or scraping noise as if you were rubbing the edge of the matchbox briskly with your fingernail back and forth. Then there would be total silence as the bird looked around. If he didn't hear or see anything out of the ordinary the ritual would start all over again.

Our strategy would be this: after hearing the so-called song, we would try to sneak up on him while he was making noise. During his scraping sound there would be time to take about three quick steps or leaps, trying, of course, to stay out of sight behind trees and then waiting motionless till he started up again. In this way we would try to get within range of his perch which would be on a tree limb about twenty or thirty feet in the air.

I remember one such hunt where I had to go across a clearing of twenty feet or so. I took my time studying the spot and figured I would get half way on my first move and clear it on the second. My calculations were correct but as I reached the center I stepped on a log hidden under the snow and my foot twisted into a bad position. The bird must have heard it too, because he just turned mute. I was miserable: head down, foot cocked unnaturally trying to stay perfectly still while those sharp little eyes and ears strained in the semi-darkness. It seemed like forever before I heard "tap" and a long time before "tap, tap." Finally he was fooled, and I was able to get to cover. From there on it was easy. Once I got in range, I waited till he was in the scraping stage before shooting. Had I missed then, I might have had another shot at him; the old-timers had told me that the bird can't hear a thing when he is making that scraping noise, so that was the time to shoot.

While rummaging at the ski factory warehouse one day, I found the kind of carbide lamp that straps on your forehead. This, I thought, would be ideal for spearing fish at night. I hunted around some more and found a can of carbide and then asked the warehouse keeper what they were used for. He didn't know. He said the lamp had been there a long time, and I could have it if there was something I could use it for. There sure was.

That fall when bird hunting started I told one of my hunting buddies what I had and suggested that we go hunting to a place about four kilometers from town. There was a small cabin there, right on the lakeshore, a sort of a community place that anybody could use. Hunting was as good there as anywhere else. My plan was to stay overnight at the cabin, fish at night and hunt during the day. I took along my homemade spear, hip boots and the carbide lamp.

It was evening when we got to the cabin. To our surprise there were already two Karelian men there who had built a fire outside and were boiling water for tea. They asked us to join them, and even though the cabin was small, invited us to stay. The cabin was about eight by ten feet with a very low ceiling, with a platform made of split logs that served as our bed. There was a stove built of rocks with no chimney that could be fired up until the rocks got hot, and then the coals and ashes were cleared out. When the smoke cleared, it was a comfortable heat source even in cold weather, as the rocks would stay hot for a long time.

We sat around the fire until about 10:00 o'clock. The Karelians were fishing, too, but not with spears. They had set out what were known as hoop nets, cone-shaped nets about six to ten feet in diameter, as well as gill nets. Any way of catching fish was legal. When it got dark, I put on my carbide lamp and my hip boots and went out to try my luck. It was a grassy shoreline, and I walked in about two feet of water so clear I could see quite a distance. The fish were spooky, but finally I was able to sneak up on a pike. After spearing it and tying it to my belt, I got a big burbot, an eel-like fish that wrapped itself around my arm when I raised it from the water. I took them both back to camp.

That got the others interested, and we fished till after midnight, spearing a few more. Early in the morning, we took off hunting while the Karelians went to check their nets. They'd had pretty good luck. We shot a few birds. Adding them to the fish it was a real nice catch.

One fall the ski factory director, Tuomainen, asked if I would take a friend of his, a Russian army officer, out duck hunting. I was willing, and so the following Sunday we took off with a small outboard to Solomon Bay, just the two of us. The boat belonged to the head bookkeeper at the ski factory. I had repaired the motor for him, so he told me to use it whenever I wanted to. It was about a three- or four-horsepower single cylinder, in pretty good shape. The boat reminded me of the kind we had on the St. Mary's River in Michigan in the twenties.

The shooting was good, and the officer was a sharp shooter. We had a fine time and, by late afternoon, a nice bag of birds, too. I suggested that we should get back home, but he kept saying, "Let's hunt some more," and so we did.

Finally I was getting worried, because I had told Sylvi that we would be back by dark, since we had plans for the evening. So I told the officer that my wife was waiting but he just brushed that off saying, "*Zhonka nye utka, nye letit kak utki*," ("a wife is not a duck, doesn't fly like a duck") so why worry? They definitely had a different attitude toward women over there. I finally persuaded him to leave because it was getting dark, and he very reluctantly agreed. He was quiet for a while on the way home, almost pouting, but then he began to discuss the hunt, and, by the time we got back, we were both in high spirits. He was very grateful to me for taking him and hoped someday we could do it again.

We made our own fine shot for hunting by melting lead and then pouring it into holes in blocks of wood to form wire the same diameter as the shot we wanted. Then we cut the wire into pieces the same length as the diameter. This we did with a cutter I had made for the purpose. It was like a paper cutter with an adjustable stop so the pieces were uniform in length. The next step was to round the pellets by putting them into a metal can about two and a half by five inches and shaking the can so the pellets would bounce around and wear into a round shape. I used to bolt the can to the eccentric on the power house steam engine for about a half hour; it would shake them back and forth till they came out smooth and round. I usually did this on a free day when the factory wasn't running so I could start and stop the steam engine while doing maintenance.

In the fall of 1935 we started to build the Finnish sled called a *potku kelkka* at the ski factory. It was very popular. We had one too, and often used it to go places like visiting Dave and Lily or into town. It had long steel runners like skates: two narrow blades ¼ inch by 1½ inches by eight feet long, with a chair up in front for a rider. The driver would stand in back with one foot on a runner, pushing and kicking with other. On a down hill he would ride with one foot on each runner. The handle bars were used for steering as well as pushing. The flexible steel blade allowed for sharp turns. The sled worked very well on the hard-packed snow of our streets in winter. This hard surface, good for sledding or skating, was known as *pääkallo keli* or "skull condition."

One evening after work, a Karelian fellow, Ronkanen, and I were going to the ski factory club house for some doings. The club house was about a half mile from the ski factory along the lakeshore, next to the ski factory garage. I was suppose to receive an award for some money-saving improvements I had made at the factory. We stopped at Ronkanen's place to get his *potku kelkka* to take into town. Before we left though, he wanted me to sample some of his homemade beer, called "*braug*," which he claimed was especially good. It was made from sugar, grain and raisins fermented under pressure. He did warn me that it was also pretty powerful stuff. So I tried some. It was sweet and didn't taste very good to me but we both had two big glasses. Then we left for the club with me driving the sled. We were going pretty fast down hill, maybe twenty or thirty miles an hour, when we met a bus coming up the hill. I steered close to the snowbank to avoid the bus. All of a sudden I found myself sliding on my stomach on the crusty snow with the handle bar in my hands but no sled! Ronkanen had made a somersault into the snow; the sled had come to a halt in a snowbank.

We were a bit banged up. Ronkanen had some blood on his nose, and my face was scratched from the hard crust on the snow. We looked over the damage and decided that we could steer the sled without the handle bar just by holding on to the uprights. Ronkanen wanted to drive; he wasn't going to depend on me anymore! So I sat in the sled, and he did pretty well until we got close to the club. There was a steeper area on the hill and a sharp turn at the bottom which we missed. Over the bank we went and right into a telephone pole. I was still sitting on the seat hugging the pole when Eino and Ben came from the garage across the road where they had been working overtime, to see what had happened. We were still determined to go to the club, but they took one look at us and sent us home in a hurry. Sylvi wasn't too harsh on me. When I looked in the mirror I could see why. My face was a real mess and it was just beginning to sting.

The ski factory had some property across Lake Onega from Petrozavodsk where workers could build summer cabins which the Russians call *dachas*. This area was known as *Pässinranta*, literally "goat's shore," and many of our friends had cabins there. During her summer vacation in 1935, which did not coincide with mine, Sylvi was able to spend five days at Heino's cabin with her friend Flossie, picking blueberries and sun bathing. But of course we wanted to build our own cabin.

The director wanted us to build on factory property, like all the others, but we wanted to be further away. We leased land from the government and got permission to build our *dacha* on a beautiful, rocky point about a half mile from the ski factory cabins. Not being on the factory property, our cabin could be built however we wanted while the factory cabins all had to be the same type of construction, and if you ever quit the factory you would have to move out. (It was possible to quit and find work elsewhere but few people did; the ski factory was a good place to work.)

We went together on the cabin with Lily and Dave and built it from logs. We picked a lot of them right there off the lakeshore. Dave knew how to hollow out one side of the log to a concave shape so it would fit snugly onto the one below. The corners were made in the Finnish style to lock them together. We worked weekends through the winter of 1935 and got the walls up. In the spring of 1936, we had a motor boat pulling a scow to bring in lumber which we'd been able to buy from a sawmill near the ski factory. We used the boards for window frames, doors, and flooring. There was no roofing material available, so Dave suggested that we make a board roof. The boards were about ¾ inch by 8 inches wide. We planed grooves along each edge about ½ inch wide and ¼ inch deep about ¾ inches from the side of the board and nailed the boards on top of the stringers as close together as possible. Then we nailed four-inch-wide boards over each seam. This way, if some water seeped in under the four-inch boards, it would drain off in the grooves and run down the slope. I don't remember having any leaks from this roof. Years later I saw some roofs like ours on old buildings in Finland.

By summer of 1936 we were able to use the cabin. We really enjoyed spending summer weekends out there with friends. It was on one of these weekends that we built the outhouse. We had four couples out that day, and when it came time to cut out the seat we looked at all the women, and decided that Inki Kent had the biggest bottom. We therefore asked her to sit on the seat so we could draw a line around her, figuring if it was big enough for her, the rest of us would be happy with it. Inki protested at first but, good sport that she was, she went along with the plan, and we had a hilarious time. All our friends contributed in some way to the cabin but Inki's share was the most fun.

Not far from our cabin lived a Karelian family by the name of Kanerva. They had a sauna built on a rocky point on the shore of Lake Onega. We were allowed to use the sauna in return for food items, vodka and such goodies. Cutting wood for the sauna each time we used it was a must. Akulina, the lady of the house, made sure we did not fail at this. She was a husky woman who ruled her family with an iron fist. Her husband, Alexander, was afraid of her and with good reason. I remember one evening when we had arrived at our cabin with our friends Eino and Sylvi Dahlstrom. Alexander came over to greet us as usual. He was down in the dumps, but, after a few drinks, he perked up and was soon singing away in a high-pitched monotone, taking a few dance steps as he sang. Just as we were beginning to enjoy his song and dance act, Akulina arrived screaming and yelling at him for drinking when there was so much work to be done. He tried to placate her, but she grabbed him by the ear and started towing him home. Now he was the one who was screaming and yelling. As far as we could hear them, he was complaining about how much it hurt and begging her to let go of his ear. To us it was funny, but to Alexander it was far from it.

One Saturday or Sunday some friends of Dave and Lily's, Vilho and Terttu, were visiting with us at the cabin. Seeing Dave and Lily coming down the path, Terttu turned to her husband and said, "Let's hide and surprise them." Our ceiling rafters were covered with sheets of plywood, some of them nailed down but some still loose. We told them to hide up there, and they quickly scrambled up. Vilho sat securely on nailed boards but Terttu, unfortunately, chose to perch on a loose piece. Just as Dave opened the cabin door, the piece of plywood gave way and crashed to the floor, leaving her, with her dress caught under her armpits, clinging desperately to a crossbeam. To say that Dave and Lily were surprised is to understate the case. We were all speechless for several moments until Vilho recovered sufficiently to come and help her down.

Realizing that she wasn't hurt, only a bit embarrassed, I got my wits about me and made us a drink to relax. Then it hit us; the more we discussed it the funnier it got.

"Biggest and best surprise I ever had," Dave declared.

We were doing quite well at this time and had hired an elderly lady, a Mrs. Mäntynen, to do our laundry while Sylvi was in school. Mrs. M. spent the summer in Pässinranta and did our washing there so we would pick it up when we were at our cabin on weekends. One day we had left a couple of suitcases of freshly laundered clothes in our cabin while visiting friends—most of our summer clothes, in fact. Before we returned, someone broke into the cabin and stole them.

We could tell immediately when we came back that they had broken in. We had American-style windows on the cabin which the robbers couldn't open. Karelian windows opened out, French style, while ours slid up. The frustrated thieves had taken off the whole frame!

What a horrible feeling. We knew we couldn't replace the clothes.

Lauri and Sylvi at their *dacha*.

Little Heikki at fourteen months.

Sylvi Dahlstrom and baby Helen.

Eino Dahlstrom.

I went to town and reported the theft to the authorities, but they did not seem concerned. After a big hassle I was able to get a couple of blood-hounds and we tried to track the thieves. We found some of the stuff that they had thrown away. We must have been close to them but we didn't catch them and were left without a large part of our wardrobe.

More Action, Fewer Words

L: The ski factory was named after Edward Gylling, the Chairman of the Karelian Executive Committee and the top man in Karelia. He would often walk in, all by himself, take a look around and stop to talk to some of the workers. Several times he asked me questions about the operation and how I felt. He never made any pretense of being better than anyone else. I liked him, and so did everyone I knew. We looked up to him. But in the fall of 1935 he was called to Moscow. We all wondered why he had to go. People were always being sent to different places, and, of course, we wondered about it, but we had learned that it was safer not to ask too many questions. We never saw Gylling in Karelia again, and his place was taken by an arrogant bureaucrat who was so paranoid that he had two fully armed bodyguards protecting him whenever he came to the ski factory.

One day we heard that a group of Russian scientists who had spent a year in the arctic were going to visit the ski factory. This created a lot of excitement. We had been reading in the newspapers about this group and the tests they had been making. Before their arrival the management went all out to prepare a reception for the Soviet heroes, even building a special platform for the elite to speak from, outdoors on the ski factory grounds.

The day they came I was having trouble with an overheated bearing on one of the ski-bottom planers. I decided to change the bearing during the festivities, so as soon as everyone was told to gather around the platform, I went to work.

It so happened that the leader of this scientific group, one Papanin, had stated that he wanted to see the factory in operation and never mind the speeches. By-passing the crowd around the platform, he headed straight into the factory and soon came upon me trying to fix the machine. He wanted to know what I was doing, and I explained as best I could. He was very pleased. He ended up praising me in front of everyone, telling them this was the way to keep production going.

"*Bolshe dyela, menshe slova,*" he said, which is an old Russian proverb meaning "more action, fewer words."

Good work was always appreciated at the ski factory, and this was encouraging to all of us who worked there. Most of us worked hard and were proud of what we accomplished. Men and women were treated fairly equally, it seems to me. A woman could go to work in the factory, or anywhere, and get the same pay as a man if she could cut the mustard.

There was one young Karelian woman in her early twenties working in the ski factory lumber yard. She was built like a wrestler, a powerful Katrinka, and she could outdo most men but was apprehensive about what the men would do if she earned more than they did. She went to the factory director and asked him if it was permissible for her to do better than the men. Since it was piecework it was easy to see how much each person produced. The director told her to do as much as she could and it would be to her credit. From then on she was a Soviet hero. They started giving her bonuses, and there were pictures of her in the newspapers as an example to others.

There were several Finnish-language newspapers in Petrozavodsk at that time. I remember one of these papers printed a picture of strikers parading in front of a Detroit automobile plant, probably some time in 1936. The paper didn't call it a strike though; they referred to it as a "hunger march" and told what a horrible time the workers in the United States were having. One of the ski factory foremen, a Russian, looked at this picture and said to me, "They don't look so hungry. See how many are overweight, and look how well dressed they are."

I made no comment knowing that it was best to keep my mouth shut. Everybody was cautious. You didn't brag. You didn't say anything that you thought could possibly be used against you, and to praise anything about a capitalist country was certainly in that category. You could be called a counter-revolutionary and people had been arrested for that.

The foreman told me a little about his childhood. He had worked in a flour mill that his father had built to grind grain for their village. After the revolution they lost everything. His father was called a *kulak*, and the government took over the mill and also their horse and cow. All they had left was the clothes on their backs. They were punished for being too ambitious.

It seemed that many of these so-called *kulaks* were just small farmers with a couple of cows who worked harder and got a little wealthier than their neighbors. My friend remembered that his father wouldn't let him go to dances* with the other young people because he always had to work.

His story reminded me of Sylvi's father, Frank Kuusisto, who owned a small farm and store on Sugar Island. He used to joke with friends that, strictly speaking, he was really a *kulak*. They would laugh about it, but I wondered what would have happened if the revolution had come to the United States. I could see that if he had been living in Russia the same way he lived in the States, he surely would have been called a *kulak* and lost everything.

It was also some time in 1936 that Sylvi came home from school in tears. She had been told that she couldn't go to school any more because we weren't Russian citizens and didn't have a Russian passport. She was preparing to teach Finnish and English and for that, she was told, she would need a Russian passport. We wondered what we should do.

Had this happened in 1937, we probably wouldn't have done it, but in 1936 things were going well for us, and Sylvi was looking forward to teaching. We went ahead and applied for a Russian passport not realizing that by doing this, we were becoming Russian citizens and thereby losing our American citizenship. I remember how shocked I was when they asked for my American passport, "Why should I give you this?" I wondered, but I did. It wasn't long before we realized what a big mistake that had been.

I only remember voting once in Karelia. When they had an election, everyone had to vote. People went from barracks to barracks opening every door to tell everyone that they must go and vote—right now. I went to the ski factory office and was given a ballot to mark but there was only one name on it, the name of the person chosen by the Party to

---

*Village dances were held on wooden bridges at that time, since they were the only places of any size with a smooth surface.

represent our district. The rest of us had no choice, but we were all expected to come out and ratify the Party's choice. It was such a farce. It really made us wonder what kind of a deal we had gotten into.

Around this time the ski factory restaurant burned to the ground leaving only a few walls standing and the brick chimney. We were allowed to scavenge some boards from the ruins for firewood and there must have been at least twenty of us out there, pulling up boards and carting them home, when suddenly the wall next to the chimney collapsed bringing the chimney down with it. One man happened to be under it; he was buried in the rubble. It took us about half an hour to reach him but we were too late. He was dead. That was the end of the free firewood. The fire department fenced it off.

Accidents also were becoming more frequent at the factory, as they were trying to speed up production and doing a lot of piecework. Many of the machines had poor safety guards. Some, in fact, had no safety guards at all, because the operators had removed them in order to work faster. I was told to put on more guards and replace those that had been taken off. Of course some of the operators were unhappy with this, but after a few weeks they got used to working with the guards, and the complaints decreased.

One machine presented a problem. There was no way to set up an ordinary guard. I designed and set up a spring that would clip you on the fingers if you pushed your hands too close to the cutters. Eager to see how it worked, I kept my eye on the girl who operated it the first day the device was on. I saw her fingers getting closer and closer to the cutter; then it sprang. She jerked her hand back and her face turned white. Quite shaken, she examined her fingers and found them all intact. Then, turning red, she raced for the mechanic's office screaming that someone had put something on her machine that scared her half to death. By then, I was in the office too, trying to keep a straight face. It took a lot of explaining to convince her that the spring was for her own good, but it worked so well we never had any more cut fingers from that particular machine.

Things were looking up at that time. Our standard of living was improving noticeably. New stores were being built, and consumer goods began to appear on the shelves. If a person had the money and time to stand in line, luxury items, such as a radio, or make-up, were available. In the fall of 1936, Sylvi began teaching Finnish language and literature. She was earning about 1,000 rubles a month—twice what I usually made with overtime, and four times the salary of the average worker. Back in the States she had earned $90 a month teaching, which was about the same wage a Ford factory worker made. I felt that the Soviets were on the right track in paying their teachers so well.

I believe it was in the summer of 1936 that the government offered glider instruction to those who were interested at a field near town, so we got a group of eight together to learn the ABCs of gliding. Our instructor was a young air force officer who taught some theory of flying and also gave us some field experience.

We would set up the glider anchored to the ground with a steel cable and a release hook. The instructor would hold on to the tip of the wing and tell the learner just how to adjust the controls. Meanwhile the rest of us would lay out a hundred foot rubber cable attached to the front of the glider. The instructor would then tell us how far to stretch out this rubber cable, say fifty steps or so. It would stretch double its length or more if fully extended. So the guy in the lead would count as we pulled it fifty steps and then stopped. Then the person in the glider was told to pull the release lever. The cable would jerk the glider about fifty to sixty feet in the air and the student would glide back to the ground. The perfect glide had to be smooth with wings level—a nice long ride and good landing.

I was the last one to take a ride, confident as usual, and the rest of them knew it so they decided to give me a real thrill. They counted fifty steps, but actually took seventy-five or more. The instructor didn't notice; he was too busy getting me started. When I released the glider I shot high up in the air and almost stalled before leveling off. Then I dove for the ground, pulled back too much, went up and then down again before managing to level off for the glide. I must have been a sight. Some of the others were doubled up with laughter. I was just happy the glider didn't get wrecked.

The hardest part for me was the direction control. I had a hard time getting over my sled riding as a kid. On a sled, when you pushed the bar with your left foot you went to the right. On the glider, it is just the opposite. We had about ten lessons and it was a lot of fun—something I have fond memories of—but then the lessons were suddenly stopped with no explanation why.

A Russian hunter friend had wanted for a long time to buy my Remington shotgun or trade me for his double barrel shotgun. I didn't want to sell, but he finally wore me down. The price was good so I gave in, but first I had to go to the border guards for permission. When I got there I was directed to an office where a man sat in full uniform with medals and the works plus a long sword at his side. Very impressive. I explained what I wanted. "Have you sold anything at the *tori?*" he wanted to know.

The tori in Petrozavodsk was what we would call a flea market where people sold used items they didn't want. It was evidently legal since it was right out in the open. I told him my wife had sold a pair of shoes and a party dress. Why did he care, I wondered.

He gazed at me for a while and then abruptly barked, "You already sold that gun!" He claimed, loudly, that I had sold the gun and then come for the permit, emphasizing his words by drawing his sword almost out of its scabbard and slamming it back in. It scared the hell out of me. He continued to do this, accusing me of selling other things illegally, always punctuating his words with the banging of his sword. Finally I was allowed to go home. The permit was never mentioned, and I was not about to bring it up again. When I told my friend I wasn't going to sell the gun because I couldn't get permission he said, "Oh you don't need permission." I probably could have gotten away with selling it without a permit, but I wanted to be up front and do things properly. It was far too easy to get in trouble over there, and I didn't want to take a chance.

Four of us at the ski factory had "boat fever." We kept asking if anyone knew of a boat engine we could buy. Finally we found an Opal four-cylinder that was so bad it had to be rebuilt. It was cheap enough, and we bought it and decided to cut it in half to make two two-cylinder engines. We had to make new piston rings, new valves, new flywheel, new timing gears; the cylinder walls had to be honed, and lots more. The pistons and flywheel we had to have cast in the Onegzavod Foundry. The honing and grinding was done at Karelian Auto. (The Karelian auto machine shop had mostly American-made machinery brought by Finnish-Americans to repair autos and trucks.)

Keijo Frilund and I built up one half of the engine. The other was made by Arne Tuomainen and another American Finn whose name I can't remember. We got our engine finished first by working evenings. I had bet the others a bottle of whiskey that it would start right off when I had it together, so one evening we gathered together at the shop to test it out. Sure enough, it started, although it sounded like a four-cycle four-cylinder engine running on just two cylinders. We celebrated so much that night that it cost them two bottles of whiskey, plus headaches the following morning.

The other two fellows got their boat built, working evenings at the ski factory and using factory equipment. They got to use the boat some, and it worked well. We didn't get ours built at all. Things were changing. Everything was tightening up, and this kind of private endeavor was discouraged.

The director of the ski factory, Elias Tuomainen, had been given a car for his own use, one of the first Ford V8s ever made. A man from Drummond Island, Michigan, had brought the car to Karelia. He was compensated for it in rubles at the rate of two rubles per dollar—a very unrealistic rate considering that white bread sold for 4.40 rubles a kilo and was ten cents a loaf in the United States, and Sylvi paid 14 rubles for a small padlock that would have been fifty or sixty cents at home.

Eino Dahlstrom, our good friend from Canada, worked as a mechanic at the ski factory garage. He was given the job of chauffering the director in the Ford. This was quite an honor and a very responsible job. One night on an icy road he rolled the car over. The body was banged up some, but the worst of it was that the transmission housing was cracked all the way around. The accident created quite a stir in town, and we were afraid Eino might even land in jail, but the director said if we could get it to run in a couple of days it would take some of the heat off.

At that time nobody would arc weld cast iron. We just had steel rod to weld with but that was our only hope. We bolted it together and put it in a forge at the blacksmith shop until it was beginning to glow. Then I started to weld about an inch at a time with the others peening it right after. We kept this up until late at night and covered it up with hot coals to let it cool slowly.

The next day Eino and Ben, another Canadian, worked at assembling the transmission while some others hammered the body into shape. By the end of the day, Eino had the car parked in front of the office. It ran okay and the heat was off.

Gasoline was in short supply and very expensive. Some of the logging trucks were converted to run on gas extracted from wood. These trucks used gasoline only for starting and warming up the motor; then they switched to wood gas or methanol. On the outside of the truck next to the fender was the firebox that the wood was burned in. Then there were two filtering tanks mounted behind the cab that coverted the smoke to gas that was piped directly into the motor. In this way the distilling process was unnecessary.

The drawbacks of these trucks were that they were less efficient, having about thirty percent less power, and they smelled bad, especially when the motor was shut off. This was because the fire would still be burning and the smoke would not be converted into gas. We usually ran these trucks all day and didn't put the fire out until evening.

The ski factory lumber yard had no tractor to haul lumber and logs around, and there wasn't room for a truck. The management asked for suggestions, and the boys from the garage suggested shortening an old model A truck and making it into a tractor. Eino Dahlstrom, Benny Laine and I took it on a contract to build. I was included to do the welding and cutting. This was a fun job for all of us. We were doing something we had never seen done, and it was quite a challenge. We would start working on it by 7:00 o'clock in the evening and work until midnight every night.

We had a half liter bottle of vodka that we called "bear juice" because there was a picture of a bear on the bottle. Several times during the evening someone would yell "bear juice" and we would stop work for a drink and a short conference. (Since we had no drawings for this project it was sometimes necessary to stop and discuss the problems we ran into.)

The job turned out to be one of the best money makers for us and also for the factory. The thing could turn on a dime, so to speak. The management was very pleased with their new tractor and we were praised for the good work. That's when Eino and I got the good idea to ask for a few days off to go to Leningrad for some relaxation. Permission granted.

Eino and Sylvi Dahlstrom, Sylvi and I, took off for Leningrad by train. We were in a festive mood. Money was plentiful, so we ate and drank the best that was available and checked into a beautiful old hotel— I think it was called the Metropole. What luxury! We had four rooms with a tub bath, a piano, overstuffed sofas and chairs and gilded tables. Everything was just grand.

The first day we walked a lot. In the evening, tired, we decided to use a taxi. From then on it was taxis, nightclubs, restaurants—nothing but the best. The only shopping we did was a pair of galoshes for Eino and a hat for me.

After three days and nights we were ready to go back and presented ourselves at the hotel desk to check out and collect our passports. The rule was that whenever you went anywhere away from your home you had to register with the police. Hotel management routinely took the passports of their guests and showed the police who was staying there. If the police wanted to question you, they simply took your passport knowing you couldn't go anywhere without it and would soon come to retrieve it.*

Eino, Sylvi and I received our passports with no problem but Sylvi Dahlstrom's, we were told, had been taken by the NKVD, the secret police, today known as the KGB. They gave us the address to go and get it.

With only a few hours until train time, the four of us took a taxi to the big, grey brick building. Eino and Sylvi Dahlstrom went in; we stayed in the taxi trying to figure out why we were being detained. For over an hour we sat there worrying about what was going on and wondering if we would miss our train. All kinds of thoughts went through our heads but we kept telling each other that of course it would all be straightened out. What's wrong with going on a trip?

Finally they came out and we dashed to the station. After we got our tickets they told us what had transpired with the police. First, the NKVD had wanted to know why we were in Leningrad since we were not on vacation. How did we get time off? What had we been doing? Did we buy anything? Meet with any friends? They couldn't see why we should be running around having fun instead of working. Apparently, the Dahlstroms' answers were satisfactory; we all returned to Petrozavodsk without any more trouble, but it was a rude ending to a fun weekend.

---

*After 1932, all citizens except peasants had to carry an internal passport. It didn't matter whether peasants had one since they weren't allowed to travel anywhere anyway. (Kort 183)

"We Like That Little One"

S: It was a great thrill for us in Karelia to get letters from America. Several people wrote to us—my father, brother Andrew, and Lauri's mother, Evi, mostly. My close friend from Sugar Island, Impi Maki, wrote quite often. She and Andrew would put little things into letters. Most of them would not reach me. In a letter I wrote her in March 1935, I lamented, "I haven't received a thing you've sent me. I just cried over that collar . . . I know it was sweet . . . somebody has it, I know. I wish you would send more little things in letters."

Andrew would put in sticks of gum and handkerchiefs; I did receive a few of those. Lauri's sister Irja wrote once to announce her coming marriage and once to announce the birth of her first baby, a boy named Lauri Andrew who died in infancy.

Bureaucrats and red tape were plentiful while we were in Karelia. During the summer of 1935 we decided to have our pictures taken. This took all summer. It was not at all what we'd been used to in the States. The very first thing one did was pay. We paid for six pictures. Then we sat for them and were told when to come for them. I did. The young lady in charge sorted through a stack of pictures asking, "Is this it?" with each one. Our pictures were not there. She just said, "Come again." I did. She spoke Russian; I could understand her, but she did not understand my Finnish and finally found someone who could translate. I asked her as sharply as I dared how many times one had to come and sit before a picture could be made. She assured me one more time would do it. We did eventually get our pictures, although I can't recall how many times we had to go to the studio.

During the summer of 1935 Lauri and I went to visit my Uncle Frank in Solomanni, about twenty miles by bus. There was a sawmill there where Uncle Frank worked filing saws. My aunt, his first wife, had died after they moved to Karelia, and Uncle had married a Karelian woman. She was a very gentle soul and treated us well. Uncle's teenage son Arvo by his first wife was living with them.

Uncle Frank and his family lived in a small, old Karelian house and kept a few animals. One of their pigs had been fattened for slaughter, and they asked Lauri to butcher it for them. Uncle's wife had become quite attached to the porker and could not bear the thought of its being hurt. Lauri assured her that when he hit the animal it would drop dead without a sound, but later she insisted she'd heard it squeal. We had a big meal that day consisting of a soup made of potatoes and, as a second course, potatoes with just a bit of meat. We were also given a piece of the pig to take home with us. Later Lauri had a chance to slaughter a pig for someone at the ski factory and again came home with a piece of pork for his labor.

Uncle Frank had always treated me like a child, and on this visit he did it again, much to my embarrassment. He and Lauri stayed up late after his wife and I had gone to bed. After a long time I awoke and, finding Lauri still missing, got up to see what was going on. There they sat at the kitchen table with a bottle of vodka between them. When Uncle saw me, he told me to go right back to bed and not bother them. I didn't dare protest.

Later I heard the story of their vodka drinking. Lauri had brought one bottle along with him, and they had sat drinking and talking about old times back in the States until, to their surprise, the bottle was empty. Uncle Frank then went to retrieve a bottle he had stashed away outdoors. It was, as it happened, forty degrees below zero Celsius that night and the vodka had actually frozen to slush. After a few minutes in the warm house, however, it cleared up and they resumed their drinking.

There was a cemetery not far from the ski factory, and I will never forget seeing and hearing my first Russian funeral. The mourners were most articulate; the weeping and wailing could be heard for quite a distance. It was mostly the women. They would throw themselves on the grave and carry on. I had never heard grief so openly voiced, and it struck me as being exaggerated and forced. Russians were apt to be more outgoing than the stoic Finns; it was normal with them. The well-known funeral march was generally played at funerals and it was very moving.

Ordinarily, I stayed at home with my schoolwork when Lauri went to the club for his band practice sessions, but now and then I would tag along with my books and papers and study in some side room. Although I'd be alone in the room, I felt compelled to stand whenever the band played the "Internationale." This song was the national anthem of the Soviet Union at the time. It was sung by workers all over the world. I'd heard it many times as a child. The Finnish people on Sugar Island sang a Finnish version of it at all their social gatherings, and it was a solemn moment fraught with deep meaning. We always stood up while singing it. I especially remember one line: *"Huomis päivänä kansat on veljet keskenään,"* (Tomorrow all nations will be brothers together). As a little child I thought it meant that tomorrow my brothers would be alone together! But the feeling of solemnity as well as exaltation associated with the "Internationale" had stayed with me, and I always had to stand whenever I heard it played. Childhood memories and feelings die hard.

Lauri worked at the ski factory throughout our stay in Petrozavodsk. He had always been a good, conscientious worker from the time he was a boy, and he continued to do his best at the ski factory. He was often rewarded for his efforts with bonuses, praise at meetings, and by having his picture in the paper. He was a *Stahanovilainen* (the Finnish term) or *Stakhanovist* (in Russian). Stakhanov was a coal miner somewhere in the south of Russia who consistently exceeded the daily norm set for the miners, sometimes even doubling the average output per man, or so we were told. He was highly praised in the newspapers, called a hero of the Soviet Union, and made an example for others to follow. The best workers, therefore, in other areas and lines of work were given the name *Stakhanovist*, in his honor. Often it was difficult to see how the work could be assessed or graded, but somehow this was done and the awards passed out. It was fine for workers who had no problem getting out a lot of work, but there were workers, too, who tried just as hard but could not accomplish as much for one reason or another. For them the *Stakhanovist* label was perhaps discouraging.

The Karelian Pedagogical Institute, which I attended, was a two-year school. During my second year, 1935-1936, we did our practice teaching at the secondary school in Petrozavodsk. Our whole class would go over to the school, and, while one of us would take over in the regular teacher's place, the rest of the class would observe. I remember my turn very well. While waiting in the hallway to enter the classroom, I began to yawn, and yawn and yawn! My classmate, Sampsa, told me that yawning was a sign of nervousness, and that I was gasping for oxygen. However, my lesson went very well. One of the things that had been stressed to us was that the pupils should be left with an interest in the next lesson. I was lucky: the children followed me out of the room, asking questions about the next day's lesson. Later, the regular teacher told me I had done a good job, and the kids had said, "We really like that little one."

The class was in literature, and the subject that day was Charles Dickens' *Oliver Twist*, which the children were studying in a Finnish translation. One of the children read from the book, and we discussed it. I recall that when she read, "*ottakaa varas kiinni*" which was the Finnish version of "stop thief," it seemed to me that the Finnish was much more formal and stiff than English. At that time most Finnish seemed to me to be just that, but, of course, once I learned to speak it more fluently, I found it wasn't always so.

In June 1936 our studies at the Institute were over. Our class made a trip to Leningrad to celebrate. I do not recall much of what we did— saw the sights, the palaces, and the parks. I do remember being glad to be back home. This was the August that we received word of my brother Andrew's death from what was known as "galloping tuberculosis." He had become ill in May and died in early June. Lauri's mother, Evi, was the one who first wrote about it. Her letter came a couple of months after he had died, and she had assumed that my father had already let us know. It was an awful blow to me. My father wrote later saying he had been afraid to tell me knowing what a shock it would be to me. Andrew and I had been very close, and his death was heartbreaking for me. I wrote to my father asking him to come to us in Karelia, but he wrote back that he was too ill to make any such plans. He was suffering from silicosis, miners' tuberculosis. I hadn't realized he was sick. He died a few months later in February of 1937. My younger brother Arvo, who had also contracted tuberculosis, entered a sanitarium where he remained for four years. He and I had little contact with each other during those years.

After graduating from the Institute in June, I waited to be assigned to a teaching job. This was a nerve wracking time for all the graduates, as we wondered where we would be sent. Many of us, at least those with families in Petrozavodsk, dreaded being sent to some small, far-away village. I was assigned to the secondary school in Petrozavodsk, called the *Suomalainen Keski Koulu* (Finnish Middle School), where I had done my practice teaching, to teach Finnish language and literature to sixth, seventh and eighth graders.

During the year that I taught at the secondary school, fall 1936 to summer 1937, I also held lectures on Finnish literature for the students at the Finnish Dramatic Theater. These students were budding actors and actresses. I did not enjoy the job. Acting being what it is, many of the students were very mindful of their looks and facial expressions, to the point where some of them spent most of the lecture time gazing at themselves in hand mirrors and, no doubt, dreaming of the time when they would be famous on stage. This proved to be very disconcerting to me.

My close friend Inkeri Letonmaki had also been assigned to teach at the secondary school, and she and I usually walked to school together. Inkeri's family had a small house all to themselves, and it was on my way to school. Her father, Lauri Letonmaki, worked for the Finnish-language newspaper *Punainen Karjala* (*Red Karelia*).[*] In the spring of 1937 he was divested of his party membership. This was a sign that he was in some kind of trouble. One morning when I stopped to pick up Inkeri she told me she would not be going to school that day. Her father, despondent over losing his party membership and fearful, no doubt, of what lay ahead, had hanged himself during the night. It was a bad time for Inkeri, her older sister, and her mother. When I visited her during the days to come, I often found her mother playing solitaire (patience). A doctor had recommended it to her to save her from a nervous breakdown.

Our class from the Institute was able to teach only one year, 1936-37. After that the government stopped the teaching of Finnish in the schools. Finnish newspapers were discontinued; we were not even supposed to speak Finnish in public. This was in line with Stalin's paranoia; he felt that the Finns were trying to make Karelia into a Finnish republic.[**]

In the fall of 1937, I was given a job teaching in an all-Russian sec-

[*]Lauri Letonmaki, editor of political works, had been Minister of Justice in Finland's 1918 revolutionary government. (Tuominen 296).

[**]On July 25, 1937, Edvard Gylling, his wife, and Kustaa Rovio were arrested in Moscow. Most of the members of the Karelian government were also arrested, and the party secretaryship was assumed by a man named Kuprianov, who reportedly said at his inauguration, "I won't sleep peacefully a single night until the last Finn has been banished from Petrozavodsk." (Tuominen 299).

ondary school. I could not make a go of it. The pupils knew no English, and my knowledge of the Russian language was not good enough. My discipline was terrible. I had several young lads in the class who continually disrupted the whole class. I repeatedly asked the principal to come and oversee my lessons and to help me with discipline, but he never would enter my classroom. I thought it was probably his first job as principal, and he was just as afraid of the kids as I was. On the other hand, perhaps he did not want me teaching there since I was a foreigner. A school friend of mine, Selma Anderson, who also had been teaching at the secondary school when the Finnish language was banned, was sent to teach English in a Russian Technicum in Petrozavodsk. She soon lost this job because she was a "foreigner," and "foreigners" were not allowed to teach in Russian schools at this time. In my case, the situation became so difficult that I finally just stayed home, and no one ever came around to ask why I didn't come back.

That same fall an NKVD man and his wife came to live in our barracks at 50 Bolotnaya Ulitsa. I don't know how we knew he was of their ranks, but, somehow, we all did. Perhaps this couple was put there to keep an eye on the Finns. The wife was quite friendly, but one look from the man's gimlet eyes made cold chills run up and down one's spine and killed any urge for a closer relationship with them.

The winter of 1937-38 was a very severe one in Karelia, the hardest we had seen. That was the winter Lauri made me a pair of *tallukkaat*— a kind of soft shoe. We used my old snowsuit that we'd brought with us from the states which was getting worn. He made a pattern, cut out as many pieces as he could of each part of the pattern, and then sewed them together. For the soles, he used some kind of tough, rubbery belting he found at the factory. The *tallukkaat* proved to be comfortable, very warm and even cute.

This was the winter we made regular use of the woolen comforter we had brought with us; other winters we had needed it only occasionally. This was also the winter the ski factory band boys had to use *pirtua* (pure alcohol) in their horns to keep them from freezing. Naturally, the players had to have firewater of some sort in themselves, too, to keep warm.

Since the Soviet Union was an atheistic country we did not celebrate Christmas as such, but we did celebrate the New Year. We had a tree and a character called Father Frost. In December of 1937 we made plans for a New Year's party. Since our home was only one room, we could not have many guests. We had asked cousin Lily and Dave, our close friends Eino and Sylvi, and also Mary and Eino who lived behind the wall from us. We wanted Benny and Miriam with us, but they had a small baby and could not go out because of her.

Although Lily and Dave had separated earlier, they were ashamed to admit this to us, and would visit us, and have us over, as if nothing had happened. They would appear at our home together, and, when we visited at their home, there was Dave. We learned of their separation much later. They both came to the New Year's party.

We planned a midnight supper with as much on the table as our purse could stand. The big thing was the tree with homemade decorations—that was great fun. As we prepared for the party we wondered what 1938 would bring.

Earlier in the fall we had become acquainted with a couple named Grandell from Detroit. Toivo Grandell worked for Karelian Auto. We liked them both immediately and told them about our party preparations. A few weeks before New Year's, he was arrested. We wondered what to do about inviting his wife. The other women coming felt that it would not do, but I happened to meet her downtown one day and told her we would like to have her if she felt like coming. She did not, probably thinking that she might spoil the party for the rest of us.

It was a subdued little group that met that night to celebrate the New Year, and had we known what terror this particular year—1938— would bring, I am sure there would have been no celebrating at all.

Toivo Grandell's arrest was most disturbing. What could he have done? Would he be released?

All of us felt the frustration of not being able to say what we thought for fear of being considered disloyal. We thought the official attitude toward Stalin—giving him credit and thanking him for any and every good thing—was ridiculous, but we would never have dared to say so in public. We were all afraid.

Someone told a little story, with a kind of wry humor that seems typically Russian, that neatly illustrated the extent of our fears. It was about a woman who went fishing with some friends and caught only a very tiny fish. This she held up with obvious disdain and said sarcastically, "Thanks to Stalin." Someone reported her, as the story went, and she ended up in jail.

How Can They All Be Guilty?

L: For the first couple of years that we were in Karelia, the whole country was on a six-day week: five days of work at seven hours a day, and the sixth was a day of rest. Then the Supreme Soviet decided to change to a seven-day week and have six eight-hour work days with the seventh day off. People on salaries would get the same weekly pay as before; those on piece work would have their pay adjusted so they wouldn't make any more than they did before. It was a losing proposition for all workers.

To make this change legal, it had to be approved by all of the workers. The government printed a pamphlet describing the changes for people to read, and then held outdoor meetings at all of the factories. Not only were the new working hours introduced at this meeting, but some new rules as well. For instance, anyone who was late to work would be fined ten percent of his or her weekly pay for the first offense. The second lateness would result in a three-month jail sentence plus a twenty percent fine. What made this even worse was the fact that there were no alarm clocks to be had in the stores.

At the ski factory meeting we were told how many more fighter planes and jumbo carriers the state would be able to acquire with the money saved by these changes. Defense of the Motherland was important. Many other things were mentioned too. I did not hear a single voice protesting during the meeting. It was only in small groups afterward that people dared to complain. There was always the fear that someone would report you. It seemed impossible to those of us who had lived in a free society that such things could happen, but they did.

Instead of complaining, we all applauded whenever we were asked to approve a change. I especially remember how Ronkanen, who was often late to work, applauded so vigorously that afterward, back in the shop, one of the Karelians told the whole gang of us that Ronkanen had just applauded a jail sentence for himself! We all had a good laugh at Ronkanen's expense and sure enough, he did get a jail sentence later. I was fortunate; we had an alarm clock, brought from the states, so I was never late.

There was one time though, when that alarm clock didn't help me. The ski factory had a boat with a ten to twelve-horsepower motor. It was made in the Soviet Union and not very dependable, but I had occasion to use it every now and then to go to the cabin at Pässinranta or to go hunting or fishing. Since I took care of it, I didn't have to get anyone's permission to use it.

One beautiful summer evening after work several of us—a Karelian fellow from the power house, the Dahlstroms, Sylvi, and I—decided to make a quick trip to the cottage. On our way we stopped at a small store across the bay to see if they had anything we could use. (We often checked the different stores around, for what they might have.) To our surprise there was a big supply of one hundred-gram bottles of vodka, about the size available on airlines. They were sealed with paper stoppers, and, once opened, the contents had to be emptied. We bought about three-dozen bottles and set them in a couple of rows on the railings on the side of the boat. As we were riding we each had a bottle on which we sipped, then another, and another . . . by the time we got to the cabin, we didn't have a care in the world.

When it came time to go back into town, the motor wouldn't start. I did everything I could think of, but all it would do was sputter a little and quit. We were really worried. It was already after midnight. If we couldn't get back in to work by seven A.M. it would mean a fine or a jail sentence or both! We worked feverishly, but that motor just would not start.

Around three o'clock in the morning, and in broad daylight (being summer so far up north), we heard the noise of a motor out on the lake. It was a speedboat racing around and coming quite near to our shore. We waved and yelled until he noticed us and came in to our dock. He was a boat captain for one of the big shots. It was such a beautiful morning, he said, that he had just decided to take a ride. We explained our predicament and offered him money, or liquor, or food if he would take us back to the ski factory dock.

He thought about it for a while and then said he would tow us back. We were very much relieved that we would not only get to work on time, but also get the boat back to town. The driver would not accept anything from us; he just said he was glad to help.

I was able to avoid the consequences of ever being late to work, but we still felt far from secure. Arrests were happening more and more often, even among people we knew. Toivo Grandell had been one of the first; we didn't know him very well. But then there were others whom we did know, and we had no idea what they could have done to warrant arrest.

Among the first from the ski factory to be arrested was a big, good-looking Finn named Kalle Soderstrom who was a good friend of ours. Just a few weeks after he had been jailed, he appeared, to our surprise, at our door, free on a technicality. Kalle was an intelligent fellow with a good sense of humor, fun to be with. He told us a little of his life history. After fighting on the Red side during the Finnish Civil War,* he was given a long jail sentence in Finland. Being young, he was not executed but he suffered from the poor conditions and lack of food. Smoking was not allowed in the jail, he told us, so he developed a method of swallowing the smoke to remove the evidence. There was one guard whom he hated for reporting the smallest infractions, so Kalle would swallow the smoke and wait to burp it up in front of the guard. The man always smelled it, but could never find a cigarette on him so he got away with it. As he told us about it, he was smoking and swallowing the smoke. Then he demonstrated burping the smoke out. We could tell this had given him a lot of pleasure amid the horrible conditions he endured in prison.

Soderstrom's situation was especially uncertain because he had skipped the border from Finland when he came to Russia and, having a jail record there, he was sure he would face a prison term in Finland if he went back. Now he was also facing the possibility of being arrested again in Russia if he stayed. I'm sure if he had known the horrors that he

---

*The Finnish Civil War was fought from January to April of 1918. The Whites, or Constitutionalists, triumphed. Many of the Reds, which included Social Democrats as well as Bolsheviks, were imprisoned in Finland. Most of their leaders fled to Moscow or Karelia after the war.

would face if he was taken again in the Soviet Union, he would have tried to escape to Finland, but he didn't. Before long he was arrested again and that was the last we ever heard of him.

It was still in 1937 when Elias Tuomainen, the director of the ski factory, was arrested and I felt real bad about that. I knew him well and just couldn't understand what he could have done. In 1938 things got even worse for the Finns in Karelia. It seemed to me that most of the people being arrested were Finns not Karelians. Our old friend Heino was arrested, as was the band director, Elis Ranta. We just couldn't understand it. We knew these people were innocent of any wrong doing. When we asked people who were party members about the arrests, they assured us that anyone who was innocent would be freed. Keijo Frilund was one who said that. I asked him point blank if all these people could actually be guilty. I remember Keijo was sitting on our sofa, legs crossed and one foot waving up and down. "They must be," he said. Maybe he believed it—until he too was arrested. He never got out.

One weekend we went to Pässinranta with Ilmi and Keijo. Keijo had just returned from a trip up north where he had served as an interpreter at interrogations of people who had been arrested. He seemed different—almost like a changed person, more somber and quieter. Ilmi said she had noticed it too. He wasn't saying much and hung around her and little Irma a lot.

We were at home late one evening when suddenly Eino and Sylvi Dahlstrom burst into our room to tell us that Benny Laine was being arrested at that very moment. The Dahlstroms had been in town and, on their way home, had walked past the barracks where Benny and Miriam lived. They had a custom of whistling whenever they went by, and Benny or Miriam would open the window and say hello. On this evening, when Eino gave his shrill whistle, Miriam yelled out the window that the police were there and were taking Benny with them. Eino and Sylvi had raced directly to our place.

We were all devastated. It was so horrible. Although we knew many people who had been arrested, this just hit us really hard. It felt like this was the end, like maybe we would be next.

Benny was a Canadian. He had been brought to Karelia by his parents when he was just a kid. He didn't mess with politics or belong to any clubs. His interests were just his job as a mechanic at the ski factory and his family. He was one of the finest fellows I had the pleasure of working with; Sylvi and I often spent evenings with the Laines and Dahlstroms and shared a drink or two. So we were really in shock to learn of Benny's arrest. His father was arrested too, and to my knowledge neither one has been heard of since. Eino told me later that Ben had told him that the secret police had talked to him about becoming a spy for them. They would have trained him for the job but he turned them down. He wasn't supposed to tell anyone about it but he did tell Eino, who kept it secret until after Benny was arrested.

Things kept getting worse. In July of 1938 we had a night of horror known afterward among the Finns as "*suuri kauhu*" (the great terror). The NKVD was everywhere that night. We spent the whole night expecting their knock at our door, but it never came. We watched from the window as gunmen took some of our good friends away.

The next morning only a couple of Karelians and one Finn showed up for work in machine repair. The others, about twenty-three men, had been arrested. I still don't know why I wasn't taken, since I was the foreman in machine repair. Usually the leaders were taken first.

One Sunday soon after, we were at our summer place with Dave. He and Lily were openly divorced by this time. We noticed a motor boat pull up and stop at the ski factory dock in Pässinranta and thought it looked like the police. We quickly took to the woods taking some pans along and pretending to pick berries. After what seemed like a long time I decided to scout around and see what was happening. Dave didn't dare go because they had already been looking for him. He warned me, too. "You go out there and the first thing you'll do is get caught," he predicted. He was right.

I headed towards the cabin still pretending to pick berries. Suddenly a group of rifle-toting secret police came around a bend in the trail and spotted me. They wanted to know my name and proceeded to look through their papers. They had a very long list, but my name wasn't on it. They were very polite then, thanked me, and told me to go on picking berries while they went on to the next cabin. I hung around watching to see when they left so the rest could come out of hiding.

Pretty soon they returned down the trail with an old Finn by the name of Lintula limping along between them. As they passed me Lintula spoke out of the side of his mouth: "*Nyt se on vientiä, sanoi papukaija kissalle.*" ("It's the end of the line, said the parrot to the cat.") The old saying fit the circumstances well. "*Lintu*" is the Finnish word for "bird." Old man Lintula in the hands of the NKVD was just like a bird in the cat's mouth.

I went back to tell Sylvi and Dave that it was safe to come out; they had gone. Dave was sure that he was on their list. He had had a premonition one night that he was in line to be arrested and had gone out and slept in his chicken coop. Most of the arrests at this time occurred at night. It was easier to find people at home then, and there weren't so many others watching. Sure enough, the police had come looking for him that very night but, fortunately, didn't think to look in the coop. Soon after, Dave went to the cabin and planned his escape. He wanted us to come along, and I might have gone, but Sylvi was afraid. "You're going to kick yourself," Dave predicted.

Vilho and Terttu went with him. They left by rowboat from Pässinranta one night, intending to go along the shore to Solomanni and then up the river as far as possible before striking out through the woods with a compass to Finland. The morning after they left, an American-Finn named Erkkila came by the cabin in another boat. "They won't get far," he said. "I reported them."

We were appalled. Maybe he did it out of fear, hoping to get better treatment for himself. His wife had already been arrested; maybe he did it for spite. It was many years before we learned what had happened to Dave.

S. One evening during the summer of 1938, in the midst of the arrests, we were returning home from the Summer Park. It was late but, being summer, not dark. As we reached our courtyard we heard the radio, from an outside speaker, blaring out the notes of the "Internationale." At the same time we saw the police rounding up people from our barracks.

Until then, the "Internationale" to us had been an expression of hope for a better world in the future, for freedom from fear. But now, hearing its stirring notes and, at the same time, being witness to a mass arrest of friends and fellow workers horrified us. How could this be? We decided to go to Ilmi and Keijo's apartment; it would be a comfort to be with friends at such a time. But as we turned to go, we saw Ilmi at their window. "Don't come here," she called to us. "They are taking Keijo."

In our own room we spent a sleepless night waiting in terror for the knock at our door. The knock never came, but we felt sure it would some other night.

After that night we just knew that Lauri would be taken too. I was terrified. We made some preparations, planned what he would take with him if he had to go. I remember going by bus one day to see Lily who had told us she had a pair of very sturdy men's boots that we could have. I cried all the way. We could not understand why these people—mostly men and mostly people we felt we knew well—were being arrested. Viktor Viiki and Albin Heino were among them. We could not believe they were guilty of any wrongdoing.

L: After the big night of arrests at the ski factory there were many women left alone. Word came that these women should get ready to move so that their rooms could be used by couples. They would be taken, we were told, to a place where they would soon be reunited with their husbands. Even women with small babies had to go. Ilmi Frilund went with little Irma, and she was so happy, fully believing that Keijo would join them. They were all taken on to a big scow at the docks and then towed to an island on Lake Onega where lime was produced for industrial use. It turned out that the women were put to work there. No husbands ever showed up. It must have been the biggest disappointment of their lives. But they weren't exactly prisoners; many of them were back in town before fall. Ilmi Frilund returned and spent the winter at Pässinranta.

One of the ladies taken to the island was Katri Lammi, an actress and singer who worked at the Finnish Dramatic Theater in Petrozavodsk. Katri was married to a well-known singer, Jukka Ahti, who had been arrested some time earlier. They used to sing together a lot, which is what they had done while the police were searching their apartment before they arrested Jukka. Those who saw Katri leave for Lime Island said she put on quite a performance, having the police pack and carry her things onto the scow. Richly dressed in furs and laces from the theater, she paraded along the dock, singing parts from operas. Once on the island, Katri got the job of driving a horse hauling stone to the dock. People said she was a real sight, dressed in the most ridiculous way—furs, lace, muffs—and acting the part of some character. I wished I had seen it.

After her divorce, my cousin Lily married a man named John. He was also arrested and charged with espionage. He was made to stand in a corner facing it, and, as the guards walked by, they hit him in the back of the head so his face would hit the wall. He said it was much worse than seeing a blow coming and bracing for it. After enduring this treatment for some time he decided to admit guilt. Whatever they asked him he admitted doing, and, when they asked for names of accomplices, he gave them names. However, he made sure to give them only names of people he knew were already dead. He made his story so believable his interrogators were pleased. He remained in jail, but there were no more beatings.

The papers he had signed detailing his "crimes" were sent to the central headquarters. It was a few months before they discovered that his stories were all lies. At that point, they let him go, and he was not arrested again. They must have had their quota filled in Karelia by that time.

But most of the people who were taken were never seen or heard from again. None of our friends who were arrested ever returned. Either they perished in the concentration camps or else they received what the Finns called a *"viiden kopekaan tuomio"* (five-kopeck sentence) which meant that they were shot. Five kopecks was the price of a rifle bullet.

The Winter War

L: In the summer of 1938 we decided that we would try to get back to the United States. Many others would have liked to leave too, but most of our closest friends did not apply being sure they would be refused. Those who did apply did not tell everyone. They were afraid they might lose their jobs.

Our first question was whether we, who were now Soviet citizens, would be permitted to enter the United States. You couldn't even apply for release from the Soviet Union unless you already had permission to enter another country. Sylvi made a trip to the American Embassy in Moscow with her friend Flossie to find out if we could return to the United States. The answer was yes.

The next problem of course, was whether the Soviets would allow us to leave. There were all kinds of forms to fill out to get permission to emigrate, and many questions to answer, such as, "Why do you want to leave?" Many people felt that it was none of the government's business why they wanted to leave, and I agreed, but the government had all the power, and we had to play by their rules. For that question, we put down that my parents were poor and getting old. They needed our support, and we had no way to help them financially from the Soviet Union. We had just finished the application when Eino Dahlstrom walked in and read it. He said that helping our parents wouldn't mean a thing to these people. But we couldn't think of anything better for an answer, so we left it the way it was and sent it in. For a long time we heard nothing about it.

We did make another train trip to Moscow though, to tell the people at the American Embassy that we had applied to leave. This time I was able to go with Sylvi. While we were there we attended an agricultural show and an air show. I remember at the agricultural show we bought sandwiches and beer and the beer bottles were covered with bees from nearby hives that were part of the show. For entertainment they had a motorcycle barrel racing act. The drivers were American women.

We took a train to the air show, which was some distance from Moscow over a vast, open field. It lasted two or three hours. All kinds of aircraft—from fighter planes to helicopters—flew right over our heads. It struck me as very dangerous. There was a huge crowd of spectators. When the show was over, a train appeared to take people back to Moscow. Everyone rushed to catch the train. We had to go around a high wooden fence demarking the air field. In the mad rush, people started climbing the fence, and it came crashing down. The train was soon covered with people hanging on all over the place. Loudspeakers kept saying that the train couldn't start with so many on it and that another train would be coming soon, but no one listened. We waited in the shelter of a building. A young girl also took refuge there, coughing blood from having been crushed in the crowd. We couldn't understand how people could act that way. Better to walk to Moscow than get caught in that wild pack. Many people were injured that afternoon, but we never saw anything in the paper about it. Papers only printed what the government wanted them to print.

One thing we did read, in all the newspapers in Karelia during the time we were there, was that Nazi Germany was a horrible, repressive country and an enemy of the working class. So in August of 1939, when Stalin and Hitler signed their nonaggression pact, we did not know what to think. We had been told that Hitler was our enemy, so for most of us this unexpected pact was hard to take. But we had one electrician in the factory who caught on real fast to this about-face. He kept walking around bragging that with Germany as our ally, "nobody can beat us now!" He seemed real happy about it. I wish I could have seen him in June, 1941, when Hitler attacked the Soviet Union.

All through the summer of 1939 we saw freight train loads of war materiel being moved north. We could see tanks, trucks and cannons on flat cars and a lot of big boxes and barrels. We didn't know what was coming until later in the fall when newspapers began to talk about negotiations with Finland. Then in the latter part of November the Russian army attacked Finland and the "Winter War" was on.

Newspapers talked about the advances the Red Army was making on all fronts, especially the eighth army. They were going to go straight across Finland—cut it in two. They did advance during the first few weeks, but then they were stopped. Finnish ski troops were behind the Russian lines cutting down trees to block their supply lines. The Russians were trapped. I heard later that Finland's strategy was to let them come just so far and then try to get them to surrender, but the Russians just hung on even though they ran out of food and supplies. A lot of them died of hunger; it was a very cold winter.

Two men from our shop went with the eighth army, and one returned after the war ended in March of 1940. He told us what a terrible time they had had. The Soviet Air Force tried to fly in supplies, he said, but half the time the drops would miss them and fall to the enemy. The Finns had powerful radio speakers in the trees and would urge them, in Russian, to surrender, offering them so much for a rifle, a tank, a machine gun, any equipment. The situation became so desperate for the Soviets that they decided to escape on foot and fight their way out. Their ammunition was low, so they had to be careful with it, and the snow was hip deep. To survive, they had to eat their horses, but they couldn't build a fire or the Finns would see it and shoot. It was a very small group that finally got out.

The Russian army was transporting fuel to the front in barrels on regular trucks. Finnish ski troops would ambush the trucks. Without even bothering to attack the driver, they would simply shoot holes in the barrels so all he could do was turn around for another load.

They brought some of the shot-up barrels to the ski factory for repair and I was given the job of welding them while two men ran hot steam through them so they wouldn't explode from gas left in the seams. These men had been in the army and were wounded so they weren't sent back to the front. They were happy to help me and did a very good job; I didn't have a single one explode.

One of the soldiers helping me had been driving a tank. He told me that when word came to attack he thought to himself, "Helsinki, here I come." But soon after he hit a mine and landed in a field hospital.

The other fellow said he was a foot soldier. He had been wounded while trying to sneak up on a bunker. He was hit by shrapnel as he was crawling through the snow. He told me about a time when his platoon was trying to cross a river. Every little while, seemingly out of nowhere, someone would get shot. All day long they couldn't get ahead. At one time they thought they saw movement across the river and started firing with everything they had: tanks, cannon, small arms. Still, some people were getting hit.

Finally, late in the evening someone spotted a sniper in a tree. They shot it down and went to look. It was a woman.* She had been sitting in a hammock with a thermos bottle, lunch, chocolate bars and a scoped rifle with plenty of ammunition. He said it was just luck that they happened to notice her, she was so well camouflaged.

The ski factory was on full-time war work by now. They increased production, so quality suffered. The skis were at best a grade three by now as were the poles and the little sleds called *pulkkas* that were used to haul ammunition to the front lines and wounded to the rear. The name *pulkka* came from Finland. They were boat-shaped sleds that the Laplanders used, pulled by reindeer. They didn't sink deeply into the snow because of their shape and being made of wood; they were light weight and ideal for the foot soldier to pull behind him.

I was collecting three rubles for each barrel I repaired, plus my salary. Sometimes I would think about how the Finns were shooting holes in these barrels and here I was, an American Finn, patching them up. Why did things like that happen? We felt pride in the Finns but didn't talk about it much, even with close friends. Someone might inadvertently say something that could get us in trouble. Over near the ski factory club house was a fenced area where Finnish prisoners were kept. I saw one man in there, and I really wanted to go and talk to him, but knew I'd better not. Somebody might see. We were still living with fear.

The Winter War lasted 105 days, ending with the Treaty of Moscow signed on March 13, 1940. Of course Finland, with 4,000,000 people was no match for the Soviet colossus with 180,000,000 inhabitants. The wonder was that the Finns were able to hang on so long and inflict so much damage as they did on the Red Army. In the end, Finland lost about ten percent of her territory. Most of the people who had lived in the ceded areas relocated within the new Finnish borders rather than live under Soviet rule.

---

*Many Finnish women helped in the war effort, though usually not at the front. They were known as the "Lottas."

What Are They Giving?

S.   By 1939 things had quieted down and we went on with our
     lives. Stalin's non-aggression pact with Hitler stunned us; we
     could not understand how a communist nation could be
friendly with a fascist country. As Lauri has written, we saw the preparations which were being made at the Finnish border as the trains rolled
by Petrozavodsk with supplies for the Red Army. The Winter War
brought various changes into our daily lives. Although the Red Army
expected to walk right through to Helsinki, precautions were taken,
nevertheless, in case of enemy air raids. We had to cover our windows
with heavy blankets when evening came and lights were turned on. We
also took turns being guards outside each barracks and wore armbands
to distinguish ourselves. Our guard duty consisted of checking all windows to make sure no light was showing through. Then, too, all radios
had to be turned in to the authorities. This was probably done to prevent
us from hearing any propaganda from the Finns or making any contact
with them.

My friend Tyyne and I had an amusing experience one day soon
after the Red Army had attacked Finland. Since we carried water by the
bucketful into our rooms and also carried slop water out the same way,
bathing at home was not easy. But we had public baths in town with dif-

ferent sections for men and women. Tyyne and I were standing in line for the bath one day when we overheard a couple of Red Army men in the other line. One of them said, "Well in a couple of weeks we will be having a bath in Helsinki." We know now that it was years before they could have had their bath, and, even then, it would have had to be as tourists, not as conquerors.

Our radios were returned to us after the Winter War, but the air-waves were often jammed by the Soviets. We did sometimes get music from Finland, and it sounded good to us. We especially enjoyed it one evening when we heard "Ain't She Sweet?" a song that had been popular when we were still in the States, sung with a strong Finnish accent.

The Finnish language was brought back into use in 1940, but as far as I was concerned, my teaching days were over. After I left the teaching job in the Russian school in 1937, I became a homebody and spent my time keeping house (in one little room?) and standing in queues (*ochereds*, in Russian) to get food.

At this time I became good friends with Tyyne Nurminen who was also a stay-at-home. Her husband, Viljo, was a party member, and I never had felt at ease with him, but Tyyne was very outgoing and friendly and a lot of fun. They had a little boy born in March of 1938 who became very dear to us. He was our little Heikki (Henry). He treated us as another set of parents and loved to be with us. To differentiate between me and our friend Sylvi Dahlstrom whom he also knew, he'd call me "*meijän syyvi*" (our Sylvi) and her, "*Dalsto syyvi*" or Dahlstrom's Sylvi.*

While Tyyne was trying to toilet train him, she came over one day and announced in triumph that she had taught Heikki a marvelous new trick. When I asked to see it, she removed his diaper, helped him stand up and lo and behold, he peed on our floor! I was not nearly as elated with his trick as she was—but I loved him dearly.

One day when Heikki was about two and a half years old, he strayed from the barracks area. Tyyne and I searched all over town and no Heikki. On the way downtown we had to cross a little river and we were fearful of what might have happened to him. Finally we went to the police and tearfully told them our story. One of them grinned at us and said, "Don't worry, those little ones always turn up. It's when your big boys are missing that you have to worry." We were disgusted with their

---

*Finns often call a person by their last name in the possessive form, followed by their first name, as in, Hokkasen Lauri or Dahlstromin Sylvi.

uncaring attitude, but Heikki did turn up, none the worse for his escapade.

Heikki was often with us at mealtime, and once, after we'd all had some potato soup, he held up his dish and said, "Give me some more of that potato water." He was right: it was potatoes, onions and water. You couldn't fool him.

During our first summer in northern Karelia, our food had consisted of dried potatoes, canned meat and porridge, bread, of course, with sometimes a bit of milk. After moving to Petrozavodsk we were able to buy more and better food, especially while the INSNAB store for foreigners was open. I remember a date-filled cooky that was delicious, and a pastry called Napolean . . . scrumptious . . . and plain shortbread-type cookies. Fresh meat was very scarce, and we would often make meatloaf from sausage which was more available. We could buy prunes, but found them inedible because instead of being dried, they had been smoked. Potatoes were diced and dried. Once on a hunting trip Lauri and Eino had the good luck to buy a quantity of potatoes, but they froze on the way home. Fruits were non-existent, as were fresh vegetables. The staples were available but we had to stand in long lines for them.

When food was in small supply, there was the tendency for people to get what they could and hoard it. Whenever we came across a food line, we would check it out. The regular procedure was this: first we found the end of the line and asked in Russian, "*Kto posledniy?*" ("Who is last?") Then we said, "*Ya za vami,*" ("I'm after you,") and, finally, asked, "*Shto dayut?*" ("What are they giving?"). Of course they weren't "giving" anything, but one was lucky to be able to buy anything at all.

Tyyne and I usually went together through these food lines. Often we would stand in line all night waiting for the store to open and "give" us a kilo of meat or sugar. In the bitter cold of winter, we would take turns going home to warm up and then returning again to our place in line. One day Tyyne told me that her husband had asked her why I was hoarding so much food. Since Tyyne was with me practically all the time buying as much, if not more, food than I did, I was incensed by the question, and she and I quarreled. We did not speak to each other or stand in any lines together for some time. Finally one day, as I turned a corner at the shopping mall downtown, I ran straight into Tyyne. Our quarrel was forgotten; we embraced and spent many an hour together again.

The scarcity of food often made people act like animals in their fear of being left without, and there was danger of being trampled under foot by those determined to get into a store the minute the doors were opened whether they had stood in line or not. I remember a time when I was in line with Sylvi Dahlstrom where people were pushing and shoving. When the doors opened a crowd swept us in, and I fainted dead away from the pressure. Several people came to my aid, however, and I got whatever was being sold without having to wait any longer.

Another time Tyyne and I were in a very unruly crowd with the most aggressive ones pushing their way in every time the door opened leaving those of us in line waiting outside. It looked hopeless. But for some reason, Lauri had come downtown to look for us, and he took it upon himself to get next to the door and stand guard, keeping the line in order until Tyyne and I got in. Then he let go, came in after us, and let the devil take the hindmost.

A crowd of people that otherwise and elsewhere was well-behaved could, if conditions were right, turn into an ugly mob with only one selfish aim: to attain whatever it was they wanted at the moment. Even law-abiding citizens could forget their scruples and join the crowd. Having been caught up in several of these hysterical groups during our stay in Karelia, I am still wary and frightened of large crowds and will not willingly join them.

Although at first the foreigners did have much better food than the natives, after INSNAB closed we were no better off. The sour black bread, "*buhanka*," in Russian, was hard on one's digestive system. Many Americans and Finns, especially Americans, developed stomach ailments. I did, and had to see doctors for help. One of them had me taking hydrochloric acid, which had to be taken so it did not touch my teeth. Normally this acid is present in one's stomach in a very dilute form but mine must have been lacking it. I have never since been told by any doctor about such a problem. The doctors in the Soviet Union were mostly women, and I remember being mighty disgusted with one of them who was much more interested in the ring I was wearing than in my complaints.

But those of us who had come to the Soviet Union to build a workers' paradise had been willing to carry on that work as best we could, in spite of the meager and nearly indigestible food and primitive living conditions. It was only when our freedom was threatened and then taken away that some of us—not all—lost our illusions and realized that our dream was not going to work.

The Family Needs Us

L: For a long time we heard nothing about our application to leave the Soviet Union. We had sent it in late in 1938. We even wrote a letter to the Supreme Soviet trying to expedite the matter. Finally in December of 1940 we received a notice to report to a certain address on a certain date in connection with our application to leave the country. When we nervously presented ourselves we were asked again why we wanted to leave. I said, again, that my parents had no way to support themselves and needed us. We were then told that our application had been approved and we had permission to leave. We would be given the necessary papers and information on how to proceed.

At first, it was hard to believe that we would actually be able to leave. When we told some of our friends about it, they cautioned us to go easy and not get our hopes up too high. As far as we know, there was only one other American-Finnish family besides us from Petrozavodsk that received permission to leave. The rest got letters saying, "You do not have enough reason to leave." We had to sign a paper that we would never return to the Soviet Union.

In spite of the skepticism of our friends, we could not help getting enthused about our return. It was in our minds every day, as was the fear that something would happen to dash our hopes. Not long after we got our permit, I got a notice to report to NKVD headquarters at a certain time in the evening. I was not told what it was all about, just to come as directed, and I was really worried. Were we going to be able to go home or not?

Arriving at the appointed time, I was directed to a room and told to wait. Soon an officer came in, introduced himself, and asked me to sit down. Then he asked me about a book by Sinclair Lewis called *It Can't Happen Here* which had been published in the States in 1935. How did I get the book, he wanted to know, what did I think of it, and did I have it now.

We had gotten that book from Ilmi Frilund. When she had to leave her rooms and go to Lime Island she asked us if we would take care of some of their books until she had a place for them. We did, of course, and the Lewis book was among them. Some time later, our band director's son-in-law came over and wanted to borrow it, and we let him have it. I told all this to my interrogator and also that I hadn't read it very well but knew that it was a fictional story about fascism coming to America. Everything I said was written down and then he read it out loud to me, and I signed it.

Then came the surprise. They brought in the young man who had borrowed the book, his hands cuffed behind his back. He was very pale, looked tired, and I noticed he did not sit until he was told to.

The interrogator introduced us and asked the prisoner to tell his version of the story about the book. He took a deep breath, then exhaled, as if he had told his story over and over. When he was through, the officer asked me if I agreed with everything he had said. I said yes, only that I had not told the young man about the book; he had asked if we had it. I made that clear because I remembered that this was what I had told him earlier. I couldn't really see what difference it made, but I knew one had to be careful, and I sensed that there had to be something they didn't like in that book.

After the prisoner was taken away the officer thanked me for coming in to talk to him and said that was all he wanted. As I was leaving I asked him what this was all about, and he said that the book was anti-Soviet and makes fun of Stalin. When I thought about it I could understand how they might see it that way because what was happening in Russia at the time was very similar to that depicted in the book: paranoia had set in and people were afraid for their lives. Actually, "it can't happen here" is exactly what we would have thought, back in 1935 or 1936, about many of the things that *did* happen in Karelia in 1937 and 1938.

In January 1941, I received orders to go to a powerhouse that was furnishing power for the Iljinski sawmill on the shore of Lake Ladoga. I was asked to do some welding on a smokestack that was in danger of collapse. Why they asked me, I don't know. I did know that if you refused, it could or would be held against you. I was told that I could negotiate my pay when I got there.

I left Petrozavodsk by train getting off at a small station about half way to Leningrad. There was an open pick-up truck waiting for me. It was about a three-hour ride and very cold, but I was prepared for it, knowing my job would be outside.

The following morning I was shown the job. There were five-eighths-inch by three-foot by six-foot supports to be welded all around the stack, but there was no welding rod made up. The first job was to cut some three thirty-seconds mild steel into lengths, make a coating to dip them into and then dry them. I had a helper to stand up the supports while I tac-welded them. Then, while I was welding, he made welding rods.

I got my power directly from the power house. There was a rheostat on the panel in the power house. Someone had to sit there and keep the current at a certain gauge reading because, when I would strike an arc, it would draw the current down. If the person wasn't on the ball, I would have a rough time. There were several women there; I asked if anyone could speak Finnish, and finally a Karelian woman spoke up, so I gave her the job.

After a few tries I found a satisfactory heat setting and explained to her that while I was welding she must keep the amp needle right on the mark. She caught on real fast, and we were a good team.

On the afternoon of the second day I started to have trouble maintaining the arc. It got worse as I went along, so I went inside to see what was wrong and found a young fellow sitting in her place at the rheostat. When I asked the foreman what was going on, he just said the old lady was back on her regular job in the lumber yard. I insisted that she be brought back, or I wouldn't be doing any more welding. It wasn't long before she showed up, all smiles. I felt better too. We put in long hours, and the work progressed satisfactorily.

The decking on which I was welding got wet when it snowed due to the heat from the smoke so they gave me a pair of rubbers to wear over my felt boots. When it came time for my pay they were going to charge me for them, but I protested, and they let me keep them. I did not have to pay for my board and room either, which was a plus, and I was given permission to shop at their special store for technical workers so my pack had candy, cookies, cigarettes and tea—things that were hard to get. They came in handy on the way back home to Petrozavodsk.

The money part I knew would be a stickler. When time came for my pay, I had it all planned in advance. So the negotiations wouldn't take too long, I merely asked for twenty percent more than I thought was a fair price. After a little bargaining, I let them cut it, and everyone was happy. The director shook hands with me, said he was pleased with the job and wished me well.

I rode back to the train station the same way, in the pick-up truck. We stopped at an old farmhouse to warm up. The lady of the house put the samovar on the table and soon we had tea. She was Karelian so I was able to converse with her in Finnish. She told me that she was alone with her four kids; her husband had been killed in the war, and the money she got from the government was so little that she had to make a little more by fixing tea water for travelers. At that time everyone carried their lunch and tea with them.

While we were having tea and lunch I saw some movement behind the brick oven they used for heating and baking. I asked her where the kids were. Sure enough, they were behind the stove where it was warm. She told them to come out, but they were so shy and afraid they would just peek out and dash back in. Finally one of them came out when I kept coaxing her with the cookies. She was pitfully thin, just skin and bones. After a lot of coaxing from me and their mother, they took a cookie and ran back to their hiding place. When it was time to go I left most of my goodies with the poor lady to feed those kids. They just got to me. I will never forget them.

I got back to Petrozavodsk on the 13th of January, Sylvi's birthday. I had been gone five days.

S. As the time came for our departure from the land that had been home for six and a half years, I became more and more nervous. Would we really be allowed to leave or would some red tape or technicality be used to keep us back? When Lauri was sent to the Iljinski sawmill, I was beside myself with worry, afraid that he would not return, that it was a trick of some kind. My friend Edla Joki stayed with me that first night to calm me down. When Lauri returned five days later, bearded and dirty, I was overjoyed to see him and felt that it was the best birthday present I'd ever received.

We sold or gave away all our belongings and most of our clothes to friends. Many of them had asked for certain things when they learned we were trying to leave, and they insisted on paying for them. I remember a lady who asked for our water kettle months before our departure. Our alarm clock, which we had brought from the States and which Lauri had repaired several times, was a thing of great value. Clocks were not available in the stores.

Our friends all stayed close to us although there was a stigma attached to folks who left, and they could have been judged guilty by association. We had a group of good, true friends there, and it was sad to leave them. I remember a group of us sitting on the floor in our room— perhaps the last night of our stay—having a farewell drink from glasses that already belonged to someone else. A glass was accidently broken and someone exclaimed, "*Sirpaleet tarkoittaa onnea.*" ("Broken glass foretells happiness.") But one of the company was more wary; he said, "You can't be sure you're out until the last railroad tie is behind you." I didn't need his warning; I was frightened enough as it was.

As far as we could tell, this group who sat with us the last night of our stay in Petrozavodsk was ideologically very much like us. They had come to the Soviet Union with their parents, most of them in their teens. They could not have been deeply imbued with communist ideas, and probably didn't understand the term any better than we did. Sure, we all knew that the communist state would be all that a worker would want and that we were striving for that in the Soviet Union. However, by this time we had seen and experienced many things that did not jibe with what we considered a workers' country. There had been arrests among friends, persecutions, the Stalin personality cult . . . how could these phenomena fit in with communism? We had questions which we dared not voice even to friends. But the questions were in our minds. These friends who sat with us that night were there to wish us well; some of them wished they could go with us, but, since they could not, they were glad for us. It hurt deeply to leave them. We had no way of knowing what terrible experiences lay ahead for them.

L: We were told we could buy tickets to the closest port in a foreign country with rubles. From then on we had to have foreign currency, which we could not obtain in Russia. Also, we were not allowed to take any rubles out of Russia, and they wouldn't have been of any value elsewhere anyway. All we were allowed to do was to change enough rubles for twenty American dollars to take with us. Think of it. After working for over six years in the country, twenty dollars, plus our few possessions, were all we had to take with us.

Since the war was on in Europe, we had to go east to Japan. So we wrote to my parents in Michigan asking them to have $50.00 and two boat tickets from Japan to California sent to the American Embassy in Kobe, Japan. Then we bought train tickets to Moscow. When we left Petrozavodsk on February 8 all we had left to our name was contained in one big suitcase except my shotgun and the clothes on our backs.

We spent that last night in Petrozavodsk with my cousin Lily and her husband, John. I had signed over our share in the cabin at Pässinranta to them. In the morning, Lily walked to the train station with us. When we got there I remembered that I had forgotten my shotgun so I went back to Lily's for it. Her daughter Viola had stayed home with her baby. She was crying, because we were leaving and probably because she would have liked to leave too. I gave her a hug, feeling really bad for her, and left again for the station with my gun. As things turned out, I should have just left the gun with Lily and John.

On the way to Moscow, we spent one day in Leningrad with our good friends Inkeri and Paul Kokko. (It was Inkeri's father who had hanged himself after being stripped of his party membership.) Paul had a young brother named Jyry who lived with them, and they also had a two-year-old daughter, a real charmer, who would crawl under the table to calm herself whenever she was disturbed. The family was doing well. Paul, who was from Detroit, was an army officer, and so they had better food and lodging than the average citizens.

Paul had done some translating during the Winter War. A Finnish army officer had been wounded and taken prisoner and was held in the hospital. He was a quadriplegic. Paul went to talk to him. As a fellow officer, he asked if there was anything he could do to help. The man looked at him hard before replying, *"Painu helvettiin sinä Ryssän kätyri."* ("Go to hell you Russian traitor.") He meant, of course, that Paul, having become a Russian officer, was a traitor to his Finnish background. Paul could understand the Finnish officer's feelings. Before we left Leningrad

Paul gave me a pair of Russian army boots that I wore all the way to Japan (where it was finally too warm). I gave him my wrist watch, and Sylvi gave Inkeri hers.

Paul also warned me that the NKVD had agents operating in the United States. He advised me to keep a low profile at first because they were dangerous and could cause us a lot of grief.*

In Moscow we stayed with Evert Muukkonen and his wife, Katri, until we could find a hotel. (Katri had gone to school with Sylvi in Petrozavodsk.) They lived in an apartment building for auto workers, as did Martha and Dave Nieminen whom we knew from Detroit. (Martha was our good friend Paul Middleton's sister.) Dave didn't like the idea that we were leaving the Soviet Union and said so. He felt that we were deserting the workers' cause. I saw him at a bus stop in Moscow, and he asked me, "Why in the world are you leaving? There's no reason to leave." I didn't even try to tell him; he was very upset and didn't want to talk about it.

We were more comfortable with the Muukkonens who felt as we did about the arrests. They knew many who had been arrested and confided to us that they believed that most of them had been innocent of any crime against the state.

The first morning in Moscow we went to the United States embassy to see if our tickets and money had arrived in Japan. The embassy staff was very nice to us. Nothing had been received but they told us to keep checking.

Then we went to find a hotel, and luck was with us. There was a long line to register, and they were calling names in order. Shortly after we arrived they called a Polish man who wanted something cheaper than the room they offered him. So then they asked if anyone else would want that room; it was 100 rubles a day. I snapped it up, and we were escorted to a very nice suite: two rooms and a bath. It must have looked odd for us to take such an expensive room. The other travelers, judging by their clothes and luggage, were quite well-to-do. We didn't have much, but what we did have was in rubles and we couldn't take it with us so we figured we might as well live it up.

As soon as we were settled, we sent a telegram to my home asking why our tickets were delayed. A few days later, when they still hadn't come, we sent another. We were really getting worried since we wouldn't be allowed to leave unless there were money and tickets for us in Japan.

---

*Kaarlo Tuomi, a former KGB agent, agrees that Paul was right in warning us.

A couple of days after the third telegram was sent, on Washington's birthday, February 22, we arrived at the American Embassy to find a lot of smiling faces. The people there had been just as concerned as we were about our tickets and were very happy to tell us that they were finally safely at the American Embassy in Japan. What a great day that was. Everyone was so nice to us.

Later we learned what had taken so long. As soon as she heard from us, my mother had gone to the telegraph office in Sault Ste. Marie, Michigan, and given them the money to send to Japan for us.* Days later she received our telegrams and took a friend with her back to town to find out why we had not received the money. They discovered that the telegraph office had never sent it! Firmly anti-communist, they just didn't want to send money to help anyone in the Soviet Union. Mother and her friend got really angry and raised a big fuss. That got some action.

We had no trouble at all at the Japanese Embassy in Moscow. They gave us visas without question after we explained why we had to travel through Japan.

Then we had to buy our tickets from Moscow to Japan and there we ran into trouble. The bureaucrat in charge at the travel agency told us that we would have to have foreign currency to buy tickets to Japan. I protested. We had been recruited to come to the Soviet Union, I said, had worked there nearly seven years and had no dollars.

"Can you prove that you were recruited," he asked.

I had no idea how to do this but he suggested that we go to the archives where we should be able to find a record of it. We were a bit dubious but there seemed to be no other way so we took off. After much walking and asking of directions we located the huge building known as the archives. An extensive search of the inside brought us to some people who worked there. When we explained what we wanted and for what purpose they were amazed. It would take weeks, they guessed, possibly months, to find the papers we wanted, if they could be found at all. We gave up and returned to the travel bureau but the answer was still no.

Believing that there had to be something we could do to get through this impasse, we told our predicament to everyone who would listen. Someone suggested we try a certain law office where we were directed

---

*The tickets and the money amounted to $600. Some of this money came from the estate left by Sylvi's father. Indians using his farm house after Arvo left paid Evi fourteen dollars per month which she banked. The rest of the money she borrowed from a friend.

to a window. We knocked and a lady slid the window open and asked if she could help.

We explained that we were leaving to go back to the United States but had no dollars and that the travel agent refused to sell us tickets for Russian money. We told her how he had sent us to the archives to obtain proof that we had been recruited to come to the Soviet Union. She appeared hardly able to believe our story. The travel agent, she said positively, had to sell us tickets, and she would personally see to it that he did. She told us to go right back and get the tickets, and she would call the agent.

So back we went to the travel bureau where we found the agent still adamant in his refusal to sell. Then back to the lady at the law office who was equally adamant that he would sell! The shuffle continued. It was on about our fourth visit to the law office, when the lady became really upset, grabbed the phone, and shouted some things I couldn't make out. Then she said to me, "You go back there right now and, if he won't sell, come right back and tell me."

I walked into the ticket office, and the agent threw the tickets across the desk at me. I threw the money back at him and walked out. I guess he just wanted to cause trouble for people who were leaving. Maybe he was even jealous. Or, just possibly, he was looking for a chance to pocket some foreign currency.

While we were staying at the hotel in Moscow a young couple came to visit us. We knew the girl from Detroit; she had moved to the Soviet Union with her parents and married a Russian fellow. He seemed very nice, and we were pleased that she had found such a good and fun-loving husband. When I mentioned to him that I was taking my shotgun back home with me, he thought I would probably not be able to get it through customs. He asked if he could buy it. I agreed to sell it and named a price. He didn't have any money on him but promised to pay the next day. The following day he called and explained that he couldn't get the money to us just then but would send it by telegram to Vladivostok, and we could pick it up when we got there. I began to smell a rat, but there wasn't much we could do. I should have known better, especially since he had stuffed a whole place setting of silverware from the hotel into his shirt when they left. When we protested he just laughed and said they'd never miss it.

This gave us one more thing to worry about. We did check the telegraph office in Vladivostok and even sent him a telegram. All we got out of the whole business was a good lesson.

We also were entitled to exchange forty rubles for twenty dollars American for landing money in a foreign port. The bank in Moscow made out a permit for us to present to customs in Vladivostok which would allow us to take the twenty dollars out of Russia. We did have another $20 American, plus some change, acquired from selling our possessions to American friends in Petrozavodsk. This we hoped to take with us one way or another.

The trans-Siberian railroad was to take us to Vladivostok, a nine-day trip with brief stops for fuel, crew changes and to pick up and unload passengers and supplies. We took a sleeping coach; our compartment had four bunks that we had to share with others. I slept in one top bunk with Sylvi in the lower. Across from us were two men: a Russian army officer and a diplomat courier traveling through Japan and the United States to England.

The coach was warm, even in forty below Celsius. After a few days we got to know our roommates better and were more relaxed. But we needed exercise. All we could do was walk the length of the coach back and forth on one side; the other side was divided into sleeping compartments.

The food in the dining car was simple: no greens, just soups, porridge, bread, and tea. We became constipated, at times so badly that we couldn't eat. Sylvi especially suffered from it. So we were counting the days.

The landscape was interesting. Thousands of miles of snow, tundra, trees, mountains, and prairie passed by. There were a few towns and an occasional village with people heavily bundled against the bitter cold. Only their weatherbeaten faces showed, what we would call the layered look.

All the towns had tiny stores called *kiosks*. They were so small that the customers didn't even go inside. They would just go to a window, or *"fortochka,"* where they paid and received their merchandise: bread, sugar or rice. The *kiosk*, which was unheated, would remain open until they sold out and then close until the next shipment. At one railroad stop I watched a woman purchase two loaves of bread from one of these *kiosks*. Having no bag, she slipped off one of her petticoats and wrapped the bread in it. Better than letting it freeze.

About two thirds of the way across Siberia, we were nearing Lake Baikal. I noticed we were getting into high country and going through a lot of tunnels. At one point we were actually headed back towards Moscow in order to get around the lake. Lake Baikal claimed the distinction of being the deepest lake in the world. We were able to buy some smoked fish at a stop near the lake—it was delicious. It looked like herring or whitefish. From Lake Baikal the railroad continued easterly to Khabarovsk where it turned south for about four hundred miles to Vladivostok, where we arrived on March 6, 1941, nine days after leaving Moscow.

We got ourselves a hotel room, but it was a real mess. There was only one toilet on our floor, and it was blocked up, stinking so bad we hated to go near it. After getting situated, we checked over our papers and had an unpleasant surprise. The paper from the bank allowing us to exchange rubles for American money to take across the border was dated to expire a few days before we were to sail.

We went first to the American Consulate both to let them know we were there and to tell them about our post-dated permit. The vice consul said there was nothing he could do about it. When I started to say more he put his finger near his lips and inclined his head toward his secretary to caution me to go easy. The secretary was a Russian, and the vice consul apparently felt that he could report our conversation to NKVD authorities who might keep us from leaving. Then he wished us good journey for the rest of the way. I read recently that Angus I. Ward was the United States consul general in Vladivostok in 1941. I wish I had known then that he was from Chassel, Michigan.

We sent telegrams to the bank in Moscow about our permit, as well as some to the gun buyer but had no results in either case.

The day before we were to leave, I asked a Polish engineer who was traveling through Russia to the United States if he would take twenty American dollars through customs for us since he had a permit. He agreed.

At customs the next day I pretended that I didn't know that the permit had expired and just handed it in. The agent took such a quick glance before telling me it was no good that I felt certain he knew in advance it would be expired, as if there was some kind of conspiracy between the bank in Moscow and the customs office in Vladivostok. I had to fork over the twenty dollars that was necessary for landing in Japan. I still had maybe two dollars in American change and the Polish engineer to fall back on.

I will never forget how it felt when we left the harbor at Vladivostok on March 11. We were moving through ice but gradually beginning to feel free as the ship pulled away from the shore. It was hard to believe that we were actually going home at last!

Immigrants Again

L: There were three classes on the Japanese ship we took to Kobe: First class was above decks, second below and the third was down in the hold. They were all displaced persons in the hold, mostly Jews from Poland running from the Nazis. I don't know how they got to Vladivostok. The men would get out on deck, form a circle and dance and sing holding on to each other. I didn't see any of the women or children join them. We heard that Japan did not accept them; they were sent back to Vladivostok on the same ship but later a Jewish organization got them to Hong Kong.

In second class we were jammed four to a small room with barely room to turn around. The Polish engineer and one other man shared our room. We slept three nights in that room, the last anchored just outside the Japanese port to wait for customs in the morning. We had had meal tickets issued on the ship. The young man who was serving was very concerned about collecting these. He kept saying "tickee no, eating no." The food was poor.

The mess hall where we took our meals had long tables seating ten or twelve, and it also served as a sitting room. As we were lounging there one evening; our Polish engineer came in. As he walked by the young waiter who was fussing with the tables, he gave him a light kick with the side of his foot. I could see the young man got very upset. He soon took off and came back with another member of the crew who appeared ready to fight. He advanced toward the engineer swinging his arms and yelling in Japanese. I was sure he would beat up on the Pole who was backing away and trying to explain that he meant no harm. Then the captain walked in and just stood there watching, apparently enjoying the proceedings. Finally the Japanese wild man gave up, and they left. Our engineer was very subdued after that. He was so scared that when we went to bed, he propped a chair against the door. To me that made about as much sense as the kicking in the first place.

On the morning of March 13th we landed in Tsuruoka, Japan. It was the most beautiful sight we had seen in years—like a fairyland. Everything was so green; fruit trees were in blossom and flowers were everywhere. The weather was warm.

Only one matter was bothering us. How would we be able to land without the $50 landing money? The Polish engineer, once on board the ship, had given me $10. He said he was short and would send me the rest of the money from Chicago, but that was the last of that ten dollars. I even reminded him by letter but he never responded. By that time, however, we were so happy to be back home that we didn't sweat the small stuff.

That morning in Tsuruoka we had ten Japanese yen given to me by the Russian diplomat we got to know on the train. We also had about twelve dollars American. The customs officials came on board ship to examine us. There were two lines: one for English speaking, the other for Russian. The English line was longer so we took the Russian.

When I was called in I found four examiners sitting around a table. They very politely asked me to sit down. The man on my left did most of the talking. He wanted to know what I thought of the Russians and what kind of mechanics they were. I said they were very poor mechanics. This brought a big laugh which made me feel better. I opened a box of expensive Russian cigarettes and offered it to the head man. As he was handing it back I motioned to him to pass it on, and when it returned to me I just pushed it over to my left.

Now we were all smoking in a relaxed atmosphere, and I knew just what to say. When they inquired about landing money I said we had 100 Japanese yen, some American money and more money at the American embassy in Kobe. They did not ask me to show any of it and wished me a pleasant trip. (We did have $50 from my parents at the embassy. If they had asked to see the 100 yen I would have pulled out the ten and claimed I thought it was a hundred. Fortunately, I didn't have to.)

We must have looked a sight as we boarded the train for Kobe, Sylvi in a fur coat and boots and I in heavy wool overcoat, fur hat and knee length boots plus a heavy shirt. The train left right on time, seemed to travel fast and arrived in Kobe at the expected minute. To us, it was amazingly efficient and clean, and we enjoyed it all. The countryside was interesting, and I relaxed from all the hassle, feeling that from then on things would get better for us.

On the 14th of March we arrived in Kobe and got a really nice room with a bath in which we luxuriated. The next morning, the cleanest we'd been for many days, we presented ourselves at the American Embassy and received the $50 that had been sent to us. They advised us to get the earliest ship we could find to the United States because so many people were leaving.

At the American President lines we learned that we were already booked on a ship leaving in three weeks. We could leave in two, however, if we were willing to take a third class berth on another vessel. We would have second class privileges. Considering how little money we had, we decided to change our tickets to the earlier boat, the S.S. *President Taft.*

We couldn't afford to stay on at the hotel but we found a nice, clean place at the YMCA for a dollar a day. There was no cooking, so we ate out: lots of rice at every meal, fish and some meat. We were so starved for fruit that we ate a big bag of it every day. The bananas seemed to be the best I'd ever tasted.

I ran into one of the other passengers on the ship from Vladivostok, a Jewish fellow who had traveled first class. He asked when we would be leaving Japan, and when I told him, offered to take us out for a sukiyake dinner.

It was a very good dinner. He and his wife were very nice to us, and we enjoyed their company, the sake, and the sukiyake very much. The meat was cooked in an electric skillet right at our table. Rice was served separately, and also some whipped raw egg. A little Japanese girl served us and showed us how to use the chop sticks. She placed them in our fingers and, giggling, motioned us to eat. I was a poor learner and got more of her attention than the rest—too much, in Sylvi's eyes. The idea was to take a piece of meat between the sticks, dip it in the raw egg and eat it. If I failed to get a piece into my mouth the waitress was right there to help.

After dinner our host got down to business. He asked if I would change some yen into dollars for him when we were leaving. There was a limit as to the amount a person was allowed to take out of the country; I think it was $100. Just before sailing, when everything was in order, a person took his yen to the bank and received dollars at the going exchange rate. This man was already dealing in the black market after only a few days in Kobe. We didn't have much money to change for ourselves so I changed fifty dollars for him. He was right at the bank door when I came out, not on the street as we had agreed.

We never felt any fear as we walked the streets of Kobe, even at night. We often stopped at little stores to shop for trinkets. The clerks would be sitting in the back; you'd have to go after them if you wanted to buy something. In the two weeks we were there we saw no crime and never a lock on a door. The money was difficult to understand; at first we simply handed over a pile of money and let clerks pick out the coins.

At that time the truck and car traffic wasn't heavy, and a lot of deliveries were done by bicycle. We saw people with six to eight pop or beer cases stacked on top of the bike rack. It was amazing how they balanced the load, and I never did get to see how they unloaded.

One day, looking around, we saw a bird store with the name *Takala* in big letters. "Must be a Finn," we thought, and went inside. There were all kinds of birds in there but only one man, and he was definitely not a Finn.

Our money was getting low so we pawned Sylvi's caracul fur coat for thirty-five dollars. Then we got her a summer coat and some silk material that was supposed to be cheaper than in the states.

Finally it was time to leave. We lined up on the dock for luggage inspection. There was no problem with ours but an American engineer near us was bringing home a samovar he had bought in Russia. The inspector opened the box and discovered a set of instructions and the price tag. These he threw in the harbor, but the samovar itself was all right to take.

Our third class sleeping quarters were bad, especially when the weather got rough. The second class food was excellent, however, and I sure enjoyed it, but poor Sylvi was seasick for many days. When seasick a person doesn't want to eat, and, if he did, he'd throw it up and get sicker.

It was evening when we arrived in Honolulu a few days later. Every place was closing up so we just walked around town a bit and sat in a park. The weather was warm and felt so nice; when we got back to the ship we took some blankets and slept up on the top deck.

The next morning we pulled out for San Francisco and in a few days hit some really rough weather. One morning I was the only one at breakfast. With four waiters at my command I really pigged out on grapefruit, eggs, bacon, sausage, cakes and coffee.

It had been March 29, 1941, when we left Japan. On the 12th of April, which was Good Friday that year, we finally sighted the Golden Gate bridge. From a distance it looked like a string pulled across the entrance to San Francisco Bay. The closer we got, the more beautiful it looked. To me it seemed like one of the great wonders of the world and held the promise of a new life for us in the future.

As we got closer the traffic became visible, and then it seemed as if our masts would not clear, but the *President Taft* slid easily under the bridge. What an unforgettable sight—the first glimpse of the good old United States of America. It is hard for me to describe the feelings I had coming home at last. I was anxious about how we would be received and how to get a job. We were quite completely broke with only a suitcase full of old clothes.

Our first stop was at the immigration station on Silver Street with all the other foreigners. Here they checked us out to see if we were fit to enter the United States. There were plenty of questions to answer, especially since we had come from the Soviet Union. At one point it was suggested that if the United States did not accept us we would be shipped back to the Soviet Union.

"Never!" I remember saying. "I will never go back. I'll jump off the ship."

It took a couple of months to get things straightened out. On the advice of one of the inspectors, I even wrote a letter to Washington explaining everything as well as I could. The fact that Hitler attacked Russia in June and the Soviet Union became our ally helped us.

Everyone at the immigration center was very nice to us, but after seven years we were really anxious to get out and start living again. It was also difficult to stay there because Sylvi was living on the women's side while I had to stay on the men's, except for a couple hours of visiting every day.

We were able to exercise in one part of the building. There was a ping pong table there that I used a lot with a German fellow and a Mexican whose skill was about even with mine. I also recall playing poker and noticing that some of the cards were marked. I told my Mexican friend about it after the game but he already knew and seemed to think it quite common. He was trying to learn the markings himself, but I thought that was too much trouble and concentrated instead on reading and making string belts.

Meals there were good—they even served desserts. Once when we had finished dinner, there was one piece of pie left, and my Mexican friend suggested that I pretend to be Russia, he would be Germany, and the pie we would call Poland. We divided the territory and thus history repeated itself.

July 28 was the day we were free to go. We called Sylvi's Aunt Anna and Uncle Charlie in Berkeley; they came right out to get us and treated us like long lost kids. Aunt Anna took Sylvi shopping and bought her things. They even took us on a trip to Fort Bragg—a beautiful drive along the Pacific coast. I enjoyed the whole trip very much. The people we visited in Fort Bragg made us welcome. They wined and dined us and kept urging us to eat more. I took them up on it, believe me. Besides a big dinner, I ate a whole smoked lobster by myself.

We spent a couple of weeks with Aunt Anna and Uncle Charlie. I registered for the draft and looked for work at the shipyards but jobs were still pretty scarce, and so we took a bus for Detroit—the last leg of our trip around the world.

Welcome Home

S: Now we were back in our native land, the United States of America, the land where we'd been born, where we'd spent our childhood and youth, the land of the free. How did we feel? We felt a deep relief, a great happiness that comes at the end of a tortuous journey. Happy and relieved . . . but still worried, not completely relaxed. Questions persisted. How would we be received by our friends? What should we tell them? Would they accept our stories? Would our government allow us to stay since, through our ignorance and thoughtlessness, we had lost our citizenship? These matters were on our minds constantly, although our general feeling was one of deep satisfaction.

We were surprised and pleased at the welcome we received from my Aunt Anna and her family in California. They took us into their home and treated us as long lost members of the family. Throughout their lives Aunt and Uncle had definitely leaned toward the left in their politics, but they showed no resentment toward us for having abandoned the fight for the workingman's cause. They even wanted us to move to California and begin our new life there. But we were eager to get back to Michigan, to Sugar Island, home.

L:
We arrived in Detroit after midnight on August 16th, and didn't feel like calling anyone at that hour so we sat in the bus station till morning. After seven years, we felt a bit hesitant to call people, not being sure how we would be received. In the morning we called some old friends named Lehtela who used to spend summers on Sugar Island. They wanted us to come to their place.

Our feet were swollen, we were dirty, the only sleep we'd had in three days was dozing on the bus, so we took hot baths and slept until some time in the afternoon. It felt so good to be clean and rested.

That afternoon Mrs. Lehtela called her daughter Valma. She welcomed us with open arms and then took us to her home. She had a brand new, beautiful house. To us, she and her husband seemed like very rich people. We wondered how they could afford it but did not question them.

Later that day we got in touch with some of our other old friends, including Ingrid and Paul Middleton who said they were planning to go to Sugar Island soon and asked if we would like to go along. That was perfect for us.

For the next few days we visited with old friends and relatives in Detroit getting to know them all over again. They were all so good to us; no one condemned us for having left the State or for coming back. They certainly made us feel that this was where we belonged. I had offers of help in getting employment, and some even offered me jobs, but we wanted to get back to Sugar Island and see my folks before deciding where we would locate.

We rode with Paul and Ingrid through the night and arrived on the island in the morning of August 20th. Everything seemed to be pretty much the same there as when we'd left. My parents' home was in worse shape and needed a new roof, which I proceeded to do as my first job.

There was a welcome-home party for us at my parents house— mostly people whom we had known for a long time. They hadn't aged much—the big change was in the kids, now in their teens. They were so grown up that I had a hard time recognizing them. We were pleased that so many came to our party—more than we had expected. They brought coffee and lunch with them and had a collection for us even though times were still hard, and no one had much money. One man gave me $2.50 that he owed me for sawmill work I had done for him before we left. Another fellow offered me a job running his sawmill for two dollars a day. A friend who was on vacation from his auto repair job down in Detroit told me to come down, and he would get me a job too.

But there was one sour note that afternoon. A fellow from the Soo made a welcoming speech. He said very little about us but got into politics, bragging about the Soviet Union. Among other things, he said that no innocent people had been arrested there. I was about to object to that but could not get a word in at that point, and so I let it go. I have regretted ever since that I did not speak up, but because I knew how my mother felt, I remained silent.

I have already said that my mother was never able to believe the awful things that had happened in Karelia. My sister Irja shared her views, and so it was very hard for us to discuss anything about the Soviet Union with her. She either would not or could not believe us when we tried to tell her our story about what was happening in Karelia and all over the Soviet Union. She would just clam up or get very upset whenever we brought it up. So with her, too, we felt it best to remain silent.

We returned to Detroit where job opportunities seemed better. Sylvi was pregnant, and I did not want her to go to work. I got a job in a gas station right away, and we rented a little room nearby. It wasn't very nice, but it was all we could afford at that time. Paul and Ingrid visited us there and afterwards invited us to come and stay with them, which we did for a few months. After that we stayed with a family named Waisanen for a while.

The life-styles of all our friends impressed us; they seemed so free to indulge in whatever they preferred to do. We were also amazed by their nice new autos and the beautiful homes with modern conveniences. This had all happened in the seven years since we had left Detroit. Their lives had improved dramatically compared to our lives in Karelia. We had worked hard but had nothing to show for it. Somehow it felt as if the revolution had happened here in the United States! Later, our friends told us they had gotten FHA government loans to build their homes. President Roosevelt, they also told us, was the man who had brought this about. He pulled the country out of the Great Depression, which had been one of the factors influencing our decision to go to Russia. It proves what a good president can do.

In February of 1942 I landed a job in a tool and die shop. Our daughter Anita was born two weeks later. The people in the shop were very good to me. They knew I had been in Russia. Only a few were interested enough to ask me how I had liked it. I would say that I didn't and would never go back. Occasionally someone would want to know how much money we made, and I would tell them, also explaining that all our pay went for food and drink.

I had registered with the draft board as soon as we arrived in California, but since I was in defense work at the tool and die company, they got a deferrment for me. I stayed with that company until my retirement in 1971.

We did not talk much about our life in Karelia with anyone over here. Once I remember when I was at our hunting camp with several friends, a fellow I had met after we came back began to ask me why I had gone to Russia and what it was like. Before I even had time to answer, an old friend of mine spoke up and told him he had no right to question me about that. It had taken a lot of guts for me to go there, he said angrily. I didn't like the sound of this argument so I just suggested we have another drink instead. I really wouldn't have minded telling them about it, but that subject always stirred up strong feelings.

S: Our homecoming to Sugar Island was most traumatic for me. My father and brother had died while we were away and I felt their loss keenly on returning to my childhood home where everything reminded me of them. The old farmhouse and hall where my father had spent so much of his time and energy were more than I could bear, and I refused to let our Sugar Island friends hold our welcome home party at the hall. One elderly woman accused me of being afraid to be seen at the hall because it had communist connections, but that was furthest from my thoughts. I was thinking only of my father and brother and my sorrow at their deaths.

My brother Arvo, the only remaining member of my family, was in a tuberculosis sanitarium at this time and would remain there for another year. He had never had the least interest in politics. We could have discussed our experiences with him but never did. Even after he came to live with us, we shied away from the subject, as we did with other people, thinking no one was interested. It was a part of our lives we would do well to forget.

But of course, we couldn't forget. What we had left was much on our minds as we adjusted to our new life in the States. The few friends we'd known in Detroit earlier welcomed us and brought us into a bigger group of their own where we soon became members in good standing. This group was made up primarily of second generation American Finns. Their parents had been active in socialist, and some, perhaps, in communist groups, but, as we have mentioned before, within the second generation Finns, class consciousness had abated. Politically, they were either Democratic or Republican depending on their circumstances. They all knew we had been in the Soviet Union, but no one questioned us because, as we later learned, they felt we were the ones who should bring it up. We, on the other hand, did not want to talk about our experiences since we felt that they did not care to hear about them. This feeling was reinforced by occasional comments such as one I remember during the war. I was with a group of women one evening when many complaints about shortages were brought up: silk stockings were scarce, bakery items were hard to come by, etc. I felt these women were pampered; they did not really know what shortages were! So I tried to tell them. When you stand all night in a queue for a pound of meat or sugar, you don't see coffee for months on end, you don't even dream of silk stockings or bakery cakes—these, to me, were shortages. One of the ladies glared at me and said, "I'm sure you didn't starve over there."

I had not intended, and could not have conveyed, any such idea. I just wanted them to know how lucky they were, and how childish their complaints seemed. But after that, I never tried to tell them of what we went through.

Occasionally, we had some contact with people connected in some way to our life in Russia. In 1941, Keijo's mother, Mrs. Frilund, came to see us. This was the first time we'd met her. She was very kind and understanding and listened to all the news we had of her son and his family. Although this was bad news—her son had been arrested, and his family evicted from their home—she did not seem to hold it against the Soviet government. It seemed, rather, that she felt these things could happen but that in time all would be corrected. Although the world was by then embroiled in World War II, she exclaimed that it was such an interesting time to be living. She evidently had a larger than ordinary view of world events, and saw everything as history in the making. The future held her interest and in connection with this, children. Children were all important to her. When we saw her again in 1946, we noticed many instances when she preferred to hear what our four-year-old Anita wanted to say than to listen to us. We do not know whether she had wished to emigrate to the Soviet Union with her son and family but if she had, and had been rejected, it could very well have because she was the kind of person whom the party in the States did not want to lose.

In 1945 we were able to get in touch with Urho and Irma Hill who were living in Sault Ste. Marie, Canada. We saw much of them over the years. Urho, having held onto his Canadian passport, was able to return to his homeland in the spring of 1938. Irma had to wait for permission to join him which did not come until the fall of that year. During the big purge at the ski factory that summer she, too, had been evicted from her room along with all those women whose men had been arrested. Because she had a small baby, she was not sent to Lime Island with the others but to a kolkhoz near Petrozavodsk where she remained until allowed to leave the country.

Urho's father had been arrested during the summer of 1938 and was never heard from again. His mother, after much suffering during the war, managed to get to the American Embassy in Moscow where she served as a cook for some time. The Embassy was instrumental in getting her back to Canada. It was war time, so they put her on an Army plane going to England. From there she eventually made her way home to Sault Ste. Marie, Ontario. Both she and Urho have since died, but Irma still lives in the Soo and we meet occasionally.

Aside from Urho and Irma we had no one with whom we could talk freely of our common experience. It was a relief to discuss these events, and I found it sad that we could not talk about them with others because they wouldn't have or couldn't have understood.

After Anita entered school, I became involved with the Girl Scouts and later on with the United Way organization (then called the Red Feather). I made many new friends among the other mothers but to none of them did I confide the fact that we had lived in the Soviet Union. These women were not involved in leftist politics; in fact, as far as I could tell, they were not interested in any kind of politics. They could not have known anything about Karelia or the issues that took us there or caused our return. I am still in contact with one friend from this period, and she does not to this day know of our life in Russia.

It took many years before we were able to regain our United States citizenship. We were technically "aliens" at that time and had to register at the post office every year. We were not supposed to travel to foreign countries, so we never visited our friends in Canada or even went to Boblo Island, a Canadian-owned amusement park in the Detroit River.

Our first application for citizenship was turned down. We don't know why. We had to have sponsors to speak in our behalf and had chosen an elderly Finnish couple whose English was not very good. We have since wondered whether they answered correctly all the questions put to them about us. They themselves were not sure that they had. Possibly, though, we were turned down simply because this was the McCarthy era when Senator Joe McCarthy of Wisconsin was leading a national witch hunt for communists in government and other influential positions. Lauri and I were called in for questioning by the Federal Bureau of Investigation once during that time. I remember that the inspector asked me if we had ever belonged to the communist party, and I said, "no." Then he asked me why I had gone to the Soviet Union. I told him I had gone because my husband went. "That's a very good answer," he told me. Lauri, who was questioned separately, was asked about several friends and acquaintances: were they communists? He said he didn't know, and we were never called in for questioning again.

We made our second application for citizenship as soon as we were allowed to do so. We took our good friend Paul Middleton and another Finnish-American who owned his own business as sponsors. This time we were granted full citizenship. It was a red letter day for us—September 29, 1953—one of the most important and happiest of our lives. We had regained our birthright. We were home at last.

We remained in Detroit for thirty years. When Lauri, whom we now call Lawrence, retired in 1971 we moved back to Sugar Island and have lived there year round ever since, with occasional trips to other parts of the United States. Twice during these years we have visited friends and relatives in Finland. Although Finland is next door to Karelia, we have not as yet ventured there due to the fact that upon our departure back in 1941 we had to sign a paper promising never to return. The reason for this has never been clear to us.

We have had a good happy life with much to be thankful for. After our return Paul Middleton and his wife, Ingrid, became our closest family friends. In 1960 our daughter Anita married their son Len. It has been a wonderful relationship all around. We lost Paul in 1981 and Ingrid this past year. We miss them very much. Lawrence and I are growing quite old, but we still get around and are enjoying our "golden years."

Having seen what can happen in a country ruled by the "Dictatorship of the Proletariat" we have become keenly aware of the personal freedom enjoyed here in the United States. In Karelia, the government decided where we could live and work—here it is a personal matter. In the Soviet Union the government kept track of its citizens by issuing passports which had to be shown to the proper authorities wherever one moved. Here a passport is needed only when leaving the country. Elections in the Soviet Union were simple: candidates were chosen from above; voters had only to approve. Here we have a real choice which often requires deliberating on the pros and cons of each candidate. People who have constantly been told what to do can find decision making difficult!

Although when we left for Karelia, we had no clear concept of what either "democracy" or "dictatorship of the proletariat" meant, by degrees we found out. Having become thoroughly disillusioned by the latter, we feel that democracy is the way to go.

We have written and talked much about the wrongs suffered by the people who were recruited to the Soviet Union from Canada and the United States. We remember the terrible things done to our friends and relatives who were innocent of any wrong doing. The Stalinist purges left their mark on all of us. We were left with a feeling of fear and hatred toward those who had committed these wrongs. A few of us escaped. We were lucky to be allowed to return to our native land to a life of ease compared to what we'd been through. I personally left with a feeling of guilt that we had somehow let our friends down. Why were we spared? We do not know to this day. Why were our friends forced to remain to face more hardships and sufferings? It was all terribly unfair. We were left with a deep feeling of sorrow and disappointment that the dream we'd had—the dream we'd worked hard to fulfill—had collapsed around us. We had been sure that, although we faced primitive conditions at first, it would all change and that our work would bring rewards in the way of a better life. At first it did. Our lives were improving. But then came 1937 and 1938. The purges. Arrests and disappearances. Prisons and labor camps. The end for thousands of fellow workers. We can never forget.

L: All in all, our life since we came back to the United States has been a happy one. We are able to say what we think without any qualms about someone being able to harm us for our beliefs. They can refute or criticize what we say, but they cannot put us in jail for saying it.

We are very interested in what is happening in the Soviet Union today and read everything we can find about it. We have a soft spot in our hearts for the Russian people and are happy to hear that they have found some freedom, which they did not have while we were there.

It is good, too, that all the horrors of the purges have come out and are common knowledge, in the Soviet Union as well as here in the United States. I have been able to go to some of those people who didn't believe me back in 1941 when I tried to tell them about events in Karelia and say, "Do you remember what I told you years ago? I knew you didn't believe me then, but now you know that I was not lying." I am glad they know that now, and we just have to forgive them for not believing us in the first place.

This openness, this *glasnost*, in the Soviet Union is a good thing but isn't there more that should be done? We have not heard of any compensation for the widows and children of those innocent people who were arrested during the purges and died in labor camps. We have not heard of any court trials of those who ordered these arrests or those who ran these slave labor camps. All that the families of purge victims have received is a document clearing their relative, posthumously, of the crimes charged. Some of those who were responsible for their deaths are still living in luxury in their townhouses and dachas. Let them stand trial in open court for their crimes. Then, after justice is done, we can go on living in friendship and harmony.

Epilogue

S: For many years after we returned to the United States we had no contact with the friends we'd left in Karelia. The war between Germany and the Soviet Union began, and the Finns in Petrozavodsk were evacuated and sent to faraway places. Those who survived the war slowly found their way back to their former homes after peace was declared. In the years since then we have heard from a few.

In 1957, the year Sputnik went up, we received a surprise letter from our seamstress friend, Edla. She wrote sending "greetings from this land of miracles" and added ingenuously that the Soviet government had instructed its citizens to send such messages to anyone they knew in other countries. From then on we corresponded sporadically with her. Her son Vilho had been in the Red Army during World War II and had been taken prisoner by the Finns. When he was returned to the Soviet Union in a prisoner exchange after the war, he was imprisoned there for having allowed himself to be taken by the enemy. This was common; a Red Army soldier does not give himself up to the enemy! During his eight years in a Soviet prison, he contracted tuberculosis. He'd been sentenced for ten years but came home when Kruschev came into power and allowed many prisoners to be freed.

In the sixties, Edla, Vilho and Vilho's wife, Evi moved to Estonia where Edla died some years later. Vilho and Evi are still there and we correspond; our letters deal mostly with events and observations having to do with our day to day lives. We hesitate to discuss politics for fear of causing them trouble.

Richie, who lived across the hallway in our barrack on Swamp Street, died in the war. His older sister Lilian has been writing to us for some years. After returning to Petrozavodsk when the war ended, she taught school and lived with her mother who died a few years ago. In her letters, Lilian has written of many amusing incidents involving us which her mother recalled. Now retired, Lilian lives quietly and seems generally satisfied with her life.

Dave and Lily's daughter, Viola, is also in Petrozavodsk. In the early seventies, she wrote that her father was still alive in Rovaniemi, Finland. In 1972 we made a trip to Finland and looked him up. We found him living with a Lapp woman who was proud of receiving visitors from America; she hoped all the neighbors had taken note of our arrival. Dave's trip across the border in 1938 with Vilho and Terttu had been hazardous and difficult—traveling mostly by night, sleeping in the woods, ever on the alert for border guards who had the authority to shoot on sight anyone who was crossing the border without a permit.

In 1977 Viola was able to make a trip to the States. Relatives here helped with technicalities such as the invitation needed by Russians in order to visit a foreign country and also assurance that these same relatives would be responsible in case of her illness or other emergencies. Viola told us that Lily had died of cancer a few years earlier. Her brother Hugo had disappeared during the war. Viola was amazed at all she saw here: the abundance of food and goods available, the cars—in many cases several in a family—the freedom with which we moved about wherever we pleased with no need to report to authorities. Since all of us had so much more than we needed, we sent her back loaded with gifts of all sorts.

Flossie, my schoolmate from the Pedagogical Institute, learned of my whereabouts several years ago, and we have exchanged a few letters. She too found her way back to Petrozavodsk after the war, married and raised a family. She is now a retired school teacher and lives with her husband, their children having grown up and married. Back in 1938, when we had decided to apply for permission to leave the Soviet Union, Flossie accompanied me to Moscow to the American Embassy to start the process. While we were there she was asked by one of the officials if she also wanted to leave the country. "I will never leave here," she replied. Her belief in the future of the Soviet Union has always appeared firm. Only recently did she wonder why her parents had gone there.

Our little Heikki had died of malnutrition while still quite young. His father, Viljo, and mother, Tyyne, died in nursing homes a few years ago. Viljo had been sent to Finland as a spy during World War II and had been caught. Upon being returned to the Soviet Union after the war, he was imprisoned there for several years. When we knew Tyyne she was a happy-go-lucky, fun loving person but, as we later learned, her war-time experiences left her very embittered.

On a more recent visit to Finland we met with Aune and Tauno Salo, another couple from our Petrozavodsk days, some of the last we'd seen there before we left. For them, too, the war had been a period of sickness and near starvation. Then after Stalin's death and Kruschev's rise to power, there was a period when it was possible for them to move to Finland to be with his elderly parents. They took advantage of this and are now living comfortably. While with them we spent many hours reminiscing and learned the fate of many of our friends.

Benny Laine's wife Miriam is still living in Karelia. So also is Inki Kent. Her husband, Walter, had perished in the war. On our last trip to Finland, we met Inki's daughter and granddaughter. My schoolmate Inkeri Letonmaki, we learned, died quite recently. The Salos also told us that the young man who had been arrested for borrowing the Sinclair Lewis book was never released.

We have never heard what happened to my Uncle Frank and his family. His daughter, who is still living here in the states, has not been able to get any information as to their fate.

My former classmate Selma Anderson, her mother, sister and son were the only others we know of who were given permission to leave at the time we were. They followed us during the summer of 1941, also by way of Japan. Selma's father and husband had died in Karelia. They had been recruited in 1931 to work in the iron mines in Siberia. By 1934, they were in Petrozavodsk where Selma attended the Pedagogical Institute and was one of our small group who met to study together. She lives now in New York; during all these years we have visited her only once, but we correspond. She has told us of the many troubles and worries she had while in Petrozavodsk and during the time she made arrangements for her return to the States.

Martha Nieminen (the sister of our good friend Paul Middleton) is still living in Leningrad. Her husband Dave and daughter Ella both died during the war. Now ninety-two years old, Martha travels a lot in the Soviet Union and makes frequent trips to Finland where she has many friends and relatives. In 1981, she made a trip to the United States. Her sister in Florida offered to take care of her if she would stay and live with her, but Martha chose to return to the Soviet Union where she had lived for fifty years and had many friends. On our last trip to Finland we met Martha and found her to be still healthy in body and mind with a great interest in world events.

Our good friends Sylvi and Eino Dahlstrom died years ago, he of tuberculosis contracted at a labor camp. Sylvi and her mother had been among the evacuees sent across the Urals for the duration of the war. After returning to Petrozavodsk, Sylvi died of heart trouble.

L: I heard that during World War II Eino had been detained at some camp for foreigners in the Soviet Union. Some NKVD big shots had stopped at the camp one day and then weren't able to get their car started when it was time to leave. When they asked if someone at the camp could start it for them, Eino had volunteered to look it over. Being a good auto mechanic (one of the best) he had it going in no time. The big shots were so impressed that they said he was in the wrong place, and let him out so he was able to go to work, thereby getting more food and better accommodations. I was glad to hear that, but I guess Eino didn't live much longer after that. I sure wish our friends could have left the Soviet Union when we did.

S: With the sister-city movement building up between the United States and the Soviet Union, we are experiencing more contact with our Russian friends. As a coincidence, the city of Petrozavodsk, where we lived, and Duluth, the American city that is home to our daughter and her family, are sister cities. Because of this relationship, we have met some people from our old home town. Furthermore, our son-in-law, Len Middleton, was able to make a trip to Petrozavodsk with one of the sister-city groups. He met several of our old friends who still live there and brought back pictures of them, along with a picture of the old barrack we used to live in: barrack 50 on Swamp Street (the street has a different name now). What memories it brought back. At present Len is urging us to make a trip with him and Anita next year, to see for ourselves what changes have been wrought since we were there. We hesitate. . . .

Bibliography

Dallin, David J. *The Real Soviet Russia.* Trans. by Joseph Shaplen. Yale University Press, 1944.

Hosking, Geoffrey. *The First Socialist Society.* Harvard University Press, 1985.

Kivisto, Peter. *Immigrant Socialists in the United States; the case of the Finns and the Left.* Associated University Presses, 1984.

Kort, Michael. *The Soviet Colossus; A History of the U.S.S.R.* Charles Scribner's Sons, New York, 1985.

Randall, Francis B. *Stalin's Russia; An Historical Reconsideration.* The Free Press, New York, 1965.

Rostow, W.W. *The Dynamics of Soviet Society.* Massachusetts Institute of Technology, 1954.

Timasheff, Nicholas S. *The Great Retreat; The Growth and Decline of Communism in Russia.* Dutton, New York, 1946.

Tuominen, Arvo. *The Bells of the Kremlin; an experience in communism.* Piltti Heiskanen, Editor. Lily Leino, translator. University Press of New England, Hanover and London, 1983.

PRAISE FOR
THE SILENT RETIREMENT CRISIS

"*The Silent Retirement Crisis: How You Can Build a Sustainable Retirement in a Potentially Broken System* is an important and timely capstone to Ms. Couyoumjian's Financial Intelligence trilogy. Ms. Couyoumjian draws the path of the American economy demonstrating how we got to where we are. Retirement is the ultimate test. The timing of *The Silent Retirement Crisis* is critical for all ages and all groups—those living the myriad challenges and insecurities of retirement and those planning in preparation thereof."

—ELLEN TUNKELROTT, Senior Contracting Manager, Raytheon

"In a world where retirement planning is often overshadowed by immediate financial concerns, *The Silent Retirement Crisis* serves as a wake-up call for individuals young and old seeking to secure their future. It not only raises awareness about the pressing issues surrounding retirement, but also offers actionable solutions. This book is a must-read for anyone who wishes to navigate the financial landscape with confidence and take proactive steps towards a secure and fulfilling retirement."

—LINDA SCIOTTI CRAFT, automotive financial analyst

"Facing your future financial retirement needs forces each of us to acknowledge our own mortality. How many years must my savings support me? How do I plan for the unknown? Will social security still be available? Where, why, when, and how should I start planning for my retirement? Stop worrying and start reading—most of your fears and questions will be answered in this book—and using your personal power to create a steady stream of income is possible. *The Silent Retirement Crisis* explains how there are many new ways to save and invest your money, enabling you to create a steady retirement income for the rest of your life."

—RONELLE INGRAM, best-selling author, *Service with A Smile*

"Besides explaining the REALM model and discussing retirement topics facing retirees, this well-researched book covers history relating to finance from the 16th century to the present. This is a great read for someone interested in finance history and/or who is near or in retirement."

—STEPHEN LUI, former QA Engineer

"This book was very insightful! A must-read! The author examines historical, political, and economic influences that hurt the average American and their retirement aspirations: when our government deregulates, greed and corruption occur; corporations have exercised profits over people and caused market crashes; capitalism favors the wealthy, not the average American. The author explains many hidden forces very simply, revealing that if we understand those forces and gain knowledge through financial literacy, we will begin to find that there are alternative ways to invest our nest egg and reverse the crisis we are experiencing in real time!"

—PAMELA WILKS, Engineering Group Manager, General Motors

"In *The Silent Retirement Crisis*, Cindy Couyoumjian expertly explains the political, economic, and financial forces that have undermined our economy and created a retirement crisis in the 21st century. More importantly, Couyoumjian offers important knowledge and a solution—an innovative investment strategy that ordinary people can use to minimize risk and increase earnings in their retirement planning. Written in a highly engaging and accessible manner any layperson can understand, *The Silent Retirement Crisis* is a must-read for anyone who wants to take control of their financial future."

—HOLLY M. HAPKE, PHD, Economic Geographer, and Director of Research Development, University of California, Irvine

THE SILENT
RETIREMENT
CRISIS

"*The Silent Retirement Crisis* is informative, educational, and very easy to understand and follow as a retirement road map. It places many subjects in one place right at your fingertips. It instructs readers to be proactive with their retirement strategy instead of leaving it to others' discretion. Couyoumjian drives home the reality of investing wisely as a basis to sustain purchasing power by keeping ahead of inflation and being aware of outside forces—especially those with negative impact. For those who value protection, sustaining value, minimum volatility, and the lowest risk to their investment, the book explains the necessities of different investment strategies and their pros and cons. For those who have already invested in the strategies suggested in this book, having a more in-depth explanation of how these investments work helps with a better understanding of financial investment."

—DAVID DANGOOR, Senior Engineering Advisor, OXY-CRC

"Cindy takes us on an adventure through the financial industry, starting with the whens, whys, and hows of our country's evolution to what it is today. Readers will have a clear understanding of how we arrived where we are, where we are going, and what to do when we get there. Our most immediate and important questions are answered with easy-to-understand concepts and examples. All the mechanics and instructions are laid out in a precise and meticulous way, so you can make an informed and intelligent decision on your journey to a secure and plentiful retirement. Remember, the more knowledge you gain, the more power you have to improve your financial future and quality of life!"

—JOHN MAJKOWSKI, financial analyst

THE SILENT

RETIREMENT

CRISIS

HOW YOU CAN BUILD A SUSTAINABLE
RETIREMENT IN A POTENTIALLY BROKEN SYSTEM

CINDY COUYOUMJIAN

with R. F. GEORGY

GREENLEAF
BOOK GROUP PRESS

This publication is designed to provide accurate and authoritative information in regard to the subject matter covered. It is sold with the understanding that the publisher and author are not engaged in rendering legal, accounting, or other professional services. Nothing herein shall create an attorney-client relationship, and nothing herein shall constitute legal advice or a solicitation to offer legal advice. If legal advice or other expert assistance is required, the services of a competent professional should be sought.

Published by Greenleaf Book Group Press
Austin, Texas
www.gbgpress.com

Copyright © 2023 Cindy Couyoumjian

All rights reserved.

Thank you for purchasing an authorized edition of this book and for complying with copyright law. No part of this book may be reproduced, stored in a retrieval system, or transmitted by any means, electronic, mechanical, photocopying, recording, or otherwise, without written permission from the copyright holder.

For permission to reproduce copyrighted material, grateful acknowledgment is made to the following:

Yale University: Photo of David Swensen from https://yaledailynews.com/blog/2020/10/27/swensen-tells-money-managers-to-increase-diversity-if-they-want-to-work-with-yale/ Reproduced by permission of *Yale Daily News*, Yale University.

Distributed by Greenleaf Book Group

For ordering information or special discounts for bulk purchases, please contact Greenleaf Book Group at PO Box 91869, Austin, TX 78709, 512.891.6100.

Design and composition by Greenleaf Book Group
Cover design by Greenleaf Book Group
Cover Image: ©iStockphoto/desnik

Publisher's Cataloging-in-Publication data is available.

Print ISBN: 979-8-88645-096-5

eBook ISBN: 979-8-88645-097-2

To offset the number of trees consumed in the printing of our books, Greenleaf donates a portion of the proceeds from each printing to the Arbor Day Foundation. Greenleaf Book Group has replaced over 50,000 trees since 2007.

Printed in the United States of America on acid-free paper

23 24 25 26 27 28 29 30   10 9 8 7 6 5 4 3 2 1

First Edition

The information contained here reflects the views of Cindy Couyoumjian and sources she believes are reliable as of the date of this publication. IFG makes no representations or warranties concerning the accuracy of any data. There is no guarantee that any projection, forecast, or opinion in this material will be realized. Past performance does not guarantee future results. The views expressed here may change at any time after the date of this publication. This document is for informational purposes only and does not constitute investment advice. IFG does not provide tax, legal, or accounting advice. It does not take an investor's personal investment objectives or financial situation into account; investors should discuss their individual circumstances with appropriate professionals before making any decisions. This information should not be construed as sales or marketing material or an offer or solicitation for the purchase or sale of any financial instrument, product, or service. The opinions of the presenter do not necessarily reflect those of Independent Financial Group, LLC, (IFG) its affiliates, officers or directors. Cinergy Financial, Inc, and IFG are unaffiliated entities.

Registered Principal offering securities and advisory services through Independent Financial Group, LLC, (IFG), a Registered Investment Advisor. Member FINRA/SIPC. Cinergy Financial, Inc., and IFG are unaffiliated entities.

This book is dedicated to all pre- and post-retirees who have to deal with the anxiety and worry about the silent retirement crisis.

This book is for all those who continue to struggle to realize one aspect of the American Dream—retirement security.

It is my hope this book offers people potentially meaningful and practical solutions that will help them not only survive but also thrive in a world full of greed and corruption.

ACKNOWLEDGMENTS

This book is by far my most ambitious to date. It is written on an epic scale to explore the macro, big-picture perspective of our broken capitalist system, which, in turn, has contributed to our silent retirement crisis. Tackling the amount of source material necessary to write it required an incredible amount of intensity and rigor. I have included more than 500 cited sources!

This book would not have seen the light of day without the love and support of all those whose steadfast commitment, tireless dedication, and unwavering support deserve not only my endless gratitude but also a public acknowledgment. To that end, I would like to thank my office staff, who have been with me for nearly 20 years. I want to begin by acknowledging Connie Hernandez, Prisma Oseguera, Thess Williams, and Danny Martinez for their superhuman effort to keep my office going. I cannot thank these four people enough for their loyalty and their unwavering support. A special thank-you goes to my marketing assistants, Charlene Ogami and Monica Milstead, for their dedication and creative insights. I also wish to thank David Lustig, who has been very helpful with my trades. And I want to thank Makenzie Frank, whose passion for learning is both inspiring and infectious. She is a special young professional who shows so much promise as a future financial advisor.

Next, with profound gratitude, I have to acknowledge my son, Kobe, who has decided to follow in my footsteps as a financial advisor. Dedicated beyond his tender years, he is currently working alongside me at Cinergy Financial.

I would be remiss if I did not thank Leticia Hewko for her tireless contribution to Cinergy Financial. Prior to joining my financial team, Leticia was a mathematics teacher for many years. In fact, she taught both my children. Her influence is so profound and far-reaching that my daughter, Claire, went on to pursue mathematics at UC Berkeley, and later at Cal State Fullerton. Leticia would later transition to become a financial advisor, and no one is happier than me. Today, she is one of the best financial advisors in the industry—exceptionally bright, analytical, and an excellent communicator.

When I was busy writing this book, it was Leticia who kept the business thriving. As a financial advisor, she always goes above and beyond, putting our clients' needs above her own. Leticia does not see dollar signs when working with clients; rather, she sees people who need her help. She may go to a senior client's home, for example, if they are unable to drive. I remember a time when Leticia went to visit a widow whose husband had recently passed simply to help her organize her home. Another time, Leticia drove to a client's home to help her use her new Apple iPhone. Leticia is an angel and a godsend who makes my life endlessly easy when I'm writing books.

Finally, this acknowledgment would not be complete without mentioning my husband, Harry. Writing books is not an easy undertaking. I spent endless days and sleepless nights doing research for this book as well as the actual writing. Harry has been my rock throughout the long and arduous process. Whenever I'm overwhelmed, it is Harry who always motivates me to keep going. Thank you, Harry, for your love, support, encouragement, and, most of all, your infectious humor.

CONTENTS

PREFACE

There is a looming retirement crisis the likes of which we have not seen in decades. The numbers alone are frightening, and what is worse is that our postpandemic world has revealed the magnitude of despair and uncertainty that is impacting multiple generations of Americans. Almost half of all Americans don't have enough money saved to cover unexpected bills. When you factor in rising health-care costs, a longer life expectancy, widespread societal uncertainty, and rampant inflation, you begin to appreciate the magnitude of our broken retirement system. We are today living through a period that I call the postpandemic economy, which is marked by heightened market volatility, high unemployment, and a bearish outlook.

This is my third book in a series of books whose overarching theme is what I call broken capitalism. My first book, *Redefining Financial Literacy*, explored the ways in which our lack of financial knowledge is hurting us as a society. In addition to noting the lack of financial awareness, I broadened our understanding of money and finances by redefining what it means to be financially literate. I argued that a more inclusive definition of financial literacy must include the historical, economic, political, and psychological forces that influence our individual and collective financial health.

My second book, *The Rise of Women and Wealth*, focused on the history of women as a marginalized other. I traced the history of patriarchy to show that women have historically been excluded from the public square. In every conceivable form of human activity, women have had to struggle in order to free themselves from a patriarchal culture that is simultaneously everywhere and nowhere: Patriarchy is everywhere in the sense that it envelops our lives in such a way that we forget that it exists as an oppressive force. It is nowhere precisely because we forget it is all around us. This, of course, is only half the story. Women today are on the verge of revolutionary political, economic, and financial change that may very well bring the end to patriarchy once and for all.

This brings me to the theme of this book, which is the silent retirement crisis. As someone who has more than 37 years of experience in the financial industry, I developed a wealth of experience dealing with people who are either on the verge of retirement or are retired. I witnessed firsthand the sense of uncertainty and despair written in people's faces and gestures. The retirement crisis is but another manifestation of our broken capitalist system that seems to reward an overwhelmingly small minority with unimaginable wealth, while the rest of us struggle to realize some semblance of the American Dream, which is quickly fading from our collective consciousness.

This sense of uncertainty about the future binds all of my clients, and most Americans, to one unmistakable reality—the fear of running out of money during retirement. Of course, a laundry list of other fears and concerns are exacerbated by a lurking, ever-present uncertainty, but all of these other fears are derived from that same worst-case scenario of running out of money during retirement. It is precisely because of this overwhelming sense of dread that I decided to write this book. I've seen more people than I care to count who never bothered to plan for retirement or whose plans were misguided or never implemented. This book grew out of a profound impulse to help Americans not only plan and prepare for a comfortable retirement but also to prosper in such a way as to leave a legacy in the form of generational wealth.

One of the things I realized about retirement has nothing to do with finances or economics. Retirement, as I came to realize, has a philosophical dimension that explains why many of us procrastinate when it comes to preparing and planning for our twilight years. Retirement is existentially linked to mortality, and many of us prefer to put off that which is inevitable by simply avoiding any active participation in managing its outcome. Obviously, any rational person would find such apathy to be absurd, but we are not always rational. Our actions are often shaped by emotions that may not be beneficial to us in the long run.

Imagine for a moment that you could go forward in time and that you could take a peek to see how things will turn out for you X years from now. While accurately predicting the future is impossible, certain scenarios in this little thought experiment can help you grasp the importance of retirement planning. If you do nothing to anticipate your retirement, then your hypothetical future could potentially be filled with greater uncertainty, an insufficient amount of money to pay for your expenses, financial losses because you didn't bother to get insurance, and little to no assets left for your heirs. You can also anticipate potentially higher inflation, living longer, and being a burden to your loved ones.

This rather unattractive portrait of your future can still be changed, however, because you have the power to potentially create the kind of future you envision. What you do today will matter tomorrow. You simply cannot afford to perpetually postpone planning for retirement, believing that things will work themselves out. If you leave things to chance, you will most likely live to regret it. I write this not from some academic perspective, but from decades of experience. One of the hardest things I have to do as a financial advisor is witness the regret people experience when they realize they waited too long to start planning for their retirement.

You might wonder why you have to worry about retirement, especially if your parents and grandparents never had to. The simple answer is that the social contract has changed.

THE OLD SOCIAL CONTRACT

One of the things I learned over the years as a financial advisor, writer, and lecturer is that the concept of retirement has changed dramatically. For much of the 20th century we had a social contract, or a cultural understanding, that if you worked hard, society would take care of you during your retirement years. Of course, this is a broad generalization, but for our parents and grandparents, that was the implicit agreement.

To better understand the importance of a social contract and how it relates to our financial reality, we first need to define it. A **social contract** is "the basic set of rules, norms, and mutual obligations that bind together individuals, firms, civil society, and the state."[1] Think of a social contract as a set of obligations and expectations that individuals have to society and vice versa. Here are some examples: Should childcare be the responsibility of families, businesses, the government, or a combination of all three? What about health care, college education, or pensions? Throughout the second half of the 20th century, both the government and corporate America took care of us through a combination of Social Security and pensions.

Retirement was traditionally envisioned in terms of a three-legged stool—Social Security; pensions; and you, the individual. But if traditional pensions are disappearing and Social Security funds might be depleted by 2034, then the burden shifts to you to plan and prepare for your retirement. Let's consider some facts about Social Security: First, the Social Security Administration's 2021 Trustee Report "estimates its combined trust funds will be depleted in 2034 based on the current way it operates."[2] Second, millennials may be hit the hardest, as they contribute the most to the fund but stand to reap the fewest benefits. To make matters worse, once Social Security reserves are depleted, "annual taxes are expected to cover only about three-quarters of the benefits."[3] Finally, one of the reasons that pensions and Social Security worked out well for our parents and grandparents is life expectancy.

When Social Security checks were first issued in 1940, life expectancy was 63 years (which is an average of both men and women).[4] Both private corporations and the government had enough money to offer retirees a reasonably comfortable retirement. This was, of course, the result of workers not living much longer beyond their retirement age. The burden placed on the individual to save was not critical to one's retirement outlook. If you wanted a more comfortable retirement, then you took it upon yourself to exercise financial discipline.

Today, though, we are living longer, which is why Social Security alone may not be enough to cover even your basic living expenses. And traditionally defined pension plans that were once widely offered by employers are being replaced by employee-funded contribution retirement plans. Again, the burden of who will care for us in our retirement years has shifted from the government and the private sector to the individual.

A NEW SOCIAL CONTRACT

Our world has dramatically changed over the past 25 years. In a single generation, the Digital Revolution altered everything in our lives. Much of this change has been positive. For example, a smartphone allows us to send text messages, purchase goods and services, order food, find directions, tweet, upload photos and videos, play games, google anything and anyone, invest, have a conference call, use a calendar, download seemingly endless apps, and—let's not forget—make a phone call from anywhere. The digital revolution has connected us in ways that were unimaginable a few years ago. However, one of the unexpected consequences of digital technology is that we are inundated by an ocean of information, which may not be a good thing. Think of a topic you might want to research. Now, put his book down and pick up your smartphone, or any smart device, and google your topic. The first thing you will notice is the number of entries that pop up on your screen. Who has the time to read even a fraction of them? What we end up doing is skimming for information, which is not the same as absorbing knowledge. I call this phenomenon the Google Mind, and you will read about it in more detail later in this book. For now, the point I want to impress upon you is that our world has changed dramatically, which is why we need a new social contract.

The scale and impact of this revolution means we need practical and meaningful change. To begin with, we need to fundamentally change our perspective of aging. As a culture, we need to embrace the generational wisdom of older Americans and ensure they are living a meaningful life with dignity and purpose. Once we as a society understand that retirement is an integral part of the American Dream, and not simply the end of it, then we can build a new social contract.

First, we need to ensure the "sustainability of Social Security benefits through necessary reforms to accommodate longer lifespans and the relative aging demographics (relative to workers entering the workforce)."[5] Second, we need to reform our health-care system to reflect our aging population, who, as you can imagine, are the most vulnerable. According to a 2021 Commonwealth Fund's International Health Policy Survey of older adults, "One-fifth of older Americans spent more than $2,000 out of pocket on health care in the past year."[6] To put this fact in perspective, older Americans today pay more for health care, and are more likely not to get care due to cost, than in other high-income countries.[7]

One of the obvious problems with the increasing out-of-pocket costs for health-care expenses is that they will eat away at your savings much faster than you anticipated.

And speaking of savings, only 36 percent of Americans believe their retirement savings are on track. Our national savings crisis existed prior to the COVID-19 pandemic, but the pandemic exacerbated the problem: One-third of Americans who plan to retire "say it will now happen later because of COVID and about 14 million stopped contributing to their retirement accounts every month as of [March 2021]."[8]

This does not, of course, absolve the government from taking action. We also need bipartisan support to address the retirement crisis. For example, the Cardin-Portman bill, which was introduced by Republican Senator Robert Portman from Ohio and Democratic Senator Benjamin Cardin from Maryland, aims to address four major challenges. The bill would expand the saver's tax credit to help low-income Americans increase their retirement savings, help those near retirement build their nest egg by increasing the catch-up retirement plan contribution limits after 60, help small businesses have access to retirement plans, and help individuals save longer by raising the required minimum distribution age from 72 to 75.[9] The good news is that important aspects of the Cardin-Portman bill, which was referred to as the Secure Act 2.0, were incorporated in the $1.7 trillion federal spending bill that was signed into law on December 29, 2022, by President Biden.[10] While more needs to be done, the changes contained in this federal spending bill will potentially improve the retirement outlook for millions of Americans.

Truth supported by facts is critical to any meaningful conversation we have about retirement. This book is the culmination of years of intense and rigorous research as evidenced by the hundreds of cited sources. Additionally, I spent years developing my potentially innovative and customizable multi-asset investment strategy known as the REALM model. This book encapsulates that research and that strategy.

It is important for you to be aware that the REALM strategy contains alternative investments, which are speculative by nature and have various risks including possible lack of liquidity, lack of control, changes in business conditions, and devaluation based on the investment, the economy, and/or regulatory changes. As a result, the values of alternative investments do fluctuate resulting in the value at sale being more or less than the original price paid if a liquid market for the securities is found. Alternative investments are not appropriate for all investors. No investment process is free of risk; no strategy or risk management technique can guarantee returns or eliminate risk in any market environment. There is no guarantee that this investment model/process will be profitable. Diversification does not guarantee profit nor is it guaranteed to prevent losses.

The book is divided into three parts. The first part offers a historical view of capitalism and demonstrates how it evolved to allow a small minority of people to gain unimaginable wealth. The second part offers a new way of thinking about money, investing, and the new social contract. The third part offers plenty of practical tips on investing and retirement planning. It is my hope that this book can help you not only prepare for retirement, but also prosper during your retirement years.

INTRODUCTION

I n my first book, *Redefining Financial Literacy*, I brought attention to important repercussions of the lack of basic financial knowledge in this country. The consequences are not simply that Americans are not saving enough, which is serious in and of itself, but also that they are making poor investment decisions and living with massive inequality, a broken retirement system, and a capitalist system that favors wealthy elites. Here are some quick facts about the lack of financial literacy and the impact it has on our lives:

- Americans rank 14th in the world in financial literacy.[1]

- Basic financial skills are generally not taught in classrooms in the United States.[2]

- 56 percent of Americans can't cover a $1,000 emergency expense with savings.[3]

- The wealthiest 10 percent of Americans own 89 percent of all U.S. stocks.[4]

- According to the U.S. Census, the average annual income for Americans 65 and older is $38,515, or $3,209 a month.[5]

The causes of our poor financial literacy are twofold. First—and most obvious—is the fact that most schools in America don't teach basic finance. Second—and this is not well known—is that the financial industry has a vested interest in keeping Americans in a state of perpetual financial ignorance. Think about your middle or high school education. Do you recall having a course on basic finance? Did you even have a single finance lesson, say, in a math or an economics class? Don't feel bad if the answer is no. You are not alone. I myself don't recall being exposed to any financial concepts in high school.

As one financial writer notes, "For many people, there are no lesson plans and no standard for minimum financial literacy. They [students] are just sent out to a world overflowing with opportunities to get into debt. At best, their financial sensibilities may come from lessons passed down from family members (sometimes the hard way), anecdotes from friends, and the occasional Google search."[6] In other words, the one subject matter that will shape and define the rest of your life is omitted from school curriculums.

As of 2021, only 21 states required some personal finance education, but that requirement does not mean that high schools must offer a stand-alone course. A single lesson about basic finance in other courses satisfies the requirement. The one bright spot, and this is something I've been pushing for, is that "25 states in the U.S. have introduced legislation that would add personal finance education in their high school curriculum."[7] Although this is encouraging news, one must still ask why state legislatures allowed generations of high school students to graduate without basic financial knowledge.

It's important here to distinguish between microeconomic and macro-economic topics. Microeconomics "is the study of decisions made by people and businesses regarding the allocation of resources, and prices at which they trade goods and services, [while] macroeconomics analyzes entire industries and economies, rather than individuals or specific companies."[8] That means microeconomics deals with everything from your personal finances to the law of supply and demand. Macroeconomics, on the other hand, includes a country's gross national product or GDP, the "total monetary or market value of all the finished goods and services produced within a country's borders in a specific time period."[9] Most elementary or high schools never touch on any of these critical concepts.

One proposal, which I support, suggests that financial literacy be taught at every grade. For K–8, basic micro concepts such as saving money, budgeting, investing, interest rates, and so on should be reinforced across the curriculum. High school students, in contrast, deserve a stand-alone course that will introduce them to both micro and macro concepts, such as the history of the stock market, the S&P 500, the Dow Jones Industrial Average, bonds, diversification, alternative investments, return on investment, 401(k) plans, Social Security, credit card debt, simple versus compound interest, credit scores, international trade, inflation, fiscal and monetary policies, the role of the Federal Reserve, recessions and depressions, and business cycles, as well as a broad overview of capitalism.

One state does offer an innovative financial literacy program that should serve as a model for the rest of the nation. In 2016 South Carolina introduced the Future Scholar Financial Literacy Program, which has been offering financial literacy education to more than 43,000 elementary students at no cost to the schools or taxpayers.[10] The success of this program is evidenced by the fact that students increased their financial knowledge of critical life skills such as responsible money choices, credit and debt, and budgeting by 42 percent. This program utilizes its own brain trust by tapping master teachers to offer professional development workshops to educators in their districts or at state educators' conferences. These master teachers assist other teachers in integrating real life financial concepts across the curriculum.

To illustrate the importance of basic financial knowledge, below is a quiz administered by the Financial Industry Regulatory Authority (FINRA) Investor Education Foundation:[11] Try answering these five questions yourself to see how well you perform.

1. Suppose you have $100 in a savings account earning 2 percent interest a year. After five years, how much would you have?

    A. More than $100

    B. Exactly $100

    C. Less than $100

    D. Don't know

2. Imagine the interest rate on your savings account is 1 percent a year and inflation is 2 percent a year. After one year, would the money in the account buy more than it does today, exactly the same, or less than today?

    A. More

    B. Same

    C. Less

    D. Don't know

3. If interest rates rise, what will typically happen to bond prices? Rise, fall, stay the same, or is there no relationship?

    A. Rise

    B. Fall

    C. Stay the same

    D. No relationship

    E. Don't know

4. A 15-year mortgage requires higher monthly payments than a 30-year mortgage, but the total interest over the life of the loan will be less.

    A. True

    B. False

    C. Don't know

5. Buying a single company's stock usually provides a safer return than a stock mutual fund.

    A. True

    B. False

Answer Key: 1. A 2. C. 3. B. 4. A. 5. B

On the most recent test administered by FINRA, only 34 percent of those who took the quiz got all five questions correct. Did you do as well as you hoped?

The other reason why we have financial insecurity is that the financial industry has a vested interest in keeping us in a perpetual state of ignorance. A recent report from the Consumer Financial Protection Bureau (CFPB) found that "for every dollar spent on financial education by financial institutions, more than $10 went to financial marketing."[12] In other words, the financial services industry spends approximately $17 *billion* annually marketing consumer financial products and services, while spending only $160 *million* on financial education, which represents less than 1 percent of how much is spent on education.[13]

What exactly does financial literacy mean? A typical definition includes "the ability to understand and effectively use various financial skills, including personal financial management, budgeting, and investing."[14] We need to broaden that understanding, however, to include the hidden forces that potentially have a direct or indirect impact on your hard-earned money. For true financial literacy, we need a big-picture view of how the financial world works.

Throughout this book you will become familiar with how historical, political, economic, psychological, and even ideological forces intersect to impact how stocks perform, why the Federal Reserve kept interest rates artificially low until recently, the effects of globalization, and your retirement outlook, among other things.

You will also become aware of hidden actors and the various risks they pose to you and your financial future. Explaining these hidden forces and actors can also help us understand why capitalism is broken, why the retirement system is broken, and why the American Dream may be out of reach for most Americans.

OUR BROKEN CAPITALIST SYSTEM

Just as there are various political systems such as democracies, dictatorships, religiously inspired systems (theocracies such as Iran), and totalitarian regimes, there are also various economic systems. These systems include capitalism, communism, and socialism. History has shown us that capitalism, while imperfect and broken at the moment, is far better than socialism. Capitalism is an economic system "in which private individuals or businesses, rather than the government, own and control the factors of production—entrepreneurship, capital goods, natural resources, and labor. Capitalism's success is dependent on a free-market economy, driven by supply and demand."[15] Capitalist systems also encourage and reward ingenuity and innovation. With socialism, in contrast, the government owns or controls much of a nation's resources. The government also determines all aspects of production. Socialism also prevents innovation because "it is thought to take away the incentive to innovate."[16]

Despite its advantages, 50 years ago capitalism gradually started becoming toxic because of an obsession with profits over ethics. As Kurt Andersen put it in his powerful and compelling book *Evil Geniuses*, capitalism became "unbalanced, unhinged, [and] decadent."[17] The architects of this mutated form of capitalism constructed an economic system that was driven by unbounded greed and extreme selfishness. These architects—politicians, economists, and legal scholars—"envisioned a new American trajectory, then popularized and arranged it with remarkable success."[18] This was made clear in an influential article written by Milton Friedman in 1970 in which the Nobel prize–winning economist attacked the idea that businesses have any ethical or social responsibility to society. He concluded that the responsibility of business is to maximize profits "so long as it stays within the rules of the game."[19] Since 1970, the rules of the game have been changed to accommodate businesses, and large corporations have been able to maximize profits without regard to social responsibility.

Legal scholars such as Robert Bork, and a Supreme Court justice, Lewis Powell, created a legal structure to encourage businesses to pursue maximum profits at any cost. Their philosophy, known as neoliberalism, "is a political and economic policy model that emphasizes the value of free market capitalism while seeking to transfer control of economic factors from the government to the private sector."[20] Neoliberalism favors free markets, less government intervention, deregulation, globalization, free trade, privatization, and artificially low interest rates set by the Federal Reserve. But it has allowed greed and corruption to get out of hand.

At the heart of neoliberal ideology is the idea that competition is what defines human relations, driving innovation and creating jobs and wealth but also producing winners and losers, giving rise to inequality over time. The problem with neoliberalism is that extreme competition is driven by extreme selfishness, creating a "me-first" attitude that is responsible for many of our social ills.

I'm not suggesting that neoliberalism alone is the cause of all our social ills. However, when you factor in other hidden forces, you begin to understand how much our world has changed over the past half century. In fact, the greatest force that has enabled neoliberalism to take off is the digital revolution. We are today living in an age of instant information and immediate entertainment. Social media platforms such as Instagram and TikTok are reducing us to narcissists who pose for selfies at every opportunity. Moreover, we live in a disposable society. When something is broken or obsolete, we have become accustomed to throwing it away and buying something new. Finally, we are living in a hyper–consumer economy that values the artificial over the substantive. Facebook, for example, changed its name to Meta to emphasize that in the future our interactions will take place in a virtual space.

This convergence of digital technology with neoliberal ideology has created a world of selfishness, alienation, isolation, drug abuse, toxic relationships, and other cultural ailments. Even the competition touted by neoliberalism has been eroded as more mega corporations dominate our economic landscape. On July 24, 2022, President Biden met with the White House Competition Council. Here is what he had to say: "What we've seen over the last few decades is less competition and more concentration that literally holds the economy back. And in too many industries, a handful of giant companies dominate—dominate the entire market."[21]

To give you an appreciation of just how powerful these corporations have become, let's compare some of these giant tech companies to the GDP of other countries. Apple, as of 2021, had a market capitalization of $2.1 trillion. (Market capitalization "refers to the total market value of a company's outstanding shares of stocks."[22]) That is greater than 96 percent of the GDP of all countries in the world.[23] Microsoft, Amazon, and Facebook monopolize the global economy in a similar way.

I noted above that neoliberalism contributed to a me-first attitude that has led to greed and corruption. Remember the 1987 film *Wall Street*? The main character, played by Michael Douglas (in an Academy Award–winning performance), summarized the neoliberal philosophy in a famous quote:

> The point is, ladies and gentleman, that greed—for lack of a better word—is good. Greed is right. Greed works. Greed clarifies, cuts through, and captures the essence of the evolutionary spirit. Greed, in all of its forms—greed for life, for money, for love, knowledge—has marked the upward surge of mankind.[24]

But greed, of course, did not turn out to be good, particularly for society. The thirst for profit over everything else has led to a series of market bubbles and crashes. From the dot-com bubble of 2002 and the 2008 global financial meltdown to the Federal Stimulus of the pandemic and artificially low interest rates, greed has had dire consequences on our financial lives.

Of course, even after accounting for the effect of greed on the world economy, some of the forces that affect our financial futures are impossible to predict. This was the case with the rise of COVID-19. The breathtaking speed with which this virus moved across the world proved devastating to the stock market. On March 12, 2020, "after President Trump banned most air travel between the United States and continental Europe, and after economies around the world started shutting down, the carnage in the stock market was even worse than Monday [March 9, 2020]. The S&P dropped 10 percent, leaving it 27 percent below its peak a few weeks earlier."[25] By March 19, 2020, the Dow Jones Industrial Average opened down 700 points. It plummeted 30 percent in a month, which was the steepest drop in history, even worse than the Great Depression. After massive market swings like that, coupled with uncertainty and higher volatility, it's not surprising that investors facing retirement have a fear of running out of money.

The American Dream, a uniquely American ideal, "is the belief that anyone, regardless of where they were born or which class they were born into, can attain their own version of success in a society in which upward mobility is possible for everyone."[26] There are those who believe the American Dream is dead, that it is too difficult to get ahead when the system is rigged against them.

I'm not one of them. I don't think the American Dream is dead, but it is certainly becoming more distant for many of us. Most Americans face structural obstacles to make a decent wage or to save for retirement. Homeownership today is increasingly out of reach; a combination of low inventory, high prices, and, now, rising mortgage rates are making it nearly impossible for young people to purchase a home. Home sales prices alone have increased by almost 30 percent since December 2019. According to the Association of Realtors, a typical home now costs $80,000 more than before the COVID-19 pandemic.[27] To make matters worse, wages, although on the rise, are not keeping up with inflation. In fact, according to the Bureau of Labor Statistics, real average hourly earnings "decreased 0.7 percent, seasonally adjusted, from March 2022 to December 2023."[28]

This brings me back to my basic point and the reason for this book: Our retirement system is broken. Retirement may be the most important component of the American Dream, and our retirement system has traditionally rested on three pillars—Social Security, pensions, and you, the individual. Two of these pillars—Social Security and pensions—may not be available to you going forward. That leaves *you* to fulfill your retirement dream. To prepare for retirement, you need to become financially literate, smarter, and aware of the hidden forces and risks that can potentially derail your plans. You need to be able to navigate a complex economic and financial landscape in order to secure a comfortable retirement.

———

I wrote this book to shine a light on the silent retirement crisis in America. Part I peels away the layers of hidden forces and the impact they have on your money. Part I also explores the political, economic, ideological, and other risks that can increase the uncertainty you will face as you get closer to retirement.

In Part II, I will explain why the traditional investment portfolio—60 percent in stocks and 40 percent in bonds—is outdated in today's complex investment landscape. Clearly, to protect yourself against the hidden forces that conspire to derail your retirement plans, you need a new way of investing. The burden is on you to realize your retirement dreams, so you need to plan and prepare. To help you do that I will introduce you to alternative investment strategies, including my innovative REALM investment strategy.

The fact that we have an avalanche of information available at our fingertips does not mean we suddenly become expert investors, however. You do not have to shoulder the burden of planning for retirement alone. In fact, I recommend that you consult a financial expert to help you navigate the often complex and seemingly impenetrable financial landscape.

In Part III, I will introduce you to potentially powerful retirement solutions that include understanding Social Security, Medicare, long-term care, tax planning, insurance planning, estate planning, 401(k)s, IRAs versus Roth IRAs, and required minimum distributions (RMDs). Part III will also help you understand portfolio recovery—the process of reviewing or assessing the elements of the entire portfolio of securities or products—which is important to help you stay on track for a sustainable retirement.

The fact that our retirement system is broken does not mean you should give up hope. This book will not only help you understand how we got into this mess, but also increase your financial literacy so that you grasp the hidden forces and risks that continue to shape your economic landscape. From a macro perspective, our broken capitalist system needs to be addressed with the immediacy and sense of urgency it deserves. In many ways, we are living through a second Gilded Age that glitters with digital technology while economic inequality persists. There are, of course, solutions to the big-picture problem, including the need to limit corporate monopolies in order to generate greater competition. However, the focus of this book is how average Americans can plan and prepare for their retirement future.

PART I

THE HIDDEN FORCES BEHIND

THE RETIREMENT CRISIS

CHAPTER 1

A BRIEF HISTORY OF CAPITALISM

"I'm a capitalist. I believe in capitalism. But capitalism only works if you have safety nets to deal with people who are naturally left behind and brutalized by it."

—THOMAS FRIEDMAN

lthough capitalism has been around in some form since the Middle Ages, it was the Protestant Reformation of the 16th century that helped give rise to our understanding of free-market economics. On the face of it, this may seem not only counterintuitive but also quite implausible. I'm sure many of you are asking yourselves how Protestantism, which elevates piety and devotion to God above all else, could contribute to something as secular as an economic system. History, of course, is not without surprises, which is why it is important for us to understand the religious roots of capitalism. But first we need a better understanding of the Protestant Reformation itself.

The word "Protestant" originates from the Latin word *protestari*, which means to "declare publicly, testify, protest."[1] The **Protestant Reformation** was a sweeping movement across Europe in the 1500s whose aim was to bring attention to the corruption of the Catholic Church. The offensive transgressions included cardinals, bishops, and abbots living a life of luxury; the lack of education for priests; and the selling of indulgences, a controversial and profitable practice that involved the issuance of a certificate by the pope declaring that a person's sins were forgiven. Many members of the clergy taught that salvation was attainable if one purchased enough indulgences.[2]

One of the people who noticed the massive widespread corruption was the German monk and teacher Martin Luther. On October 31, 1517, in Wittenberg, Germany, Luther "published a document he called Disputation on the Power of Indulgences, or 95 Theses,"[3] so named because it contained 95 ideas. At the heart of Luther's argument against the ongoing corruption was a direct challenge against "the Catholic Church's role as intermediary between people and God, specifically when it came to the indulgence system."[4] Luther rejected the idea that one could simply buy forgiveness; rather, he believed that salvation is a gift from God given to those who have faith.

It is important to remember that Martin Luther did not want to break away from the Catholic Church. His intention was to *reform* the Church, which is why historians call the movement he started the Protestant Reformation. Unfortunately, the Church was not receptive to the challenges. Three years after Luther posted his 95 Theses, Pope Leo X issued a decree "condemning Luther and banning his works. Defying the Pope, Luther publicly burned the decree. The break with the Church was then complete. In January 1521 Pope Leo X excommunicated Luther."[5]

The Holy Roman Emperor, Charles V, then offered Luther one final chance to recant, to take back his teachings. In 1521 at a meeting (called a "diet") in Worms, Germany, he refused to do so. He said, in part, "I do not accept the authority of Popes and councils. My conscience is captive to the word of God. I cannot and I will not recant anything. Here I stand, I cannot do otherwise."[6] The emperor declared Luther an outlaw and encouraged anyone to kill him without punishment.

Martin Luther at the Diet of Worms in 1521[7]

Remember, Luther did not set out to form a separate, distinct branch of Christianity. But after the Church rejected Luther and threatened him with death, he set out to forge a new Christian identity. He translated his 95 Theses from Latin into German, translated the Bible from Greek to German, and elaborated on his view of Christianity. His ideas were spread throughout Europe by the printing press, which had been developed around 1450. By 1523, a million copies of Luther's pamphlets were in circulation. (Prior to the invention of the printing press, books, pamphlets and, of course, the Bible had to be copied by hand, which may partly explain why many Catholic clergymen were illiterate.)[8]

To grasp how the Protestant work ethic contributed to the early development of capitalism, it is important to understand how the idea of individualism emerged from Martin Luther's challenge to the Church. It arose because "Protestantism encouraged people to 'find God for themselves.' It taught that silent reflection, introspection, and prayer were the best ways to find God. This form of religious self-reliance, unintentionally, and over many years, encouraged Protestants to adopt a more 'individualistic' attitude to their religion by seeking their own interpretation of Christianity."[9] It is this individualistic attitude that became the foundational seed of capitalism.

Although we take individuality for granted today, there was a time when the very idea of a person amassing wealth was a foreign concept. Most people had little hope of improving their lives, but the Protestant work ethic offered a blueprint that would evolve into a free-market system.

Martin Luther emphasized that individuals could read and interpret the Bible; the French-born reformer John Calvin would go one step further by elevating hard work to the level of Christian virtue. Under Calvinism, work became a religious calling—a vocation. ("Vocation" comes from the Latin *vocare*, which means "to call"; priests, for example, were "called" to the ministry directly by God. Another word similarly suggests that the language of capitalism goes back to religious concepts. "Industry," for example, which now connotes factories or the Industrial Revolution, actually comes from the Latin *industria*, which means "diligence, or hard work.") Calvinists and other Protestants worked for the glorification of God. Moreover Calvinism, like Lutheranism, eliminated the need for a priest or a church hierarchy. For these Protestants, the individual stood alone before God.

The theological framework of Calvinism is based on the idea that God has already decided who will be saved and who will be damned. According to Calvin, most people are born in a state of sin and are unable, despite living a moral life, to escape eternal damnation. However, a select few people are predestined to everlasting life. Here is where Calvinism becomes difficult to understand: Although most people are damned, we *all* must lead a moral life as if we are one of the few chosen to receive eternal life. You must live your life under this assumption. And living a moral life rests on the idea of self-discipline and hard work. For those in the 16th century who believed in Calvinism, work was not performed to gain wealth or to become greedy. As I noted above, work was meant to glorify God.

This powerful connection between religion and economics was first observed by the German historian and sociologist Max Weber. In what is perhaps his most famous work, *The Protestant Ethic and the Spirit of Capitalism*, Weber argued that the Protestant ethic practiced particularly by Calvinists but also by Lutherans, Methodists, Baptists, and Quakers elevated hard work and self-discipline to central pillars of religious faith. Weber made an important distinction between the pursuit of wealth and the systematic achievement of profit through economic activity. He pointed out that a simpler form of economic activity, known as mercantilism, has existed throughout history—in "Babylon and Ancient Egypt, China, India, and Mediaeval Europe. But only in the West, and relatively in recent times, has capitalistic activity become associated with the rational organization of formally free labour."[10]

Weber meant that labor—the work that people perform—had to become systematic, routinized, managed, disciplined, and efficient, and he elaborated on the concept of a "calling," which explains the relationship between the accumulation of wealth and the lack of interest in material things. This calling gave people a moral obligation to engage in hard work, with a purpose not for material riches but for the glorification of God.[11] Thus, there was a theological importance to work, expressed as "God does not exist for men, but men for the sake of God."[12] This religious interpretation of hard work would, however, become more and more secular over time.

As the religious meaning attached to work faded, the pursuit of wealth simply became its own goal. As to how the Protestant ethic evolved in the United States, Weber says: "In the field of its highest development, in the United States, the pursuit of wealth, stripped of its religious and ethical meaning, tends to become associated with purely mundane passions, which often actually give it the character of sport."[13] Sports are competitive activities, which, one might argue, are one of the key pillars of capitalism. This begs the question: Was America born as a capitalist society?

The short answer is yes. As Daniel T. Rodgers argues in his book *As a City on a Hill: The Story of America's Most Famous Lay Sermon*, the Puritan concept of self-discipline was an important factor in the early development of capitalism. According to Rodgers, "The careful accounting and control of the self that the Puritans valued was only one of the cultural traits on which capitalist economies have thrived. Others, like the risk-taking and labor exploitation on which the tobacco and slave economy of early Virginia was founded, could be successfully capital-generative as well. Capitalism's identifying features lie as much in its institutions of trade, property law, and labor as in the inner ethos that captured Weber's imagination."[14] When you have strong discipline, coupled with risk-taking and labor exploitation, you begin to develop a blueprint for capitalism.

In addition to self-discipline, the Puritans in New England engaged in trade and commerce, which created wealth, but not for the glorification of God. In fact, wealth "was a sign of value. Wealthier men like John Winthrop played a vastly outsized role in public affairs in the Massachusetts colony. Land distribution was sharply skewed in favor of the wealthy as well."[15] In many ways this early unequal wealth distribution in colonial America, which took place well before the beginning of the Industrial Revolution, may have been the earliest form of inequality in American history.

ADAM SMITH

Considered the father of modern capitalism, Adam Smith was a Scottish philosopher and political economist.[16] In his most important book, *An Inquiry into the Nature and Causes of the Wealth of Nations* (simply referred to as *The Wealth of Nations*), published in 1776, Smith "recommended leaving economic decisions to the free play of self-regulating market forces."[17] It is important to point out that Smith removed God from his economic philosophy and added the more scientific idea of "self-regulating forces." As you can see, by the time we get to Adam Smith in the 18th century, God was excluded from the conversation about economic affairs. That removal would help usher in selfishness and greed as powerful drivers of capitalism.

In *The Wealth of Nations*, Smith outlines the foundation of modern capitalism, though he never actually used the term. In fact, the word "capitalism" would not be widely used until the late 19th century. The phrase Smith uses is "commercial society," which conveys the idea that economic activity represents one aspect of the human condition. Smith makes it clear that "the moral character of a people is the ultimate measure of their humanity." By the mid-20th century, that idea would fade as the emphasis turned to profits.

Wikimedia Commons

Adam Smith

What Smith *does* focus on in his book are the critical structures of capitalism, which include the division of labor, free trade, self-interest in exchange, the limits on government intervention, price, as well as the general structure of the market.[18] The kind of capitalism that believes that the less government intervention you allow, the better economic success you will have is called "laissez-faire,"[19] a French term that simply translates to "leave alone." Some economists and scholars falsely attribute laissez-faire to Adam Smith. But in *The Wealth of Nations*, which runs to more than 1,000 pages, Smith never used the term. He actually believed in some government involvement. In fact, he claimed "that all corporations and the greater part of corporate law had been passed to keep prices, wages, and profits higher than they would be with free competition. Furthermore, these laws were supported to increase their profits at the expense of the public. Second, Smith argued that any time businessmen meet together they are likely to conspire against the public good."[20]

What Smith meant was that if you leave businesses to their own devices, they will become endlessly greedy without regard to the public good or society as a whole. While economists and scholars today argue that Adam Smith favored free markets without government intervention, I believe that's a false reading of his ideas. Smith was, above all else, a philosopher. Seven years before publication of *The Wealth of Nations*, Smith published *The Theory of Moral Sentiments*, which he considered to be his greatest work.[21] In it Smith holds "greed, selfishness, and egoism with disdain."[22] For him, our capacity to feel more for others and less for ourselves, to limit our selfish desires, "constitutes the perfection of human nature."[23]

Now, if God is removed from moral considerations, how then does human nature become less about greed and more about distributing wealth more equitably? In the past, the idea of God, along with the morality that was derived from such beliefs, kept human selfishness, greed, and other vices in check. And although Adam Smith had contempt for greed, he never noted the absence of God as a major causal factor. So how did systematic diminishment of God in the public square of ideas contribute to a broken capitalist system?

THE EXCLUSION OF GOD FROM PUBLIC LIFE

The decline of God in public life began with the Scientific Revolution and the birth of modern philosophy. Men such as Nicolaus Copernicus, Galileo Galilei, and Sir Isaac Newton reshaped our understanding of the world by offering physical explanations. Philosophers such as the Scottish empiricist David Hume and the French thinker René Descartes would also slowly hammer away at the idea of God. Descartes used what is called methodical doubt to establish absolute knowledge. He doubted everything—his own existence, the existence of the world, mathematics, and even God. But unlike Hume, Descartes was a religious man. After establishing his own existence with the famous "I think, therefore I am," he brings God back into the equation to guarantee that the world exists. Other thinkers of the time didn't bother; it would only be a matter of time before philosophers and men of science would ignore God completely.

Wikimedia Commons   *Wikimedia Commons*

René Descartes   *David Hume*

To better appreciate God's exclusion from our public consciousness, let me tell you a famous story that intersects with history, mathematics, and science. By the early 19th century, science had emerged as the dominant source of knowledge. In 1802 the French mathematician, physicist, astronomer, and philosopher Pierre-Simon Laplace gave Napoleon Bonaparte—who had once been his student at the military academy—a copy of his book on astronomy. After Napoleon finished reading the book, he invited Laplace to the palace. He congratulated his former teacher and "expressed his astonishment at not seeing God mentioned in the manuscript. Laplace's famous answer tells it all: 'Sir, I have no need for that hypothesis.'"[24] The mathematician had no need for God to explain how the universe operated.

There are far-reaching implications here that go beyond science. During the 19th century, three leading thinkers—Karl Marx, Sigmund Freud, and Friedrich Nietzsche—transformed our world and in the process further diminished the idea of God in the public mind. Marx developed a communist ideology that "called for a worker revolution to overturn capitalism."[25] God was nowhere to be found in his socialist writings. In fact, Marx called religion "the opium of the people," which was his way of saying that religion kept people in a perpetual state of ignorance.[26] Next, Sigmund Freud, the father of psychoanalysis, came along to say that God is the projection of our childish fears about the unknown.[27] Last, the German philosopher Friedrich Nietzsche declared that "God is dead," which was his way of telling us that faith in God is no longer possible. His solution was that we need a new moral system without God.[28]

Wikimedia Commons

Karl Marx

Wikimedia Commons

Sigmund Freud

Wikimedia Commons

Friedrich Nietzsche

Now, what does all this have to do with capitalism? As the diminishment of God in the public square of ideas gave rise to the selfish accumulation of wealth for its own sake, as opposed to the glorification of God, capitalism began to thrive under a different set of moral values. That would enable a select few to become leaders of industry. And greed and the selfish desire to amass wealth would result in a capitalist system with unequal wealth distribution, a broken capitalist system (and by extension, a broken retirement system). Capitalism today is designed to benefit the wealthy few who have the wealth and power to change the laws to enrich themselves and their corporations.

These historical lessons drive home the idea that to repair our broken capitalist system, structural change needs to occur. We as Americans need to curb the boundless greed that has enabled a select few to amass unimaginable wealth at the expense of everyone else. What we need today is an ethical capitalist system that drives innovation and improves our standard of living, while maintaining a social conscience. While we pursue this, however, I can also offer you actionable steps that you can take to plan your retirement future today. I believe the American Dream is still available to us all.

CHAPTER 2

THE INDUSTRIAL REVOLUTION AND THE FIRST GILDED AGE

"We can have democracy in this country or we can have great wealth concentrated in the hands of a few, but we can't have both."

—LOUIS D. BRANDEIS

The forces of progress, scientific innovation, and capitalism converged to create the Industrial Revolution and the first Gilded Age, a period in American history defined by greed, corporate and political corruption, and inequality on a mass scale. Beginning in the 17th century, the Scientific Revolution, which drew on the work of Polish astronomer and mathematician Nicolaus Copernicus, the Italian astronomer and inventor Galileo Galilei, and the English mathematician and physicist Sir Isaac Newton fundamentally reshaped how we looked at the world.

Newton, in addition to all of his other extraordinary achievements, combined the absolute certainty of mathematics with reliable observation and measurement to arrive at the modern scientific method.[1]

The influence that Newton had on technological innovation and industrial development was not immediate or obvious. He revolutionized the world with the introduction of something that we all take for granted today—the idea of facts, which served as foundational pieces for the Industrial Revolution. A fact "was a precise statement whose truth could be verified by an independent observer."[2] Prior to the Scientific Revolution, people engaged in beliefs, superstitions, and myths as a way of understanding the world. The scientific method included facts and experimentation and made it possible not only to understand the world but also to manipulate it with technology. This was the intellectual blueprint of the Industrial Revolution.

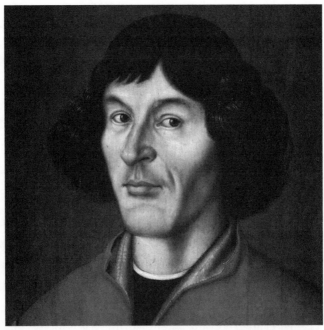

Wikimedia Commons

Nicolaus Copernicus

Wikimedia Commons

Galileo Galilei

Wikimedia Commons

Sir Isaac Newton

By the 19th century, science became useful, practical, and profitable. Industry incorporated scientific experimentation to improve efficiency and products. It was during this time that we witnessed the "rise of the engineer, who sought to apply scientific knowledge to practical matters."[3] Along with engineers, inventors relied upon science to innovate and create optimism about the future. The list is long, and though you may not recognize the names of all these inventors, you certainly know their inventions: James Watt and the steam engine (1769); Eli Whitney and the cotton gin (1793); Thomas Moore and the first wooden icebox (1802); George Stephenson and the first patented steam engine locomotive (1814); Samuel Morse and the telegraph (1844); Elias Howe and the sewing machine (1846); Alexander Graham Bell and the telephone (1876); Thomas Edison and the phonograph (1877), as well as the incandescent light bulb (1880); Nikola Tesla and the electric motor (1887); Orville and Wilbur Wright and the airplane (1903); and Henry Ford and the Model T (1908).[4]

One of the driving forces behind the Industrial Revolution was the idea of progress. You might be surprised to learn that this concept—the idea that society is evolving and moving toward better technological and economic conditions—was first introduced in the 18th century and later popularized in the 19th century.[5] The very structure of the modern world—from the European Enlightenment to the philosophy espoused by the American Founding Fathers—was based on the concept of progress.

If the modern world was filled with promise and opportunity, however, it also contained economic despair and the unequal distribution of wealth. The first Gilded Age magnified the oceanic separation between the wealthy few and the economic struggles of everyone else.

THE FIRST GILDED AGE

The term "Gilded Age" was first introduced by Mark Twain and Charles Dudley Warner. In fact, it was the title of their 1873 novel, *The Gilded Age: A Tale of Today*, which explored the greed and corruption of the era between 1870 and 1900.[6] It was a powerful metaphor for something that glitters with gold on the outside but in reality is something quite different beneath the surface.

The **Gilded Age** was a period in American history that represented image over substance. It was a time when the privileged few engaged in ostentatious wealth while the rest of the country struggled to simply survive. Let me tell you a brief story that perfectly captures this time period. Caroline Schermerhorn Astor belonged to one of the wealthiest families in America. With a net worth of $1.5 billion (adjusted for inflation as of February 21, 2022), Caroline Astor was regarded as the matriarch of New York high society.[7] After she died in 1908, her Fifth Avenue mansion was sold at auction in the 1920s and "many were disappointed to find out that her dinnerware was only gold plated and not solid like most believed."[8]

This was an age of "greed and guile: of rapacious robber barons, unscrupulous speculators, and corporate buccaneers, of shady business practices, scandal-plagued politics, and vulgar display."[9] Yet the Gilded Age was also a time of unprecedented change. The second half of the 19th century witnessed the creation of the modern industrial economy; a national transportation system; technological innovation such as the phonograph, telephone, radio, automobile, electric trains and trollies; the mass circulation of newspapers; and the rise of sports as entertainment, among other things.[10]

The continental United States was now connected by rail, the number of factories increased, and people moved from farms to growing cities in search of better economic opportunities. They came not only from small-town America, they also traveled from Europe. In fact, nearly 12 million immigrants came from Germany, Ireland, and England seeking personal freedom or to escape from political and religious persecution.[11] Yet not everyone was able to improve their standard of living. As factories grew in size and number, there was a need for more low-wage unskilled workers.

Life for the millions who came to the big cities was harsh. Factory work proved to be unforgiving. When you consider that "the conditions of work— low wages, long hours (the twelve-hour day was not uncommon), harsh conditions, abusive managers, and high accident rates on the job—sparked repeated protests at places of employment and in workers' communities across the nation," you begin to understand how the Gilded Age benefited an overwhelmingly small number of industrialists who amassed unimaginable wealth while millions of people suffered the indignities of inhumane work.[12] Who were these industrialists, and how much control did they have over America's growing industrial economy?

The men who exercised an extraordinary amount of power and control over economic and political affairs were known as robber barons, a term that highlights their greed and corruption. The economic force that enabled these robber barons to exploit workers, destroy their competition, and unethically amass an unimaginable amount of wealth was laissez-faire capitalism.

Remember that "laissez-faire" translates to "allow to do." In economic terms, that means the government should keep its hands off the market. During the Gilded Age, this political philosophy was called liberalism. It is important to distinguish how we use liberalism today, which is the idea that government intervention in the economy is necessary to solve social problems. In the late 19th century, liberalism had the opposite meaning. Liberals during the Gilded Age "opposed most government intervention in the economy or labor relations."[13] The lack of government regulations created an economic environment that favored those who were ruthless in matters of business. Both individuals and corporations were encouraged to defeat their competition by any means, thanks to a philosophy with a biological connection.

In 1859 the British naturalist Charles Darwin published his groundbreaking and controversial book *On the Origin of Species*, which was an instant best seller.[14] Darwin argued that organisms have certain characteristics that make them adapt to their environment. Those organisms that better adapt, evolve; those that cannot, die out.[15]

One person who was immediately influenced by Darwin's theory of evolution was the English philosopher, biologist, and sociologist Herbert Spencer. It was Spencer who first introduced the expression "survival of the fittest" in his 1864 book *The Principles of Biology*. Spencer wrote that what he meant by "survival of the fittest" is "that which Mr. Darwin has called 'natural selection.'"[16] What Spencer did next had a far-reaching impact on how people understood sociology and economics during the late 19th century.

Wikimedia Commons

Charles Darwin

Wikimedia Commons

Herbert Spencer

Spencer generalized Darwin's theory of evolution to include human behavior. He believed that the biological mechanism of survival of the fittest applied to society itself. He called this **Social Darwinism**, which is the nonscientific belief that the social world is a "competitive jungle requiring ruthless competition for limited resources, in which only the 'strongest' survive. Social Darwinism takes a negative view of human nature, holding that people are inherently selfish and that cynical manipulation is an acceptable route to get ahead."[17]

Do you see the implication here for capitalism? Many people, particularly the robber barons of the Gilded Age, used Social Darwinism to "justify laissez-faire economics and the minimal state, which were thought to best promote unfettered competition between individuals and the gradual improvement of society through the 'survival of the fittest.'"[18]

Wikimedia Commons

Andrew Carnegie

Wikimedia Commons

John D. Rockefeller

Wikimedia Commons

J. P. Morgan

Wikimedia Commons

Cornelius Vanderbilt

During the Gilded Age, Social Darwinists believed in the kind of capitalism that allowed for extreme competition. They "opposed government handouts, or safety regulations, or laws restricting child labor."[19] There were no laws at the time that regulated child labor or the safety of children, who often worked up to 18-hour days.[20] These giants of industry, including Andrew Carnegie, John D. Rockefeller, J. P. Morgan, and Cornelius Vanderbilt, embraced Social Darwinism to justify their monopolistic, cutthroat, win-at-all-costs attitude toward capitalism.

Although Social Darwinism offered these titans of industry a ready-made philosophical system to justify their greed and hypercompetitive spirit, there was one problem. Most Christians at the time did not accept Darwin's theory of evolution and found Social Darwinism distasteful. To reconcile their Christian beliefs with Social Darwinism, Andrew Carnegie and John D. Rockefeller, for example, believed that successful people possessed the necessary skills, given to them by God, to compete in business.[21] Many of these robber barons believed they were destined to build their corporate empires by any means simply because they were destined to win. To do so, these giants of the Industrial Revolution had to control the political reality of their day.

Wikimedia Commons

Bosses of the Senate

Their corporate monopolies controlled the economy, and, as I noted earlier, when greed and unlimited power converge, it is only a matter of time before corruption becomes the norm. In the Gilded Age, corporations "bribed politicians to ensure government policies favored big businesses."[22] Corporate bosses offered senators and congressmen bribes to write and pass legislation favorable to their enterprises. The "Bosses of the Senate" cartoon perfectly captures the political reality of the Gilded Age. Notice the fat businessmen looming over the Senate, as if they are dictating the legislative process while senators appear as feeble employees of the rich and powerful.

This blatant in-your-face mockery of American democracy would define the patronage system, which was a way for presidents to repay their friends and supporters by handing out political posts. Let's look at how this collusion between a so-called free-market system and politicians impacted average Americans. I like the word "collusion" because it perfectly captures the secret or illegal cooperation between the wealthy elites and government officials. Consider that "by 1890, the wealthiest 1 percent of American families owned 51 percent of the country's real and personal property, while the 44 percent at the bottom owned only 1.2 percent."[23] With this type of inequality you can begin to imagine the power these giants of industry exerted on local, state, and the federal government. In many ways, democracy was being undermined for the sake of selfish profits on a massive scale.

How is all this relevant today? History has a stubborn habit of repeating itself. You would think that 150 years after the first Gilded Age, we would have learned a thing or two about how to make capitalism more just and fair for everyone. But capitalism moves in predictable cycles. Whenever capitalism is unregulated, or poorly regulated, greed and corruption emerge. When capitalism is put in check, more people have an opportunity to experience the American Dream.

CHAPTER 3

THE RISE OF NEOLIBERALISM: PROFITS OVER PEOPLE

"The very design of neoliberal principles
is a direct attack on democracy."

—NOAM CHOMSKY

The prefix "neo" means new. So the term "neoliberalism" refers to the new liberalism that gained prominence in the 1970s. During the Gilded Age, liberalism was the economic ideology that favored free-market capitalism while limiting government intervention. Liberalism would rise again to take us once more on a path of greed, selfishness, and unimaginable corruption. In fact, the neoliberalism of the past 50 years has had a direct impact on our current broken capitalist system and, by extension, our broken retirement system. Corporate monopolies, the uncertainties of the Social Security system, the disappearance of pensions, corporate buybacks, the volatility of the stock market, artificially low interest rates set by the Federal

Reserve, and even cultural problems like our divorce rate, selfish attitudes, and narcissistic behavior can all be attributed to the rise of neoliberalism.

Neoliberalism got its start in Europe shortly after World War II, when leading historians, philosophers, and economists came together to form what we today call think tanks. These think tanks, which were, and continue to be, closed to public input, have had far-reaching consequences on the modern world order.

In April 1947, 39 economists, historians, and other intellectuals came together in the picturesque ski resort of Mont Pèlerin, which overlooks Lake Geneva. The purpose of the meeting, which was organized by the Austrian economist Friedrich Hayek (who would win the Nobel Prize in Economics in 1974), was to discuss the new liberalism in a postwar Europe. The attendees included the economist Milton Friedman, who would win the Nobel Prize in Economics in 1976; the Austrian-British philosopher Karl Popper; and the economist George Stigler, who would win the Nobel Prize in Economics in 1982. One of the concerns these men shared was a "decline of belief in private property and the competitive market."[1] To address what they perceived as a global threat, these men decided that they would, on their own, create a new world order that would "favor a very particular brand of capitalism."[2]

Wikimedia Commons

Friedrich Hayek

Wikimedia Commons

Milton Friedman

Karl Popper

Think of the significance of this meeting for a minute. These men wanted not only to strengthen capitalism in a postwar world that had witnessed the horrors of Nazism, totalitarianism, and dictatorships, but they also had a particular vision of what capitalism should be. There is a certain male-centered arrogance in these men's belief that they could shape the global economic future. Remember that classical liberalism had proven to be a spectacular failure during the Gilded Age. Why would a group of very smart men want to bring it back?

The answer to this question turns out to be counterintuitive. The neoliberalism of the Mont Pèlerin Society wanted greater government intervention, not less, and not the type you might assume. In other words, the neoliberalism that emerged from the Mont Pèlerin Society advocated for maximum market freedom and minimal intervention from the state. The exception to this rule, a disingenuous one in my opinion, is that governments should intervene only to defend markets, protect private property, and uphold capitalism. Over time, neoliberals would ask for greater government intervention, such as bailing out banks and companies that are too big to fail. This pattern of government bailouts became the norm in the early to mid-2000s when neoliberal economists wanted the state to "intervene to ensure the existence of markets. Activities such as bailing out the banks in 2008, privatizing public services, and making markets in technology such as 5G are all neoliberal acts of state which a purely classical liberal perspective may not advocate for."[3] Of course, this neoliberal ideology is misguided and self-serving. The argument was, and continues to be, based on the idea that the state should intervene in the free market only in so far as it protects corporate interests. So how and why did these men spread an ideology that favored the interests of corporations and dictators instead of championing the economic needs of the people?

It's important here to recap events from earlier in the 20th century. The free-wheeling capitalism of the Gilded Age and lack of government regulations had ended in what is perhaps considered the greatest economic disaster in American history. In 1929 the stock market crashed and ushered in the Great Depression. Clearly, classical liberalism had failed spectacularly. When President Franklin Roosevelt took office in 1932, in the depths of the Depression, he immediately began to offer several far-reaching welfare programs to get people back on their feet, and Congress enacted massive reforms and regulations. However, the neoliberals didn't learn much from the failures of classical liberalism. The one lesson they seemed to have taken away from the crash of 1929 and the Great Depression was the notion that the government needs to intervene only in so far as it does not allow big businesses and large banks to fail.

Despite the numerous disagreements among the members of the Mont Pèlerin meeting, most of the attendees did agree on one idea: that the monumental task of spreading free-market economies across the globe would take time. It was Friedrich Hayek who made the prophetic remark that "the battle of ideas would take a generation before it was successful."[4] In fact, by 1971 (exactly one generation after Mont Pèlerin) neoliberalism had started to take hold in the United States, Britain, and other countries that you wouldn't have imagined, such as Chile. The first step in spreading neoliberal ideology was the establishment of think tanks all over the world. Powerful groups like the Institute of Economic Affairs, the Adam Smith Institute, the Heritage Foundation, the Cato Institute, and many others can trace their lineage back to the first Mont Pèlerin meeting of 1947.[5]

The initial purpose of these think tanks was twofold: First, these neoliberal groups wanted to establish an alternative to the dominant Keynesian economic system of the postwar world; second, they hoped to establish policy that could be presented to governments all over the world. Keynesian economics, named after the British economist John Maynard Keynes, says that markets do not have the natural ability to restore themselves to some kind of equilibrium or balance and that government regulation is periodically needed to bring back balance.[6]

As you can see, these two philosophies are directly opposed. On the one hand, neoliberalism advocates for little to no government intervention, unless that intervention is aimed at rescuing businesses when they fail. On the other hand, Keynesian economics accepts the fundamental premise that capitalist economic systems experience cycles that require government intervention to bring them into balance.

In addition to creating economic policy that would influence powerful world leaders like Ronald Reagan and Margaret Thatcher, some neoliberals decided to use their own personal influence to bring about economic change. One such memorable example took place in 1977 when Friedrich Hayek visited Chile to spread his neoliberal ideology. The person in power at the time was Augusto Pinochet, one of the most brutal dictators in Latin American history. During his 17-year rule, Pinochet killed more than 3,000 opponents, tortured thousands more, and forced tens of thousands into exile.[7] Despite the brutality of Pinochet's regime, Hayek justified his involvement by saying, "Sometimes it is necessary for a country to have, for a time, some form of dictatorial power."[8] This is a truly remarkable statement when you consider how neoliberalism started.

One of the intellectuals who attended the 1947 Mont Pèlerin conference was Karl Popper, who two years earlier had published *The Open Society and Its Enemies*, which strongly warned against totalitarianism and dictatorship. Among Popper's editors was Hayek himself. The influence that Popper had on the Mont Pèlerin conference cannot be underestimated. The original aims of the conference included a profound concern for "disappearance of 'human dignity and freedom' especially 'freedom of thought and expression.'"[9] It's baffling to think that Hayek helped articulate those goals, yet went to Chile to ask a brutal dictator to adopt a neoliberal economy. Putting aside the moral hypocrisy for a minute, we can ask if this economic experiment in Chile worked.

According to Milton Friedman, who had attended Mont Pèlerin, the neoliberal experiment in Chile was "the miracle of Chile." The only problem with that assessment was that Chile under Pinochet looked nothing like an economic miracle. In fact, "Chile's GDP [gross domestic product] grew by 2.9 percent annually during the dictatorship, putting Pinochet in eighth place of the nation's past ten governments, between 1958 and 2018. Annual inflation was 79.9 percent, the second highest of the past ten governments. Unemployment averaged 18.0 percent, the highest figure in any Chilean government of the past 60 years."[10] You don't have to have a degree in economics to understand that the neoliberal experiment in Chile was an absolute disaster. Economic inequality was also astonishing: "28.1 percent of the total income is concentrated among 1 percent of the population, making

Chile one of the world's most unequal nations."[11] Friedman should have referred to Chile as the neoliberal nightmare.

MISGUIDED GENIUSES

As I noted above, Friedrich Hayek's prediction that it would take a generation for neoliberalism to take hold in Europe and America was prescient. But in order for neoliberalism to become the dominant economic ideology of the late 20th century, three historical forces had to come together at the same time. First, economists had to be powerful enough to exert influence on the highest levels of government. Second, a legal structure had to create a blueprint for corporate monopolies. And third, Americans had to be sold on the idea that social problems could only be solved by free-market forces. Let's begin with the rise of economists as powerful agents of misguided change.

During the late 1940s and early 1950s, economists played a marginal role in shaping economic decisions. There is an interesting story about a young economist by the name of Paul Volcker who worked in the basement of the Federal Reserve in the early 1950s. His job was to crunch numbers for the people who made decisions. Evidently Volcker told his wife that he saw little hope of ever moving up in his career. At the time, the Federal Reserve's leadership was made up of bankers and lawyers, with not a single economist. The Fed's chairman was William McChesney Martin, a former stockbroker. McChesney once told a visitor that he "kept a small staff of economists in the basement of the Fed's Washington headquarters. They were in the building, he said, because they asked good questions. They were in the basement because 'they don't know their own limitations.'"[12] In fact, this contempt for economists was shared by President Franklin Roosevelt, who dismissed John Maynard Keynes, arguably "the most important economist of his generation, as an impractical 'mathematician.'"[13] Eisenhower, too, would later urge Americans to keep technocrats (by which he meant economists) from power.

So widespread was the disdain for economists that Congress rarely consulted them, and the courts often ignored economic evidence as irrelevant.

But a revolution was brewing. It would only be a matter of time before economists sat at the seat of power, where they not only advised policymakers but were also responsible for shaping policy. Paul Volcker would rise to become the chairman of the Federal Reserve in 1978. And another economist—Milton Friedman of the University of Chicago—would become a central figure in shaping American policy.

In 1962 Friedman published *Capitalism and Freedom*, in which he covered such widely varied topics as floating exchange rates, the abolition of medical licenses, school vouchers, and a negative income tax.[14] The book sold more than half a million copies and has been translated into 18 languages, making Friedman an academic celebrity and a sought-after advisor by such leaders as Richard Nixon, Ronald Reagan, and Margaret Thatcher, to name a few. Eight years later Friedman published a *New York Times* article that revealed his neoliberal views clearly and concisely. In "The Social Responsibility of Business Is to Increase Its Profits," Friedman offered a framework for corporate behavior. He wrote, "There is one and only one social responsibility of business—to use its resources and engage in activities designed to increase its profits so long as it stays within the rules of the game, which is to say, engages in open and free competition without deception."[15]

Friedman was suggesting that if businesses followed the rules of the game, then all would be well. But what if the rules of the game were written by those with a singular interest in maximizing profits for the elite few? What happens when the rules of the game marginalize the vast majority of people who have little to no input in how the rules are applied? This is the failure of neoliberalism: An ethical impulse toward others is ignored for the sake of profits. It was disingenuous of Friedman to suggest that business has no input in how the rules of the game are written. There was another flaw in Friedman's argument: The idea that capitalism is driven by the need for maximum profits is a myth.

Let's now briefly examine how the legal blueprint was created to accommodate a monopolistic free-market capitalism. In 1971 a Virginia tobacco industry attorney by the name of Lewis F. Powell wrote a memo in support of businesses coming together to defend their corporate interests. Powell argued, "Business must learn the lesson . . . that political power is necessary; that such power must be assiduously cultivated; and that when necessary, it must be used aggressively and with determination— without embarrassment and without the reluctance which has been so characteristic of American business."[16] This fateful memo would catch the attention of President Nixon, and two months later Nixon nominated Lewis Powell to the U.S. Supreme Court. Powell's memo was, in effect, a call to arms for businesses to defend their mission of free and open competition without government regulations. Both Milton Friedman and Lewis Powell set the stage for less government regulation, which, by the end of the 20th century, would contribute to the second Gilded Age. Powell's memo was a rallying cry for businesses to use their power to fight for free-market competition; Robert Bork would go on to offer the legal framework that would enable them to succeed.

Wikimedia Commons

Lewis F. Powell

Wikimedia Commons

Robert Bork

If Milton Friedman was behind the political ideology of neoliberalism, then Robert Bork was the legal scholar who justified corporate greed and corruption by advocating for corporate mergers and monopolies. Some of you may remember when President Reagan nominated Bork to the U.S. Supreme Court in 1987. The nomination was contentious and prompted heated debates in the Senate. In response to Bork's desire to roll back civil rights, he became one of only four Supreme Court nominees (along with William Rehnquist, Samuel Alito, and Brett Kavanaugh) to be rejected by the American Civil Liberties Union.[17] Many Democrats opposed Bork because of his opposition to the federal government's claim that it had the authority to impose voting-fairness standards on individual states. Bork also advocated for the executive branch's having far more power than the legislative or judicial branch.

Despite the fact that Bork was not confirmed as a Supreme Court justice, his judicial influence on antitrust laws was extraordinary. He played a "critical role in recreating the antitrust laws of the original Gilded Age. During that period, antitrust enforcers largely allowed corporations to merge and control markets in, for instance, chemicals, steel, telegraphs, and tobacco."[18] Bork's impact on corporate America remains broad and far-reaching in its implications for the average American. His 1978 book, *The Antitrust Paradox*, has shaped antitrust laws for several decades. Witness the fact that "the Department of Justice and Federal Trade Commission today mostly leave Google, Walmart, and other businesses across the economy alone and seek to suppress the collective action of workers in the service economy."[19]

From the early 1970s into the 1980s economists such as Milton Friedman and legal scholars such as Robert Bork became the architects of an economic worldview that favored corporate power over and above government regulations. In *Evil Geniuses*, Kurt Andersen describes a "kind of secret history that happened in broad daylight; starting in the early '70s," he writes, "a band of conservative economists and pro-business groups, terrified of the progressive movements of the 1960s, drew up plans and blueprints for a version of America in which big corporations and Wall Street would be liberated from regulation and labor unions and antitrust laws, allowing the free market to sort out the winners from the losers."[20] This vision of American corporate power has largely been realized at the expense of the average person.

Neoliberalism as an economic ideology, coupled with Robert Bork's legal framework to support corporate monopolies, has helped create a world where less than a handful of global corporations control how we interact and consume information in the digital age. Think about how much you rely upon the services of Apple, Amazon, Google, and Facebook. Consider that "Amazon controls a third of the cloud business, 44 percent of e-commerce, and a staggering 70 percent of the smart-speaker market. Google controls 90 percent of search. Facebook has become a conduit for political disinformation and Apple a symbol of conspicuous consumption and ruthless brand protection. As tens of thousands of small and not-so-small businesses face bankruptcy in the wake of the [COVID-19] pandemic, all four companies continue to thrive."[21] In many ways, these four corporations helped create the second Gilded Age.

Now let's look at how neoliberalism was sold to the American people. Kurt Andersen explains that the message had to be simple, emotional, and relatable. After the turbulence of the 1960s, a time of political, social, and cultural change, Americans were longing for the simpler times. By the 1970s, they looked back longingly at the 1950s. What neoliberals sold to the American people was nostalgia, packaged and delivered, according to Andersen, in the form of television programming.

Hollywood "revived and celebrated the recent past in a big way, right away, with nostalgia-fests like *American Graffiti, Happy Days,* and *Grease.*"[22] How exactly does nostalgia connect with neoliberalism? Nostalgia tends to romanticize the past and distort what actually happened. For many neoliberals, this feeling became associated with the concepts of rugged individualism and self-reliance, fostering a tendency to conservatism. The overly simplified economic idea of a "rich-get-richer" system was dressed up in "old-time patriotic drag," according to Andersen, "by portraying low taxes on the rich and unregulated business and weak unions and a weak federal government as the only ways back to some kind of rugged, frontiersy, stronger, better America."[23]

To be sure, whenever political, economic, or any other kind of ideology preys upon our emotions, reality becomes distorted. Andersen points this out when he identifies the period between the mid-1940s to the early 1970s as economically fair and more democratic.[24]

The more you understand how and why our capitalist system is broken, the more likely you are to protect yourself against the seemingly insurmountable forces working against you. Knowledge gives us agency to change mind-sets and make different choices, including those that affect your retirement and your financial future.

Greed and selfishness change human behavior for the worse. Greed has a nasty habit of slowly corrupting our consciousness. Regardless of your religious affiliation or moral background, greed will always be tempting. Greed lurks behind us, waiting to strike. According to Marriam-Webster, greed is a "selfish and excessive desire for more of something (such as money) than is needed."[25] Now think about the corporate executives who are not only driven by greed but also are encouraged to maximize profits by any means. Once again the question is how to protect yourself against these powerful forces of greed and corruption. You do that first by understanding the nature of the forces and how they interact with each other to impact your hard-earned money. Second, you open yourself up to alternative investment strategies that will potentially protect you from these powerful forces.

There are real-world consequences of an economic ideology that enriches the wealthy few, while leaving the rest of us struggling. From the dot-com disaster of the late 1990s to the housing bubble of the mid-2000s and the subsequent global financial meltdown of 2008, neoliberalism has left in its wake one economic catastrophe after another. History always repeats. Today we are living through a second Gilded Age, also known as Gilded Age 2.0.

CHAPTER 4

UNCONTROLLED CAPITALISM: THE SECOND GILDED AGE

"I've never been antiregulation.
I've always believed that raw,
unregulated capitalism doesn't work."

—HENRY PAULSON

O n some level, we can all identify with a feeling of unease about our financial reality. Beyond persistent worries about paying bills, saving money for a rainy day, buying a home, or even planning for retirement, we may sense that something is out of whack with an economic system that enriches a select few, while keeping everyone else in a perpetual state of struggle. If you have ever felt like this, you are not alone. In a 2020 Edelman survey, "57 percent of people worldwide said that 'capitalism as it exists today does more harm than good in the world.'"[1] Still, despite the problems of capitalism, and there are many, it is the best economic system we have, when you compare it to socialism or other central planned economies.

There are hidden historical, political, and economic forces that impact your retirement. According to a Gallup poll, 56 percent of Americans own stocks. This includes individual stocks, as well as those that are part of a mutual fund or retirement savings account, such as a 401(k) or IRA.[2] It is important to understand that stocks are generally riskier than other assets such as bonds, or alternative assets like real estate.[3]

Before we discuss why stocks tend to be relatively risky investment vehicles, we need to distinguish between two concepts—market corrections and market crashes. A **stock market correction** is defined as a drop between 10 percent and 20 percent in a market index such as the S&P 500 or Dow Jones Industrial Average. **A market crash**, on the other hand, is defined as a prolonged market decline that is greater than 20 percent.[4] Since the market crash of 1929, there have been four additional market crashes: the 1987 Black Monday crash, the 1999–2000 dot-com bubble, the 2008 financial crisis, and the 2020 pandemic crash. Each of these involved market declines of more than 20 percent. The dot-com crash of the early 2000s was particularly notable because the tech-heavy NASDAQ Composite Index plummeted 76.81 percent.[5] In addition to these crashes, there have been 28 market corrections over the past 50 years.[6]

So why are stocks potentially riskier investments, especially when you want a strategy to prepare for retirement? It's because there are powerful hidden forces that influence the direction of the stock market.

UNCONTROLLED CAPITALISM

Let's begin with uncontrolled capitalism. As the phrase implies, this refers to few or no government regulations, which, too often, increases the possibility of corporate greed. Whenever we have had uncontrolled capitalism, we experienced higher inequality, widespread corporate monopolies, and stock market crashes.

In the Gilded Age, you recall, the level of corruption was so pervasive that large corporate monopolies openly bribed members of Congress to look

the other way when it came to rampant greed. Without government intervention, a few corporations were able to dominate the economic landscape
by eliminating the competition.

One glaring example involved Andrew Carnegie's U.S. Steel Corporation.
Between 1887 and 1904 "a total of nine steel companies were consolidated,
and the corporation was able to practice ruthless tactics to monopolize the
industry without consequences from the government."[7]

With uncontrolled capitalism you create an environment where there is
"no economic stability because greed and overproduction cause the economy
to have wild swings ranging from times of robust growth to cataclysmic
recessions."[8] In other words, uncontrolled capitalism encourages greed for
both the individual and corporations. In the 1920s, when banks were not
regulated, uncontrolled capitalism would lead to one of the greatest economic crises in American history.

IRRATIONAL EXUBERANCE

Have you ever experienced greed? Of course you have. If you have ever gam-
bled, or played the lottery, or even dreamed of making millions, you know
what greed feels like. Greed is the ultimate expression of our self-centered
orientation to the world. And it leads to the concept of irrational exuberance,
a phrase introduced by former Federal Reserve chairman Alan Greenspan. In
a 1996 speech, "The Challenge of Central Banking in a Democratic Society,"
Greenspan posed the following question: "But how do we know when irrational exuberance has unduly escalated asset values, which then become
subject to unexpected and prolonged contractions?"[9]

We can think of irrational exuberance as widespread economic optimism. When investors "start believing that the rise in prices in the recent
past predicts the future, they are acting as if there is no uncertainty in the
market, causing a feedback loop of ever higher prices."[10] In other words,
when investors start acting on the belief that asset prices (for example
stocks or real estate) will only continue to rise, they create a frenzy of activity that in many cases creates a self-fulfilling prophecy, where prices do go
up in the short term. However, there is a steep price to pay. When asset

prices go up quickly, they tend to form market bubbles, which eventually burst. Then the market crashes.

A classic case of irrational exuberance was the 1929 stock market crash. Some of the forces that led to a sustained market bubble included a strong and vibrant economy that resulted from the mass production of products and improved advertising techniques. That is partly why the decade between World War I and the massive stock market crash is referred to as the Roaring Twenties. Everything was changing, from cultural norms to technological innovation, and the American Dream seemed to be within most people's reach. From 1922 to 1929, the gross national product (GNP) grew at an annual rate of 5 percent; wages, for a small number of Americans, increased by 15 percent; and unemployment never exceeded 5 percent.[11] But something else was happening during the 1920s that would have dire consequences.

The banking system during the 1920s was largely uncontrolled. Of the 24,000 banks in the country, only one-third belonged to the Federal Reserve.[12] There was no distinction made between commercial banks and investment banks. This led to "improper banking activity—the overzealous commercial bank involvement in stock market investment, [which] was deemed the main culprit of the financial crash."[13] Improper banking activity meant that commercial banks not only offered questionable loans to people who could ill afford them, but they also actively engaged in their own stock market speculation. Think about how reckless this was for the economy as a whole. These were respected banking institutions that had a fiduciary responsibility to manage and take care of property for others.[14] During the 1920s, thousands of banks failed in that obligation by giving out loans to people who used the stock market as a form of gambling and also actively engaged in highly speculative investments themselves.

CONTROLLED CAPITALISM

Shortly after the stock market crash of 1929, the government had to address many of the underlying causes of the failure. When President Franklin Roosevelt took office in 1932, he immediately started addressing the economy. In his first inaugural address on March 4, 1933, Roosevelt had this to say about the rampant greed that defined the previous decade: "Finally in our progress toward a resumption of work we require two safeguards against a return of the evils of the old order; there must be a strict supervision of all banking and credits and investments; [and] there must be an end to speculation with other people's money."[15]

Roosevelt was calling for two layers of protection against the greedy behavior of banks. First, the institutions needed to be regulated and held accountable for their actions. Second, banks needed to stop engaging in market speculation using other people's money. To avoid returning to the evils of the old order—such as commercial banks that engaged in speculative investments and "became greedy, taking on huge risks in the hopes of even bigger rewards"[16]— the president pushed for greater regulation of the banking system.

One of the first legislative changes that came out of the Great Depression was the Glass-Steagall Act of 1933, which was designed to separate commercial banks from investment banks. It was signed into law by Roosevelt as part of the New Deal programs. Another piece of legislation, the 1933 Banking Act, created the Federal Deposit Insurance Corporation (FDIC), which aimed to restore trust in America's banks by insuring depositors' money.

In a broader sense, when the Great Depression hit, it became quite clear that government intervention was needed to help the United States recover. Roosevelt's New Deal programs "attempted to curb the excesses of untrammeled capitalism through such policies as setting minimum wages, regulating working conditions, promoting labor unions, and bolstering retirement security."[17] These programs would help usher in Fordism, which would give more people access to the American Dream.

FORDISM AND THE AMERICAN DREAM

Do you remember the metaphor of the three-legged stool? Retirement traditionally stood on three legs—government (Social Security), private pensions, and the individual. From the 1940s to the 1990s, the retirement burden was upheld by Social Security and private pensions. Over this 50-year period, a new form of economic growth helped give rise to the postwar boom and, by extension, a strong, viable middle class. This type of growth became known as Fordism. It offered mass consumption, sufficient wages to support families, job stability, and rising incomes. "Fordism extended well beyond the factory walls; it reshaped the spatial and demographic configuration of cities; it ignited bouts of economic development, industrial concentration, and social conflict."[18]

The years between the mid-1940s and the mid-1990s were a time when controlled capitalism proved to be favorable to the average American. Capitalism was given a framework by which it could benefit more people. In this era, in particular, the American Dream, which was largely defined by homeownership, was becoming attainable by more people. During the 1950s, for example, the average household income was $4,237, and the average price of buying a home was $8,450, which represented two years of household income. Although home prices increased to $23,450 by the 1970s, they were still affordable, just 2.4 times the average family's annual income.[19] My point here is that when you put limits on capitalism, you improve the quality of living for millions of people.

THE POLITICS OF GREED

Let's suppose that you are not yet convinced that whenever greed is allowed to flourish, capitalism favors the wealthy few, while simultaneously hurting average Americans. Perhaps you like neoliberalism because you like the idea of a free-market economy. The story I'm about to tell you might change your mind, or at the very least force you to question your beliefs.

Remember the Glass-Steagall Act? As it turned out, this important piece of legislation would not survive the test of time. In 1999, the act was repealed by the Clinton administration, which would contribute to the dot-com bubble of the early 2000s, as well as the 2008 global financial meltdown.

In 1998 the Travelers Group, one of the largest insurance and financial services companies in the world, announced a merger with Citicorp, which was primarily a commercial bank. What made this proposed merger unprecedented was not simply the scale of the merger, which was valued at $140 billion, but rather the fact that Congress had to repeal the Glass-Steagall Act of 1933 to accomplish it. The two corporate giants actually announced their merger before Congress formally changed the law.

How was the merger made possible, if the Glass-Steagall Act was still the law? The short answer is corporate influence. In order to ensure that Glass-Steagall would be repealed so the merger could go through, both companies poured millions of dollars into the election campaigns of Republicans and Democrats alike. In fact, according to Arthur Levitt, a former banker and chairman of the American Stock Exchange, and the chairman of the Securities and Exchange Commission from 1993 to 2001, "It was apparent that the protections of Glass-Steagall had already largely eroded. But Congress at several times, nearly passed a bill to do away with Glass-Steagall. It was clear that it was a question not of whether but when Glass-Steagall would go. Millions of dollars were pouring in the campaign coffers of senators and congressmen who were set to do this."[20]

As you can clearly see, when politics and money become intertwined, greed and corruption are the inevitable outcome.

On September 23, 1998, "the Board of Governors of the Federal Reserve (the 'Board') approved the application by Travelers Group Inc. ('Travelers') to become a bank holding company by acquiring Citicorp."[21] And once that merger was given the green light, it would only be a matter of time before the dot-com bubble burst and the 2008 global financial meltdown occurred. Whenever corporations use their financial power to change laws to conform to their vision of greater profits, then capitalism becomes unfair and unjust. In fact, democracy itself suffers, because corporations dictate the legal landscape by which they operate.

FROM THE DOT-COM BUBBLE TO THE REAL ESTATE BUBBLE

The late 1990s were a period of rapid technological change. In many ways they marked the beginning of the digital revolution. Companies both large and small were rushing to gain an online foothold, in part because having

a web presence meant that businesses were forward looking and techno-
logically savvy. But the race for online supremacy was both intense and
unforgiving. This was the Wild West phase of the internet, and only a select
few would emerge as corporate giants. In the process, greed would help create one of the greatest economic bubbles in history.

The possibilities of making money online seemed endless, and hundreds of companies were created seemingly overnight. Remember irrational
exuberance? The frenzy of activity surrounding new websites captured the
imagination. The competition was so intense that some companies started
to make money on initial public offerings (IPOs) by hyping the value of
a company before it even proved itself. One of the more glaring examples
was Priceline.com, launched in April 1998, after its founder, Jay Walker,
recognized a problem with the way traditional airline seats were sold. He
noticed that approximately half a million airline seats went unsold every day.
Priceline entered this space by asking customers what they were willing to
pay for these unused seats. This early online model of tickets sales worked
beautifully. Consumers benefited from cheap airline tickets, and the airlines
sold their excess inventory.

Priceline became an overnight sensation. The emphasis, however, was not
on creating a viable business model; rather, it was about hype and creating
brand awareness. Prior to the IPO in March 1999, the company spent more
than $20 million on clever advertising. Their spokesperson was William
Shatner of *Star Trek* fame. The hoopla worked. The IPO went from $16 per
share to $162.37 per share just one month later. This represented a whop-
ping 914 percent gain in one month.[22] What's my point? Many of these
start-ups didn't care as much about making a profit as about hyping their
product or service in order to rake in profits from their IPOs.

Greed, however, was not the only driver behind the dot-com bubble.
Not surprisingly, there was also corruption, as was evident in the stories of
Enron and WorldCom. Founded by Kenneth Lay, Enron was one of the
largest energy companies in the world, but it had to file for bankruptcy when
the fact was revealed that executives were cooking the books by inflating
profits. Similarly, Bernie Ebbers, the cofounder and CEO of WorldCom,

the largest telecommunications company in the United States in the late 1990s, was found guilty of enhancing the firm's balance sheet. Both Enron and WorldCom are today considered the largest accounting scandals in American history.[23]

The greed and corruption were, of course, unsustainable. As many start-ups failed and new sources of capital dried up, the excitement turned to panic, and the dot-com bubble burst. The stock market crash wiped out $5 trillion in value between March and October 2002.

You would think that corporations would have refrained from engaging in questionable business practices after that. Unfortunately, things got worse quickly.

Another market bubble was forming. This time it was in real estate. Banks were only too eager to lend money to people whose credit was suspect. These types of loans became known as subprime loans, and they became possible after the Glass-Steagall Act was repealed and banks were allowed to act like hedge funds. Hedge funds are not a specific type of investment; rather, these funds pool money from participants to "invest in costly, high-risk, high-reward securities and other opportunities."[24]

Millions of Americans took advantage of the subprime loans, and on September 29, 2008, the real estate bubble burst and the stock market crashed. The Dow Jones Industrial Average fell by 777.68 points in intraday trading, the largest point drop in history until 2018. As a result of bad lending practices, many banks, hedge funds, and insurance firms suddenly found themselves holding worthless investments. Millions of Americans simply walked away from their homes when they couldn't afford to pay their mortgage.

Many banks, including some large ones, were now in danger of failing. But the mess introduced a new phrase in our vocabulary: "too big to fail." The government decided it couldn't let the large banks fail, so they bailed them out. On October 3, 2008, Congress established the Troubled Asset Relief Program (TARP), "which allowed the U.S. Treasury to bail out troubled banks [in the amount of $700 billion]."[25] The following year, on February 17, 2009, Congress passed an additional $787 billion stimulus package known as the American Recovery and Reinvestment Act.[26] Not only did the government reward the bad behavior by banking executives, but this governmental practice kept happening, either through the U.S. Treasury or the Federal Reserve.

THE SECOND GILDED AGE

So far in this book you've read about the birth of capitalism, the Scientific and Industrial Revolutions, the first Gilded Age, the rise of neoliberalism, and controlled versus uncontrolled capitalism. When Milton Friedman wrote his *New York Times* piece in 1970, he argued that the only goal of business was to maximize profits, *as long as businesses played by the rules.* History, of course, has shown us that Friedman's seemingly noble condition is laughably absurd and misleading.

Though businesses, in large part, do play by the rules, they have always had a hand in bending the rules to their advantage. In the Gilded Age, for example, when a few corporations flourished as a result of rapid technological changes, they were able to exert considerable influence over Congress to ensure that laws were enacted to protect their power.

Something similar has happened over the past 25 years. In a single generation, the digital revolution radically changed our world, and many economists and historians identify today's era as the Gilded Age 2.0. The parallels between the two periods are both striking and disturbing. Both experienced unprecedented technological change. The telephone today is now the smartphone. The phonograph is now digital music apps. Newspapers and books have been replaced with instantaneous access to information in our pockets or on our wrists. Even the internal combustion engine is disappearing in favor of clean electric vehicles.

The Vanderbilts, Morgans, Rockefellers, and Carnegies of the past have been replaced by Jeff Bezos, Steve Jobs, Mark Zuckerberg, Elon Musk, and Bill Gates, to name a few. And while our new Gilded Age is beautiful on the outside, we can see massive inequity between those who are on the forefront of the digital revolution and everyone else.

The big five tech companies—Google, Apple, Facebook (Meta), Amazon, and Microsoft—had a stock market value, as of July 30, 2021, of $9.3 trillion, which is more than the value of the next 27 most valuable U.S. companies combined. These are monopolistic behemoths who dominate their respective industries. Apple, for example, posted a profit over three months (May 30, 2021, to July 30, 2021) of $21.7 billion, which was double the combined annual profits of the five largest U.S. airlines in prepandemic 2019.[27]

As for personal wealth, the second Gilded Age has produced 2,750 people who have more wealth than half the planet. Given that the global population (as of June 1, 2022) was 8 billion people, a simple division reveals that .0000344 percent of the wealthiest individuals have more wealth than nearly 4 billion people. The wealth gap today is "roughly as wide as it was more than a century ago when the [first] Gilded Age led to massive disparities between rich and poor."[28] One of the reasons for this massive wealth inequality is our current lobbying system.

CORPORATE LOBBYING AND POLITICAL CONTRIBUTIONS

James Madison, one of the framers of the Constitution and the fourth president of the United States, warned us against factions, noting that their single-minded focus on a common cause may undermine the interests of the community. Madison considered these factions—what we today call interest groups or lobbyists—dangerous and referred to them as the "tyranny of the majority."[29] Madison was correct to be concerned with the dangers of special interest groups who spend massive amounts of money to help create rules, policies, and laws that help them maximize profits.

We can see this happening. During the first quarter of 2022, lobbyists collectively spent more than $1 billion.[30] In very simple terms, "the main purpose of lobbying is to influence legislation or regulation in favor of a company or industry."[31] Below is a list of the largest industry lobbyists and how much they spent in the past 24 years, including 2021.

- Pharmaceuticals/health products ($5.17 billion and $356.6 million in 2021)[32]

- Insurance industry ($3.3 billion and $152.9 million in 2021)[33]

- Electric utilities ($2.83 billion and $112.2 million in 2021)[34]

- Electronics manufacturing ($2.82 billion and $179.5 million in 2021)[35]

- Business associations ($2.7 billion and $121.5 million in 2021)[36]

- Oil and gas ($2.56 billion and $119.3 million in 2021)[37]

- Hospitals/nursing homes ($2.09 billion and $118.6 million in 2021)[38]

- Miscellaneous manufacturing ($2.07 billion and $105.1 million in 2021)[39]

If you add up the amounts spent by these eight industries, you get the astronomical sum of $23.54 billion, yet for many corporations the extraordinary cost is justified as a necessary expenditure to increase profits.

We have to distinguish between bribery and lobbying. Although both seek a favorable outcome, there is a subtle difference. While bribery is "considered an effort to buy power; paying to guarantee a certain result; lobbying is considered an effort to influence power, often by offering contributions."[40] The obvious difference, of course, is that bribery is illegal, and lobbying is not.

The difference rests on two words: "buy" versus "influence," though in both cases, money is used. Of course, whenever corporate money enters the political arena, the potential for corruption increases dramatically. Remember the Watergate scandal, which led to Richard Nixon's resignation as president? What you may not be aware of is that, as a result of Watergate, "the Securities and Exchange Commission (SEC) and the U.S. Department of Justice (DoJ) began investigating the sources of Nixon's illegal campaign contributions and discovered that hundreds of U.S. companies had bribery slush funds on hand in order to curry favor with legislators and other officials."[41] This massive and widespread form of corruption would lead to stricter rules governing the flow of money from corporations to politicians.

In 1977 Congress passed the Foreign Corrupt Practices Act (FCPA), which barred "corporations and some foreign companies operating in the U.S. from making such [briberies]."[42] If you think this act eliminated, or at the very least reduced, corporate corruption, think again. In 2008 Kellogg Brown & Root, now known as KBR, Inc., was charged by the Department of Justice with offenses under the FCPA, "including paying hundreds of millions of dollars to secure a natural gas plant construction contract to Nigerian officials."[43] KBR pleaded guilty and paid $402 million in fines, plus $177 million to the SEC. Its CEO, Jack Stanley, was also sentenced to 2.5 years in prison in 2012. This type of in-your-face corruption became even more widespread after 2010.

On January 21, 2010, the U.S. Supreme Court issued a ruling in *Citizens United v. Federal Election Commission* that overruled an earlier decision that prohibited independent expenditures by corporations.[44] In effect, this ruling freed corporations to fund political candidates and dark-money campaign committees, which are organizations that do not have to disclose the identity of their donors.[45] This fateful Supreme Court decision would open the floodgates of political campaign contributions.

Dark-money committees have "pumped billions of dollars into politics" from outside sources that are supposed to be unaffiliated from political candidates or parties.[46] Today, "wealthy donors flexed their expanded political power by injecting unprecedented sums into elections," all without having to report their identity.[47] In fact, since 2010 independent groups have spent the most amount of money in the history of U.S. elections. Hidden political forces like these are having an impact on market volatility, creating fear, uncertainty, and doubt—as well as a real risk to your money.

FROM HIDDEN FORCES TO REAL RISK

The overarching theme of this book is quite simple: The retirement system is broken as a result of our broken capitalist system. You can't separate these two ideas. In other words, if capitalism were working the way it should, we would not have a retirement crisis on our hands. We would also have far less inequality than we currently do, more people would have guaranteed pensions, and Social Security would not be threatened with insolvency by 2033.[48]

These hidden forces are important to understand because they lead to real economic and political risks. Your hard-earned money is impacted by them. It doesn't matter if your money is in a savings account, a 401(k) plan, stocks and bonds, or other investments, there are always risks to be aware of. The more you learn about the risks that affect your money, the better you will be at managing them.

CHAPTER 5

FROM HIDDEN FORCES TO ACTUAL RISK: RETIREMENT UNCERTAINTY

*"You must gain control over your money or
the lack of it will forever control you."*

—DAVE RAMSEY

Our complex, globally interconnected world is governed by hidden forces—political, economic, and financial. These forces are all around us, and if we are to better understand what our financial future—specifically our retirement future—will look like, we better understand them. Moreover, the risks associated with such forces are very real, because they impact what happens to our money.

Today, more than ever before, we need to grasp how these risks affect retirement planning. As the retirement burden has shifted to us, we need to better understand how political and economic risks influence how much money we save, our investment strategy, how much money to withdraw during retirement, when to start planning for retirement, and so on.

WHAT IS FINANCIAL RISK?

Risk in financial terms is "the chance that an outcome or investment's actual gains will differ from an expected outcome or return. Risk includes the possibility of losing some or all of an original investment."[1] In simpler terms, suppose you invest $100 in stocks. You are hoping or expecting that your initial investment will go up in value (perhaps to $130). However, after a period of time, your initial investment of $100 may drop to $70. The risk is that your outcome will be different from your expectation. Some of the things that can impact investment risk include the historical behavior of your assets (for example, stocks), as well as some technical measurements like standard deviation, which is a measure of volatility of asset prices in relation to historical averages.

Two of the most important macroeconomic risk factors affecting your hard-earned money are economic and political risk, but there are others as well—ideological risk, correlation risk, globalization risk, and others. These risks don't exist in isolation; rather, they interact with each other. I want to concentrate on economic and political risks because they have the potential to threaten Social Security, underfund pensions, and contribute to the possibility of investors potentially running out of money. Economic risk generally involves decreased government regulations, which shifts market control from government to corporations. Political risk involves tax policy that favors the wealthy few, as well as the Federal Reserve's practices of reducing or increasing interest rates to stimulate the economy or creating bailouts and buybacks at times of instability.

ECONOMIC RISK

Economic risk "refers to the likelihood that macroeconomic conditions (conditions in the whole economy) may affect an investment or a company's prospects domestically or abroad."[2] From a global perspective, economic risk may include government policy or regulations, political instability, fluctuations in exchange rates, and so on. We have seen that when you remove government regulations, you increase corporate greed, which may potentially impact your investment. Although it is easier to identify economic risk in hindsight, certain obvious historical conditions have contributed in the past. Recognizing these can help us understand and manage macroeconomic risks in the future.

For example, let's look at asset bubbles. The one thing that history has taught us about market bubbles is that they burst. In fact, evidence suggests that bubbles "accompanied by strong lending booms tend to be followed by more severe crises."[3] This happened during the 1920s when banks offered loans to people to purchase stocks and again during the early 2000s when banks and other lenders extended subprime loans to millions of Americans who they knew would default on them.

Historically, then, we can see the correlation between economic risk and deregulation. "Without regulation, a free market creates asset bubbles. That occurs when speculators bid up the prices of stocks, houses, and gold. When bubbles burst, they create crises and recessions."[4]

Deregulation is defined as a "reduction or elimination of government power in a particular industry, usually enacted to create more competition within the industry."[5] From my experience, people often assume there is a correlation between regulation/deregulation and political or ideological leanings—for example, that Republicans want less regulation and Democrats embrace greater regulations. This is a false narrative; both political parties have played an important role in the gradual deregulation of America's economy since the 1970s. The two leading think tanks—the Brookings Institution, which leans to the right, and the American Enterprise Institute, which leans to the left—both actively advocated for less regulation throughout the 1970s and 1980s. Academic economists on both sides were also influential.

As an example, Alfred E. Kahn, a Cornell University professor of economics and an expert on deregulation, was heavily involved in the Democratic Carter administration's efforts to deregulate transportation.[6] During the Republican

Nixon administration, a comprehensive proposal was designed to deregulate rail and truck transportation. Under the Reagan administration, a strong push was aimed at rolling back environmental regulations. Although Reagan "developed his anti-government ideas long before he ever met [Milton] Friedman," it was Friedman who gave him the ideological justification.[7]

Deregulation did not come only from Congress or presidential action. It also came from the Federal Reserve. In 1986 the Federal Reserve reinterpreted the Glass-Steagall Act and decided that 5 percent of a commercial bank's revenue could come from investment. In 1996 the Federal Reserve raised that to 25 percent. The following year the Federal Reserve ruled that commercial banks could engage in underwriting, which is the method by which corporations and governments raise capital in debt and equity markets. As you can see, the Glass-Steagall Act was gradually chipped away to the point where commercial banks and investment companies were now merging. In 1999, the Gramm-Leach-Bliley Act was passed under the Democratic Clinton administration, overturning Glass-Steagall completely.

We have already seen how repealing the Glass-Steagall Act in 1999 contributed to the dot-com bubble and market crash of 2002 and later the real estate bubble, which led to the financial crisis of 2008. Also part of the financial fiasco were high-yield bonds (known as junk bonds), which pay a higher interest rate because of their lower credit ratings. By 2008 junk bonds had lost a staggering 26.17 percent of their value in just one year.[8]

Two years after the financial crash of 2008, Congress passed the Dodd-Frank Act, which restricted subprime mortgage lending and derivatives trading. However, this example of government oversight would not last long. In May 2018 the Trump administration "exempted small and regional banks from Dodd-Frank's most stringent regulations and loosened rules put in place to prevent the sudden collapse of big banks."[9] Notably, this bill had bipartisan support; both Republicans and Democrats voted for it.

When Trump signed the Economic Growth Regulatory Relief and Consumer Protection Act in 2018, he essentially allowed banks to engage in risky investments. To be more precise, banks with less than $10 billion in assets no longer had to comply with the Volcker Rule, which prohibits banks from "conducting certain investments with their own accounts."[10] As some of these regulations are eased and certain banks are exempted, you start to create a regulatory environment that is similar to the 1920s when banks used depositors' money to engage in speculative stock market investments.

THE SEC AND STOCK BUYBACKS

Companies may increase economic risk by engaging in stock buybacks and stock options that affect their balance sheet inequitably. A **stock buyback**, also known as a "share repurchase," simply refers to a company's buying back its shares from the market using its own cash reserves.[11] One of the immediate benefits of a stock buyback is that a company effectively removes some of its stock shares from the market, reducing the number of outstanding shares and increasing the ownership stake of the stakeholders. There are also tax benefits to shareholders, whose share values are not taxed, as opposed to their dividend payments, which are taxed as income.

Stock options, which are sometimes used to attract employees to a company, are a form of compensation. **Stock options** "give an employee the right to buy, or exercise, a set number of shares of the company stock at a preset price, also known as the grant price."[12] Exercising a stock option simply means you can purchase the option stock at the exercise price.

In these cases, the term "employee" doesn't necessarily mean lower-level workers. Stock options are "offered to key employees and top management,"[13] and many of these executives receive preferential tax treatment, since the IRS treats gains on such options as long-term capital gains. The other, more important, benefit of stock options for company executives is that if a company's stock rises, their shares will also rise. This leads to some rather interesting connections between stock buybacks and executive stock options.

Kurt Andersen, in *Evil Geniuses*, poses an important question: "How much do executives, each being paid with stock and options worth millions and sometimes hundreds of millions, use buybacks simply to enrich themselves?"[14] According to Sarah Williamson, Ariel Babcock, and Allen He, in an article posted to the Harvard Law School Forum on Corporate Governance,

"The rise of buybacks has been riddled with controversy. Academics, practitioners, and politicians alike have maligned the use of buybacks, taking issue with their potential contribution to income inequality."[15] If you are wondering why there hasn't been any prosecution of companies engaged in such deceptive practices, the answer lies with the Securities and Exchange Commission (SEC).

In 1982 the SEC issued Rule 10B-18, whose aim was to reduce the liability for companies who repurchased shares of the company's common stock.[16] Here is the problem with this rule: It failed to "define what might constitute unacceptable deception of fraud when it came to buybacks, so in the [forty years] since, no company has been prosecuted for abusing the practice."[17] This is why, according to Andersen, as soon as a buyback becomes public, "the average executive sells five times as many of his or her shares as usual. 'When executives unload significant amounts of stock upon announcing a buyback, they often benefit from short-term price pops at the expense of long-term investors.'"[18] In other words, executives "use share buybacks to manipulate stock prices for their own benefit, and no one else's."[19]

BOEING BUYBACKS AND GOVERNMENT BAILOUTS

When the COVID-19 pandemic began in 2020, many industries were affected severely as a result of public health measures that were taken to mitigate the spread of this deadly virus. Because of border closures, travel restrictions, and wide-scale lockdowns, the airline industry was one of the hardest hit sectors. It would only be a matter of time before the Federal Reserve bailed out the airline industry, particularly companies like Boeing, whose corporate greed and mismanagement had left it strapped for cash during the emergency.

The idea of the government bailing out private corporations is nothing new. In 2008, during the height of the financial crisis, the Federal Reserve took steps to prevent the collapse of large financial institutions. As we've noted, banks such as Bear Stearns, Bank of America, Citigroup, and

AIG were considered "too big to fail," which prompted the $700 billion Emergency Economic Stabilization Act (EESA) of 2008. Similarly, when the 2020 pandemic-related economic shutdown occurred, "the Fed 'bailed out' companies to avoid failure. These were no longer 'financial institutions' getting bailed out either, but companies like Boeing (BA) . . . These companies [had] spent years using their capital and debt to execute 'share buybacks' to enrich insiders."[20]

Prior to the pandemic, Boeing and other airlines had spent "more than $90 billion in buying shares." Boeing alone spent more than $43 billion buying back stock in order to boost its share price.[21] This artificially inflated share price would benefit the company's top executives. Despite the fact that Boeing CEO David Calhoun "publicly announced that he would decline pay in 2020, he still received stock options with an estimated worth [in 2020] of $21 million."[22]

Before the government bailed out Boeing and other corporations, it did demand certain conditions. President Donald Trump, to his credit, agreed with Democrats that Boeing and other public corporations couldn't take taxpayer money to buy back their stock in order to increase its value.[23] Some of the other restrictions imposed by the government on the emergency loan programs included a limit on CEO pay, a halt to dividend payments, and a priority on employee retention and workers' payroll.[24]

Boeing and other companies like Exxon nevertheless managed to find a way to access government money without restrictions. As the pandemic economy came to a halt, the corporate debt market, controlled by the Federal Reserve, came to a halt as well. In 2020 the Federal Reserve announced it would "buy up to $20 billion in corporate debt to thaw out the frozen market."[25] This allowed companies to borrow money by selling off their debt.

It also allowed companies like Boeing and Exxon to avoid the restrictions on CEO salaries, the size of layoffs, and the protections on workers. They were able to engage in future stock buybacks as well. Not surprisingly, after Boeing secured billions of dollars in backdoor bailouts, the company cut more than 26,000 jobs and announced that future job cuts would be coming.[26]

CORPORATE CORRUPTION: FROM BALANCE SHEETS TO COOKING THE BOOKS

As we've seen, uncontrolled capitalism can create a corporate culture of greed, corruption, and fraud. **Corruption** is defined as "dishonest behavior by those in positions of power, such as managers or government officials. Corruption can include giving or accepting bribes or inappropriate gifts, double-dealing, under-the-table transactions, manipulating elections, diverting funds, laundering money, and defrauding investors."[27] The most important thing to understand about corruption, aside from the ethical considerations, is that it destabilizes the market.

Businesses will often justify corrupt practices by telling themselves it's the cost of doing business. In fact, large American corporations often do business across the globe, where corruption is a common practice. One of the largest examples of bribery had to do with Alcatel-Lucent SA, a giant French-American landline network. The case involved a "complex series of money transfers between shell companies and to consultants, resulting in payment being made to foreign officials."[28] (A shell corporation is a "corporation without active business operations or significant assets."[29] Although these corporations are not illegal, they are sometimes used illegitimately in order to disguise business ownership from law enforcement or the public.) In 2010 Alcatel-Lucent settled the bribery case with the Department of Justice by agreeing to pay $137 million, including $45 million to the SEC.

A more subtle form of corporate corruption is cooking the books—"the act of falsifying financial information about a company."[30] Why do it? A company may want to avoid paying taxes or wish to keep investors happy. Perhaps a company wants to see its stock price rise, attract new investors, or obtain a loan.[31] The most important reason a company may want to use this illegal activity is to "prove" to investors it is profitable. Cooking the books may also involve what are commonly referred to as "creative accounting" methods, which have become illegal since 2002. Below are some examples:

- Counting money intended for retirement pay as part of assets to offset large debts[32]

- Counting inventory that has already been sold[33]

- Recording extra expenses to raise customer confidence, even when a company can ill afford these extra expenses[34]

All these practices are essentially a form of deception designed to mislead potential investors. Some of the largest accounting scandals in American history have included Enron, WorldCom, Tyco, HealthSouth, Freddie Mac, AIG, Lehman Brothers, and Bernie Madoff.

In 2001 Enron Corporation, one of the largest U.S. energy, commodities, and services companies, used creative accounting methods to hide billions of dollars of bad debt, while simultaneously inflating the company's earnings. Once exposed, the scandal resulted in shareholders losing more than $74 billion; the share price went from $90 to less than $1 within a year. The following year, WorldCom, which was the second largest telecommunications company, inflated its assets by almost $11 billion. The scandal resulted in 30,000 job losses and $180 billion in losses by investors.

In the prosecutions that followed, Enron's CEO, Jeff Skillings, and former CEO Ken Lay were found guilty. Skillings was sentenced to 24 years in prison, and Lay died before serving any prison time. In the case of WorldCom, its CEO, Bernie Ebbers, was sentenced to 25 years in prison.[35]

U.S. TAX POLICY AND THE PERPETUATION OF GREED

There is something fundamentally wrong when billionaires pay significantly less in taxes (in terms of percentage) than average Americans. As you might imagine, most Americans do not have huge bank accounts to draw on. In fact, thanks to post pandemic inflation, "64 percent of Americans are living paycheck to paycheck."[36] Recently, the median household income was $70,000 annually. According to the tax code, this group paid 14 percent of their income in federal taxes.

The amount of federal taxes Americans must pay increases as income rises. For example, in 2021 "the highest income tax rate, 37 percent, kicked in this year [2021], for couples, on earnings above $628,300."[37] That seems reasonable. As income goes up, people should pay a higher percentage of taxes. The only problem is that as income gets into the hundreds of millions or billions of dollars, the tax burden decreases dramatically.

Here are some recent examples. On June 8, 2021, an explosive article by the nonprofit organization ProPublica revealed that Jeff Bezos, the richest man in the world at that time, "'did not pay a penny' in federal income taxes."[38] If you are thinking this must be an isolated incident, you would be wrong. Tesla founder Elon Musk, who was the second richest person in 2018, similarly paid zero federal income tax.

ProPublica conducted a groundbreaking analysis of the taxes paid by the 25 richest Americans—billionaires like Warren Buffett, Bill Gates, Rupert Murdoch, Mark Zuckerberg, Jeff Bezos, and Elon Musk—in relation to how much Forbes estimated their wealth had grown between 2014 and 2018. The results were astounding. Between 2014 and 2018 these Americans had a collective net worth of $401 billion. Over the same period, this group paid a total of $13.6 billion in federal income tax. While on the surface this seems to be a staggering sum, it only amounts to a true tax rate of 3.4 percent.[39]

How is this possible? It happens because the wealthiest 1 percent of Americans tend to have their wealth tied up in stocks, while the majority of Americans may have their money in a bank. Here are some disturbing numbers: "The wealthiest 1 percent of households in the U.S. own more than half of all the publicly-traded stock in the market, according to Federal Reserve Data, and the bottom 50 percent own less than 1 percent."[40] As the value of stocks continues to rise, the wealth of this overwhelmingly small group of Americans goes up dramatically. However, as long as they don't sell their stocks, they don't have to pay income taxes.

The ultrawealthy utilize other legal methods to bring down their income tax rates as well. These billionaires can afford to hire certified public accountants and tax lawyers to report "previous losses" or deduct their philanthropic giving. In fact, according to the Department of the Treasury, "the wealthiest Americans may be deducting as much as $163 billion in income taxes every year."[41] The ultrawealthy have the financial means to not only preserve their wealth, but to also expand their wealth across generations.

THE FEDERAL RESERVE

The Federal Reserve is one of the most powerful financial institutions in the world. Acting as the central bank of the United States, the Federal Reserve has a board of governors made up of seven individuals who are appointed by the president and voted upon by the Senate. These board members, who serve seven-year terms, have the following responsibilities:

- Analyze domestic and international economic development[42]

- Supervise and regulate the 12 Federal Reserve banks[43]

- Oversee America's payments system[44]

- Oversee and administer most consumer credit protection laws[45]

Although there had been early attempts to establish a central bank—Alexander Hamilton, the first secretary of the treasury, helped establish the first national bank, known as The Bank of the United States—the Federal Reserve system was established by Congress through the Federal Reserve Act, which was signed into law in 1913 by President Woodrow Wilson. The system "created the dual mandate to maximize employment and keep inflation low. The Federal Reserve was thus given the power over the money supply, and by extension, the economy."[46] Therefore, the Federal Reserve controls monetary policy, which includes the ability to regulate interest rates.

The Federal Reserve has used interest rate policy for decades to keep credit flowing. It does this by adjusting its target for the funds rate, which influences the short-term rates that banks charge each other for overnight loans.

THE FED BALANCE SHEET

For many years after the 2008 financial crisis, the Federal Reserve maintained artificially low interest rates through a process known as quantitative easing (QE) in which the Federal Reserve purchased large quantities of bonds or other securities on the open market. One result is that when interest rates are down, safe investments such as money market accounts, certificates of deposit (CDs), Treasury notes, and corporate bonds don't offer much in terms of a return. This forces investors to seek out riskier investments like stocks.[47] To fully grasp how quantitative easing works, it helps to understand the Federal Reserve balance sheet.

The Fed's balance sheet is "a statement listing the assets and liabilities of the Federal Reserve system. Details of the Fed's balance sheet are disclosed in a weekly report called 'Factors Affecting Reserve Balances.'"[48] During quantitative easing, the Federal Reserve purchases bonds, which reduces the supply of bonds in the open market, driving bond prices up and bond yields down and also increasing the assets on the Fed's balance sheet. After the financial crisis of 2008, the Fed's balance sheet increased to about $4.5 trillion in assets.

Before the COVID-19 pandemic, the Federal Reserve had begun to reduce its balance sheet. However, as a result of the pandemic, the balance sheet almost doubled to $9 trillion. Then in 2022, in response to the post-pandemic inflation, the Federal Reserve again started to shrink its balance sheet through a process called quantitative tightening (QT), which can raise interest rates and lead to chaos in the markets. Although it is difficult to know for sure what the effects of quantitative tightening will ultimately be, the Federal Reserve has been warning the market about its intentions to continue to raise interest rates.[49]

When the Federal Reserve increases interest rates, it unleashes a chain reaction of unpleasant events. Financial institutions have to pay more to borrow money from the government, and banks and other lending institutions pass on these higher rates to customers. Interest rates on credit cards and mortgages with variable interest rates go up, and that, along with double-digit inflation, means that households have less disposable income. As a result, business revenues and profits go down, limiting corporate profits and hindering growth, which can lower the price of stocks. As more companies' share prices drop, the entire stock market falls, along with key indexes like the Dow Jones Industrial Average and the S&P 500. As the economy slows down, it enters a recession.

Although you might be tempted to blame one political party over another for these events, in fact both parties are culpable.

THE POLITICS OF NEOLIBERALISM

Republicans and Democrats alike have played a significant role in increasing economic risk. Although Republicans embraced neoliberalism during the 1970s, by the 1990s the Democrats "celebrated deregulation as an economic good that resulted when governments could no longer interfere with the operations of markets. It hailed globalization as a win-win position that would enrich the West (the cockpit of neoliberalism) while also bringing an unprecedented prosperity to the rest of the world."[50]

The political elites of both parties agreed that deregulation was the best thing to happen since sliced bread. As Kurt Andersen points out in *Evil Geniuses*, "The Washington left was tweaking and improving the political economy in good faith, finding common ground with the reasonable good-faith Washington right, which still existed."[51] Both political parties accepted the idea that less regulation was a good thing for capitalism to thrive. But if both political parties shared the same political economic outlook, then what separated the left from the right?

What happened was the development of two very different moral directions. On the right, conservatives have embraced what is sometimes referred to as a "neo-Victorian" moral framework, which celebrates "self-reliance, strong families, and disciplined attitudes toward work, sexuality, and consumption."[52] On the left, a more liberal set of moral principles include an acknowledgment of our racist past, feminism, multiculturalism, and an overall sense of pluralism and gender freedom. Despite these differences, however, both perspectives have embraced a free-market-style capitalism that creates economic risk.

POLITICAL RISK

It is time to examine the role of political risk. Remember, there is always a "degree of uncertainty and/or potential financial loss inherent in an investment decision. In other words, whenever you invest your money, you don't know for sure if you'll receive the desired returns or experience unexpected losses."[53] Understanding different types of risks can potentially help you manage the degree of uncertainty or loss in your investment decisions.

Political risk refers to the "political decisions within a country that might result in an unanticipated loss to investors."[54] Since we live in a globalized world, political risk, also known as geopolitical risk, refers to the instability affecting investment returns that result from a "change in government, legislative bodies, other foreign policymakers or military control."[55] While it is important for you to understand geopolitical risk, particularly when you invest in companies that deal with other nations, my emphasis on political risk involves *domestic* political decisions.

DOMESTIC POLITICAL RISK

Very little has been written about domestic political risk. In my research the closest thing I found was a scholarly article from 1982 about the relationship between domestic political risk and the valuation of stocks. So I'm going to introduce my own definition: **Domestic political risk** refers to the political decisions and actions of government institutions such as Congress, the Federal Reserve, Department of the Treasury, and other domestic agencies that can potentially impact your investments.

I've already discussed the Department of the Treasury's corporate bailouts and the Federal Reserve's policy of quantitative easing. We've also seen how decisions of government have affected the stock market and led to bubbles that burst with disastrous consequences.

In considering your strategy for retirement you should be aware that market bubbles are cyclical. In fact, there is something known as the bubble theory, which states that "market prices, especially commodity, real estate, and financial asset prices, occasionally experience rapidly rising prices as investors begin buying beyond what may seem like rational prices."[56]

Although the market bubble theory is a perfectly rational explanation of how bubbles form, let me introduce another idea that will help you understand these bubbles. I call this idea the Universal Law of Controlled Greed (ULCG). I'm calling it "controlled greed" because market bubbles form in an economic environment that is controlled (or manipulated) by a powerful force like the Federal Reserve. When this powerful force creates the conditions that make it easy and cheap to borrow money, our irrational exuberance, which is basically greed, takes over our decision-making, and we buy. As prices go up, bubbles form, which leads to a crash. The Universal Law of Controlled Greed points out that things do not typically end well for those who are highly exposed to bubble formation.

Ultimately the politics behind these events affect your retirement. Let's say you are five to ten years from retirement, and like millions of people, you utilize the 60/40 investment strategy, with 60 percent of your assets in stocks and 40 percent in bonds. Low interest rates make it cheap for you to borrow money and purchase more stocks, which continue to rise in price. When the stock market bubble bursts, however, you lose a substantial amount of your investment.

Think of bonds as shock absorbers for your portfolio. When stocks go down, bonds can pick up the slack. But in a low-interest-rate environment, low-yield bonds won't provide enough for retirement. The answer is to explore diversification and alternative asset classes that can potentially mitigate your losses.

How Economic and Political Risk May Have Contributed to Fear and Uncertainty

- : https://money.yahoo.com/retirement-americans-run-out-money-214436546.html

Macroeconomics can help you understand political and economic risk.

THE POLITICS OF MISDIRECTION

Both Democrats and Republicans have contributed to the retirement crisis. From the trickle-down Reaganomics of the 1980s, Clinton's North American Free Trade Agreement (NAFTA), and the repeal of the Glass-Steagall Act to the greed behind the dot-com bubble and the fraudulent subprime loans that led to the global financial crisis of 2008, both parties have been culpable. And although Republicans and Democrats alike have presented themselves as the champions of average Americans, they are all guilty of the politics of misdirection. While both political parties have been busy blaming each other for everything from economics to family values, most Americans have been struggling to make ends meet.

There is an economic reality behind the headlines. Your retirement future, in large part, depends on your understanding the hidden forces and risks that can potentially derail your retirement future. Remember, the retirement burden is now on your shoulders. The more knowledge you gain, the more potential you have to improve your retirement future.

PART II

A NEW WAY
OF INVESTING

CHAPTER 6

FROM A THREE-LEGGED STOOL TO A FOUR-LEGGED CHAIR

"It's not the days in life we remember,
rather the moments."

—WALT DISNEY

For several generations, the three-legged stool—Social Security, pensions, and financial initiatives by individual workers—has defined our retirement model. From the early 1940s to the early 1980s, the retirement burden rested upon Social Security and pensions. Since the 1980s, however, that has shifted to the individual. The days of working for the same company for much of your life, then retiring with a pension and Social Security have become the stuff of nostalgia. Unfortunately, when the retirement burden shifted to the individual, people were not prepared. Both the federal government and the private sector have failed to help the American people improve their financial literacy.

The old social contract promised American workers a relatively secure retirement in exchange for decades of loyal and dutiful work. The government offered Social Security, and the private sector provided pensions. Average Americans didn't need financial knowledge in order to secure their retirement. Now Americans have been left to their own devices to plan for retirement, but their financial awareness has remained unchanged.

In my first book, *Redefining Financial Literacy*, I argued that Americans lack the financial literacy necessary to thrive in a complex, globally interconnected world. According to a June 2022 *New Reality Check: Paycheck to Paycheck Report*, 61 percent of Americans overall were living paycheck to paycheck . . . in other words, almost two-thirds of the U.S. population, or about 157 million people, have little to nothing left over at the end of the month."[1] I believe the lack of financial literacy is a root cause.

One glaring reason why Americans struggle with financial literacy is that our educational system does not take it seriously. Only seven U.S. states require high school students to take a personal finance course in order to graduate.[2] That is shameful.

Society seems to be telling us that we are responsible for our own retirement, but it will not help equip us with the basic knowledge necessary to navigate our complex financial landscape, which would enable us to have the retirement we deserve. That is one of the fundamental messages of this book: The silent retirement crisis is the result of a broken social contract. So we have to ask: What have people been doing to plan and prepare for retirement?

WHY THE 60/40 MODEL IS POTENTIALLY DEAD

To deal with their retirement burden, most individuals have come to rely on the 60/40 investment model. It remains the dominant investment philosophy; though, as you'll see, it is potentially dead. The 60/40 portfolio means you invest 60 percent of your money in stocks and 40 percent in bonds. Part of what makes this strategy attractive to both average investors and professional financial advisors is the ease by which you allocate your hard-earned money. The simple-to-use model is static. There is no need to change or adjust your asset allocation. You "set it and forget it."

The 60/40 portfolio is based loosely on the rigorous academic work of the Nobel Prize–winning economist Harry Markowitz. In 1952 Markowitz published "Portfolio Selection" in *The Journal of Finance*. This single academic paper introduced Modern Portfolio Theory to economists and would fundamentally change the way people and institutions invested.

The reason the 60/40 stock-bond formula worked well was because of negative correlation. This occurs when one variable (say, stocks) moves in the opposite direction of another variable (say, bonds). For many years this negative correlation between stocks and bonds held up, and individual and institutional investors enjoyed great returns. That's because, with 60 percent of assets in stocks there was an unnecessarily high exposure to a volatile asset; the 40 percent in bonds was designed to protect against losses from stock market volatility.

Here is an example: Suppose the stock market is going well and you are making excellent returns. In this scenario, bond yields, which are negatively correlated to stocks, will have lower yields. Now look at the opposite case. Stocks are going down. This is where the 40 percent in bonds offers some protection, since bond yields would move up. Now if stocks and bonds have a positive correlation, meaning they move in the same direction, then investors have no protection against risk. Another way to think of negative correlation is that stocks and bonds hedge each other.

Stocks and bonds are positively or negatively correlated because they reflect macroeconomic conditions. Some of these conditions include interest rates, inflation, gross domestic product (GDP), unemployment, trade wars, and so on. Economic conditions are often cyclical in nature, which suggests that the 60/40 portfolio will experience periods of low, or even negative, returns.

During the Lost Decade (2000–2009) the 60/40 portfolio returned a meager 2.3 percent, and when you adjust for inflation, the real return was an alarming negative .3 percent.[3] From 2011 to 2021, the 60/40 approach generated an impressive 11.1 percent nominal return and, after adjusting for inflation, that was a 9.1 percent real return.[4] But it would be a grave error to assume these types of returns will continue throughout the 2020s. As the saying goes, you can't assume that past performance will predict future outcomes.

The 60/40 model, it hasn't been working so well recently: From January 2022 to June 2022, the 60/40 portfolio was "down nearly 18 percent . . . [which] is the worst start to a year since 1976, according to an analysis from Bespoke Investment Group."[5] Moreover, according to the professionals at Bank of America, Morgan Stanley, and J.P. Morgan, the 60/40 portfolio is dead.[6]

A PARADIGM SHIFT AWAY FROM 60/40

There are some important reasons why the 60/40 portfolio may not be an effective investment strategy moving forward. These reasons include:

- Increased positive correlation between stocks and bonds

- Interest rates

- Increased volatility

- Sequence-of-return risk

- Lower withdrawal rates

Increased positive correlation will occur whenever there is inflation and slow growth, which is why in 2022, and possibly beyond, stocks and bonds will move positively to each other.[7] Inflation during the first half of 2022 was the worst since 1970.[8]

When inflation occurs and the Federal Reserve raises interest rates to bring it under control, corporations find it difficult to raise capital, which means they cut back on growth. Profit expectations are revised downward, and future cash flows drop. This ultimately leads to stock prices dropping.[9] Also, when interest rates rise, bond prices fall. Higher interest rates are not an attractive financial environment for the 60/40 portfolio.

When the Federal Reserve takes an aggressive stance to combat inflation, the stock market becomes more volatile. Remember, stock market volatility reflects the degree to which stock prices move. A stock whose price fluctuates wildly—hitting new highs and lows or moving erratically—is considered highly volatile,[10] posing a greater risk for the investor.

Age	INVESTOR A "UP" MARKET			INVESTOR B "DOWN" MARKET		
	5% Annual withdrawals	Annual return	Year end value	5% Annual withdrawals	Annual return	Year end value
60	——	——	$1,000,000	——	——	$1,000,000
61	$50,000	5%	$1,000,000	$50,000	-25%	$700,000
62	$50,000	28%	$1,230,000	$50,000	-14%	$552,000
63	$50,000	22%	$1,450,600	$50,000	-10%	$446,800
64	$50,000	-5%	$1,328,070	$50,000	16%	$446,288
65	$50,000	20%	$1,543,684	$50,000	21%	$516,628
66	$50,000	19%	$1,786,984	$50,000	5%	$492,460
67	$50,000	23%	$2,147,990	$50,000	-16%	$363,666
68	$50,000	9%	$2,291,309	$50,000	8%	$342,760
69	$50,000	16%	$2,607,919	$50,000	14%	$340,746
70	$50,000	23%	$3,157,740	$50,000	24%	$372,525
71	$50,000	22%	$3,802,443	$50,000	14%	$374,679
72	$50,000	-26%	$2,763,808	$50,000	5%	$343,412
73	$50,000	-15%	$2,299,237	$50,000	-15%	$241,901
74	$50,000	5%	$2,364,199	$50,000	-26%	$129,006
75	$50,000	14%	$2,645,186	$50,000	22%	$107,338
76	$50,000	24%	$3,230,031	$50,000	23%	$82,087
77	$50,000	14%	$3,632,235	$50,000	16%	$45,221
78	$50,000	8%	$3,872,814	$45,221	9%	$0
79	$50,000	-16%	$3,203,164	$0	23%	$0
80	$50,000	5%	$3,313,322	$0	19%	$0
81	$50,000	21%	$3,959,120	$0	20%	$0
82	$50,000	16%	$4,542,579	$0	-5%	$0
83	$50,000	-10%	$4,038,321	$0	22%	$0
84	$50,000	-14%	$3,422,956	$0	28%	$0
85	$50,000	-25%	$2,517,217	$0	5%	$0

The table above is a hypothetical chart of investing $1,000,000 in an "up" market and a "down" market.

The 60/40 portfolio is also affected by what's known as sequence-of-return risk, an important consideration when planning for retirement. **Sequence-of-return risk** is "the risk of receiving lower or negative returns early in a period when withdrawals are made from an investment portfolio."[11] In other words, the timing of your withdrawal, particularly during retirement, is potentially risky. Let's suppose you are retired, and you start withdrawing assets during a bear market, when stock performance is falling. Your portfolio will run out of money. The best way to understand sequence-of-return risk is through an example.

The table shows a hypothetical $1 million investment in stocks and bonds, in a 60/40 stock-and-bond portfolio. The table examines what happens to a million dollars invested (the nature of the investment is not relevant here) over a 25-year period. Investor A begins to withdraw a fixed 5 percent of the initial $1 million until she reaches the age of 85 (25 years). The left side of the table represents Investor A who begins to withdraw her money during a bull (up) market. On the right side of the table is investor B who begins to withdraw his money during a bear (down) market. Notice that after 25 years, investor A has a balance of $2,517,217. I want you to contrast this with investor B, who by year 18 has balance of $0. The important point that you need to understand is that when you decide to withdraw your money will determine how much you have left after a set number of years. You need to consider the economic environment before you decide to withdraw. If it is a bull (up) market, you will potentially have more money at the end of your withdraw cycle than what you started with. Conversely, if you withdraw you money during a bear (down) market, you may potentially lose your entire principle at some point.

Another problem with the 60/40 portfolio is the "4 percent withdrawal rule." This guideline was created in the 1990s by California financial planner William Bengen. In 1994 "Bengen recommended a 4 percent withdrawal rate in tax-deferred accounts for the first year of a 30-year retirement, making adjustments in subsequent years according to inflation."[12] If you're thinking a 4 percent withdrawal rate is unrealistic in today's economic environment with hyperinflation, then brace yourself. For those retirees who will depend on cash savings, the maximum withdrawal rate is 2.7 percent. If your investment is all in stocks, then your maximum withdrawal rate is 2.9 percent. Last, if you have a portfolio that has 40 to 60 percent in stocks, your withdrawal rate is 3.3 percent.[13] Clearly the 60/40 portfolio will not get you the withdrawal rate you will need throughout your retirement years.

To recap, now that the retirement burden has shifted to individuals, the three-legged stool is not viable. What's needed is a fourth leg to create stability and continuity. This fourth leg is a financial advisor who will help you prepare for retirement. The advisor, however, has to understand different investment portfolios, including alternative investment strategies, not just the 60/40 portfolio. The 60/40 split offered strong returns for many years, but it may not offer the same robust returns going forward as it once did.

LOOKING AHEAD

It's vital that we move from a broken three-legged stool to a stable four-legged chair.

First, we can no longer rely on Social Security, which may go insolvent by 2034, at which time retirees will receive a smaller portion of their benefits.[14]

Second, pensions are both underfunded and largely utilize the potentially ineffective 60/40 portfolio. That approach to investing may no longer offer you protection in today's market conditions. Retirees and those approaching retirement are today not only dealing with 40-year-high inflation "but also the 'biggest shock to their retirement portfolios since the worst stretches of the Financial Crisis.'"[15]

In both a low-interest-rate environment—like the one prior to COVID, where the Federal Reserve kept interest rates artificially low—or a high-interest-rate environment (which is what we have in 2023), the 60/40 portfolio may fail many of your retirement dreams. According to the Employee Benefit Research Institute, 40 percent of all U.S. households, where the head of the household is between 35 and 64, are expected to run short of money in retirement.[16]

Which brings us to the third leg of the retirement stool—the individual. Though your financial literacy may have been minimal in the past, you can alter that. You have powerful choices that can potentially offer you consistent growth and better income, while managing risk. I call this new investment mind-set DIG, which is an acronym for:

Diversification

Income

Growth

If the 60/40 portfolio today is demonstrably ineffective as a vehicle for sustained income, then diversification is the answer. Diversification will offer you assets that go beyond the traditional stocks, bonds, and cash. These new assets, which have recently been made available to the average investor, are known as alternative investments.

To navigate this new financial landscape, you need to hire a qualified and experienced financial planner who can help you understand portfolio construction, diversification, asset allocation, and other more complex investment strategies. This financial professional is the fourth leg of a stable chair.

As an investor, it's important to remember that you can't control hidden macro forces like inflation, low interest rates, wars, oil prices, supply chain problems, and so on. However, you *can* control asset allocation that takes diversification and alternative assets into account.

CHAPTER 7

DAVID SWENSEN AND UNIVERSITY ENDOWMENTS

"I believe the greatest teachers
create thinking students."

—DAVID F. SWENSEN

The idea that hidden forces affect our financial decisions, particularly investment decisions, is shared by some of the biggest institutional investors in history. Have you ever wondered how America's Ivy League universities grow their money to build more facilities, maintain high levels of academic excellence, offer scholarships to disadvantaged students, and ensure that their university will be around for years to come? The answer is that they do it through university endowments. Endowments don't just rely on donations from alumni and the general public; rather, they invest their money to generate greater returns. Universities hire experts to manage their endowment funds.

Yale University's endowment fund manager—the late David Swensen

One of the best people to do that was Yale University's endowment manager, David Swensen. When Swensen took the job in 1985, the fund was valued at $1.3 billion. Since that time "it has grown to $31.2 billion, passing those at both Princeton and the University of Texas and trailing only Harvard."[1] With returns like these, Swensen, who died on May 5, 2021, became the most sought-after financial guru in the academic world. His impact and influence were so far reaching that many of his apprentices have gone on to run endowments at other schools and nonprofits.

Although Swensen was not a household name, he generated astronomical returns for Yale. An academic who held a PhD in economics, Swensen turned Yale's investment methodology on its head. Prior to 1985 Yale largely followed the 60/40 investment model, which offered predictable results without significant growth. Swensen quickly realized that the key to generating greater returns while managing risk was diversification. He started by investing "in all kinds of things: real estate, timber, shampoo, and soap companies in Asia. He put seed money into technology start-up companies . . . Basically, he built a table with 10 legs: very stable even if a few legs get wobbly or fall off."[2] Swensen operated on a set of beliefs that guided him toward unimaginable success.

David Swensen believed that "the knowledge base that provides useful support for investment decisions knows no bounds. A rich understanding of human psychology, a reasonable appreciation of financial theory, a deep awareness of history, and a broad exposure to current events all contribute to development of well-informed portfolio strategies."[3] As you can see, Swensen was talking about the hidden forces that can potentially affect stock prices—volatility, how much interest you will pay on your home mortgage, car loans, the gas you put in your car, the food you put on the table, and a host of other financial transactions. When it comes to retirement, which involves long-term planning, it is important to have a good understanding of these forces.

DAVID SWENSEN'S INVESTMENT PHILOSOPHY

David Swensen was one of the first to adapt the Modern Portfolio Theory to the multibillion-dollar juggernaut that is the Yale Endowment Fund. Swensen recognized that university endowments have a much longer time horizon than individual investors. Rather than focus on the reactive, short-term approach of the stock market, "Swensen delved into private assets, which afford greater access to management, and insight into their strategies as well as value drivers. He realized that private assets that required rigorous research and have no active exchange offered a premium to patient investors who could forgo the need for immediate liquidity."[4]

In other words, what Swensen realized was that long-term financial security was possible when institutional investors, including university endowments, diversify their portfolios by adding alternative asset classes. Swensen, along with his longtime collaborator, Dean Takahashi, expanded the 60/40 portfolio to include alternative assets "such as hedge funds, real estate, timber, and private equity."[5]

Ten years before taking over the endowment fund, Swensen had been a graduate student studying economics at Yale. One of his advisors was the Nobel Prize–winning economist James Tobin, who, along with Harry Markowitz, influenced Swensen's investment ideas. During a 2018 reunion speech, Swensen had this to say about his diversified portfolio: "For a given level of return, if you diversify you can get that return at lower risk. For a given level of risk, if you diversify you can get a higher return. That's pretty cool! Free lunch!"[6]

Swensen's view of the relationship between diversification and level of risk comes from Tobin's portfolio selection theory, which seems commonsensical but still had to be proven mathematically. Tobin argued that "investors balance high-risk, high-return investments with safer ones so as to achieve a balance in their portfolios."[7] That means if you diversify your investment by adding alternative asset classes, you can get strong returns while lowering risk. Or, for a given level of risk, you can get higher levels of returns.

This sounds very simple, but the devil is in the details.

Swensen not only had to find viable alternative assets, but he also had to determine what percentage to assign to each asset class. He had to balance safe assets like bonds and real estate with more risky assets like U.S. stocks, international stocks, and emerging markets. Below is a sample allocation devised by David Swensen. Keep in mind that it is for a large university endowment.

Here's the sample Yale model:

- 30 percent in the total U.S. stock market—30 percent of assets held in the portfolio are invested in a highly diversified U.S. stock exchange-traded fund (ETF) with exposure to a wide range of sectors and stocks with various market caps.

- 15 percent in the international stock market—15 percent of the portfolio's assets are invested in an investment-grade fund that's centered around international stocks across a variety of regions, sectors, and market caps.

- 5 percent in emerging markets—while investing in emerging markets can be risky, it can also be a source of significant growth. Swensen allocated 5 percent of the portfolio to these opportunities in order to tap into the profit potential without accepting too much risk across the portfolio as a whole.

- 20 percent in real estate—20 percent of the portfolio is invested in real estate by way of real estate investment trusts (REITs). These funds attract funding from a large group of investors to purchase real estate like office buildings, apartment buildings, cell towers, and other infrastructure. When the owned real estate is leased, profits are divided among investors.

- 15 percent in intermediate-term Treasury bonds—getting into the fixed-income side of the portfolio, 15 percent of the portfolio's assets are invested in intermediate-term Treasury debt securities. These are generally U.S. Treasury bonds with terms between 3 and 10 years.

- 15 percent in Treasury inflation-protected securities—the final 15 percent of the portfolio's assets are invested in Treasury inflation-protected securities (TIPS), which generally increase with inflation and decrease with deflation, hence the term "inflation-protected."[8]

Swensen's investment philosophy, which has come to be known as Swensen's Approach, is unique in that it "stresses allocation of capital in Treasury inflation protection securities, bonds, real estate funds, emerging market stocks, domestic stocks, and developing world international equities."[9] The key aspect is **asset allocation**, which "refers to the long-term decision regarding the proportion of assets that an investor chooses to place in particular classes of investments."[10]

In his 2005 book *Unconventional Success*, Swensen writes, "Asset-allocation decisions play a central role in determining investor results. A number of well-regarded studies of institutional portfolios conclude that approximately 90 percent of the variability of returns stems from asset allocation, leaving approximately 10 percent of the variability to be determined by security selection and market timing."[11]

The endowment portfolio philosophy is "based on high allocations to alternative assets," which are largely responsible for Swensen's success.[12] It is important to note that many of these alternative assets that Swensen utilized were, until very recently, not available to the retail (average) investor. For a long time, they were only available to high-net-worth individuals and large institutional investors like university endowments.

Over his 35-year tenure as Yale's endowment manager, Swensen consistently outperformed the stock market with considerably less risk. In their book *The Ivy Portfolio*, Mebane Faber and Eric Richardson offer powerful evidence to support Swensen's endowment model. "Not only did the Yale endowment outperform stocks by over 4 percent per year, it did so with 33 percent less volatility and only one losing year (a measly -.2 percent in 1988)."[13] In addition, the Yale endowment model has consistently outpaced inflation.

The net result is that endowment managers reap income from multiple asset classes, as well as multiple strategies. If one asset or strategy falters, it can be adjusted without impacting the portfolio as a whole. The success of university endowment funds is staggering: "The top 20 endowments grew more than 9 percent annually on a real basis (after inflation) between 1992 and 2005. As of 2007, the two largest endowments, belonging to Yale and Harvard, have grown to $35 billion and $22 billion in size, respectively."[14] These results also suggest that the rich universities are getting richer while the rest of the schools are falling behind.[15]

Endowments have similarly outperformed corporate pension funds over the same period. This success was partly due to the fact that the "share of alternative [asset classes] rose from 11 to 21 percent."[16] As endowments continued to become more diversified by investing in alternative assets, fees concomitantly declined, thus making them more affordable for everyone, including the individual investor.

Swensen created his endowment approach in part to mitigate against the inherent risk of stock market fluctuations, as well as to hedge against inflation due to low interest rates on bonds. What makes the endowment strategy such a powerful investment vehicle is the flexibility and malleability of its multi-asset class allocation structure. The endowment model offers institutional investors customizable strategic balance to meet long-term needs. Similarly, the retail investor may potentially benefit from a customized model that can be suitable for long-term retirement goals.

The endowment strategy is predicated upon two important factors: First, a wide variety of assets that are designed and managed to deliver results across different time horizons, and second, rebalancing. This rebalancing protects the endowment portfolio against market turbulence and unforeseen punctuated moments of market volatility.

Rebalancing investments may cause investors to incur transaction costs and, when rebalancing a non-retirement account, taxable events will be created that may increase your tax liability. Rebalancing a portfolio cannot assure a profit or protect against a loss in any given market environment.

Endowments also plan for, and anticipate, timely exits within each type of investment, while fulfilling the income needs of the investor. They do this by reallocating asset classes. For example, the Yale Endowment Fund "dramatically reduced the Endowment's dependence on domestic marketable securities by reallocating assets to nontraditional asset classes."[17]

This forward-thinking strategy enables endowments to support both income and longevity. Individual investors, however, should consult with a qualified and experienced financial advisor before adapting the endowment model to their own situation. It is also incumbent upon every financial advisor to confirm that individual investors are suitable for the endowment-like model as a complement to a broader portfolio.

Certainly these strategies hold lucrative potential for individual investors. One of the important benefits of the endowment approach is the possibility of offering individual investors more income over a longer retirement. Given that we are living longer, we must start to think like the large institutional endowments, which operate under the assumption they will be around forever. As an individual investor, your goal is to support your own time horizon. To do that, you need a diversified approach.

CHAPTER 8

ALTERNATIVE INVESTMENTS AND WHY WE NEED THEM

"The true depth of understanding and maturity as a practitioner is how we apply what we've learned to our lives."

—DAVID F. SWENSEN

I t's time to take a deep dive into alternative investments—what they mean, their history, and how they fit in a multi-asset-class portfolio. An **alternative investment** is a "financial asset that does not fall into one of the conventional investment categories. Conventional categories include stocks, bonds, and cash. Alternative investments can include private equity or venture capital, hedge funds, managed futures . . . commodities, and derivative contracts. Real estate is also often classified as an alternative investment."[1]

David Swensen, as fund manager for the Yale University Endowment, began by lowering the fund's percentage allocated to stocks and bonds, reducing each to 15 percent. With the combined allocation of 30 percent in stocks and bonds, he had 70 percent to allocate to alternative investments. This approach worked out quite well; the Yale Endowment Fund went from $1 billion in 1985 to $31 billion in 2020.[2]

Be advised that alternative investments are speculative by nature and have various risks including possible lack of liquidity, lack of control, changes in business conditions, and devaluation based on the investment, the economy, and/or regulatory changes. As a result, the values of alternative investments do fluctuate resulting in the value at sale being more or less than the original price paid if a liquid market for the securities is found.

The recent popularity of alternative investments has allowed the retail investor the opportunity to invest like billion-dollar institutions. Although this is a recent phenomenon, investing in instruments other than stocks, bonds, or cash has a long history. From commodity trading that originated around 4500 BC to the speculative Dutch tulip bubble in the mid-1600s and onward, people have always explored alternative investments. The use of alternative investments as structured financial mechanisms, though, occurred much more recently. Andrew Winslow Jones is credited with developing the first hedge fund in 1940, and less than 10 years later, private venture capital was introduced. By 1960 the first real estate investment trust, which I'll discuss later in this chapter, was created.[3]

THE DEMOCRATIZATION OF OPPORTUNITY

Political democracy, at least in its idealized form, is designed to offer all citizens an equal opportunity to participate. When it came to investing, however, the financial world was far from democratic. Average Americans were excluded from the same potential opportunities that made a small group of wealthy individuals and institutions ultrarich. I'm not suggesting there was any kind of conspiracy. Rather, there were systemic problems that had to be resolved before alternative investments became available to a wider pool of retail investors.

Some of the reasons alternative investments were reserved for institutional investors and high-net-worth individuals included lack of technology, mathematical limitations, and lack of regulations. The thinking at the time was that financial players like pension funds and university endowments were better suited to understanding and managing the complex, highly risky, and apparently illiquid investments.

Then, at the turn of the 21st century, something changed the paradigm of alternative investments. On the eve of the digital revolution, two forces converged—mathematics and computing power—in such a way as to open up alternative investments to everyone. For example, the development of Gaussian copula theorems in 2000 helped investors price complex financial products such as derivatives and structured securities.[4]

Before the year 2000, institutional investors had to deal with the problem of pricing certain asset classes and structured securities, and most computers were still not powerful enough to handle massive amounts of data. In my opinion, however, the belief that ultrarich investors, endowments, pension funds, and so on were better able to understand and manage the complex, often high risk, and illiquid nature of alternative investments was misguided. While it is true that institutional investors and ultrarich individuals had the resources to deal with the complex issues of alternative investments, I believe the retail investor should have had the same access and opportunity to invest as the big players.

To be fair, the financial literacy of average Americans was at the lower end of the spectrum in relation to other industrialized nations. Americans were simply not very good at understanding simple financial concepts, let alone complex financial instruments. Nevertheless, there were pioneering financial experts, such as myself and others, who engaged in rigorous research and study to master complex financial structures. Despite the fact that some financial experts were in a position to construct multi-asset portfolios for retail clients, government regulations enabled the large institutions and ultrarich investors to basically keep their monopoly on alternative investments.[5]

When it came to real estate investment trusts (REITs), it took an act of Congress to make them possible. The Federal Real Estate Investment Trust (REIT) Act was signed by President Eisenhower in 1960. It "blended the features of real estate and stock-based investing to establish a new means of generating income."[6] Other regulations would follow.

For example, following the 1974 stock market crash, the **Employee Retirement Income Security Act (ERISA)** became a federal law "that sets minimum standards for most voluntary established retirement and health plans in private industry to provide protection for individuals in these plans."[7] Four years later ERISA was updated to lift earlier restrictions that kept pension funds from investing in privately held securities, which meant pensions could now invest in alternative investments on behalf of their workers.[8] Some of the problems that led to the enactment of ERISA included pension plan mismanagement and downright corruption.

THE IVORY TOWER

If there is one thing that connects university endowments, pensions (which themselves are large institutional investors), and high-net-worth individuals, it is that they all operate in an ivory tower, removed from the realities faced by average Americans. The term has often been used in a derogatory manner to suggest that anyone who studies, teaches, or does research in a university is somehow sheltered or insulated from the harsh reality of everyday life. I want to make it clear, though, that I'm not using the ivory tower label in a pejorative manner. After all, much of our knowledge about Modern Portfolio Theory, Swensen's Yale Endowment model, general economic theories, political theories, history, and so on, comes from the ivory tower. There are times, however, when knowledge developed in the ivory tower is slow to reach the average person. The theoretical knowledge that was largely developed by economists— for example, in Harry Markowitz's 1952 paper "Portfolio Selection"—did not reach a wider audience until five decades later.

I believe that there are occasions when we have to push the ivory tower to bring their innovations to the rest of us. It bothers me greatly that universities used their own research and knowledge about investing to benefit only themselves. Inequality has always been a problem for capitalism, and if the ivory tower found an investment strategy that worked, efforts should have been made to spread this knowledge to average Americans.

By the mid-2000s I was certain that I didn't want to continue using the 60/40 portfolio as an investment model. After reading Swensen's *Pioneering*

Portfolio Management, I knew that adding alternative structures was the answer I was waiting for. One problem, of course, was the lack of available alternative assets for the retail investor. But I knew that I could use REITs, since they had been available since 1960.

There are two types of REITs: traded REITs and nontraded REITs. Publicly traded REITs trade on an exchange just like stocks. One of their attractive qualities is a low barrier of entry, which means that average investors can take advantage of them. (If an asset class becomes available but the barrier of entry is $100,000, then you still exclude millions of people from investing.) Nontraded REITs, as the name implies, do not trade on an exchange. They are illiquid in the sense that investors have to hold their investment for a longer period of time. Also, nontraded REITs used to have a high entry point; however, by 2017, the Blackstone Group, which is the largest investment firm in the world, offered a nontraded REIT with an entry point of $2,500.[9] Once this alternative asset became available, I added it to my clients' portfolios.

Another asset class that started to become popular in 2009 was business development companies (BDCs), which invest in small- and medium-size companies. What made BDCs popular with the retail investor were high profit potential, diversification, and transparency.

I spent endless hours on the phone with various companies asking about the different products they offered. I wanted to know when they might lower the barrier of entry for the average investor. My task over the years has been to actively find low-barrier-of-entry asset classes that would be suitable for my clients. In many ways, I was at the forefront of bringing the ivory tower down to earth.

JIMMY HOFFA AND THE CORRUPTION OF PENSIONS

Change—whether political, economic, or financial—is often slow. It is important to understand that prior to ERISA, many private pensions suffered from gross mismanagement and outright fraud. A case in point was the 1963 closing of the Studebaker automobile plant in South Bend, Indiana.

As a result of mismanagement, more than 4,000 employees lost some or all of their promised pension-plan benefits.[10]

It wasn't just mismanagement that undermined pension plans. Pension plans worked because money was deducted from workers' paychecks and invested. Over time, pensions became large institutions that were open not only to mismanagement but to outright corruption.

If you watched Martin Scorsese's epic film *The Irishman*, which was loosely based on Jimmy Hoffa's dealings with the Mafia, you got a sense of the corruption with the pensions of the International Brotherhood of Teamsters. In 1964, Hoffa, who was president of the union, was found "guilty on four of 21 counts in what the government called a $25 million scheme."[11] Hoffa, along with six others, had fraudulently arranged $25 million in loans from the teamster pension fund and diverted $1.7 million for their own personal use. He was sentenced to 13 years in prison but only served four years before President Nixon commuted his sentence in 1971.

Hoffa's story is interesting in its own right, but the point here is that when you place your trust in pensions, you are putting your future in jeopardy. Many pensions rely on the outdated 60/40 investment strategy. In addition, the regulatory protections for pension funds may no longer have the same impact they once did.

When ERISA was passed by Congress in 1974, its purpose was to safeguard "the establishment of private retirement plans."[12] ERISA worked well for many years, but it faces extraordinary challenges today. These include "the breakdown of the traditional 'three-legged stool' of retirement security—employer-sponsored pensions, individual savings, and government-run Social Security. They include changing economics in which employers are unwilling or unable to offer traditional pensions and in which employees cannot afford to save much on their own after paying bills."[13] Clearly, the economic landscape for workers has changed.

ERISA, too, "has changed dramatically, as defined benefit pension plans have been largely replaced by defined contribution plans, which shift the onus for retirement planning from employers to individuals."[14] This is why I've repeatedly stressed the need for financial literacy. Pensions are fast becoming extinct, and if you continue to rely upon your pension to safe-guard your future, you will be in for a rude awakening.

One of the reasons pensions are changing is that corporations are unwill-ing to accept the responsibility of taking care of their employees. In fact, "nearly two-thirds of pension funds are considering dropping guaranteed benefits to new workers within five years."[15] While there are systemic rea-sons for this, including "declining union power and the rise of 401(k)-style defined-contribution plans, which require workers to kick in their own funds for retirement,"[16] there is something more sinister at work here.

Corporations have embraced the philosophy outlined by Milton Friedman in his 1970 *New York Times* article. As noted earlier, Friedman wrote, "There is one and only one social responsibility of business—to use its resources and engage in activities designed to increase its profits so long as it stays within the rules of the game, which is to say, engages in open and free competition without deception."[17] But the fundamental problem with Friedman's argument is that the rules of the game have been written by the businesses themselves, and they marginalize the vast majority of people who have little to no input in how the rules are applied. This is the failure of capitalism: It has always lacked an ethical impulse toward others, ignoring average Americans for the sake of profits.

THE DOUBLE-WHAMMY EFFECT

When you rely on pensions and Social Security to take care of you through-out your retirement years, you come up against a double whammy. Believing that your pension will protect you ignores history. Consider that "U.S. state pension funds collectively earned an annualized asset-weighted average return of 5.87 percent between fiscal year-ends June 30, 2000, and June 30, 2018, 'badly trailing' the 7.75 percent aggregate annualized asset-weighted assumed actuarial rate of return."[18] What does this mean? For nearly 20 years (2000–2018) state pension funds returned roughly 6 percent, which is nearly a 2 percent shortfall. You might think that 2 percent is insignifi-cant, but the "2-percentage point shortfall contributed greatly to a decline in pension funding ratios . . . from close to unity (100 percent) in 2000 to 73 percent as of June 30, 2018."[19]

Perhaps you feel that 73 percent is better than nothing, but here is the problem: Today we are living longer than ever before, so the cumulative effect of pension shortfalls will dramatically impact your retirement.

Here's what we are up against: We know that Social Security and pensions may not be able to take care of our retirement needs. Pensions are underfunded and, because they largely invest in a 60/40 portfolio, have historically performed worse than college endowment funds. Pensions have also historically been prone to corruption. Meanwhile, corporations are no longer offering pension plans, because they are only interested in maximizing profits.

The retirement crisis is the result of intersecting and overlapping forces that converged to create doubt, uncertainty, fear, and inaction. As a result, we keep putting our retirement planning off. We are either busy, or we may not want to take on this responsibility of planning and preparing.

Now that the burden has shifted to you, the average American, to plan for your own retirement, what you need now more than ever before is financial literacy. You need to protect yourself by taking charge of your financial future. As someone who's been in the financial industry for more than 35 years, I'm often asked if things could get worse. My short answer is no. I actually believe things will get better. There is a new approach to investing that can generate consistent returns while managing risk.

TAKING RESPONSIBILITY

I believing it's possible for ordinary Americans to make the fundamental changes that are necessary. First, you need to educate yourself. No one is going to do that part for you. Financial literacy is now a social imperative.

The second thing you need to do is to work with a qualified and experienced financial professional who can offer invaluable advice and bring focus to your retirement planning. If you're wondering why you need to educate yourself when a financial advisor can plan your retirement for you, understand that when it comes to your financial future, you need to be an active participant in the process. Becoming educated will, at a minimum, help you ask the relevant questions when selecting a financial advisor.

If you don't understand some very basic things about how the economy works or how macroeconomic forces, like inflation, can impact your ability to save or invest, then it will be difficult for you to ask important questions. If you've never heard of multi-asset-class investing or heard anything about alternative investments, then you will not be able to ask your advisor about them.

You will be doing yourself a great disservice if you don't start educating yourself. And there's an actual cost: According to a National Financial Education Council 2021 survey, "[the] lack of financial literacy cost Americans a total of more than $352 billion in 2021."[20] These are staggering financial losses that can easily be avoided by improving your financial literacy.

And what are the benefits of financial knowledge? First and foremost, financial literacy creates less worry and uncertainty over money. Of course, uncertainty is a fact of life, particularly our financial lives. However, the more knowledge you gain, the more you can control certain aspects of your financial future. While we cannot control inflation, unemployment, or interest rates, we can control how much we save or how we invest. Financial literacy empowers us to take charge.

Here are some of the things financial knowledge allows you to do:

- Save for retirement
- Create and stick to a balanced budget
- Purchase a home
- Select insurance
- Reduce expenses
- Invest
- Buy a car
- Save for college
- Manage debt

- Use credit cards

If you want greater peace of mind, less worry, and less uncertainty in your decision-making process, then do yourself a life-changing favor and become more financially aware. Reading this book is a powerful first step toward financial literacy.

CHAPTER 9

THE RISE OF DIGITAL ASSETS

"Bitcoin has no power, no authority that can decide on its fate. It is owned by the crowd, its users. And it now has a track record of several years, enough for it to be an animal in its own right. Its mere existence is an insurance policy that will remind governments that the last object the establishment could control, namely the currency, is no longer their monopoly. This gives us, the crowd, an insurance policy against an Orwellian future."

—NASSIM NICHOLAS TALEB
(FROM *THE BITCOIN STANDARD*)

C ryptocurrency is one of those topics that many people, particularly older people, find difficult to understand. I generally divide those who do understand crypto into three groups. The first group are the computer experts who are fascinated by the technical side of digital currency.

This group grasps such technical concepts as blockchain technology, mining Bitcoin and other cryptocurrencies, electronic wallets, burn mechanisms, and other ideas that will make your head spin. The second group is interested in trading or investing cryptocurrency. This group is not so into all the computer jargon, although many investors and traders do get the basic idea behind digital currency. The third group combines the technical sophistication of the first group with the financial awareness of the second group.

In many ways, the rise of cryptocurrency was the unwitting result of the digital revolution, which is perhaps the most sweeping, socially disruptive, and concentrated form of societal change—more powerful than the Scientific Revolution and the Industrial Revolution combined. R. F. Georgy, in his book *Notes from the Café*, warned us about the effects of living in an age where information is the dominant intellectual currency, social media the source of endless distractions, and algorithms the wave of the future.

The digital age is also transforming our lives in ways that challenge the institutional control of money by banks and governments. The recent introduction of cryptocurrency to our digital vernacular is changing the transactional nature of money. Cryptocurrency is a digital currency that operates independently of banks and uses encryption technology to generate units of currency and verify the transfer of funds. While there are thousands of cryptocurrencies available today, the oldest and most dominant is Bitcoin.

Traditional financial dealings involve your bank. If you want to buy a car or a home, you need to go through a bank. If you need a credit card, you go through the bank. If you want to pay for groceries or dinner at a nice restaurant, you may use a debit card or credit card, both of which require a bank. If you want to see your monthly transactions, you can access this information online through the bank. The bank keeps track of all your purchases.

Say you want to purchase movie theater tickets. You may buy and pay for them online. You can go to an ATM and withdraw some cash to buy your ticket, or you can use your credit or debit card at the box office. Again, you need a bank to facilitate your transaction. On the face of it, the bank makes our lives easier. But all this convenience comes at a cost. With certain banks, using your ATM has a fee attached. Your credit card has an interest rate that can be as high as 25 percent, or even higher, depending on your credit score.

Think about a car purchase. If you go the bank to obtain a car loan, the bank will charge you interest that can add up to thousands of dollars over the life of your loan. This is the way we have dealt with money for a long time.

Cryptocurrency at its most basic level is designed to eliminate the bank by allowing people to pay for goods and services directly. Think about those movie tickets. Many national movie theater chains, like AMC, now accept cryptocurrency. You simply pay for your tickets with Bitcoin, Ethereum, or Shiba Inu.

According to Investopedia, a **cryptocurrency** "is a digital or virtual currency that is secured by cryptography, which makes it nearly impossible to counterfeit or double spend. Many cryptocurrencies are decentralized networks based on blockchain technology—a distributed ledger enforced by a disparate network of computers."[1] Cryptography is "the study of secure communications techniques that allow only the sender and intended recipient of a message to view its contents. The term is derived from the Greek word *kryptos*, which means hidden."[2] The cryptography is designed to make your online financial transactions safe.

The definition mentions blockchain technology, which is based on a ledger. People have been using ledgers for centuries. A well-organized ledger will help you keep track of how much you spend on a certain date. Because most of us use banks, our monthly statements are a form of ledgers where you can check your spending history. Bank statements also offer us proof that we did indeed spend X amount of money on a certain date. If cryptocurrency is designed to remove banks as the middlemen for our transactions, then we need a way to keep track of our transactions.

This is where the blockchain comes in. A **blockchain** is a "distributed database or ledger that is shared among the nodes of a computer network."[3] What's a **computer node**? "A node is any physical device within a network of other tools that's able to send, receive, or forward information."[4] Think of the personal computer or laptop you have at home. Your computer is the most common node that connects you to other computers around the world. The blockchain acts as a highly sophisticated ledger where all of your transactions can be stored. When thousands of people are using cryptocurrency to pay for goods and services, and banks are no longer available to keep track of all these transactions, different people around the world have to use the blockchain to keep track of these transactions. These people are known as miners, and their job is to solve mathematical problems. They are rewarded for their work by being paid in cryptocurrency.

A BRIEF HISTORY OF CRYPTOCURRENCY

I believe there are historical forces that converge in such a way as to create progress and innovation. A historical convergence in a certain period can generate sudden breakthroughs or moments of great insight. The early 2000s were a period in history defined by concentrated technological change. This was when the digital revolution was unfolding all around us. From the internet to smart technology (the iPhone was introduced in 2007), from social media to sophisticated apps, our world was changing at a breathtaking pace.

Along with these rapid technological changes came economic forces that would soon converge with the technological innovations. The 2008 global financial meltdown—which was partly a result of the repeal of the Glass-Steagall Act almost a decade earlier—left our banking system on the precipice of complete collapse. Banks that were "too big to fail" had to be bailed out by the federal government.

As for the historical convergence, during 2008 many people, not only in America but around the world, became distrustful of banks. It was only a matter of time before digital technology offered a way to sidestep banks completely by creating a digital peer-to-peer payment system. This was the cultural and technological environment behind the birth of Bitcoin. The digital technology enabled a sweeping paradigm shift in how we view money.

The search for a peer-to-peer electronic cash system ended when a computer programmer, who went by the name of Satoshi Nakamoto, introduced the radical idea that people no longer needed the powerful banks to control their lives. On November 1, 2008, Nakamoto sent an email to a cryptography mailing list (a mailing list reserved for cryptographers) to announce that he had produced a new electronic cash system that was fully peer-to-peer, with no trusted third party. Nakamoto "copied the abstract of the paper explaining the design, and a link to it online."[5] The paper, "Bitcoin: A Peer-to-Peer Electronic Cash System," introduced the functionality of the Bitcoin blockchain network.

Think of a blockchain as a record of transactions made in Bitcoin or another cryptocurrency and maintained across several computers that are linked in a peer-to-peer network. While this may sound rather technical, it was a revolution in the making.

The promise of Bitcoin was too fantastical to believe. We had all become accustomed to dealing with "evil" banks, simply because there were no alternatives. How were the banks going to be removed entirely from the day-to-day transactions we take for granted? Bitcoin promised to offer a payment network with its own native currency; it used a sophisticated method for members to verify all transactions without having to trust any single member of the network. And unlike past attempts at creating digital cash, Bitcoin worked. Bitcoin not only had the potential to revolutionize the way we transact money, but it also was transforming our understanding of money itself.

For thousands of years people used bartering, also known as in-kind transactions, to trade goods. This gave rise to the idea of the double coincidence of wants, which simply means that both parties in a transaction have to agree to sell and buy each commodity. As an example, think about a waitress who is paid with food. The waitress has rent to pay, but her landlord does not accept food as a form of payment. Both the waitress and the landlord lack an agreed-upon medium of exchange. One of the main problems of in-kind transactions was the improbability of the wants or needs occurring at the same time and place.

Bartering also created problems of time constraints. Let's say you want to trade fruit with rice. A trade could only occur when both fruit and rice were available at the same time and place. By introducing a medium of exchange—money—you can sell your fruit whenever it is available, then take the medium of exchange and buy rice whenever it is on the market. The invention of money largely solved the double-coincidence-of-wants problem.

BITCOIN AND THE MULTIMILLION-DOLLAR PIZZA

On May 22, 2010, a Florida man by the name of Laszlo Hanyecz traded 10,000 Bitcoins for two large pizzas from Papa John's. This transaction had its roots in a lighthearted exchange of ideas on a newly developed online forum where people could freely discuss various topics such as cryptocurrency, Bitcoin, the blockchain, and so on. On that fateful day, Laszlo Hanyecz asked members of the forum to help him purchase two large pizzas.

The only catch was that Hanyecz would pay for the pizza using Bitcoins—10,000 Bitcoins to be precise. Hanyecz asked the members of the forum to purchase the Papa John's pizzas for him using fiat money (money backed by the government) and, in exchange, Hanyecz would pay the person 10,000 Bitcoins. A British gentleman accepted the offer, spent $25, and delivered the two pepperoni pies to Hanyecz, who promptly electronically transferred 10,000 Bitcoins to the other man for his trouble. Bitcoins seemed basically worthless at the time. In fact, they were worth a paltry $41. The British gentleman actually made a profit of $25 buying and delivering the pizza to Hanyecz.

What makes this story more remarkable was the nonchalant attitude Hanyecz exhibited when ordering his pizza. The ad he placed in the forum simply stated, "I'll pay 10,000 Bitcoins for a couple of pizzas . . . like maybe 2 large ones so I have some left over for the next day. I like having left over pizza to nibble on later. You can make the pizza yourself and bring it to my house or order it for me from a delivery place, but what I'm aiming for is getting food delivered in exchange for Bitcoins where I don't have to order or prepare it myself."[6]

None of the members in this forum, certainly not Hanyecz, had any clue as to how much Bitcoins would soon be worth. Within nine months (February

2011), Bitcoin would reach parity with the U.S. dollar. In other words, with a single Bitcoin valued at $1, the two pizzas would have been worth $10,000. Five years later, on the fifth anniversary of the pizza purchase, the two large pizzas were valued at $2.5 million. In July 2019 Bitcoin reached a price of $13,125, which meant the two large pizzas had soared to $131,250,000.

In August 2021 the price of Bitcoin reached an all-time high of $68,500. The two large pepperoni pizzas would then have been valued at an unimaginable $685,000,000. Although hindsight is 20/20, the giving away of 10,000 Bitcoins may perhaps be the biggest financial blunder in history. But Mr. Hanyecz might feel a little better knowing that during the crypto winter of 2022, the price of Bitcoin plummeted. By August of that year the price of Bitcoin stood at $21,503.24, which means the two large pizzas were down to $215,032,400. Despite the massive correction in price, Mr. Hanyecz's 10,000 Bitcoins would still have made him a multimillionaire.

One obvious lesson here is that history often presents us with opportunities of a lifetime and only those who have the vision to anticipate what is to come will benefit in unimaginable ways. Bitcoin had what you might call less than humble beginnings. Below is a timeline of important dates in its story:

- January 3, 2009: With the genesis block—the first block in the Bitcoin blockchain—50 Bitcoins are generated.

- January 9, 2009: The first version of Bitcoin (known as Bitcoin v0.1) is issued.

- May 22, 2010: In the first purchase with Bitcoins, Laszlo Hanyecz buys two large pizzas for 10,000 Bitcoins. At the time, each Bitcoin was valued at 0.0025 cents.

- March 2015: One Bitcoin was worth between $200 and $300.

- November 28, 2017: Bitcoin reaches $10,000.

- December 15, 2017: Bitcoin reaches $17,900.

- August 2021: Bitcoin reaches an all-time high of $68,500.

- June 18, 2022: Bitcoin crashes to $17,599.

BITCOIN AND THE POWER
OF BLOCKCHAIN TECHNOLOGY

The topic of cryptocurrency can be intimidating. Part of the reason why it's difficult to understand this new form of digital currency is its esoteric vocabulary, which includes such words as blockchains, crypto mining, nodes, virtual wallets, and public and private keys, among others.

The architecture behind Bitcoin is the blockchain, which is simply an electronic record of all online activity. As we've seen, you can think of it as a ledger or database. Just as banks need to keep track of all patrons' activity, the cryptocurrency community needs to keep track of all peer-to-peer transactions around the world.

This is a monumental undertaking that requires thousands of people around the world to record each transaction on a blockchain, which is distributed across and manipulated by a large number of nodes (computers), in contrast to its being held by a single authority or party. A single block electronically records the most recent transaction, which is both viewed and shared by anonymous users. A block is a permanent store of records, which, once written, cannot be altered or removed. Each of these transactions, or blocks, are connected sequentially to form a blockchain.

Now, these blocks are not automatically added to the blockchain. A verification process needs to be put in place. Without such a process, anyone could simply add fictitious transactions. In order to verify transactions, a proof-of-work system was introduced. This was a measure designed to deter abuses of the computer system, such as spam.

Verifying each block within the blockchain calls for some effort on the user's part. As an analogy, think of websites you visit that want to make sure you are human and not a machine. Most of these websites use what is known as the CAPTCHA system to distinguish between humans and machines. You may have used this, for example, if you've ever been asked to type the letters in a distorted image.[7]

Bitcoin relies upon a similar, yet more complex, system to verify the authenticity of each block in the blockchain. Users must solve complex mathematical problems that require the use of sophisticated computers, in a process called mining. Why would anyone spend such time, effort, and money (the amount of electricity needed by miners is extremely high) to verify the individual blocks being added to the blockchain? There is an incentive: Miners are rewarded with Bitcoins for their effort.

The only way to release Bitcoin, or other cryptocurrencies, into circulation is by rewarding miners for their efforts to verify transactions on the blockchain. When Bitcoin was first mined in 2009, each miner was rewarded 50 Bitcoins for solving a single block in the blockchain. The number of Bitcoins available is not endless. In fact, it has been predetermined that the total number of Bitcoins will be capped at 21 million. This begs the question: Does one have to be a miner to obtain Bitcoins? The answer is no. You can purchase Bitcoin by using fiat money (USD or any other government-issued currency) or by trading it on an exchange. As we've noted, Bitcoins have monetary value, which can be converted to the U.S. dollar or other currencies.

As Bitcoins became more valuable, the number of coins rewarded to miners was reduced by successive halves over the next several years. For example, in 2012, miners were rewarded 25 Bitcoins for successfully completing a block. By 2016 miners were rewarded 12.5 Bitcoins, and by 2020, the amount was reduced to 6.25 Bitcoins.[8] Another way of thinking about this is that for every 210,000 blocks completed, on an average of four years, the reward offered to miners was cut in half.

The importance of Bitcoin halving is that it reduces, "the rate at which new coins are created and thus lowers the available amount of new supply.[9] Halving reduces the rate at which new coins are created. This is important from an investment perspective since a low or finite supply can create high demand, thus pushing prices higher. The increase in value after each halving is not immediate; in many cases it takes months for the price to dramatically go up. Since the creation of Bitcoin in 2009, there have been three halvings—in 2012, 2016, and 2020.

- November 28, 2012: The Bitcoin block reward for miners was reduced from 50 BTC to 25 BTC. The price of Bitcoin at the time was a paltry $12. After one year, the price soared to $1,031.95.[10]

- July 9, 2016: The Bitcoin block reward for miners was reduced from 25 BTC to 12.5 BTC. Bitcoin at the time was trading at $650.96. After 526 days, Bitcoin exploded to $20,089.[11]

- May 11, 2020: The Bitcoin block reward was reduced from 12.5 BTC to 6.25 BTC. In the midst of the COVID-19 pandemic, Bitcoin was trading at $8,787. Eighteen months later, Bitcoin skyrocketed to an unimaginable $66,000.[12]

The next Bitcoin halving will take place on March 10, 2024, and the final Bitcoin halving will happen in 2140, at which point Bitcoin will reach the maximum supply of 21 million.[13]

BITCOIN AS A STORE OF VALUE AND PORTFOLIO DIVERSIFIER

You may have heard that gold is a store of value, but what does this term mean exactly? A **store of value** is "an asset class that does not lose its value over time like fiat, which is relatively volatile."[14] **Fiat money** is government-issued currency; the U.S. dollar is fiat money.[15] But fiat money is not considered a store of value because over time inflation will reduce its purchasing power.

Suppose you place $1,000 in your mattress in 1980. Decades go by, and you completely forget about the trove of dollars. Let's further suppose that you decide to do a good deed and donate your mattress to Goodwill. Over the next several decades, the mattress is sold several times. Finally, in 2022, a college student buys this old and not so hygienic mattress. While doing homework, the student—who happens to be studying finance (good for her)—notices a tear on the side of the mattress. Bored with her finance textbook, the student decides to enlarge the tear to see what is inside the mattress. Much to her surprise, she finds dozens of $20 bills. She is rich, or so she thinks.

After counting the money (twice), she realizes she has $1,000. However, once you factor inflation, in order to equal the goods and services she could have bought with $1,000 in 1980, she now needs $3,595.58.[16] The dollar lost a considerable amount of value in 42 years. The lesson here is that fiat currency is not a good store of value during inflationary times. In deflationary times, however, it is a good store of value.

One way for people to counter the negative effects of inflation is to invest in other asset classes like stocks and bonds. The problem with these assets is that they experience cycles of boom and bust. Moreover, though stocks and bonds used to be negatively correlated—if stocks went down in price, bonds went up to protect your investment—more recently they have been positively correlated, meaning that price movement occurred in tandem.

In addition to cash, stocks, and bonds serving as stores of value, another popular store of value is gold. Although it is considered one of the oldest stores of value, gold is also subject to market conditions. For example, from May 1980 to March 2002, gold lost 75 percent of its value. Despite these setbacks, which may and do occur, the durability, rarity, mobility, and convertibility—as well as emotional appeal—are some of the reasons that have helped gold outlast several monetary systems and stand the test of time."[17]

Keep in mind that gold had thousands of years to develop, mature, and gain the trust of individuals, institutions, and governments. Bitcoin has been around for little more than 10 years, yet despite its infancy, it has quickly startled the world with its realized and unrealized potential. Of course, Bitcoin and the larger cryptocurrency landscape are highly volatile and dangerous to invest in if you don't have a thorough understanding of this emerging asset class.

Bitcoin's volatility is due partly to its meteoric rise as an alternative asset class. As noted above, at the beginning of 2017, Bitcoin was worth less than $1,000, and by December of that year, it had exploded to $20,000.[18] Part of what makes an asset a desirable store of value is that it serves "as a medium of trade, allowing it to be converted as needed. Bitcoin is exchangeable due to its fungibility, portability, divisibility, and widespread adoption."[19] Another important consideration in Bitcoin's rise to investment prominence is institutional adoption.

According to Todd Crosland, CEO of CoinZoom, "Worldwide crypto adoption jumped by over 800 percent in 2021 alone."[20] It's not just that large financial institutions like banks and hedge funds have adopted Bitcoin; countries are beginning to consider adopting Bitcoin as legal tender. In September 2021 El Salvador became the first country in the world to make Bitcoin an official currency alongside the U.S. dollar. In January 2022 other countries, including Panama, Guatemala, Paraguay, and Honduras, were exploring adoption as well.[21] Bitcoin is quickly becoming mainstream.

When large institutional investors like hedge funds, pension funds, and university endowments like those of Harvard, Yale, and Brown adopt Bitcoin, that tells you that the crypto market is no laughing matter.[22] In fact, "in 2021 alone institutional inflows into crypto markets reached a record USD 9.3 billion—a 36 percent increase from 2020."[23]

Despite the crypto winter of 2022, where Bitcoin lost 68 percent of its value from its peak, large hedge funds are continuing to invest in the crypto space. Although 57 percent of hedge funds allocated less than 1 percent of their total assets under management, a wise decision given the current crypto bear market conditions, two-thirds of these institutional investors planned to increase their exposure by the end of 2022.[24]

In addition to being a store of value asset class, Bitcoin can be a portfolio diversifier. As the name implies, a portfolio diversifier is an asset class that expands possibilities beyond cash, stocks, and bonds and can possibly reduce the overall risk in a portfolio. Real estate or private credit are examples, and Bitcoin can be a great diversifier as well, as long as it is done responsibly and under the direction of a financial expert who has knowledge of and experience with cryptocurrency.

Some institutional investors see Bitcoin, and cryptocurrency in general, as portfolio diversifiers. This is significant because there was a time not long ago when institutional investors viewed Bitcoin as a speculative gamble.[25] Another significant outcome of institutional investors' embracing Bitcoin as a diversifier is that "market perceptions toward Bitcoin and cryptocurrencies are changing. These changes indicate that Bitcoin's role in the economy is maturing. It is no longer considered a fringe asset but a mainstream financial asset. This perception is only likely to grow with time, as adoption increasingly becomes mainstream."[26]

BITCOIN AS A 60/40 DIVERSIFIER

There are some people today who may have some or all of their assets in cryptocurrency, which, in my opinion, is dangerous, risky, and irresponsible. You may know some of these people. You may also hear some anecdotes of people who made a substantial return by investing exclusively in Bitcoin or other cryptocurrency. I believe this is a form of gambling, which I strongly encourage you to avoid.

A study conducted by Bitwise, a leader in crypto index funds, revealed that adding between 1 percent to 2.5 percent Bitcoin "to a portfolio of 60 percent stocks and 40 percent bonds from 2014 to 2020 added 1 percent to 2.3 percent to annual returns without significant increase in portfolio volatility or drawdown."[27] Adding a relatively safe amount of Bitcoin to a 60/40 portfolio can potentially result in better returns without an increase in volatility.

UNIVERSITY ENDOWMENTS AND BITCOIN

University endowments have done extremely well for their institutions by investing in alternative assets to stocks and bonds, but it was not until recently that endowments entered the crypto space by adding Bitcoin and other digital assets to their multi-asset portfolios.

According to CoinDesk, a news site specializing in crypto news, "Harvard University, Yale University, Brown University and the University of Michigan are among schools whose multibillion-dollar endowments have begun buying cryptocurrency directly on exchanges."[28] Many other endowments are "allocating a small portion to crypto, and most have been in for at least a year."[29]

University endowments are not only buying and holding cryptocurrency, they are also now accepting gifts in the form of Bitcoin. For example, in December 2021 the University of California Berkeley's Blockchain Lab received a gift of $50,000 in the form of Bitcoin from the Echo Link Foundation. That amount actually pales in comparison to the massive gift given to Pennsylvania's Wharton School—an anonymous gift in the amount of $5 million, all in Bitcoin.[30] Now, before you assume that I'm telling you this in order to defend Bitcoin, you would be wrong. I'm telling you this so that you can be careful if you invest in Bitcoin or other cryptocurrencies on your own.

THE CRYPTO WINTER

The year 2022 was not particularly kind to cryptocurrency. The crypto winter brought with it digital devastation. Bitcoin fell by more than 60 percent from its record highs. Despite these massive losses, millions of people have not given up on the digital technology. In fact, 56 percent of consumers say they are somewhat interested in buying cryptocurrency within the next year. Almost 42 percent of millennials are either very or extremely likely to buy crypto in the next year. Part of what is driving this is Fear of Missing Out (otherwise known as FOMO).[31]

But if you are investing on your own and decide to put 100 percent of your money into Bitcoin, Ethereum, Dogecoin, or Shiba Inu, you stand to lose everything. You don't have to believe me. Simply google "people who lost everything in crypto," and you will find thousands of entries. Before investing in cryptocurrency, you need to consult with a qualified financial expert who is experienced with this asset class.

BITCOIN ETFs

Despite the growing popularity of Bitcoin, it is still, in my opinion, too volatile to directly purchase Bitcoin or trade it on your own with an exchange. It might help here to review the concept of exchange-traded funds.

An **exchange-traded fund (ETF)** is a "type of pooled investment security that operates much like a mutual fund. Typically, ETFs will track a particular index, sector, commodity, or other assets, but unlike mutual funds, ETFs can be purchased or sold on a stock exchange the same way that a regular stock can."[32]

A **mutual fund** is a financial vehicle that pools assets from shareholders who "mutually" invest in securities such as stocks, bonds, money market instruments, and other assets.[33] Mutual funds are run by professional money managers who decide which securities to buy. Investors in a mutual fund thus have exposure to a diversified set of asset classes. Along with diversification, other benefits of mutual funds include low cost, convenience, and professional management.[34] Some of the downsides of ETFs include high expense ratios and sales charges, management abuses, tax inefficiency, and poor trade execution.

Bitcoin ETFs, which track Bitcoin futures contracts, started trading on October 19, 2021. "A **futures contract** is a legal agreement to buy or sell a commodity asset, or security at a predetermined price at a specified time in the future."[35] Michael Sapir, CEO of ProShares, marked the launch of the first Bitcoin ETF as a milestone in the ongoing evolution of ETFs. He said, "1993 is remembered for the first equity ETF, 2002 for the first bond ETF, and 2004 for the first gold ETF. 2021 will be remembered for the first cryptocurrency-linked ETF."[36]

In addition to ETFs acting as vehicles for retail investors to add cryptocurrency to their portfolio without actually trading directly, corporations are doing the same thing. According to Bitcoin Treasuries (bitcointreasuries.org), most publicly listed companies that purchase and hold Bitcoin on their balance sheets are companies that specialize in cryptocurrency or blockchain firms.[37] In February 2021 Tesla became the highest-profile company to shift some of its cash on its balance sheets to Bitcoin, making a whopping $1.5 billion bet on the digital currency.[38] It is important to note that Tesla lost $204 million on Bitcoin overall; though it gained back $64 million through trading.[39]

One bit of potentially good news about Bitcoin ETFs is that Grayscale, which manages the world's largest Bitcoin fund, is trying to get the Securities and Exchange Commission (SEC) to approve its flagship fund (the Grayscale Bitcoin Trust) as an ETF. If the SEC approves Grayscale's request, the Grayscale Bitcoin ETF will be a part of a spot-exchange traded fund in the market. In this case the new fund would track the spot market rather than futures contracts. This would broaden access to "Bitcoin and enhance protections while unlocking $8 billion in value for investors."[40] As of this writing, the SEC has yet to approve Grayscale's request.

Cryptocurrency in many ways is in the Wild West of digital currency. This is a period in which governments and regulators will try to regulate how exchanges operate, how Bitcoins ETFs will evolve over time, and how large exchanges like Coinbase and Binance will survive in a marketplace filled with potential abuse, like hackers who steal Bitcoin and other cryptocurrency from people's accounts.

In other words, these are volatile times for the industry, both in terms of price and safety of customer funds. Once again, I urge you to not enter the crypto space without thoroughly studying it and without having a qualified and experienced financial professional helping you. Retail investors cannot simply read a few online articles and naively believe they can invest on their own. You need a professional on your side.

Bitcoin, in my opinion, will likely continue to be a highly volatile asset class. Although in a study by Digital Assets Strategy, Bitcoin exhibited lower volatility than 112 stocks of the S&P 500 in a 90-day period, this statistic is misleading and can easily be misinterpreted.[41] Bitcoin is generally more volatile than stocks, which is why I treat this maturing asset class with caution, and you should as well. If you think cryptocurrency in general—and Bitcoin in particular—represents a get-rich scheme, you may end up losing your shirt . . . and quite a bit of money. The only way, in my opinion, to adopt Bitcoin is as a diversifier in a multi-asset-class portfolio.

PART III

THE RETIREMENT
SOLUTION

CHAPTER 10

VINDICATION

"Sometimes it is the people who no
one imagines anything of, who do the
things that no one can imagine."

—ALAN TURING

Following the stock market crash of 2003, which was the result of the dot-com bubble, many of my clients lost a great deal of money. Devastated and full of doubt and uncertainty, I began to question the financial industry and my place in it. Doubt is a crippling feeling that freezes you into inaction. Once it finds its way into your soul, you start to question everything, including your identity.

I was so distraught that I was ready to leave the financial industry. That's when I went to see my pastor for guidance. I told him what happened and how I was feeling. The wisdom he imparted was invaluable. First he asked me a few simple questions. Was I a truthful person? I immediately answered, "Yes, of course I am." He then proceeded to ask me other questions in rap-id-fire fashion. Did I have integrity? Did I care about my clients? Did I have passion for what I do? I answered yes to all of his questions. Then he looked me in the eye and told me that I had a moral obligation not to leave my clients. In fact, he said I had a moral obligation not to leave my clients of tomorrow, as they would need guidance. His final words to me were so powerful they jolted me out of my all-consuming doubt. He told me to move forward by embracing the divine spark of ethical engagement in order to help others.

Setbacks are defining moments that present us with opportunities. How we respond to these opportunities determines our existential value in the world. The choices we make in the face of setbacks are binary. We can either allow the setback to define us, or we can take charge of our own destiny and transform ourselves into something that transcends our preconceived limitations.

Shortly after the 2003 stock market crash, and after a great deal of soul searching and reflection, I chose not only to continue to help my clients, but also to fundamentally change my investment strategy. Once I recognized the fundamental flaws in the 60/40 investment portfolio, I set out to find an innovative investment strategy that was flexible and adaptable to our complex and globally interconnected world. I spent endless days and sleepless nights doing research in order to find a strategy that could potentially withstand unexpected market forces.

I spent years searching for an investment strategy that would help my clients prepare for retirement. The one thing I knew for sure was that the 60/40 portfolio was vulnerable to unexpected market swings. As I was doing my research, I came across an academic paper called "Portfolio Selection" by Harry Markowitz, which, I must confess, I found to be not only scholarly, but also mathematically dense. Markowitz made one statement, however, that caught my attention: "Diversification is both observed and sensible; a rule of behavior which does not imply the superiority of diversification must be rejected both as a hypothesis and as a maxim."[1] In other words, portfolio diversification was and is superior to stocks and bonds alone.

It was the rigorous research by Markowitz, who went on to win the Nobel Prize in economics, that pointed me in the right direction. The problem I had to solve was twofold: Should I abandon the 60/40 portfolio completely and construct an entirely new portfolio, or should I retain stocks and bonds by lowering their allocation and adding new asset classes? This problem proved to be more difficult than I imagined. My intuitive sense that the 60/40 was broken would be vindicated later, since "analysts from major firms like Bank of America, Morgan Stanley, and JP Morgan have all proclaimed the death of the 60/40 rule."[2]

I would later conclude that stocks and bonds have value in a portfolio if we reduce their allocation. Having 60 percent of one's assets in stocks is simply too high of a risk for most investors. The challenge was to reduce the stock-bond allocation and add other asset classes that would give my clients better returns than the outmoded 60/40 split.

According to Markowitz and his Modern Portfolio Theory, all investment portfolios have two characteristics that exist in a state of tension—risk and return. If you want a higher return on your investment, you will have to accept higher risk. When I was developing my REALM model, however, I wanted what others told me was impossible: higher returns *without* the higher level of risk. The solution to this problem was buried in the Modern Portfolio Theory. According to Markowitz, it is possible for an investor to "construct a portfolio of multiple assets that will result in greater returns without a higher level of risk."[3] The multi-asset-class approach now had rigorous, mathematically supported evidence.

It is important for you to understand that the REALM strategy contains alternative investments, which are speculative by nature and have various risks including possible lack of liquidity, lack of control, changes in business conditions, and devaluation based on the investment, the economy, and/or regulatory changes. As a result, the values of alternative investments do fluctuate resulting in the value at sale being more or less than the original price paid if a liquid market for the securities is found. Alternative investments are not appropriate for all investors. No investment process is free of risk; no strategy or risk management technique can guarantee returns or eliminate risk in any market environment. There is no guarantee that this investment model/process will be profitable. Diversification does not guarantee profit nor is it guaranteed to prevent losses.

The pieces for my model were coming together. I knew I needed to expand the 60/40 model to include other asset classes. I also knew that the more assets I added, the better returns I would get without increasing my clients' risk. At this point I had an important epiphany. If we started with an investor's desired level of expected return, we could construct a portfolio with the lowest possible risk that was capable of producing that return.[4] The implication is profound and far reaching.

For decades, portfolios were simply given to clients. There was a certain mystique surrounding them, as if they were developed in a secret lab. Portfolio construction is now flexible and customizable, however, and I realized that retail investors should have a great deal of input in how their portfolio is put together. First, no two investors are exactly alike. Each one has a different time horizon—the period of time one expects to hold an investment until the money is needed. Investors also have different tolerances for risk, liquidity needs (having access to your money), and other unique characteristics. Given this information, a qualified and experienced financial planner can help you create a portfolio that meets your specific situation.

With this understanding I was ready to create a multi-asset-class model. What was still missing was the type of asset classes I could utilize. This is where David Swensen entered the picture.

It was sometime in early 2010 that I stumbled upon Swensen's work. His book, *Pioneering Portfolio Management*, sounded promising until I read the subtitle—*An Unconventional Approach to Institutional Investment*. That stopped me, because my clients were all retail investors. I had no need for a book about how institutions invest their money.

I decided to read it, nevertheless, and I was absolutely riveted by Swensen's analysis. Although the book was over 400 pages, I read it in a single sitting. The text made me dizzy with ideas, but I also felt a profound sense of vindication for my belief that the 60/40 portfolio needed to be expanded.

One of the things that I found profoundly interesting on a personal level was the fact that Swensen had been influenced by Markowitz and Modern Portfolio Theory and had become, as far as I was able to determine, the first endowment manager to introduce a multi-asset-class portfolio. Reading Swensen's book gave me the missing piece for my portfolio: alternative investments. The challenge for me—and it was monumental in scope—was how to adapt his institutional model to the average retail investor who had no access to alternative investments. For many years, those were only available to institutions and high-net-worth individuals.

Over time, as a result of technological change and mathematical innovations, alternative asset classes started to become available to the retail investor. Computing power revolutionized the financial markets by making it possible to track, store, and analyze large amounts of data. Mathematical innovations like the Black-Scholes formula made it possible to price complex financial products like derivatives and structured securities.

Eventually the retail investor gained the same access to alternative assets that large endowments and high-net-worth individuals had enjoyed for decades. The playing field was becoming more even, and average Americans, perhaps for the first time in history, had the potential to earn higher returns while managing risk.

WELCOME TO MY WORKSHOP

If you walk into my office today, you will find it to be the epitome of understated elegance, with a cabinet exhibiting my awards in the lobby, perfectly appointed bookshelves, and a desk that projects confidence and utilitarian value. The back rooms, where all my financial professionals and research assistants work, are neatly organized into separate offices and workstations. For many years, however, the very same space looked more like a college research library, a place my assistants called "Cindy's Workshop."

The place was filled with books, as I researched investment strategies, retirement planning, financial concepts, basic economic theory, and economic systems. There were works like Adam Smith's classic *The Wealth of Nations*, volumes on Modern Portfolio Theory, Benjamin Graham's *The Intelligent Investor*, John R. Nofsinger's *The Psychology of Investing*, and dozens of other books.

I also devoured articles, including "Portfolio Selection" by Harry Markowitz, "The Social Responsibility of Business Is to Increase Its Profits" by Milton Friedman, and countless others. I spent two decades immersed in rigorous study. There were years when I worked 16-hour days. I would meet with clients in the morning, then carve a few hours in the afternoon for reading and research. After going home and preparing dinner for my family, I would retire to my study and read until midnight, then get up and go to my office at six a.m.

The results of those years of study are largely the subject of the preceding sections of this book. I began to embrace the idea of including alternative assets in the portfolios I designed for my clients.

During my years of research there were not many books available on alternative investments. One of the few that were available—and the most comprehensive at more than 700 pages—was *The Handbook of Alternative Assets* by Mark J. Anson, which introduced me to an entirely new world of investment opportunity.

Once I had begun to work out my new theoretical framework, the challenge was to add more asset classes to the 60/40 portfolio. The one alternative structure that was immediately available to my clients was **real estate investment trusts (REITs)**. Although publicly traded REITs "move closely with stock market patterns," I found that nontraded REITs "can be largely uncorrelated to stocks."[5] This meant that nontraded REITs were a potentially powerful source of diversification. But my REALM model did not suddenly come into existence once I added nontraded REITs to the traditional 60/40 portfolio.

The new model was limited by what was available at the time for retail investors. As other structures became available to the retail investor, I still spent an extraordinary amount of time studying them before adding them to a client's portfolio. For example, in 2009, once business development companies (BDCs) were offered by FS Investments—a publicly traded business development company formerly known as Franklin Square Capital Partners—I did careful research and added this structure to my clients' portfolios.

A **business development company** is an "organization that invests in small- and medium-sized companies as well as distressed companies."[6] It's a closed-end fund, which is a "type of mutual fund that issued a fixed number of shares through a single initial public offering (IPO) to raise capital for its initial investments. Its shares can then be bought and sold on a stock exchange."[7]

By 2017, FS Investments had also introduced the first interval fund for the retail investor, which, again after careful analysis, I added to an evolving multi-asset-class portfolio. An **interval fund** is a "closed-end fund with shares that do not trade on the secondary market. Instead, the fund periodically offers to buy back a percentage of outstanding shares at net asset value (NAV)."[8] Now, I don't want to get overly technical here. My point is that as new asset classes became available, I researched their suitability and added them to my constantly evolving portfolio.

That doesn't mean I was randomly adding more asset classes. The process of developing a new investment model was far more nuanced. I had to think about asset allocation, which is "an investment strategy that aims to balance risks and reward by apportioning a portfolio's assets according to an individual's goals, risk tolerance, and investment horizon."[9] Asset allocation is a strategy in itself. Using an asset allocation methodology does not guarantee greater or more consistent returns, or against loss; it is a risk management method.

The thing about a multi-asset portfolio is that you have to balance and rebalance the asset allocation with the type of structure, or asset class, you are using. Let's suppose client A has $100,000 to invest. Client A is in her mid-50s. She has a low-risk appetite and a limited time horizon because she wants to retire in 10 years. Given this information, I may put 20 percent in stocks, 20 percent in bonds as a hedge, and perhaps 20 percent in nontraded REITs and 20 percent in BDCs. This leaves 20 percent for tactical investing, which provides hedging and liquidity.

Now, is this a fixed investment portfolio that I can use with others? The answer is no, it is not. What has distinguished my evolving REALM model is customizability.

No two clients are exactly the same. I have hundreds of clients, and my team and I have to construct a customized portfolio for each one. Each client has different parameters, such as risk profile, retirement goals, time horizon, and so on. I use this information to construct a unique asset allocation plan. But the plan is not fixed for all time. Periodically I have to adjust the allocation or introduce different structures as circumstances change. But there is also one other important consideration.

THE POWER OF THREE

Once I had a basic multi-asset-class model in place, I still intuitively felt something was missing. I spent several years thinking about this issue, always trying to perfect my model so I could protect my clients the best way possible.

One day—it must have been in 2017—I was with a client explaining my multi-asset-class model, which still had no official name. As I stood up and started writing on the whiteboard in my office to explain the process, the client, an engineer, asked me a question that I had never considered: How do all these different asset classes interact with each other? Dumbfounded, I looked at him, praised his question, and told him that I would have to think about that for a while.

The client was so impressed with my honesty that he told me he would make a deal with me. If I could work this problem out, he would sign with me immediately. Armed with this challenge, I set out to discover how these different asset classes interact with each other. Although it felt like an eternity, I spent about a week trying to work out the solution. It was grueling work. I spent 18 hours per day thinking about this problem. It was not something I could find through research. The Yale Endowment model used varying allocations, but there was nothing about how the allocations interacted with each other.

After a week, I was no closer to a solution than when I started, but I wasn't about to give up. I assembled my team and started to describe my multi-asset-class model in detail, but they couldn't help me either. Frustrated, I told them to go home for the day.

I also went home tired and dejected, but my daughter, Claire, who was starting college, happened to be there. She was excited about a lecture she had in her government class that described our tripartite system of government: the three branches that are the executive branch (the presidency), the legislative (Congress), and the judicial (the courts).

This three-part system creates checks and balance between each branch so that one branch never becomes too powerful. That's when I had one of the most profound epiphanies of my life. It came to me how different asset classes interact with each other. I gave Claire a big hug and retreated to my home office, where I rushed to my whiteboard and drew three intersecting circles: a Venn diagram.

As I stared at the circles, I realized I had my answer. My multi-asset-class system cannot be static; rather, it has to be dynamic and flexible enough to accommodate change. As I searched for examples, I realized there are certain asset classes, such as alternative products, that require a range of liquidity, from limited liquidity to illiquidity. (**Liquidity** "refers to the efficiency or ease with which an asset or security can be converted into ready cash without out affecting its market price."[10]) Other asset classes, like stocks and bonds, are passive; you set them and forget them. **Passive investing** is a strategy "to maximize returns by minimizing buying and selling."[11]

Finally, I realized that I needed a tactical approach that involved absolute return. **Absolute return** "is the return that an asset achieves over a specified period. This measure looks at the appreciation or depreciation, expressed as a percentage, that an asset, such as a stock or a mutual fund, achieves over a given period."[12] In other words, absolute return is interested in the return of a particular asset without comparing it to any other measure or benchmark.

The tactical sphere places the emphasis upon protection for my clients, and it also offers liquidity that balances the limited liquidity and illiquidity of alternative assets. Remember, my driving force all along was to develop an investment portfolio that could potentially generate high, durable income while managing risk. Instead of bonds acting as a hedge, I use managed futures. And in place of using a 60/40 stock/bond allocation, I can now use a 60/40 allocation in stocks and managed futures. According to the Chicago Mercantile Exchange, some of the advantages using managed futures include:[13]

- Diversification

- Low correlation to stocks, bonds, and real estate

- Reduced overall portfolio volatility

- Returns in any economic environment

- Accessible to most investors

Managed futures are a "type of alternative investment vehicle. They are similar in structure to mutual funds, except that they focus on futures contracts and derivative products."[14] The term "refers to a 30-year-old industry made up of professional money managers who are known as commodity trading advisors, or CTAs."[15] In my opinion, managed futures act as a better hedge against stocks than bonds. They can potentially mitigate the risk in a portfolio if stocks underperform. My opinion is supported by numerous academic studies regarding the effects of combining traditional asset classes with alternative investments such as managed futures.[16]

There is tremendous strength in this kind of a dynamic tripartite system. As I said, the idea was sparked by my daughter's excitement over the American government's system of checks and balances. The idea actually originated with the French enlightenment thinker Baron de Montesquieu, whose work influenced the ideas of our Founding Fathers, including Thomas Jefferson and James Madison. What is remarkable about this interlocking system of government is the fact that it has not only survived but also thrived for 235 years.[17]

A tripartite system also appears in philosophy: Plato's theory of the soul includes the appetitive, the spirited, and the rational. The appetitive involves bodily desires, the spirited deals with our passions and emotions, and the rational seeks truths by using logical thinking. Each of these three elements exists in tension with the other two aspects.

There are also tripartite systems in modern psychology. Think of Freud's tripartite human personality—the id, the ego, and the superego. The id is our animalistic side, interested only in bodily pleasures; the superego is the moral center of our psyche. The ego is caught between the id and superego, always trying to bring the two into harmony.

Finally, you can find tripartite systems in nature, including in the study of "genuine tripartite nonlocality (GTN) and the genuine tripartite entanglement (GTE) of Dirac fields in the background of a Schwarzschild black hole."[18] That's a mouthful, but it simply means that tripartite systems can be used to understand black holes.

Tripartite systems are important because they demonstrate how powerful forces work together to counter each other. The tripartite system in my REALM model potentially maximizes returns while managing risk. The tactical side offers a hedge against stocks. The alternative asset circle, with its range of limited liquidity to illiquidity, offers returns for long-term investing. Finally, the passive circle offers lower allocations of stock/bond assets.

However, these three interlocking circles are in constant motion. My tripartite system is fluid, reflecting changing circumstances in the economy or with my clients. Asset classes can be tweaked, moved around, and altered according to client needs. Here are some of the benefits of a tripartite approach:

- Diversification of your portfolio

- Potentially enhanced returns

- Potentially durable income sources

THE BIRTH OF REALM

How did the REALM name come about? Several years ago, around 2018, my friend and partner, Leticia Hewko, and I were out having coffee. We started to discuss the multi-asset-class model that I had developed. Leticia has an uncanny ability to analyze words and create acronyms that reflect their meaning. As we were brainstorming, she spelled out the acronym in all capital letters: **RETAIL ENDOWMENT**-Like **ALLOCATION MODEL**. She then proceeded to break down the model. First, she said, we know the model is designed for the retail client. Now we have an R in place. Next, she pointed out that though our model is exactly like the endowment model, it is nevertheless only endowment-like. That added an E. And how does our model differ from Yale's? Leticia immediately said, "Allocation!" Then she inserted an L for "like" and finished with M for "model. That's how REALM was born—over a cup of coffee.

Another thing I love about this acronym is that one of the meanings of "realm" has to do with a special area of knowledge. In this sense, REALM is apropos, since it describes a new way of thinking about investing.

I wanted to offer my clients the potential for high, durable income through dynamic diversification. To that end, I have dedicated years of my life developing an investment portfolio based on rigorous research and mathematical rigor, one that is similar to the multi-asset-class portfolios used by billion-dollar university endowments. The driving force behind all of that work was, and continues to be, the protection of my clients.

CHAPTER 11

THE REALM MODEL:
A WORLD OF
POSSIBILITIES

"An investment in knowledge
pays the best interest."

—BENJAMIN FRANKLIN

Note: The REALM strategy contains alternative investments, which are speculative by nature and have various risks including possible lack of liquidity, lack of control, changes in business conditions, and devaluation based on the investment, the economy, and/or regulatory changes. As a result, the values of alternative investments do fluctuate resulting in the value at sale being more or less than the original price paid if a liquid market for the securities is found. Alternative investments are not appropriate for all investors. No investment process is free of risk; no strategy or risk management technique can guarantee returns or eliminate risk in any market environment. There is no guarantee that this investment model/process will be profitable. Diversification does not guarantee profit nor is it guaranteed to prevent losses.

A ccording to the Financial Industry Regulatory Authority (FINRA), "All investments can carry some degree of risk. Stocks, bonds, mutual funds, and exchange-traded funds can lose value—even their entire value—if market conditions sour. Even conservative, insured investments, such as certificates of deposit (CDs) issued by a bank or credit union, come with inflation risk."[1]

This highlights one of the fundamental ideas in finance—the relationship between risk and return. The greater amount of risk an investor is willing to take on, the greater the potential return. Each investor has a risk profile that determines his or her willingness and ability to withstand risk.

Here's a simple example of risk versus return. Treasury bonds are considered one of the safest investments, but they offer you a lower rate of return than corporate bonds because a corporation is considered more likely to go bankrupt than the United States government. And precisely because the default risk of investing in a corporate bond is higher is why investors can receive a higher rate of return.[2]

Although risk is an inevitable part of our financial lives, it does not mean there is nothing we can do about it. In fact, one of the most important challenges facing individual investors, institutional investors, and financial advisors is the development of risk-management strategies. One way they do that is by focusing on the relationship between volatility and risk. **Volatility** is a "statistical measure of the dispersion of returns for a given security or market index. In most cases, the higher the volatility, the riskier the security."[3] You can measure volatility by using standard deviation.

Standard Deviation

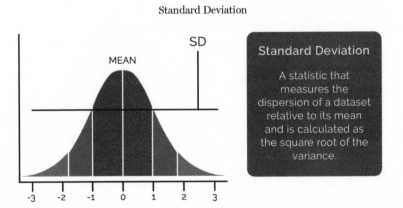

Standard Deviation

A statistic that measures the dispersion of a dataset relative to its mean and is calculated as the square root of the variance.

Standard deviation is a "statistic that measures the dispersion of a data set relative to its mean and is calculated as the square root of the variance."[4] The 0 in the middle of a standard deviation graph represents the **average**, also known as the **mean**. The positive numbers to the right of 0 and the negative numbers to the left of 0 are known as **deviations**. The farther away you are from the middle (0), the higher the deviation.

We can apply standard deviation to the annual rate of return of an investment to get a sense of the investment's historical volatility.[5] For example, a volatile stock has a high standard deviation, while a stable blue-chip stock typically has a low standard deviation. An index fund may have a low standard deviation compared to its benchmark index, as the fund's goal is to replicate the index.[6] Investors who have a low-risk profile will generally prefer less-than-average volatility, which translates to a lower standard deviation.

Standard deviation is a tool that helps you better understand your tolerance for volatility, which in turn helps you better assess your risk profile (i.e., your risk tolerance).

While the concept of investment risk has a clear definition, *the amount of risk* each of us is willing to accept involves some level of subjectivity. How do you know how much risk you are willing to tolerate? There are self-assessments available online, or you can consult a qualified and experienced financial advisor to help you understand your own risk tolerance. This is one of the reasons it's so important to have a financial advisor.

Another way of understanding your risk tolerance is to determine your aversion to risk. If you have a strong desire not to see the value of your investment account decline, then you are risk averse and have a low willingness to take on risk. The opposite, of course, is also true. If you want the highest possible return on your investment, then you have a high willingness to take on risk.[7] In other words, if you don't like to take risks with your hard-earned money, you are risk averse. Similarly, if you want potentially higher returns, then you are someone who tolerates higher risk. It is important to understand that any investment you make carries risk. Other factors that can help you determine your unique risk tolerance include:[8]

- Time horizon: The time frame for your investment is a major consideration for how much risk you are willing to accept. For example, someone who has a 15-year time horizon may take on more risk when compared to someone who will need their assets in five years.

- Goals: The goal of financial planning is not necessarily to accumulate the maximum amount of money. Rather, you want to determine the amount of money needed to achieve certain goals. Your investment strategy should reflect those goals, which in part will determine your risk tolerance.

- Age: It is obvious that the younger you are, the more risk you can take. This goes back to one's time horizon. Young people will have more years to earn more money and more time to withstand market fluctuations.

- Portfolio size: A larger portfolio can take on more risk than a smaller one. For example, a $1 million portfolio will be less affected by risk than a portfolio valued at $100k. If the value of your portfolio drops, the percentage is much less in a larger portfolio than a smaller one.

- Comfort level: Some people are naturally more comfortable taking on greater risk, while for others, market volatility can be quite uncomfortable. Based on how much risk an investor can tolerate, there are typically three categories to describe risk tolerance.

    › **Aggressive**: An aggressive investor is someone who can handle the sudden swings of the market. Aggressive investors tend to be wealthy, experienced, and have a diversified portfolio.

    › **Moderate**: This type of investor tends to have a lower tolerance for risk. A moderately risk-averse investor will typically set a percentage of loss he or she can handle. This investor will balance risky investments with safe asset classes.

    › **Conservative**: This investor type is risk averse and will not engage in risky investments at all. A conservative investor will prioritize avoiding losses above making gains.

PORTFOLIO DIVERSIFICATION AND RISK

We all have a level of risk tolerance that we are comfortable with, but our personal exposure to risk can be managed and potentially mitigated. Standard deviation can be used to judge how risky an asset is. Another strategy for potentially lowering risk is **diversification**, which is a "technique that reduces risk by allocating investments across various financial instruments, industries, and other categories."[9] Although diversification does not guarantee against loss, most investment professionals agree that diversification is perhaps the most important consideration in achieving long-term financial goals while potentially minimizing risk.[10]

Minimizing risk for my clients was why I developed the REALM model, which rests on the fundamental idea that a diversified portfolio can potentially lead to higher risk-adjusted returns. Creating a multi-asset-class portfolio was not enough. I knew I had to make a model that was flexible, adaptable, and customizable for each of my clients.

STRUCTURE VERSUS FUNCTION

When you hear the word "structure," what comes to mind? You might think of a shape or form of something, like a house or a building; or you might think of the design or organization of something complex like a car or computer. According to Google's Oxford Languages dictionary, a **structure** refers to "the arrangement of and relations between the parts or elements of something complex."[11] The key word here is "arrangement." If you arrange different parts, or elements, and these parts are related in some way, then you have created a structure.

Structures can be found in nature, or we can create them. Think of a beautiful flower and the arrangement of its petals, or a suspension bridge with its suspender cables, main cables, and deck.

Intimately connected to structure is **function**, which, according to the Cambridge Dictionary is "the way in which something works or operates."[12] How are structure and function related? The simple answer is that structure determines function. Here's an example from biology: The human body is made up of trillions of cells. Many of these cells, of course, have different structures. Skin cells are different from muscle cells, which are different from brain cells, also called neurons.

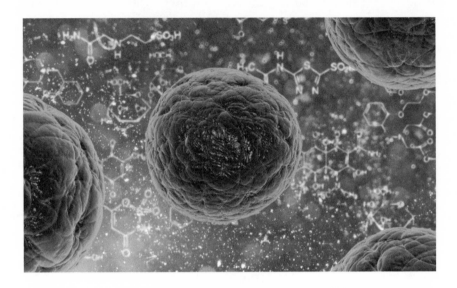

High resolution image of a human cell juxtaposed
with a series of chemical reactions[13]

Think of the human cell as a factory with different departments that carry out specific tasks. Cells are the basic unit of all living things. Each cell carries out complex chemical reactions necessary to sustain life. Again, the structure of each cell will determine its function. For example, the human brain has some 80 billion cells called neurons. These neurons communicate with one another using electrochemical signals that move across hairlike structures called dendrites. If neurons had a different shape, say spherical, then there would be no electrochemical signals sent from one neuron to the next.

This idea of structure determining function is found throughout nature. Let's now apply this fundamental concept to the structure of the REALM model.

THE STRUCTURE OF REALM

The REALM® Model

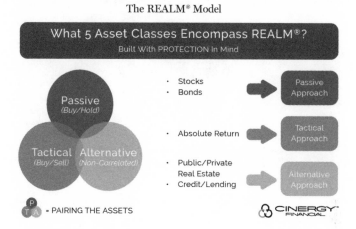

The structure of my REALM® Model with three intersecting circles and five asset classes

The structure of REALM involves three interlocking circles, with each circle having a function that impacts the other two. These three circles include a passive strategy, a tactical strategy, and an alternative strategy. In addition to three interlocking circles, the REALM model utilizes five asset classes: stocks and bonds under the passive strategy, absolute return under the tactical strategy, REITs and credit lending under the alternative strategy.

Notably, the REALM structure is not static. I purposely designed the structure of REALM to be dynamic, to change in response to economic conditions and to my clients' financial reality.

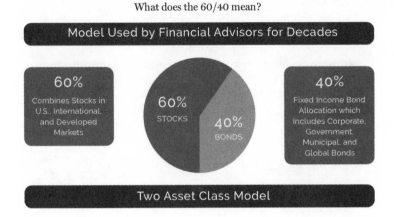

The 60/40 portfolio is a simple two-asset-class model that is static and inflexible

Let's compare the REALM structure to that of a 60/40 portfolio, which is much simpler. This is a two-asset-class model with a fixed allocation of 60 percent in stocks and 40 percent in bonds. There is nothing dynamic about this model. Its simplicity is what originally made it attractive, but from a structural point of view, the simplicity makes it a liability in today's economic environment of high-interest inflation.

If structure determines function, then a simple binary structure of stocks and bonds may not generate the kind of functionality that the REALM model is capable of. The structure of the 60/40 portfolio does not allow for dynamic diversification, which can potentially offer higher durable income opportunities while managing risk.

THE FUNCTION OF REALM: DYNAMIC ASSET ALLOCATION

The structure of an investment portfolio will largely determine its function. In the abstract, a complex portfolio structure may not necessarily produce a desired outcome. For the REALM model, however, I tried to construct a portfolio with the potential to generate high durable income while managing risk.

To begin with, its five asset classes allows for **dynamic asset allocation**, which is a "portfolio management strategy that frequently adjusts the mix of asset classes to suit market conditions."[14] Adjustments typically involve reducing positions in asset classes that perform poorly and adding positions to the best-performing assets. This approach can help protect you from the risks of sudden downturns in the market, and has the potential to achieve returns that go beyond a targeted market such as the S&P 500 index.

The concept of dynamic asset allocation lends itself to a similar concept known as **dynamic diversification**, which I define as an active ongoing diversification of assets that change over time in response to market conditions or the changing circumstances of retail investors. It is not enough to simply diversify; you also need to continually monitor your diversification.

THE THREE PILLARS OF REALM: AN INTEGRATED STRATEGY

The REALM® Approach Based on Three Integrated Strategies

A Multi-Strategy Approach Aimed at Providing STRENGTH and STABILITY to Withstand Uncertain Markets

DYNAMIC DIVERSIFICATION

| I PASSIVE | Balance | II TACTICAL | Sustainability | III ALTERNATIVE |

The structure of REALM creates balance and sustainability.

The three pillars of REALM—Passive, Tactical, and Alternative Assets—form an integrated strategy that structurally supports dynamic diversification. By using these three approaches, I can offer my clients five asset classes: stocks, bonds, absolute return, commercial real estate, and private equity. The amount I allocate (as a percent of the total portfolio) to each of these assets is, in part, dictated by economic conditions. Economic conditions may also determine whether I use traded or nontraded REITs and BDCs. This is why it's so important to understand macro, big-picture economic forces. Let's quickly review the REALM model:

Three Strategies	Five Asset Classes
1. Passive	1. Stocks
2. Tactical	2. Bonds
3. Alternative	3. Absolute Return
	4. REITs
	5. Private Credit

PASSIVE STRATEGY

Passive assets refer to the 60/40 stock/bond approach but at a much lower allocation. One of the benefits of passive investing is, of course, its buy-and-hold strategy, which is a long-term approach. I prefer to use **low-cost index funds**, which are "pooled investments with low expense ratios, or annual management fees."[15] Low-cost index funds minimize costs while potentially generating superior returns over time. Similarly, bond funds, which may be mutual funds, ETFs, or closed-end funds, invest in bonds or other types of debt securities. One of the benefits of bond funds is that they "provide instant diversification for investors for a low required minimum investment."[16]

TACTICAL STRATEGY

The tactical strategy involves the use of short-term, liquid assets that protect gains in accounts that investors can tap as needed. Tactical investments are designed to take advantage of short-term market fluctuations but always with protection to minimize losses. **Tactical investing** is an "active portfolio-management strategy that changes the percentage of asset class categories to capture current market strengths or mispricing."[17] The tactical strategy is critical to the REALM model given that the "60/40 portfolio has returned 5 percent on average over the last 100 years, so [the current] drawdown has erased more than two years of average returns."[18] If tactical moves are done correctly, investors will potentially benefit from better outcomes.

ALTERNATIVE STRATEGY

The alternative strategy involves the addition of alternative assets to a well-designed multi-asset-class model, such as REALM. As we've noted, an alternative asset is any asset class that does not include stocks, bonds, or cash, and these exist on a spectrum of limited liquidity to illiquidity. These asset classes have the potential to deliver greater returns than a simple stock/bond/cash portfolio (the 60/40 model). Alternative assets such as interval funds add time as an active investment factor and require a commitment of months or even a couple of years. Specific alternative structures include daily net asset value (NAV) funds, nontraded preferred stock, interval funds, business development companies (closed-end funds), nontraded real estate investment trusts (REITs), private placements, credit/lending, venture capital, and commodities and credit/lending.

Alternative Structures

Alternative structures or products have a range of liquidity from limited liquidity to illiquid.

I want to clarify that when I use the term "specific alternative structures," I mean the actual alternative products that I offer my clients. Economic conditions will determine my allocation strategy as well as my preference for traded versus nontraded products such as REITs and BDCs.

It is important for all investors to understand what is meant by **three degrees of liquidity**. It refers to the fact that certain asset classes offer a range of liquidity from liquid to moderately liquid to illiquid. A liquid asset can be easily and quickly converted into cash. Liquid assets include cash or cash equivalents such as stocks, bonds, money markets, and CDs. Other assets, such as nontraded BDCs and REITs, offer relatively limited liquidity. Finally, private placements tend to be illiquid, which means you have to hold on to them longer.

Liquid alternative assets—alternative vehicles that aim to be more accessible to retail investors—may include net asset value funds, nontraded preferred stocks, and interval funds.[19]

NET ASSET VALUE (NAV)

The **net asset value** of an investment company is "the company's total assets minus its total liabilities."[20] Here's a simple example: If an investment company has securities and other assets valued at $100 million and total liabilities of $10 million, the investment company's NAV is $90 million.

The important thing to understand is that the NAV will change daily. One day it might be $90 million, then $100 million the next, and $80 million the day after that.[21] Once companies determine their daily NAV, this amount is divided by the number of shares outstanding to get "the per share value of the fund, which makes it easier to be used for valuing and transacting the fund shares."[22]

Mutual funds "collect money from a large number of investors, then use that money to invest in securities, such as stocks, bonds, and money market instruments. Each investor gets a specified number of shares in proportion to their invested amount. The pricing of each share is based on NAV [net asset value]."[23]

PREFERRED STOCK

There are two types of stocks—common stocks and preferred stocks. **Preferred stockholders** "have a higher claim to dividends or asset distribution than common stockholders." Common stockholders have voting rights in corporate governance, while preferred stockholders have limited or no voting rights.[24] When it comes to dividends, preferred stock holders have priority over common stockholders. Preferred stockholders have limited voting rights, compared to common stockholders. Preferred stocks have the following characteristics:[25]

- Equity ownership of a company
- Tradable on public exchanges (for public companies)
- Nontraded for private companies
- Have first right to dividends
- Have no voting rights
- May have the option to be converted to common stock
- Receive better treatment during liquidations

Some of the advantages of preferred stocks include higher dividend returns and a "callable feature, which means that the issuer has the right to redeem the shares at a predetermined price and date as indicated in the prospectus."[26] Like any other investment, there are risks involved with preferred stocks, which may include the loss of capital.

INTERVAL FUNDS

An **interval fund** is a "type of closed-end fund with shares that do not trade on the secondary market."[27] **Closed-end funds** "offer a particular number of shares after raising a fixed amount of money through an IPO (initial public offering). The rules of interval funds make this alternative asset largely illiquid. What makes these funds attractive to investors are the high yields. In effect, you give up liquidity for potentially higher yields. Below are some characteristics of interval funds:[28]

- Interval funds are typically offered for sale daily by the fund at the current net asset value (NAV).

- The minimum investment of an interval fund is typically between $10,000 and $25,000, and they have expense ratios as high as 3 percent.

- Interval funds tend to offer higher returns than open-end funds. Also, their ability to invest in alternative types of assets helps increase interval-fund yields.

- Due to restricted selling opportunities, an interval fund should be considered a long-term, mostly illiquid investment.

TRADED AND NONTRADED REAL ESTATE INVESTMENT TRUSTS (REITs)

As the name implies, **nontraded real estate investment trusts** are "not listed on public exchanges and can provide investors access to inaccessible real estate investments with tax benefits."[29] Because they do not trade on a securities exchange, nontraded REITs are illiquid. REITs deal with commercial properties, and property acquisitions might be made through a blind pool, where the investors do not know the specific properties that are being added to the program's portfolio. Some of the advantages of nontraded REITs include:[30]

- High potential payout

- Significant tax benefits

- Equity ownership of real property

- Portfolio diversification

You also need to be equally aware of the risks of nontraded REITs, which include:

- Non traded REITs are not publicly traded, which means investors are unable to perform research on their investment. The result is that it is difficult to determine the REIT's value.[31]

- Lack of liquidity: It is important to understand that non traded REITs are illiquid, which means there may not be buyers and sellers in the market available when you want sell. In many cases, nontraded REITs can't be sold for a minimum of seven years.[32]

- Nontraded REITs need to pool money to buy and manage properties, which locks investor money.[33]

- Fees: Investors have to deal with upfront fees which are between 9 percent and 10 percent—and sometimes 15 percent.[34]

As the name implies, **traded REITs** are "publicly traded on major securities exchanges, and investors can buy and sell them like stocks throughout the trading session. These REITs typically trade under substantial volume and are considered very liquid instruments."[35] Traded REITs tend to be more risky than private or nontraded REITs. To minimize risk, I offer my clients nontraded REITs, though I may also offer a combination of traded and nontraded REITs.

TRADED AND NONTRADED BDCs

Within private credit, the recent rise of business development companies (BDCs) has created a new sector of alternative asset classes. I currently offer my clients both traded and nontraded BDCs. The former trade on an exchange, which means they are fairly liquid and transparent. Private BDCs are referred to as nontraded BDCs and aren't exposed to the risk of share-price volatility. They also tend to have heavy fees, low liquidity, and little transparency.[36] To minimize risk, I offer my clients a combination of traded and nontraded BDCs.

PRIVATE CREDIT

Private credit is an "asset class comprised of higher yielding, illiquid investment opportunities that covers a range of risk/return profiles. This includes debt that is secured and senior in the capital structure with fixed income like characteristics and distressed debt that has very equity-like risks and returns."[37] What exactly does that mean? Private credit is the process through which nonbank lenders offer loans to small- and medium-sized companies that are considered noninvestment grade. Think of a time when you applied for a loan. The bank checks your credit, which is based on your credit score. (FICO credit scores range from 300 to 800.) The higher your credit score, the more likely you are to get a loan with excellent terms.

Similarly, small- and medium-size companies have their own creditworthiness known as investment grade. Investment ratings companies like Standard and Poor's and Fitch use a unique letter-based system to quickly convey to investors whether a bond carries a low or high default risk and whether the issuer is financially stable. For example, Standard and Poor's highest rating is AAA. A bond is no longer considered investment grade if it falls to BB+ status. Moody's, on the other hand, uses uppercase and lowercase letters to assign credit ratings such as Aaa, Aa, A, Baa, Ba, B, Caa, Ca, C, with WR and NR as withdrawn and not rated, respectively.[38]

Private credit creates what is known as "senior secured debt." When a company obtains private credit, it is because they have a low credit rating and pose a higher risk to the lender. The debt the company incurs is known as a senior debt, meaning that if a company goes bankrupt, the issuers of senior debt—the lenders—have seniority in terms of repayment. In other words, the lender of the private credit must be paid first. Private credit funds "serve as a diversifier in a private market portfolio as debt is less correlated with equity markets."[39]

INDEX FUNDS

Is there a way for average investors to have broad market exposure with low operating expenses and low portfolio turnover? The answer is index funds.

An **index fund** is a "type of mutual fund or exchange-traded fund (ETF) with a portfolio constructed to match or track the components of a financial market index, such as the Standard & Poor's 500 index (S&P 500)."[40] An index fund is basically a pool of money collected from "big and small investors that is passively managed. Its strategy is simple: follow the moves in a designated widely known market index."[41] Some advantages of index funds include the following:[42]

- Index funds seek to match the market, not beat it.

- Investors can easily gauge performance, because the funds track widely used benchmarks. For instance, if the S&P 500 rises 0.5 percent on any given day, the index fund will rise by almost the same amount.

- There's minimal trading activity—only what's necessary to match any adjustments to the composition of the index-computer programs, and it's done without human intervention.

- Minimal trading means low turnover in the fund, low maintenance, and very low fees; for example, the most popular S&P 500 funds charge about 0.025 percent, or 25 cents per $1,000 invested.

I use index funds to give my clients broad market exposure. Index funds offer the average investor exposure to markets with a much lower barrier of entry. They act like a combination of hedge funds, a way to hedge risk. Index funds:[43]

- Can lower risk through diversification

- Have low expense ratios

- Offer strong long-term returns

- Are ideal for passive, buy-and-hold investors

- Lower taxes for investors

Hedge funds are "private investment partnerships that use a variety of non-traditional strategies, many of them considered too risky by more conventional fund managers, with the objective of delivering exceptional returns." The risks are reduced by using an approach called—you guessed it—hedging. It was not long ago that hedge funds required a minimum investment of $1 million. However, this high barrier of entry has gone down recently with minimum investments now starting at $100,000.

PRIVATE PLACEMENTS

Private placements involve the sale of "stock shares or bonds to pre-selected investors and institutions rather than on the open market."[44] When a company wants to raise capital for expansion, one popular avenue to take is for the company to sell shares, or a fractional amount of ownership, to the public. A company does this by a process known as an initial public offering (IPO). If a company wants to raise capital but does not want to become publicly owned, then private placement is another option.

One of the advantages of private placement is that it allows start-up companies to raise funds much faster than by going public. In addition, raising money through private placement avoids public scrutiny and regulations. The "light regulation of private placements allows the company to avoid the time and expense of registering with the SEC. That means the process of underwriting is faster, and the company gets its funding sooner."[45]

BENEFITS OF THE REALM MODEL

I constructed the REALM model in order to protect my clients from sudden market corrections and uncertainty. I spent years studying and researching an investment portfolio that can potentially offer robust returns while managing risk. The resulting tripartite system of passive, tactical, and alternative strategies, along with five asset classes, serves as a dynamic system that can diversify your portfolio and offer enhanced returns.

Adding Alternative Investments to the 60/40 Model Potentially Provides

- Solid Historical Return
- Potentially Lower Volatility
- Potentially Higher Income

Source: https://www.financialsamurai.com/the-60-40-portfolio/

Note: Past performance is no guarantee of future results.

By adding alternative investments—which have a lower correlation to traditional assets like stocks, bonds, and cash—to your portfolio, you could potentially generate solid historic returns with lower volatility and higher income. The REALM model is also potentially superior to the outdated and ineffective 60/40 portfolio. Since "interest rates have risen, the attractiveness of a 60/40 portfolio should be higher . . . [yet] a 60/40 portfolio increased by only 2.47 percent (YTD 1Q 2021) compared to a 6.17 percent increase in the S&P 500 during the same period. Given the huge decline in bonds, the underperformance of a 60/40 portfolio is to be expected."[46]

Given that the burden has shifted to each one of us to plan and prepare for our own retirement—whatever *your* vision of retirement is—you need to start preparing for it *now*.

One of the difficult aspects of my job is to talk to people who are close to retirement who have not prepared for it. The REALM investment model can potentially help you achieve your retirement vision. Investments alone, however, are not the only component of retirement planning.

CHAPTER 12

INSURANCE AND TAX STRATEGIES FOR RETIREMENT

*"The biggest adventure you can take is
to live the life of your dreams."*

—OPRAH WINFREY

Note: This material is not intended to replace the advice of a qualified tax advisor, attorney, accountant, or insurance advisor. Consultation with the appropriate professional should be done before any financial commitments regarding the issues related to the situation are made.

Please keep in mind insurance companies alone determine insurability, and some people, for their own health or lifestyle reasons, are deemed uninsurable.

Our lives are punctuated by stages. That is the nature of what it means to exist. We are born, go through childhood, get an education, work, get married (or develop partnerships), struggle to realize some aspect of the American Dream, and finally retire with a sense of dignity and the belief that we have lived a life of purpose and meaning. Of course, we are not solitary creatures. We are social beings whose lives often revolve around the family. In this respect, we live for others. We work hard all our lives in the hope that our children will realize a greater potential than our own.

Clouding that noble goal of generational self-improvement lies a set of existential fears. Will we have enough money to sustain our retirement? If our worst fear is realized and our money runs out, then what will become of us? The last thing we want, as we get older, is to become a burden to our children. For both men and women, work endows our lives with not only purpose and meaning but also independence. There is something about being free— socially, politically, and economically—that gives us agency in the world.

Agency gives us the capacity to choose how we want to live our life. It is the perceived loss of agency that scares us about being a burden to others. Think of agency as existing on a continuum. As we get older, our physical and mental abilities begin to decline. We can't do the things we did for decades with the same ease. For example, for some of us, driving, particularly at night, becomes more and more difficult. We might be forced to depend on others to drive us. This loss of movement limits our freedom.

If we do not anticipate what is coming, we may find ourselves in situations that are uncomfortable and difficult. This is why it's so important to have a broadly defined risk-management strategy whose purpose is to hedge against sudden life changes that could potentially undermine everything we have worked hard to build.

RETIREMENT RISK-MANAGEMENT STRATEGIES

I'm sure you've heard the term "risk management" in casual conversations. You may associate the phrase exclusively with managing *investment* risk. **Risk management**, however, has a much broader meaning, which "includes steps you can take to minimize the risks to your financial plans— not just stock market risk, but also inflation risk and longevity risk. It includes protecting your finances from other risks—such as the risk to your family if you die early and your income stops, or you become sick and injured and unable to work, or that your home or car will be damaged in a disaster or accident."[1]

Certainly, our lives are defined by uncertainty. It was the French philosopher Jean-Paul Sartre who said, "Man is a being hurling himself towards the future."[2] In other words, human beings are always projecting themselves into the unknown. But if we couldn't imagine the future with ourselves in it, there would be no need to plan or prepare for anything. Even if we look ahead, we cannot predict with any degree of acceptable accuracy how exactly our lives will unfold. You need a risk-management strategy to protect yourself from an uncertain future. Let's start with life insurance.

LIFE INSURANCE

Insurance generally is defined as a "contract, represented by a policy, in which a policyholder receives financial protection or reimbursement against losses from an insurance company. The company pools clients' risks to make payments more affordable for the insured."[3] Thus insurance acts as a hedge against financial losses that may result from the insured or their property.

Like any other type of insurance, life insurance is a contract between an insurer (typically a large corporation) and a policy owner (you). More specifically, "a life insurance policy guarantees the insurer pays a sum of money to named beneficiaries when the insured dies in exchange for the premiums paid by the policy holder during their lifetime."[4] There are two types of life insurance policies, and it's important to know the different choices available to you.

- Term life insurance: This type of insurance is largely defined by the number of years attached to it. You can choose 10-, 20-, or 30-year term life insurance. One thing to keep in mind when deciding on which term to select is the balance between affordability and long-term financial strength.[5] Within this canopy are three different types of term life insurance.

> › Decreasing term life insurance: As the name implies, this is a renewable life insurance with coverage decreasing over the life of the policy at a predetermined rate.[6]

> › Convertible term life insurance: This kind of term life insurance gives you the flexibility to convert a term policy to permanent insurance.[7]

> › Renewable term life insurance: In this type of life insurance, you are given a quote for the year your policy is purchased. Premiums increase annually. This is the least expensive term life insurance available during the early years of the policy.[8]

• Permanent life insurance: This type of insurance stays in force throughout the insured's lifetime. It is typically more expensive than a term life policy, and it, too, has different versions.[9]

> › Whole life insurance: This type of policy accumulates a cash value. You, the policyholder, can use the cash value as a source of loans or to pay policy premiums.[10]

> › Universal life insurance (UL): This kind of permanent life insurance contains a cash value component that earns interest. Premiums are flexible in the sense that they can be adjusted over time and designed with either a level or increasing death benefit.[11]

> › Variable universal life insurance: This permanent life insurance policy allows the policyholder to invest the policy's cash value in an available separate account.[12]

> › Indexed universal life insurance (IUL): This kind of policy is often presented as a cash value insurance policy that benefits from the stock market without the risk of loss during a market downturn. An indexed universal life insurance gives you permanent coverage, as long as premiums are paid. What makes IUL different from other permanent life insurance policies is that the cash portion of

your policy earns interest based on the performance of an underlying stock market index.[13]

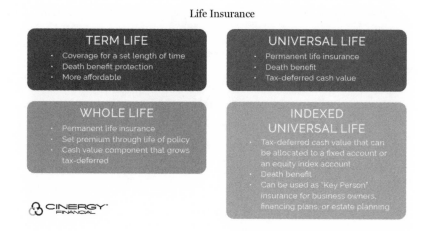

Life Insurance

Types of life insurance policies that are potentially important to your retirement plan

Taking out a life insurance policy is a selfless act that we can perform so as not to leave our loved ones in a dire financial situation. Below are some of the benefits of having life insurance—some obvious, others less so.

- Life insurance payouts are tax-free: Many people may not be aware of this benefit, which can potentially save your beneficiaries thousands of dollars. Let's suppose person A takes out a life insurance policy. If person A dies while the coverage is in effect, the beneficiaries will receive a lump-sum death benefit. Life insurance payouts are not considered income for tax purposes; therefore, beneficiaries don't have to report the money when they file their tax return.[14]

- Your dependents won't have to worry about living expenses: Experts generally recommend that a life insurance policy be equivalent to 7 to 10 times one's annual income. This is to ensure that those who depend on your income will not have to worry about living expenses or other life expenses, like college tuition.[15]

- Life insurance can cover final expenses: The national median cost of a funeral, which includes a viewing and a burial, was $7,848 in 2021. This is a staggering sum, given that Americans do not have enough savings to cover a $400 emergency expense. A life insurance policy can relieve your family of this burden. Your beneficiaries can use money from your life insurance policy to pay for your funeral expenses.[16]

- You can get coverage for chronic and terminal illnesses: Many life insurance companies offer what are known as riders or added provisions that amend the terms of a basic policy. For example, an accelerated benefits rider allows you to access some or all of your death benefits under certain circumstances. Let's suppose you are diagnosed with a terminal illness and are expected to live less than a year. Under these circumstances, you can use your death benefit while you're still alive to pay for your care.[17]

- Life insurance policies can supplement your retirement savings: Those who purchase a whole, universal, or variable life insurance policy can use the accumulated cash value to cover expenses such as buying a car or putting a down payment on a home. You can also tap into these funds during your retirement years.[18]

LONG-TERM CARE

Long-term care is an umbrella term that describes a "variety of services and supports for those who can no longer care for themselves due to age-related impairments."[19] Some of the services include assisted living, nursing home care, in-home care, as well as adult day-care centers. It might surprise you to learn that 70 percent of us will require long-term care at some point, and long-term care is an expensive proposition.

For example, a private room in a nursing home currently costs $297 per day or $9,036 per month. A semiprivate room in a nursing facility is $260 per day or $7,908 per month. Assisted living is $168 per day or $4,500 per month.[20] These are astronomical prices that will quickly deplete your hard-earned savings or investment account, which is why it is important to consider long-term-care insurance (LTC insurance).

Obviously, these prices are out of reach for average Americans. Medicare will pay for doctor visits, hospital stays, and prescription medication, but it will *not* pay for long-term care. Medicaid does pay for long-term care, but there is a condition that many people may not be aware of.

Medicaid "is a joint federal and state program that helps low-income Americans of all ages pay for the costs associated with medical long-term custodial care."[21] However, if you qualify for Medicaid, you should be aware of the fine print: Although you do not have to sell your home before moving into a long-term care facility, "that does not mean [your home] is completely protected. The state will likely put a lien on the house the resident is living in and attempt to recover the property after the resident has passed away."[22] A federal law "requires the state to attempt to recover the long-term care benefits from a Medicaid recipient's estate after the recipient's death."[23]

Let's suppose you own your home but due to declining health or an unforeseen injury, you need to spend time in a long-term-care facility (nursing home), either temporarily or permanently. During your stay, you and your loved ones are comforted by the fact that Medicaid is taking care of the bills. However, the state where you received Medicaid will likely put a lien on your home in order to recover some or part of the cost of your long-term-care expenses.

Long-term-care insurance "covers all or part of assisted living facilities and in-home care."[24] Many experts recommend that people start shopping for long-term-care insurance between the ages of 45 and 55. As a financial advisor, I believe that long-term-care insurance should be an important part of your retirement plan to protect yourself from the high costs of extended health care. Of course, the earlier you purchase long-term-care insurance, the cheaper it will be.

LTC RIDERS

Today, you can combine a life insurance policy with long-term care (LTC) with what is known in the industry as a rider. **Riders** are simply "additional benefits that can be bought and added to a basic life insurance policy."[25] A long-term-care life insurance rider is "a policy addition that slightly changes how your life insurance works, allowing you to use part or all of the policy's death benefit for long-term care while you are alive."[26] One benefit of combining life insurance with long-term care is that it covers two needs in one policy. The rider can help you pay for long-term-care expenses that traditional health insurance doesn't cover, such as a home health-care worker, long-term-care facility, or a nursing home. An LTC rider does not pay for expenses covered by health insurance policies like doctor visits, hospital stays, or prescriptions.

When searching for a life insurance policy with a long-term-care rider, you need to get an amount of insurance that will cover all your assets: your home, car(s), investment accounts, and retirement accounts. If your combined assets are worth $1 million or more, you should get a policy with at least $1 million coverage.

Think of a rider as customized coverage. There are perhaps seven companies today that offer life insurance with a rider. Always be sure to read the fine print before buying a life insurance policy with a rider. You should also sit down with a qualified and experienced insurance advisor to help you evaluate the benefits of riders and to choose one best suited to you and your family.

UMBRELLA INSURANCE

Another form of insurance you should consider is an **umbrella policy**. This is "extra liability coverage which goes beyond the limits of the insured's home, auto or other liability coverage. It provides an additional layer of security to those who are at risk of high loss if they injure someone else, or someone's property."[27] An umbrella policy will typically kick in when your base liability limits have been reached.

Suppose you are in a car accident. Unfortunately the accident was your fault, and several people were injured. The medical bills come to a whopping $350,000, which exceeds the limits of your liability car insurance by $100,000. In this hypothetical situation, you would be responsible for the balance, which could put your home and savings at risk. An umbrella policy would protect your assets in liability situations that you may not be able to control, covering a wide range of liability issues including:[28]

- Bodily injury to others

- Property damage to others

- The legal costs to defend you in lawsuits

- Other lawsuits such as defamation, libel, slander, and invasion of privacy

- Liability situations that happen outside the U.S.

THE THREE BUCKETS OF TAXATION

We all know the saying that the only things certain in life are death and taxes. Certainly taxes are an unavoidable fact of modern life, with our economic lives today revolving around a seemingly endless array of state and federal taxes. We are taxed on the gas we use, on goods and services we purchase, on our home, our income, and several other categories. These taxes can be financially exhausting and can potentially derail your investment and retirement plan. It's important for everyone to have a basic understanding of how taxes work. I'm not suggesting you become a tax expert, but you need to familiarize yourself with the ways taxes can impact your retirement planning.

First, a little background: It might surprise you to know that the idea of a tax on income is a relatively new concept in American history. The federal income tax was introduced in 1913 to help finance World War I. Taxes on income were based on a marginal rate model that increased with income. For example, when the federal income tax was introduced in 1913, the marginal tax rate was 1 percent on income of $0 to $20,000, 2 percent on income of $20,000 to $50,000, 3 percent on income of $50,000 to $75,000, 4 percent on income of $75,000 to $100,000, 5 percent on income of $100,000 to $250,000, 6 percent on income of $250,000 to $500,000, and 7 percent on income of $500,000 and more.[29]

As you can see, the federal income tax rate was progressive. Over time the rate would increase considerably. During World War II, the marginal tax rate reached an astronomical 94 percent. The current tax rate was signed into law in 2017 and has a range of 10 percent to 40.8 percent.

You also need to be aware of your state income tax laws. Some states have implemented a flat tax rate, where everyone is charged the same rate, regardless of income level.[30] There are those who believe that the federal government should also adopt a flat tax rate, which would tax everyone, both individuals and corporations, at the same rate. Those who oppose such a flat-tax system argue that it results in high-income taxpayers paying less than they should, which in turn contributes to greater inequality.

Below is a chart of the federal income tax rates from 1913 to 2022.

Top Federal Tax Rates

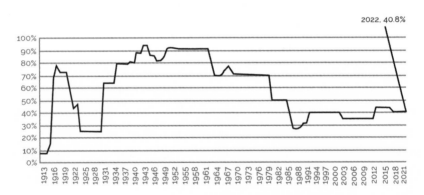

Federal tax rates from 1913 to 2022 [31]

TAX-EFFICIENT INVESTING

When it comes to investing, taxes can "take the biggest bite out of your returns."[32] The good news is that if you are willing to learn basic tax-efficient investing strategies, you can minimize your tax burden and maximize your bottom line. Here are some observations and tips:

- Taxes can be one of the biggest expenses and take the biggest bite out of your returns.

- Tax-efficient investing becomes more important when your tax bracket is higher.

- Investments that are tax efficient should be made in taxable accounts.

- Investments that are not tax efficient are better off in tax-deferred or tax-exempt accounts.

- Tax-advantaged accounts like IRAs and 401(k)s have annual contribution limits.

The Schwab Center for Financial Research "evaluated the long-term impact of taxes and other expenses on investment returns, and while investment selection and asset allocation are the most important factors that affect returns, the study found that minimizing the amount of taxes you pay also has a significant effect."[33] There are two reasons for this. First, when you pay taxes, you lose the money you pay, and second, you lose the potential growth your money could have generated if it were still invested.[34]

There are two types of investment accounts—taxable accounts and tax-advantaged accounts. A brokerage account, for example, is taxable. These accounts are good candidates for investments that lose less of their returns to taxes. Tax-deferred accounts, on the other hand, such as an individual retirement account (IRA), 401(k), or Roth IRA are generally better for investments that lose more of their return to taxes.[35] An important aspect of tax efficiency is placing your investments in the right account.

THREE BUCKETS OF MONEY

It's time to discuss the three categories of taxable assets, or three types of money. These include:

- Taxable money

  › Savings accounts

  › Money market accounts

  › Individual stocks and bonds

- › Mutual funds

- › Brokerage accounts

- Tax-deferred growth

  - › 401(k)s, 403(b)s, 457s

  - › Traditional IRAs

  - › Tax-deferred annuities

  - › I Bonds and EE Bonds

- Tax-free income

  - › Roth IRAs

  - › Roth 401(k)s

  - › Properly designed cash-value life insurance

  - › Municipal bonds

3 Types of Money

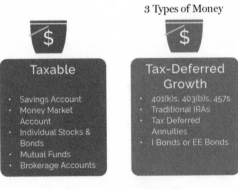

*Income from investing in municipal bonds is generally exempt from federal and
state taxes for residents of the issuing state. While the interest income is tax-exempt,
any capital gains distributed are taxable to the investor. Income for some investors
may be subject to the Federal Alternative Minimum Tax (AMT).

TAXABLE MONEY

Let's start with your savings account. Although you may not be earning significant money in your savings account, you need to know that "any interest earned on a savings account is considered taxable income by the Internal Revenue Service (IRS) and must be reported on your tax return."[36] It's not just your savings account that will be taxed on any interest earned; you will also be taxed on high-yield savings accounts, certificates of deposit (CDs), and money market deposit accounts. Although savings accounts are typically not thought of as investments, the IRS will consider the interest you earn—which may not be much—taxable. Your bank will send you a 1099-INT at the beginning of each year showing you the interest you earned for the previous year. If the amount is greater than $10, you are responsible for the taxes even if you do not receive a 1099-INT.

Money market accounts, which are also taxed, are interest-bearing accounts at a bank or credit union. Most money market accounts pay a higher interest rate than typical savings accounts. Just like other savings accounts or certificates of deposit, the interest earned is taxable. The federal income taxes "due on savings account interest are calculated as a percentage of your taxable income according to the current federal income tax brackets. These range from 10 percent to 37 percent depending on your income level."[37]

In addition to savings accounts, individual stocks and bonds are also taxed. The profits that result from the sale of any capital assets, such as stocks, bonds, and real estate, are viewed as capital gains. If you are an investor who sells stocks within one calendar year of buying them, your gains will be taxed as ordinary income. Your gains are referred to as short-term capital gains and, depending on your adjusted gross income (AGI), the tax rate could be as high as 37 percent.[38] Profits from the sale of bonds are also considered capital gains and are also taxed.

Although mutual funds are taxed, the process is more complicated than for other sources of income. The way mutual funds are treated for tax purposes has a lot to do with the type of investments within the fund's portfolio.[39] Generally speaking, the distributions you receive from a mutual fund must be declared as investment income. The determination of how much tax you will pay will depend on the type of distribution you receive, the duration of the investment holding, as well as the type of investment. Based on these and other factors, your distributions may be subject to your ordinary tax rate, or you might be eligible to pay the lower capital gains tax. Other distributions may be tax-free.

TAX-DEFERRED GROWTH

Although this is an oversimplification, the concept of tax-deferred growth is based on the idea of "earn money now, pay taxes later." I don't know of many people who enjoy paying taxes to the IRS. If given a choice, many of us would prefer to hold off on paying our taxes for as long as possible. Tax-deferred growth allows you to do just that. **Tax-deferred growth** "refers to investment earnings—such as interest, dividends, or capital gains—that accumulate tax-free until the investor takes constructive receipts of the profits."[40] Let's look at an example of a tax-deferred investment versus a taxable investment.

Suppose you have a single tax-deferred investment that earns 8 percent gross annual interest over a period of 30 years. After 30 years this single investment has grown to more than $750,000. Once you withdraw this amount, you pay 28 percent in taxes, which leaves you with an amount greater than $540,000. Now, let's suppose you paid 28 percent in taxes every year you had this investment. Over the same 30-year period, you would receive an after-tax amount of $400,000. The tax-deferred approach would have earned approximately $140,000 more than the annually taxed version. The reason for this is the compounding effect over a 30-year period.[41]

Some examples of tax-deferred growth include 401(k)s, 403(b)s, 457s, traditional IRAs, and tax-deferred annuities, as well as I bonds or EE bonds. In a traditional **401(k) plan**, which is an employer-sponsored retirement account, employee contributions are tax deferred. You pay the taxes on "contributions and earnings when the savings are withdrawn."[42] Another retirement plan with tax-deferred benefits is the **403(b) retirement account**. This plan is designed for "certain employees of public schools and other tax-exempt organizations. Participants may include teachers, school adminis-trators, professors, government employees, nurses, doctors, and librarians."[43] Similar to the 403(b) plan is the **457 plan**, which is a tax-deferred retirement savings plan offered to employees of local and state governments, as well as some nonprofit organizations.[44]

Another example of tax-deferred growth accounts is a traditional **individual retirement account (IRA)**, which allows "individuals to direct pre-tax income toward investments that can grow tax-deferred."[45] The IRS will not assess a capital gain or dividend income tax until you make a withdrawal. There are contribution limits that you need to be aware of. For example, for those under age 50, the contribution limit is $6,000 for 2021 and 2022; $7,000 for those 50 and older. There is also a required minimum distribution (RMD), which must begin at age 72 (73 if you reach age 72 after December 31, 2022).[46]

There are other tax-deferred growth opportunities, such as deferred annuities. An **annuity** is a "contract between the contract holder—the annuitant—and an insurance company."[47] Under this contract, an insurance company prom-ises to pay the owner (you) a regular income, or a lump sum at some date in the future. Annuities have several tax advantages. For example, "during the accumulation phase of an annuity contract, your earnings grow tax-deferred. You pay taxes only when you start taking withdrawals from the annuity."[48] If you fund your annuity through an IRA, you might be entitled to a tax deduction for your contribution. An IRA-funded annuity is known as a qualified annuity.

Remember, the contributions you make to annuities grow tax deferred until you withdraw funds. There are several types of annuities, including fixed, indexed, and variable. **Fixed annuities** provide "a predictable source of retirement income, with relatively low risk."[49] A fixed annuity gives you a specific amount of money every month for the rest of your life or a pre-defined period of 5, 10, or 20 years.

Another type of annuity is an indexed annuity, which is also known as a fixed-indexed annuity. An **indexed annuity** is like a fixed annuity with some additional investment growth. In other words, you are guaranteed a "certain minimum return, plus a return pegged to any rise in the relevant market index, such as the S&P 500."[50] An indexed annuity is regulated by state insurance commissioners as an insurance product, and in most states, agents must have an insurance license as well as a securities license to sell them.

TAX-FREE INCOME

There is another category of income: tax-free income. One such retirement vehicle is a Roth IRA. The primary benefit of a **Roth IRA** is "that your contributions and the earnings on those contributions can grow tax-free and be withdrawn tax-free after the age 59½ assuming the account has been open for at least five years. In other words, you pay taxes on money going into your Roth IRA, and then all future withdrawals are tax-free."[51] This is the key difference between a traditional IRA and a Roth IRA—both IRAs are funded with after-tax dollars; however, with a Roth IRA, once you start withdrawing funds, the money is tax-free.

Unless certain criteria are met, Roth IRA owners must be 59½ or older and have held the IRA for five years before tax-free withdrawals are permitted. Additionally, each converted amount may be subject to its own five-year holding period. Converting a traditional IRA into a Roth IRA has tax implications. Investors should consult a tax advisor before deciding to do a conversion.

Similar to Roth IRAs, many companies offer Roth 401(k) retirement accounts alongside traditional 401(k) plans. In a traditional 401(k) plan, you contribute pretax dollars and choose from a variety of investment options. Your contributions and potential earnings are tax deferred until you withdraw money. In a **Roth 401(k) plan**, you make contributions to your plan with money that has already been taxed. Any earnings you make grow tax-free, and you don't pay any taxes when you take withdrawals.[52] Understanding the different types of 401(k) plans could potentially save you thousands. For example, if you are young and in a low tax bracket but expect to be in a higher tax bracket over time, then a Roth 401(k) could potentially be a better choice for you.

Another investment vehicle that can offer you tax-free income is a properly designed cash value life insurance policy. One reason to purchase cash value insurance is to have access to the money that builds up within the policy. When you pay premiums, your money goes to three places: cash value, the cost to insure you, and policy fees and charges. The money within the cash value account grows tax-free, based on the interest or investment gains.[53] One important aspect of life insurance is that the payout to your beneficiaries is tax-free. However, if a beneficiary is not named, or is deceased, the death benefit goes into the estate of the insured and becomes taxable along with the rest of the estate.

Finally, government agencies may issue bonds to fund public projects, and these municipal bonds have a federal tax-free status; the interest payments are not taxed by the IRS. A **municipal bond** is "a loan to a state or local government or an entity under its control."[54] The interest you earn from municipal bonds is not taxed at the federal level. Some states do not tax municipal bonds, but some will, so you will need to check the state where you live.

CHAPTER 13

A RETIREMENT ROAD MAP: A QUICK GUIDE

*"A good financial plan is a road map
that shows us exactly how the choices
we make today will affect our future."*

—ALEXA VON TOBEL,
CEO OF LEARNVEST.COM

Think of a financial road map as a diagnostic tool to determine where you are today in terms of your financial health and what you need to do to achieve your retirement goals. One of the most important steps you can take now is to sit down and make a budget. Once that is in place, you can create a retirement checklist. Most people procrastinate when it comes to making a budget, perhaps because they don't want to delve into the details of their discretionary (nonessential) spending!

RETIREMENT BUDGET

A retirement budget is essential because it offers you a realistic, quantifiable overview of your essential expenses in relation to your income. While it is true that most people spend less per month after they retire, a retirement budget still needs to account for the fact that we are living longer today. You also need to be aware that companies today are moving away from defined benefit pensions—the traditional retirement model, which guaranteed you a certain amount of money throughout your retirement—to defined contribution plans that are subject to market ups and downs.[1] It's important to keep these facts in the back of your mind when you sit down and create a budget.

Here are some of the important steps in creating a budget:

- Get organized: Start by writing down your vision of how you want to live in retirement. Next, note how much income you are bringing in and how much debt you are paying off. Begin by adding up your average monthly expenses, like your mortgage, car payments, credit card payments, cable, telephone, electric bills, student loans, and so on. You also want to look at your year-end bank statements, which will give you an itemized statement of how much money is coming in and how much money you are spending. Once you do this, you will have a clearer picture of where you financially stand today in relation to your retirement vision. Your bank statements will also help you identify which expenses you may no longer need once you retire. For example, a large chunk of your expenses may be work-related, such as gas, extra care for your car, buying lunch at work, and so on. Once you retire, you will no longer have these.

- Essential expenses: As the name implies, essential expenses are those things that you cannot do without. According to Fidelity Retiree Health Care Cost Estimate, "an average retired couple age 65 in 2022 may need approximately $315,000 saved (after tax) to cover health care expenses in retirement."[2] This is why later in this chapter I will discuss sudden medical emergencies and how to protect yourself when they occur.

Let's look at four essential expenses in retirement.

- Health care: When you consider the need for $315,000 to cover health-care expenses, you might ask, "What about Medicare?" Well, although you might be covered by Medicare, "your supplemental premiums and out-of-pocket costs may continue to rise."[3] Given this disturbing trend, over half (54 percent) of the approximately 455 respondents who participated in a survey by Willis Towers Watson (WTW), which employs 8.2 million people, say their health-care costs will be over budget.[4] Many of us fail to read the fine print when we get Medicare or other insurance policies. It's only when we get an out-of-pocket bill that may run in the thousands of dollars that we find out we are not prepared.

- Housing: If your home is paid off, that doesn't mean there are no further expenses related to it. You still have to worry about property taxes, utilities, and home maintenance and repair. There is a general rule that says you should budget 1 percent of your home value for general upkeep and repairs.[5] That does not take into account your annual property taxes. I recommend budgeting 1.5 percent for expenses relating to your home.

- Transportation: Although you will be driving much less when you are retired (unless of course you travel across the country every year), your transportation costs will not necessarily go to zero. You need to budget for gas, car maintenance and repair, or public transportation. If you are thinking of buying a new or used car during retirement, then you need to factor in that expense as well.

- Food: You probably will not be eating lunch with colleagues, but you still need to factor in your food expenses. Although it may seem trivial, the cost of food has risen recently, and grocery bills can add up.

There are several budgeting apps that you can download. These apps will make the budgeting process easier than sitting down with a pencil and paper. These apps will store your information and tell you if you are on track toward retirement. Below is a list of the best budgeting apps for 2023.[6]

- Mint: This free app, available in the Apple store and on Google Play, tracks your expenses and places them in budget categories. Mint also helps you pay down debt, save more money, and track your goals.

- Goodbudget: This is another free app available in the Apple store and on Google Play. The app is based on the envelope budgeting system, where you portion out your monthly income toward specific spending categories (called envelopes), but it does not connect to your bank account. You manually input account balances (from your bank's statements), as well as cash amounts, debt, and income. Once you do this, you assign money toward each envelope.

- Personal Capital: This free app in the Apple store and on Google Play lets you connect and monitor your checking, savings, and credit card accounts, as well as IRAs, 401(k)s, mortgages, and loans. You can customize these categories and see the percentage of total monthly spending each category represents.

Once your budget is in place, it's time to start a retirement checklist, which ensures that you understand the various components of your retirement finances—income sources, debt consolidation, insurance, retirement calculator, sequence of return risk, and so on. Below is a retirement checklist that can help you map out your retirement preparedness.

- Savings: This perhaps is one of the most important items on your checklist. The earlier you start saving, the better off you will be in retirement. A good rule of thumb is to save 15 percent of your pretax income. After analyzing an enormous amount of national spending data, Fidelity Investments concluded most people will need between 55 percent and 80 percent of their preretirement income to maintain their lifestyle in retirement. So is saving 15 percent each year enough? The answer will depend on several factors, including when you start saving, as well as other income sources you may have. One of the things I do with new clients is go over their savings habits, as well as other factors to help them achieve their retirement goals.[7]

- Retirement calculator: A retirement calculator helps you calculate where you financially stand today in relation to your retirement goals. You can use it to map out different paths that will help you reach your retirement target. There are numerous retirement calculators online, but you'll need to do your homework to determine which calculator works best for you. Most calculators will ask you to input your retirement plan assets such as pensions, investments, Social Security, 401(k), and savings. Other calculators may also ask you about your investment asset allocation and alternative income sources. The calculator will then give you an idea of how much retirement cash flow your resources might be able to support. Remember, a financial calculator is only one tool among many.

- Withdrawal strategy: One of the more complicated aspects of retirement planning is figuring out a withdrawal strategy. As you will see, there are several strategic tax advantages that you need to be aware of when tapping certain accounts. I've mentioned that traditional IRA and 401(k) withdrawals are taxed as ordinary income, while Roth IRA accounts will generally not be taxed as long as you follow certain rules. You also need to be aware of the effects of withdrawal rates in a bear market. For many years, the safe withdrawal rule was 4 percent from your nest egg during the first year of retirement; then the amount would adjust for inflation every year after. However, today "the highest safe withdrawal rate is 3.3 percent for a 60/40 portfolio."[8] That's certainly not enough to cover your retirement expenses, especially during a bear market.

- Sequence-of-return risk: Another important concept to consider when mapping out your retirement plan is the sequence-of-return risk. This "refers to the possibility that low returns in an investor's retirement can deplete his or her portfolio just as they start spending their nest egg."[9] You and your financial advisor need to factor this into your plans. Imagine that we are in a bear market (as of this writing, we are certainly in a bear market), when your investment returns are not as high as they were during a bull market. In these conditions, as you start to withdraw funds from your investment account, you will deplete your account faster than if you started withdrawing funds during a bull market.

	Retiring at the beginning of an up market				Retiring at the beginning of a down market		
Year	Investment Value	Withdrawals	Return	Year	Investment Value	Withdrawals	Return
0	$100,000	N/A	N/A	0	$100,000	N/A	N/A
1	$103,000	$5,000.00	8.00%	1	$90,000	$5,000.00	-5.00%
2	$109,330	$5,000.00	11.00%	2	$79,600	$5,000.00	-6.00%
3	$124,000	$5,000.00	18.00%	3	$62,660	$5,000.00	-15.00%
4	$136,371	$5,000.00	14.00%	4	$52,647	$5,000.00	-8.00%
5	$147,735	$5,000.00	12.00%	5	$45,541	$5,000.00	-4.00%
6	$156,031	$5,000.00	9.00%	6	$42,818	$5,000.00	5.00%
7	$168,195	$5,000.00	11.00%	7	$40,816	$5,000.00	7.00%
8	$178,332	$5,000.00	9.00%	8	$39,489	$5,000.00	9.00%
9	$185,816	$5,000.00	7.00%	9	$38,883	$5,000.00	11.00%
10	$190,106	$5,000.00	5.00%	10	$37,328	$5,000.00	9.00%
11	$177,502	$5,000.00	-4.00%	11	$36,807	$5,000.00	12.00%
12	$158,302	$5,000.00	-8.00%	12	$36,960	$5,000.00	14.00%
13	$129,557	$5,000.00	-15.00%	13	$38,613	$5,000.00	18.00%
14	$116,783	$5,000.00	-6.00%	14	$37,860	$5,000.00	11.00%
15	$105,944	$5,000.00	-5.00%	15	$35,889	$5,000.00	8.00%
	Average Return: 4.0%				Average Return: 4.0%		

Despite having the same average annual return, Investor #1 has $70,055 more than Investor #2 due to their sequence of returns

Comparative example of withdrawing funds in
a bull (up) market versus a bear (down) market[10]

Notice the investor who withdrew funds at the beginning of a bull market has $70,055 more after 15 years than the investor who withdrew funds at the beginning of a bear market. One way to counter sequence-of-return risk is to increase your investment time horizon. This gives your investments time to recover from a bear market. Another way to mitigate against sequence-of-return risk is to have other sources of income, like annuities with lifetime income benefits.

- Risk tolerance: This is an important consideration to add to your retirement checklist. To recap, risk tolerance simply refers to the amount of risk you are willing to accept given the volatility in the value of an investment. You can use the measure of standard deviation to manage risk and make better informed decisions. The goal is to mitigate risk.

- Preretirement questionnaire: Like the retirement calculator, a preretirement questionnaire will help organize and clarify your retirement goals. One of the first things I do before sitting down with new clients is give them a questionnaire to help me better understand their risk tolerance, time horizon, budget, investment mind-set, income, debt, and several other areas that are important to retirement planning. There are also questionnaires available online, but I strongly urge you to sit down with a qualified and experienced financial advisor to fill one out. Some typical questions include:

  › What are your goals for retirement?

  › Are you ready to leave your job?

  › Do you know your pension value?

  › Are you in good health?

  › Have you considered the tax implications of your retirement plan?

  › Do you have a clear idea of how much income you will need in retirement?

  › Where do you want to live in retirement?

  › Do you have an estate plan in place?

  › Do you have a health directive?

> › Do you have a life insurance policy? If so, do you have one with a long-term-care (LTC) rider?

> › Do you have funeral arrangements in place?

> › Do you have other sources of income?

> › When do you plan on taking Social Security?

These and other questions can be answered on a 0-to-5 scale, which is what I use with my clients.

Once you have a better understanding of what a retirement road map should look like, it's time to explore various forms of retirement income. There are practical considerations for those of you who have pensions. For debt-reduction strategies you should also be aware of other income sources such as guaranteed annuities and rental income, a second mortgage, and a reverse mortgage. Some or all of these income streams will not only benefit you in retirement, they may also protect you against sudden medical expenses.

If retirement is fast approaching and you find yourself financially unprepared, then you may want to consider the following income sources:

- Pensions

- 401(k)

- Social Security

- Medicare

- Annuities

- Rental income

PENSIONS

When employers, unions, and other organizations pool their contributions, they create what is called a **pension fund**. These funds form some of the largest institutional investors in the world. Pension funds are typically exempt from capital gains tax, and portfolio earnings are either tax deferred or tax exempt. Also, if you are part of a defined pension plan (traditional pension), you have certain rights under the Employee Retirement Income Security Act of 1974 (ERISA). This federal law establishes guidelines that retirement plan fiduciaries must follow to protect the assets of private-sector employees.[11]

Although traditional pensions are quickly disappearing and being replaced with 401(k) plans, millions of people rely upon them. For example, according to the 2021 Census, "over 6,000 public sector retirement systems exist and manage $4.5 trillion of portfolio assets for 14.7 million working members. In addition, roughly 15 percent of private employees in the U.S., are covered by a defined-benefit plan today according to the Bureau of Labor Statistics."[12] There is a key difference between pensions and 401(k) plans: A traditional pension places the burden of retirement on employers, while a 401(k) shifts this burden to employees. Below is a brief summary of pensions:[13]

- A pension is a retirement plan that requires an employer to make contributions to a pool of funds that are set aside for an employee's retirement benefit.

- There are two main types of pension plans—defined benefits and defined contribution plans.

- A defined benefit plan guarantees a set monthly payment for life (or an employee can take a lump-sum payment upon retiring).

- A defined contribution plan creates an investment account that grows throughout the employee's working years. The amount is available to employees upon retiring.

- Pension funds are primarily funded by the employer, while 401(k) plans are primarily funded by the employee.

Under a defined pension plan, it may take some amount of time for an employee to begin to accumulate and earn the right to take pension assets. This is known as **vesting**, and it may depend on the number of years of service you have accumulated with your employer. Typically, enrollment in a defined pension plan occurs automatically within one year of employment. If you leave a company before retirement, you may lose some or all pension benefits, which is why it is important to ask questions and get all the pension details from your employer.

Most defined pension plans meet internal revenue code 401(a) and ERISA requirements, which means that most of these plans fall under a tax-advantaged status for both employers and employees. The contributions that employees make to the plan come off the top of their paychecks—that is, out of an employee's gross income—which effectively reduces the employee's taxable income. Also, taxes on your earnings are deferred until you begin withdrawals during retirement. The benefit of deferred taxes means that you can reinvest dividend income, interest income, and capital gains, which generate a much higher rate of return over years.[14]

Finally, if you are in a defined pension plan, you have two choices when it comes to distributions—monthly payments for the rest of your life or one lump sum. Certain plans allow you to do both; you can take some of your money as a lump sum and the rest can come in the form of monthly annuity payments. Monthly annuities can be offered as a single-life annuity for retirees only or as a joint-survivor annuity for the retiree and spouse. It is theoretically possible that a pension fund does not have enough money to pay what it owes you. This is where the Pension Benefit Guarantee Corporation (PBGC) could pay a portion of your monthly annuity up to a legal limit. For 2022, the monthly PBGC maximum for a straight-life annuity for a 65-year-old retiree was $6,204.55.[15]

If you choose the lump-sum option for your pension you can avoid the potential yet unlikely danger of your pension plan going broke. You can invest your money and potentially earn a greater rate of return. The danger here, of course, is that you can run out of money, which will leave you with no guaranteed monthly income. You need to make this decision with a qualified and experienced financial advisor. One of the things an advisor can help you with is a pension-maximization analysis, which factors in such important variables as your:[16]

- Age

- Current health and projected longevity

- Current financial situation

- Projected return for a lump-sum investment

- Risk tolerance

- Inflation protector

- Estate-planning considerations

401(K) ROLLOVERS

A **401(k) rollover is** "when you take funds out of your 401(k) account and move them into another tax-advantaged retirement account."[17] Rollovers most commonly occur when you get a new job with a new retirement plan. You can typically roll a 401(k) into an individual retirement account (IRA) or another 401(k). You can easily roll a traditional 401(k) into a traditional IRA or a Roth 401(k) to a Roth IRA. In most cases, you can do a direct rollover, which is also referred to as a trustee-to-trustee transfer. This method simply involves your 401(k) provider wiring funds directly into your new IRA provider, or your provider can write you a check that you deposit into your IRA.

A rollover may have hidden tax benefits. For example, rolling your 401(k) into a Roth IRA can potentially help you avoid required minimum distributions (RMDs) that come with a Roth 401(k). It is important to note that the Secure Act 2.0, which was passed on December 23, 2022, increased the age in which required minimum distributions begin to age 73. In other words, "If you turn age 72 in 2023 or later, a minimum distribution is not required until the year you turn age 73. However, if you turned age 72 in 2022 or earlier, you are required to continue taking your minimum distributions as before." A 401(k) rollover into an IRA might be particularly attractive to people with high incomes who cannot otherwise save in a Roth IRA. Some reasons it may be a good idea to roll over your 401(k) include:[18]

- Account consolidation

- Access to more investment choices

- Lower fees

One feature of the modern job market is that we change jobs more frequently than ever before. Keeping track of different 401(k) accounts can be tedious, and it's possible to forget about some of your 401(k) plans after you leave several jobs. By the end of 2021 "there were nearly 25 million forgotten 401(k) accounts worth about 20 percent of all 401(k) assets in the U.S., according to estimates by Capitalize, a financial services company that specializes in 401(k)s."[19] Consolidating all your accounts into a single account will avoid losing track of them and may also reduce your management fees.

If you roll your 401(k) into an IRA, you can potentially "expand your investment choices to include a broader range of funds, exchange traded funds (ETFs) or even individual stocks and bonds."[20] This gives you more control over your portfolio, particularly if you use a self-directed IRA that allows you to invest in alternative assets like real estate.

Finally, a 401(k) rollover into another 401(k) or an IRA can potentially save you thousands over the life of your account. If your current 401(k) plan charges you a high administrative fee, you need to consider a rollover. According to "401(k) research firm BrightScope and the Investment Company Institute (ICI), the average 401(k) fees amount to 0.96 percent of all assets the plan manages. That's almost $1 in annual fee per $100 you invest in your 401(k)."[21] By consolidating your 401(k)s, or rolling over to an IRA, you might be able to eliminate administrative fees and reduce the expense ratios you pay.

In certain cases, you might be *required* to roll over your 401(k). For example, if you don't meet a minimum balance requirement, typically $5,000, your employer may require you to roll your 401(k) into a different account. Also, if your employer changes 401(k) providers, your account may not automatically roll over, or if it does, your new provider may have requirements you can't meet or they may not provide the services you want.[22]

SOCIAL SECURITY

Your Social Security is based on your work history. The minimum qualifica-tion for Social Security is that you typically need to earn 40 credits, although exceptions are made for those who become disabled at a younger age.

A credit represents a certain amount of earnings; you can earn up to four credits each year. In 2022 "the amount needed to earn one credit was $1,510. You can work all year to earn four credits ($6,040), or you can earn enough for all four in a much shorter length of time."[23] When you are ready for Social Security, you simply fill out an application online or at your local Social Security Administration office. The government will then verify your information to determine if you qualify.

The minimum age you can apply for Social Security is 62, provided you have completed 40 credits. The size of your benefit will depend on your average indexed monthly earnings (AIME), as well as the age at which you begin benefits. Your average indexed monthly earnings are used to determine your primary insurance amount (PIA) and is calculated by "taking into con-sideration the 35 years that represent an individual's top earnings. Those top earnings are then indexed to factor in wage growth and averaged to produce a monthly figure."[24]

You can take your full retirement benefit when you reach full retirement age (FRA). When Social Security started in 1935, the full retirement age was defined as 65 years old. Today, the FRA has been raised to 67 for anyone born in 1960 or later.

Let's look at how to calculate your Social Security benefits. Suppose you start claiming benefits at age 66. If your full monthly benefit is $2,000, then you get the full amount of $2,000 per month. If you claim your retirement at age 62, then you will receive 75 percent of your full monthly benefit, which comes out to $1,500. This does not mean your benefit will increase once you reach 66. That is the amount you will get for life. The amount will increase due to the cost-of-living adjustments (COLAs), however. On the other hand, if you wait until the age of 70 to claim your benefits, you get an extra 8 percent per year, or 132 percent of your original amount, which is $2,640 per month, using our example.[25]

You also need to be aware of spousal benefits. Spouses who didn't earn enough credits to qualify for Social Security on their own are eligible to receive benefits starting at age 62. If you take retirement before reaching full retirement age, your spousal benefits will also be reduced. If one spouse dies, the surviving spouse is entitled to receive the higher of their own benefit or their deceased spouse's benefit.

There may be taxes on benefits. Your Social Security benefits may be partially taxed if your combined income reaches certain thresholds. The Social Security Administration defines **combined income** as "your adjusted gross income + nontaxable interest (for example, municipal bond interest) + half of your Social Security benefits = combined income."[26]

For example, if your federal tax return as an individual and your combined income is $25,000 to $34,000, then you may have to pay income tax on up to 50 percent of your benefits. If your combined income is more than $34,000, you may have to pay tax on up to 85 percent of your benefits. Regardless of how much you make, the first 15 percent of your benefits are not taxed.[27]

MEDICARE

Medicare is a U.S. government health insurance plan for people aged 65 or older. The plan also covers younger people with disabilities and patients with end-stage renal failure. As a national program that subsidizes health care for seniors, Medicare offers four components: Medicare Part A, Part B, Part C (also known as Medicare Advantage), and Part D for prescription drugs. Below is a brief overview of the different components:[28]

- Part A covers hospital insurance, skilled nursing facilities, hospice, and in-home care.

- Part B covers doctor's visits, outpatient care, preventive screenings, home health care, and durable medical equipment.

- Part C, which is also known as Medicare Advantage, involves Medicare-approved plans by private companies to offer Medicare Part A, Part B, and usually Part D.

- Part D covers prescription drugs.

To qualify for Medicare, you simply need to have legally lived in the United States for at least five years and be age 65 or older. Enrollment in Part A and B is automatic for those who receive Social Security benefits. The premium for Part A is free if the insured, or their spouse, contributed to Medicare for 10 or more years through their payroll taxes. Medicare is largely funded by payroll taxes under the Federal Insurance Contributions Act (FICA). As of 2022, "FICA payroll taxes paid by employees include a 6.2 percent Social Security tax on annual earnings below $147,000 ($160,200 in 2023) and a 1.45 percent Medicare tax on all taxable earnings."[29]

You do need to sign up for Medicare coverage during your initial enrollment period, or you may have to pay a late enrollment penalty for Parts A, B, and C. These penalties are added to your monthly premium; they are not a one-time late fee. Some people who do not qualify for a premium-free Part A coverage will have to pay for the premium; however, if they do not buy coverage when they become eligible, the monthly premium will go up by 10 percent. It's important to be aware of your enrollment period.[30]

ANNUITIES

An annuity is a contract you purchase from an insurance company, designed for long-term investing. The values will fluctuate based on investment option performance. Annuities have restrictions and limitations; fees and charges will vary based on the product. Any withdrawals may be subject to income taxes and, prior to age 59½, a 10% federal penalty tax may apply. Please remember that investing involves risk, including possible loss of principal. Investors should be aware that investing based upon a strategy or strategies does not assure a profit or guarantee against loss. There is no assurance that any strategy will achieve its objectives. All guarantees and protections are subject to the claims-paying ability of the issuing insurance company.

If you are looking for a dependable source of retirement income, then an annuity might be an excellent choice. **Annuities** are "insurance contracts that guarantee regular income payments in the future, in exchange for payment(s) now."[31] The period when you make contributions to an annuity is called the accumulation phase. You have the ability to add to your annuity gradually or in one lump sum. When you start receiving payments from your annuity contract, you've entered the distribution phase.

There are two types of annuities—a fixed annuity and a variable annuity. A **fixed annuity** "provides a predictable source of retirement income with relatively low risk. You receive a specific amount of money every month for the rest of your life or another period you've chosen, such as 5, 10, 15, or 20 years."[32] Fixed annuities offer the security of a guaranteed return. Regardless of whether the insurance company that issued you the annuity earns a sufficient return on its own investment, your monthly payment should be the same. Benefits of having a fixed annuity include predictable investment returns, guaranteed minimum rates, tax-deferred growth, and guaranteed income payments.[33]

In a variable annuity, your account balance and your payments fluctuate based on the performance of the market. In this respect, a variable annuity is similar to an individual retirement account (IRA). Both a **variable annuity** and an **IRA** "are retirement savings accounts that offer tax-deferred growth for your investment."[34] Benefits of variable annuities include maximizing tax benefits, potentially accelerating growth through stock market gains, lifetime income, and guaranteed death benefits.

One potentially attractive add-on with a variable annuity is the living-benefit feature. Although this option is available at an additional cost, it is worth the money to receive the guaranteed benefits it offers. As the name implies, the **living-benefit feature** "is intended to guarantee protection of the principal investment and the annuity payments or guarantees a minimum income over a specified period to you and your beneficiary."[35] Variable annuities carry a variety of fees. For example, there are surrender fees if withdrawals are made before certain periods; mortality and expense risk charges, which are fees the insurer charges for any loss that it might suffer as a result of unexpected events, such as the death of the annuity holder; administrative fees; and underlying fund expenses.[36]

Insurance companies also offer indexed annuities. These annuities are not considered securities, so they are not regulated by the Securities and Exchange Commission (SEC) or the Financial Industry Regulator Authority (FINRA). Indexed annuities are regulated by state insurance departments. In an **indexed annuity** "you invest an amount of money (premium) in return for growth potential based on the returns of a linked market index (e.g., the S&P 500 index); protection against negative returns of the same linked market index; and in some cases, a guaranteed level of lifetime income through optional riders."[37] An indexed annuity offers its owner, also referred to as an annuitant, the potential to earn higher yields than fixed annuities when the markets perform well, as well as protection against market declines.

RENTAL INCOME

Perhaps one of the most powerful vehicles to generate retirement income is owning a rental property. Although some people don't think of rental property when they are preparing for retirement, these can potentially be an excellent source of additional income. While it is true that being a landlord involves active management and extra responsibilities, having a consistent rental income can potentially supplement your retirement funds. Rental real estate can potentially generate substantial passive income.[38]

As a general rule, you may want to consider purchasing a rental property several years before you decide to retire. Suppose you rent a property out for $1,500, and your costs of owning the property—property taxes, insurance, HOA fees, management fees, repairs and maintenance, as well as mortgage payments—come to $1,200. That leaves you with $300 in cash flow per month. If you use this extra cash to pay down your mortgage faster, you can enjoy a cash flow of $800 per month. If there is a sudden medical emergency, you can even sell the property at a higher price than when you purchased it.

Since 1991, the average annual home price increase has been 4.3 percent, according to the FHFA. Since 2000, the average rate was 4.7 percent, and since 2012, the average rate was 7.7 percent.[39] If you are patient and purchase a rental property during a bull market, you will potentially benefit even more.

You also need to be aware of the drawbacks of owning rental property. Some of the disadvantages include:

- Lack of liquidity: Real estate is not a liquid asset and even in the hottest markets it can take several months to complete a sale.[40]

- Rising taxes and insurance premiums: While your mortgage interest rate may be fixed, there is no guarantee that taxes will not rise faster than you can increase your rent.[41]

- Difficult tenants: This is a major drawback for rental real estate. You could, unfortunately, wind up with renters who are needy, or demanding, pay late, run the water 24 hours per day, and so on. Worse yet, renters can be destructive, which can lower your property value.[42]

Suppose you purchased a rental property in 2011 for $150,000. Ten years later, in 2022, according to the S&P CoreLogic Case-Shiller Home Price Index, that home you purchased could be worth $295,000, nearly doubling your investment. Rental real estate can also offer tax advantages, including annual depreciation, which can potentially offset your annual taxable income. (Depreciation is the act of deducting a portion of the property's value each year to reflect general wear and tear over time.) However, this depreciation will work negatively when selling the rental property, as all the net proceeds will be treated as capital gains dollar for dollar in the year the property is sold. If the rental property is inherited, then a new appraisal will reset the value of the property as the new basis of the property value.[43]

DEBT-REDUCTION STRATEGIES: A SECOND MORTGAGE

For many people who are quickly approaching retirement, or are already in retirement, a second mortgage, also known as a home equity loan, can help cover sudden and unexpected emergencies or serve as a debt consolidation strategy. Americans tend to accumulate a great deal of debt. According to the Federal Reserve, "American households hold a total of $16.51 trillion in debt – which is up $2.36 trillion since the end of 2019, just before the COVID-19 pandemic."[44] Your home equity is the difference between the value of your home and what you owe to the lender. You can use a home equity loan (second mortgage) to pay off other higher-interest debts like credit cards, student loans, or any other higher–interest rate debts.[45]

There are generally two types of second mortgages—fixed-rate loans and home equity lines of credit (HELOCs). As the name implies, a **fixed-rate second mortgage** is an equity loan offered at a fixed rate over a period of typically 5 to 15 years. The interest rate remains the same for the life of the loan. A **home equity line of credit** offers an adjustable, or variable-rate, loan and works like a credit card. Borrowers are preapproved for a certain amount of money and can withdraw the money using a credit card or special checks.[46]

Although the interest paid on second mortgages used to be deductible, the Tax Cuts and Jobs Act of 2017 removed the ability to deduct the interest starting in 2018. The only exception is if you use your second mortgage to "buy, build, or substantially improve" the home that secured the loan.[47]

Where second mortgages are concerned, you need to be aware of some pitfalls. For some people, second mortgages can be "an easy solution for a borrower who may have fallen into a perpetual cycle of spending and borrowing, spending and borrowing—all the while sinking deeper into debt."[48] This cycle of borrowing and spending is so common, lenders call it "reloading."

REVERSE MORTGAGE

Just like a second mortgage, a reverse mortgage can be a valuable tool to help you face unexpected emergencies. A **reverse mortgage** is a "loan for homeowners aged 62 and older who want to borrow against their home equity without having to make monthly payments."[49] Although a reverse mortgage is not ideal for everyone, it does offer powerful solutions for certain seniors. In a reverse mortgage, a lender makes payments to you based on the equity of your home. You can choose to get a lump sum, monthly payments, or a line of credit. The interest and fees are rolled into the balance each month, which means that the amount you owe grows over time, thus decreasing your equity. You maintain the title to your home, however, and the balance isn't due until you move out or die. Below are some advantages to a reverse mortgage:[50]

- It creates cash flow for retirees who have built up considerable equity in their home.

- You are able to stay in your home.

- You can continue to pay off the mortgage on your home or use the proceeds from a reverse mortgage to pay off your existing home loan.

- The IRS does not count a reverse mortgage as income. Unlike distributions from a 401(k) or IRA, a reverse mortgage is not taxed.

Your heirs are protected if the value of your home ends up being less than what is owed on the reverse mortgage. If this occurs, your heirs don't have to worry about paying the balance. You also need to be aware of the disadvantages of a reverse mortgage, which include:

- You could lose your home to foreclosure: It is important to remember that in order to qualify for a reverse mortgage, you need to be able to afford your property taxes, homeowners insurance, HOA fees, and other costs. If at any time you become delinquent on these expenses, or spend the majority of your time living outside your home, you could default on your reverse mortgage and lose your home.[51]

- Your heirs could inherit less: Homeownership is typically a path to building generational wealth. When you have a home mortgage, it requires the home to be sold in order to repay the debt. In other words, when you die, your heirs will be required to pay the full loan balance or 95 percent of the home's appraised value, whichever is less.[52]

- It's not free: Although you are not required to make payments with a reverse mortgage, there are other expenses associated with one. You need to keep up on your tax payments, insurance, and HOA fees, as well as pay an upfront insurance premium, which is usually 2 percent of your home's appraised value. You will also need to pay origination fees at closing. Now, you do have the option of rolling these costs into your loan balance, but you this means you receive less money.[53]

- Reverse mortgages are complicated: You need to read the fine print, as there lots of rules and caveats to reverse mortgages. These loans come with many risks and may not be worth the extra cash.[54]

To qualify for a reverse mortgage, you need to own your home outright or have sufficient equity. You should compare quotes from at least three different lenders and receive reverse mortgage counseling to gain a better understanding of how the process works. You also need to be aware of the cost. For example, home equity conversion mortgages (HECMs), which are the most common type of reverse mortgage, have several one-time fees and ongoing costs. In addition to the interest you will pay, there are origination fees, closing costs, and mortgage insurance premiums.[55] A reverse mortgage is not for everyone, which is why you need to do your due diligence and learn as much as you can before committing yourself to this type of loan.

––––––––––

Retirement planning is much more involved than simply saving your money or choosing the right investment strategy. Retirement itself is a broadly defined conceptual framework that involves risk management, various insurance policies, tax-efficient investing, and multiple income sources. The quick reference guide in this chapter will help you understand the importance of having multiple income streams to help you thrive during your retirement years.

CHAPTER 14

ESTATE-PLANNING TIPS

"We are born weak, we need strength; helpless, we need aid; foolish, we need reason. All that we lack at birth, all that we need when we come to man's estate, is the gift of education."

—JEAN-JACQUES ROUSSEAU

The tax information and estate planning information contained herein is general in nature, is provided for informational purposes only, and should not be construed as legal or tax advice. We do not provide legal or tax advice. We cannot guarantee that such information is accurate, complete, or timely. Laws of a particular state or laws that may be applicable to a particular situation may have an impact on the applicability, accuracy, or completeness of such information. Federal and state laws and regulations are complex and are subject to change. Changes in such laws and regulations may have a material impact on pre- and/or after-tax investment results. Always consult an attorney or tax professional regarding your specific legal or tax situation.

For some, the word "estate" conjures up images of mansions, fancy cars, and huge investment portfolios. The fact of the matter is that estate planning is not just for the ultrawealthy or the elderly. Everyone, regardless of status or age, can benefit from estate planning.

Another misconception people have about estate planning is they confuse it with drafting a will or trust. Although both a will and an estate plan provide instructions for how your assets should be handled after your death, an estate plan is a broader legal instrument that encompasses several directives. An **estate plan** is a "collection of documents and includes a will, guardianship designations, healthcare power of attorney, and a personal letter of intent, outlining your wishes, should you die or become incapacitated."[1] Below are five reasons why everyone needs an estate plan:

- It goes beyond a will.
- It will save you time and money.
- You will avoid paying big taxes.
- It protects children.
- It protects your wishes.

As a broadly defined legal instrument, an estate plan can include durable powers of attorney to appoint an individual or individuals to make "medical and/or financial decisions on your behalf [should you be] unable to provide instructions yourself."[2] A medical directive will outline the medical treatment you want, or don't want, should you become incapacitated. An estate plan will include beneficiary designations that will identify who will receive money, which may be from various financial instruments, including life insurance policies, retirement accounts, and annuities. Estate planning may also contain one or more trusts to help facilitate passing property to your heirs, which may potentially provide important tax benefits.

Estate planning can save your beneficiaries time, money, and protracted headaches. If you die without an estate plan in place, or at a minimum, a will, then from a legal perspective you have died intestate, "and the laws of the state where you live and own property determines what happens to your assets and who gives them away."[3] In this eventuality, the probate court will name a representative to distribute your assets. In most cases, the surviving spouse or another close family member is appointed as the administrator of the estate. If there is no family member available or willing to take on this responsibility, then the state will name a public trustee to distribute your assets according to state law.

The probate process can be lengthy and difficult. If, for whatever reason, you neglect this very important aspect of your retirement plan, those you love will have to contend with a slow-moving court system. During the probate process "no one can touch your assets or carry out directives. They're frozen until the court system combs through every detail of your estate, applies state laws, pays off debts, and makes decisions about how to allocate your assets."[4] If those headaches are not enough incentive for you to embark on estate planning, then the issue of taxes might be the wake-up call you need.

While it is true that federal estate taxes typically apply to the ultrawealthy, you do need to be aware of state taxes. First, if you are fortunate to be leaving behind a sizeable estate, the federal estate tax exemption is $12.06 million per person (or $24.12 million for a couple in 2022). As far as state taxes, your heirs and beneficiaries may, depending on the state where you live, pay inheritance taxes. As of 2022 "twelve states and the District of Columbia impose an estate tax, and six states impose an inheritance tax."[5] For example, Massachusetts and Oregon tax estates valued at more than $1 million. In Nebraska, heirs (depending on their relationship to the decedent) may pay inheritance tax on anything over $10,000.[6]

The terms "estate tax" and "inheritance tax" are often used interchangeably, but they refer to two different types of taxes. An **estate tax** is "calculated based on the net value of all the property owned by a decedent as of the date of death. The state's liabilities are subtracted from the overall value of the deceased's property to arrive at the net taxable estate. Any resulting tax bill is paid by the estate."[7] An **inheritance tax**, on the other hand, "is calculated based on the value of individual bequests received from a deceased person's estate. The beneficiaries are liable for paying this tax, though a will sometimes provides that the estate should pick up this tab as well."[8] You also need to be aware that the states that collect an estate tax offer exemptions. In those cases, only the net value of an estate that exceeds the exemption amount is taxed. The estate tax takes priority, and the tax comes off the top of the estate before any bequests are made to beneficiaries from anything that remains.

An estate plan can also protect your minor children should you die without a surviving spouse. As with your assets, if you do not have an estate plan in place, the probate court will appoint a legal guardian or conservator to look after your children. In this case, a guardian would typically be a grandparent. If a grandparent does not want to take on this responsibility, or there are no grandparents available, then a family friend can petition the court to be appointed as the guardian. In certain rare cases where a minor child has no surviving family members, or a third party does not petition the court, then the child becomes a ward of the state and enters the foster care system.[9]

An estate plan can also have benefits for you while you are alive. A typical estate plan may include a durable power of attorney and health-care proxy to make sure your wishes are carried out should you be temporarily or permanently incapacitated. There are important distinctions that you need to be aware of when it comes to a durable power of attorney and a health-care proxy. A **health-care proxy** "grants the authority to make medical decisions, and a power of attorney grants the authority to make financial decisions."[10] In both legal instruments, you appoint people to make important decisions in case you become incapacitated. The legal definition of incapacity will vary from state to state, and you should consult an elder-law attorney about the specific definition in your state.

A health-care proxy will speak on your behalf concerning medical care in case you can't make such decisions. Such an agent is known by several names—medical proxy, medical power of attorney, health-care representative, or health-care agent. One very important responsibility for a health-care proxy is end-of-life care. If you are in a coma or on life support, for example, your health-care proxy may have to make a difficult decision to "ensure the doctors comply with [your] stated wishes about being kept on life support."[11] A health-care proxy can also be durable, which means your health-care agent has the power to make medical decisions on your behalf even if you didn't explicitly state your wishes prior to being incapacitated.[12]

WILLS, LIVING TRUSTS, AND REVOCABLE TRUSTS

A **will** is a legal document that "directs the distribution of your assets after your death to your designated heirs and beneficiaries."[13] A will may also include instructions concerning decisions after your death, such as the appointment of an executor of the will or directions for your funeral and burial. A will may also include the appointment of a trustee to hold assets for minor children until they reach majority or a specified age. As a legal document, a will must be signed and witnessed as required by state law and must be filed with the probate court in your jurisdiction. The document is publicly available in the records of the probate court that oversees its execution.[14]

Living trusts, by contrast, are legal arrangements "that provide for the transfer of assets from their owner, called the grantor or trustor, to a trustee. They set the terms for the trustee's management of the assets, for distributions to one or more designated beneficiaries, and the ultimate disposition of the assets."[15] The trustee is a fiduciary who is obligated to carry out the trustor's wishes according to the terms of the trust documents and solely in the best interest of the beneficiaries. Unlike a will, a living trust becomes effective upon the transfer of assets. A living trust "can be created during a grantor's lifetime [or] a trust may be a 'testamentary trust' created after death in accordance with directives in the decedent grantor's will."[16]

Another legal instrument that you should be aware of is a **revocable trust**, which is a type of trust "whereby provisions can be altered or cancelled depending on the wishes of the grantor or the originator of the trust."[17] Throughout the life of the trust, income can be earned and distributed to the grantor. It is only after the death of the grantor that property is transferred to the beneficiaries of the trust. A revocable trust offers the living grantor both flexibility and a living income, and it protects your privacy. Unlike wills, which are subject to a public probate process, a revocable trust is private.

In order to create a revocable trust, you need to establish a written agreement or declaration that appoints a trustee to manage and administer the property of the grantor (you). One flexible aspect of a revocable trust is that you have the freedom to name a competent adult, a bank, a trust company, or even yourself to act as trustee throughout your lifetime. You then place your assets, including investments, bank accounts, and real estate, into your trust. Once your assets are transferred, you no longer own these assets. They are part of the trust. You retain control of the assets, however, even though they no longer belong to you.

Some of the benefits of having a revocable trust include:[18]

- You avoid probate.

- Revocable trusts are flexible and changeable.

- They protect privacy.

- They eliminate challenges to the estate.

- Assets are segregated.

- They control a guardian's spending habits.

- There is continuous management.

- They minimize estate taxes.

A revocable trust will help you avoid a potentially lengthy and costly probate process. As with a living trust, a revocable trust allows you to make changes to the trust while you are still alive. If you value your privacy, a revocable trust helps keep your assets private. You can preempt any legal challenges to your estate by specifically disinheriting anyone who poses a challenge to your wishes. You can segregate your assets. This may become a useful arrangement for married couples with substantial assets that were acquired prior to the marriage.[19]

A revocable living trust can also help control a guardian's spending habits for the benefit of minor children. You can designate someone to act on your behalf should you become incapacitated, and the trust can automatically appoint a trustee to oversee your financial affairs without the need to obtain a durable power of attorney. A revocable living trust can include continuous management, which can potentially allow your accumulated wealth to grow for multiple generations. In other words, this instrument can help you create generational wealth.[20]

In and of itself, a revocable living trust is not good at minimizing taxes, but you can add provisions to the document to transfer your wealth by establishing a credit shelter trust (CST) in the event of your death. The credit shelter trust helps reduce estate taxes that exceed the combined estate tax exclusion amount. Assets placed in the trust "are generally held apart from the estate of the surviving spouse, so they pass tax-free to the remaining beneficiaries at the death of the surviving spouse."[21]

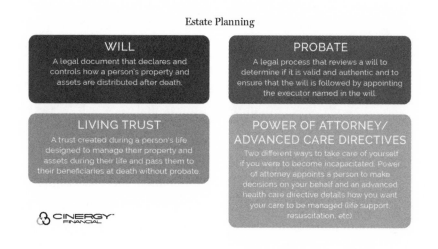

Estate Planning

WILL
A legal document that declares and controls how a person's property and assets are distributed after death.

PROBATE
A legal process that reviews a will to determine if it is valid and authentic and to ensure that the will is followed by appointing the executor named in the will.

LIVING TRUST
A trust created during a person's life designed to manage their property and assets during their life and pass them to their beneficiaries at death without probate.

POWER OF ATTORNEY/ ADVANCED CARE DIRECTIVES
Two different ways to take care of yourself if you were to become incapacitated. Power of attorney appoints a person to make decisions on your behalf and an advanced health care directive details how you want your care to be managed (life support, resuscitation, etc)

CINERGY FINANCIAL

Having a will or living trust can help you potentially avoid probate.

RETIREMENT TIPS—A REFERENCE GUIDE

It's important to remember that retirement planning begins with a vision of how you want to live your retirement years. However, having a vision or a goal without a detailed plan will not work. As the saying goes, the devil is in the details, and the success or failure of any retirement vision will depend on the details of your financial plan. A sound and effective retirement plan encompasses several elements that go beyond Social Security, 401(k)s, savings accounts, or investment strategy. It must include some form of life insurance, risk-management strategies, tax-efficient strategies, estate planning, and an ongoing your financial educations. **The earlier you start planning for retirement, the more likely you will be to achieve the conceptual vision you've held in your mind for many years.**

Let's recap some important retirement steps you need to take now:

- You can save for your retirement through various tax-advantaged and taxable accounts. Many of these accounts are offered by your employer or through a brokerage firm or bank.[22]

  › Tax-advantaged accounts are offered through different vehicles. For example, 401(k)s and IRAs are tax-deferred accounts, which means you don't have to pay taxes on your contributions or earnings that accrue over time. Income tax is due only on the money you withdraw during retirement. Also, traditional IRAs and 401(k)s are funded with pretax dollars, which means you get a tax deduction for your contributions for the year you made the contribution.

  › In a Roth 401(k) and Roth IRA, your money is funded with after-tax dollars. Although you cannot deduct your contributions, you don't pay taxes on any withdrawals you make during retirement.

  › Taxable accounts are funded with after-tax dollars, and your contributions are not tax deductible. You will pay taxes on any investment income or capital gains for the year you receive it.

- Start saving and investing early. (I can't stress this enough.)

  › The power of compounding will help you reinvest your earnings continuously to build your account value quicker.

  › Make saving and investing a lifelong habit.

  › When it comes to investing, you will have time to recover from losses.

> › You will have more experience and learn to ask relevant questions when it comes to your investment decisions.

- Do not underestimate the power of compound interest.

  > › You can benefit tremendously from the power of compound interest.

  > › Suppose you invest $10,000 at the age of 20 and it grows at a 5 percent interest rate each year until you retire at age 65. If you continuously reinvest, or compound your gains, you will have $90,000.

- Calculate your net worth.

  > › To help you determine where you financially stand in relation to your retirement goal, calculate your net worth. To do that, you simply subtract your liabilities (what you owe) from your assets (what you own).

  > › Your assets typically include cash, or cash equivalents like savings accounts, Treasury bills, and CDs. Other assets include stocks, mutual funds, ETFs, real property, alternative investments such as REITs, BDCs, interval funds, cryptocurrency, and so on. Personal properties like vehicles, boats, jewelry, and household furnishings are also considered assets.

  > › Liabilities are debts that include your mortgage, car loans, medical bills, credit cards, and student loans.

  > › Calculate your net worth once a year to determine if you are moving in the right direction toward your retirement goal.

- Establish measurable goals that collectively get you closer to your broader goal of retirement. Each goal you write down needs to be assessed in terms of its achievability.

Retirement is not a sprint; it is a marathon. Remember, the retirement burden has now shifted to each one of us. Those who plan and prepare for retirement will be rewarded with a much easier transition toward their golden years. If you do not take retirement planning seriously, you may find yourself working longer or depending more on your children. Our economic system is unforgiving to those who fail to properly plan.

CHAPTER 15

THE GOOGLE MIND: WHY YOU NEED A FINANCIAL PLANNER

"Information overload is a symptom
of our desire to not focus on what's
important. It is a choice."

—BRIAN SOLIS

The Scientific Revolution and the Industrial Revolution changed the world. Today we are again living through one of the most powerful cultural revolutions in history. The digital revolution has fundamentally changed our lives in a single generation. Much of the change has been both sweeping and positive. Consider how much you rely upon your smartphone.

The digital revolution has had numerous other benefits, of course, particularly in the fields of medicine, scientific research, ecommerce, education, and other areas of human endeavor. But we don't often talk about the unintended consequences of the digital revolution. For example, although we have a near infinite supply of information, we do not read critically as we once did. We live today in what I call the Google Mind—a world of fleeting images and ephemeral ideas.

One of the disturbing consequences of not reading with the intent to gain knowledge is that ideas don't stay in our mind for very long. We consume vast amounts of information, but we don't retain much of it. In fact, our memory is being affected because of digital technology. Why bother memorizing phone numbers or other seemingly trivial details in our lives if our smartphone can do that for us? And we merely skim for information, which is quite different from reading to learn something of substance. Think about how much information you consume in a single day. Simply check the search history on your smartphone, laptop, or desktop. You might be surprised how much time you spend consuming information. Now try to remember the details of one of the items of information you searched.

Information is not the same thing as knowledge. Knowledge requires effort and sustained focus. Since the burden rests upon each of us to prepare for our golden years, and given that our financial knowledge is lacking, we now have to rely on our own efforts to learn about the complex world of finance. We can google any topic imaginable and scroll though articles on stocks, bonds, index funds, annuities, CDs, IRAs, 401(k)s, investment strategies, cryptocurrency, volatility, investment risk, and so on. While on the surface this may seem admirable, it can lead us to the misleading conclusion that we have gained critical insights into how the markets and the financial world generally operate.

THE DUNNING-KRUGER EFFECT

One of the disturbing consequences of our Google-ized world is that vast amounts of information can lead us to believe that we know far more than we actually do. This is known as the **Dunning-Kruger Effect**, which is a "cognitive bias whereby people with limited ability in a given field tend to greatly overestimate their own competence."[1] Introduced in 1999 by psychologists

David Dunning and Justin Kruger, this predilection leads people to falsely believe that they know more about certain subjects than reality would reveal. This is not about dumb people who lack any awareness of their own ignorance. Rather, "it's mostly about all of us when it comes to things we are not very competent at."[2]

In the more than two decades since the Dunning-Kruger Effect was introduced, the digital revolution has radically changed our world. We're now drowning in an ocean of information. Why bother remembering anything of value if our smartphone can access such information in seconds? There's also the fact that the Google Effect, which refers to our growing dependence on the internet for instantaneous information, fools us into believing we have expanded our knowledge of the world.

Thanks to our shiny little smartphone, we rely on the internet from the time we wake up in the morning until we go to sleep. The totality of human knowledge, it seems, rests in the palm of your hand, and you might be tempted to believe that such knowledge belongs to you. In fact, studies show that people mistake the internet's knowledge for their own. What the internet has done to us is allow us to have a superficial awareness of a wide variety of topics but no in-depth knowledge of a single topic. Even the superficial knowledge is faulty and filled with errors, as our memories become more dependent on Google and other virtual warehouses of information.

THE EDELMAN TRUST BAROMETER

For more than 20 years, the Edelman Trust Barometer has published an annual report on the level of trust the public has toward governments, the media, corporations, and nongovernmental organizations (NGOs). Following the COVID-19 pandemic, it showed that the majority of us no longer trust these institutions. For example, only 42 percent of the world population say they trust the government; 46 percent trust the media. To make matters worse, 67 percent believe their country's leaders are purposely trying to mislead them or saying things that are false or gross exaggerations. Moreover, 67 percent also believe journalists are misleading them, and 63 percent believe that business leaders are also misleading them. According to the Edelman Trust Barometer, "Government failure has created an over-reliance on business to fill the void, a job that private enterprise was not designed to deliver."[3]

THE WHY BOTHER EFFECT

While it is important to always have a healthy level of skepticism, having complete distrust of institutions can also lead us to what I call the Why Bother Effect. And that has dangerous consequences.

Our capitalist system is broken, and neoliberalism, as an ideology, has exerted an extraordinary amount of power that was, and continues to be, used to influence laws and regulations to favor corporate greed and corruption.

All of this means we need new ways of thinking about retirement. You need to take action *now* in order to secure your retirement future. You cannot afford to be frozen in place or to surrender your future by deciding it isn't worth the bother. The actionable steps laid out in Part III can help you prepare for your retirement future.

The Why Bother Effect can keep you frozen in place. If you recall, during the early part of my career, many of my clients lost money as a result of the stock market crash of 2003. I was devastated and became unable to act. I felt the weight of my fiduciary responsibility and contemplated leaving the financial industry. Only after some deep soul searching did I decide to continue helping people with their finances.

It might seem easier to accept the world as it is and surrender your fate to forces that are seemingly out of your control. The problem with this way of thinking is that your inaction can potentially have a negative impact on your retirement years, and by the time you decide to wake up, it might be too late. You cannot afford to be frozen in place by mistrust. You need to be aware and skeptical, because that's when you start taking action.

Remember, the paradigm has shifted. The social contract that once promised us retirement benefits is gone. It is up to all of us today to take responsibility for our own future. Now is the time for you to make your retirement vision a reality by taking the first steps toward your own goals and dreams.

THE FOUR-LEGGED CHAIR

While the burden of retirement planning is now on your shoulders, you don't need to do it alone. Most of us don't have the time to devote to a rigorous study of markets, and what little time we do have we spend skimming for information. To help you navigate the complex world of investing, get help from an educated and experienced financial advisor. As I've pointed out earlier in this book, what we need is not the wobbly three-legged stool of the past but a solid and steady four-legged chair.

After all, when you are sick, do you not seek the services of a health professional? What if you need legal representation, do you not seek the services of a legal expert? But when it comes to financial planning and investing, many of us feel comfortable trying it ourselves. Men, in particular, have a tendency to exaggerate their financial skills. A survey by Money Crashers revealed some interesting differences between men and women when it comes to investing.

- Men are two times more likely than women to believe their investment returns beat the broader stock market.[4]

- The majority of men (59 percent) prefer to manage their own investments, while women prefer to use a financial advisor.[5]

- Men's favorite asset class is stocks, while women prefer real estate.[6]

- Nearly three-quarters (74 percent) of men reported they invest in the stock market, compared to only 51 percent of women.[7]

- Yet women make better investors then men.[8]

  › Women have more patience than men when it comes to investing.

  › Women have less need to prove themselves.

  › Women are more willing to admit mistakes.

  › Women trade far less than men.

  › Women research more diligently.

When it comes to investing, apparently the greatest obstacle is not the market; rather it is our psychology. Of course we are rational animals, but in certain circumstances human emotions can be far more powerful than reason. This is particularly true when it comes to investing. A 2018 study published in the *Journal of Financial Planning* found that "investors who use a behavior-modified approach to investing that removed emotion saw returns up to 23 percent higher over 10 years."[9] Emotions can, and often do, overpower our rational decision-making process, which can undermine our retirement goals.

In particular, we are prone to the psychology of limitations, which is a set of emotional, cognitive, or behavioral forces that individually or collectively serve as powerful barriers to reaching our predefined goals and objectives. Some examples of these limitations include:

- Irrational exuberance
- Fear of missing out (FOMO)
- Overconfidence
- Echo chambers
- Loss aversion
- Recency bias
- Lack of knowledge
- Losing sight of the big picture
- The Google Mind

Let's briefly explore some of these psychological limitations. Irrational exuberance occurs when there is "widespread and undue economic optimism. When investors start believing that the rise in prices in the recent past predicts the future, they are acting as if there is no uncertainty in the market, causing a positive feedback loop of ever higher prices."[10] According to this positive feedback loop, you believe a price of an asset—let's say, stocks— will rise. When the price does rise, you interpret that as proof, or positive feedback. You decide irrationally to continue with this belief until the asset bubble bursts, causing you to lose a substantial amount of money.

Another form of irrational investing comes from a herd mentality, **the fear of missing out (FOMO).** It's the feeling that you are missing out on something important or that others are "having more fun, living better lives, or experiencing better things."[11] The problem with this attitude is that it may force you to make important financial or investment decisions without rational consideration. You may have heard about the latest stock that "everyone" is buying or the latest cryptocurrency coin that will make you rich overnight. When we react in an emotional knee-jerk reaction to what others are doing, we typically make bad decisions.

An opposite reaction is an unjustifiable sense of confidence. Overconfident people tend to believe the future will be exactly as they envision it. In order to gain affirmation, or find others with similar beliefs, investors may go online to find groups who share their view. These groups reinforce our beliefs instead of challenging us to think more critically. They are essentially echo chambers that transmit information among individuals with similar opinions while simultaneously hindering the transmission of information from those with different opinions.[12] Think of chat groups on Facebook, LinkedIn, Reddit, or other social media platforms, and ask yourself if you've been tempted to join such groups because they reinforce your worldview.

Another reason I advise people not to invest on their own is loss aversion. No one, of course, likes to lose money, in part because our brains feel pain more strongly than pleasure. In other words, "losing $100 feels twice as bad as gaining $100."[13] If we feel losses much more acutely than gains, then, when the markets are down, we may be more inclined to sell because we fear we will lose more. Remember, however, that past performance is no guarantee of future results. This leads to the idea of recency bias, which is the belief that past performance *will* mirror future outcomes.

Perhaps the most important, and potentially most dangerous, psychological limitation is our lack of knowledge of the financial sector. As I've pointed out before, our educational system has failed us when it comes to financial literacy, and that lack of knowledge can have a negative impact on your ability to save, invest, and plan for your retirement.

Here's how lack of knowledge, coupled with overconfidence, can hurt you. Despite the fact that investors often hear the mantra "never put all your eggs in one basket," that's exactly what they do. Instead of diversifying their portfolio, investors may devote 60 percent, 70 percent, or more of their funds to stocks, which tend to be more volatile than other asset classes. In many ways, lack of knowledge makes us stubborn and sure of ourselves when all of the rational evidence tells us to behave differently. The irony, of course, is that having an overwhelming supply of information at hand does not make us any smarter. The Google Mind may actually contribute to our lack of understanding, by causing us to lose sight of the big picture.

Retirement planning demands the big picture, because it involves long-term goals. When we start carrying our retirement road map, we often run up against irrational behavior that, over time, causes us to lose sight of the entire financial landscape. We need a financial professional to monitor our behavior or advise us to take a different course of action.

And once you recognize that you need the services of a qualified and experienced financial professional, you have to be careful how you select that person. Choosing an advisor who is right for you may have life-changing implications.

Here are some of the important questions to ask when considering a financial professional:

- Are you a fiduciary?
- What is your fee structure?
- What services do you provide?
- What is your professional experience?
- What is your investment philosophy?

You may have heard of the term "fiduciary" without fully understanding what it means. The word is derived from the Latin *fiducia*, which means confidence or trust. In finance, **fiduciary** simply means that professional advisors are required to put the needs of their clients above their own. You need to be able to work with an advisor you trust.

It is important to understand how fee structures work. Advisors can charge an hourly or a fixed fee. Some advisors charge on assets under management (AUM), which is a percentage of the investments managed on your behalf. You also need to ask if your advisor receives commissions on common financial products like annuities, insurance, mutual funds, and other products he or she recommends.

It will help to balance the information on fees with how much professional experience your advisor has. What are their credentials? How many years has he or she worked in the financial industry? Did your advisor publish any articles or books on topics of financial relevance? Last, and most importantly, what is your advisor's investment philosophy? Does your advisor understand the importance of diversification strategies that go beyond stocks and bonds? Has your advisor dealt with alternative investments? Does your advisor understand university endowments and how they work? All these are important considerations in choosing the right person.

A CITY UPON A HILL AND THE AMERICAN DREAM

When the Puritans left England in 1630 with a fleet of 11 ships, they embarked on a new life in a land that would one day serve as beacon of hope for millions of people around the world. On their flagship, the *Arabella*, John Winthrop, a lawyer and a founder of the Massachusetts Bay Colony, delivered one of the most powerful sermons in American history. In many ways, it established the foundation for what would later become known as the American Dream, as you can see in this short excerpt:

> For we must consider that we shall be as a city upon a hill. The eyes of all people are upon us. So that if we shall deal falsely with our God in this work we have undertaken, and so cause

> Him to withdraw His present help from us, we shall be made
> a story and a by-word through the world.[14]

What Winthrop is saying is that the Puritans' new colony would be an example for all others. From the very beginning of America's unfolding narrative, people looked to us as an example of an individual's freedom to make something of yourself, to be better than what society dictated. America was the place to remake yourself and to improve your lot in life through hard work and a belief in what is possible.

Winthrop's sermon was largely forgotten over time, until President-elect John F. Kennedy delivered an address to a Joint Convention of the General Court of the Commonwealth of Massachusetts in 1961. He said, "We must always consider that we shall be as a city upon a hill—the eyes of all people are upon us. Today the eyes of all people are truly upon us—and our governments, in every branch, at every level, national, state, and local, must be as a city upon a hill—constructed and inhabited by men, aware of their great trust and their great responsibilities."[15]

Kennedy was not the only president to reference the theme of a proud nation that stands as a symbol of hope for people around the world. In his 1989 farewell to the nation, Ronald Reagan also referenced America as a proud city, crediting the phrase "a city upon a hill," to Winthrop but embracing it as his own. In his final address to the nation, Reagan said, "I've spoken of the shining city all my political life, but I don't know if I ever quite communicated what I saw when I said it. But in my mind it was a tall, proud city built on rocks stronger than oceans, wind-swept, God-blessed, and teeming with people of all kinds living in harmony and peace; a city with free ports that hummed with commerce and creativity. And if there had to be city walls, the walls had doors and the doors were open to anyone with the will and the heart to get there. That's how I saw it, and see it still."[16]

If there is one message that I take from Reagan's powerful speech, it is the idea that America has open doors to anyone who has the will and heart to get here. In my opinion, America also needs to open its doors to those who are here and who have worked hard all their lives. We need to tackle the problem of inequality. We need to make capitalism more inclusive. Neoliberalism has been a failure. Neoliberal ideology, supported by both Democrats and Republicans, has largely benefited corporate profits at the expense of average Americans. Our retirement crisis today is, in large part, the result of our broken capitalist system.

Capitalism has failed us over the past 50 years or so. The American Dream has become more elusive for people both young and old. Many of us seem to work longer hours for less pay. But it doesn't have to be that way. The American Dream—and, more specifically, the retirement dream—is possible. All you need to do is change your thinking and take action now. If you procrastinate about your retirement future, you may pay a heavy price later.

There is something strange about the way we think about our lives. When we are young, we feel there is plenty of time to think about our retirement. Life, however, has plans of its own, and time seems to move more quickly as we get older. Before we know it, retirement is upon us, and we wonder where the time went.

The very idea that time is your friend is a comfortable illusion. The only way to beat the passage of time when it comes to retirement is to start planning early. Time is on your side only when you realize how quickly it can deceive you. Let me tell you something from my experience of dealing with clients who are either in or on the verge of retirement. The two concepts of the American Dream and the retirement dream are intertwined. If you are having difficulty realizing your own definition of the American Dream, you will also have difficulty realizing your retirement dream. Yet both are attainable if you start improving your financial literacy.

I cannot stress enough the importance of financial literacy, which was the focus of my first book, *Redefining Financial Literacy*. You cannot begin to imagine how much money Americans lose as a result of poor financial literacy. According to a survey by the National Financial Educators Council (NFEC), the average adult loses $1,389.06 annually due to a lack of financial knowledge. If you multiply this amount by 40 years (assuming we work from the age of 25 to 65), you would lose $55,562.40 throughout your working life. Collectively, poor financial literacy cost Americans $352 billion in 2021.[17] This is a staggering sum.

You can protect yourself now by becoming more educated about the financial world, but poor financial literacy is but one part of our economic problems. Our capitalist system needs to move away from corporate dominance and toward a more people-driven economy.

I truly believe that capitalism needs to evolve to reflect our collective capacity to share the benefits of our economic life. I like the word "peoplism," a term that was recently coined by Alec Reed, the author of *Capitalism is Dead: Peoplism Rules*. Reed argues that after centuries where money and capital have served as the driving economic force, a paradigm shift is underway. This sea change embraces *people* as the driver behind innovation and progress. In many ways, peoplism is an unintended consequence of the digital revolution. And although I've argued here and in my previous books that the digital age has presented us with serious problems, I believe the future will present opportunities that were unimaginable a generation ago.

As the digital age advances beyond offering us an endless supply of information and social media that celebrates mediocrity, people will emerge as the dominant currency. I envision a time when many of us will have some level of creative and economic control over our lives. Our capacity for entrepreneurial innovation will find platforms that will deliver goods and services that will rival giant corporations. Today we live in an age where people matter. Now that the retirement burden has shifted to us, we have to plan and prepare for our own retirement. As the digital revolution continues to unfold, we will take on the responsibility of being our own agents of change.

OUR SPIRITUAL IMPULSE: LOVE, LEGACY, AND LIBERATION

One of the things I noticed about America over the past decade or so is the loss of our spiritual impulse toward each other. I'm not using this term "spiritual impulse" in a religious sense. I'm using it to describe how Americans relate to one another. We no longer have the spiritual impulse to love and care about one another. We are so politically divided today that we no longer care about our common humanity. We yell at one another because of political disagreements. We live in a world of alternative facts, a world where the truth no longer matters. Both the right and the left are so entrenched that a civil conversation seems to be out of reach.

For many of us, politics has become a combat sport. Some on the right no longer want to acknowledge basic facts, and some on the left want to cancel anyone who disagrees with them. Democracy cannot survive in an environment where love, respect, and human dignity are missing. When I say that Americans have lost their spiritual impulse toward others, I mean we find ourselves spiritually lost in a world that is harsh and cruel.

I deal with clients of all political persuasions, and politics has never corrupted my relationship with them. Throughout my books, I've criticized and praised both Republicans and Democrats equally. Many of my readers have wondered about my political leanings. Let me reveal it now. My political leanings are people. My political viewpoint is to help people realize their American Dream and their retirement vision.

One aspect of my work that I cherish is helping people leave a legacy. Certainly retirement is a kind of liberation from a lifetime of work. But retirement is also about leaving a legacy to your loved ones. I'm sure most of you want your children and grandchildren to be better off than you. This is another reason why you need to start planning early.

Leaving a legacy is one of the greatest gifts you can give to your loved ones. It is also an affirmation of a life that deserves to be remembered. For some of us, leaving a legacy to society as a whole is the kind of gift that can help countless others. I love the three Ls—love, legacy, and liberation. If America is to reclaim its lofty status as a city upon a hill, it needs to recapture its spiritual impulse toward others. We need to celebrate each other rather than tear ourselves apart over issues that in the grand scheme of things are not as important as our shared values.

NOTES

PREFACE

1. Minouche Shafik, "The Pandemic and Our Broken Social Contracts," project -syndicate.org, January 21, 2022. https://www.project-syndicate.org/onpoint/new -social-contract-needed-for-21st-century-by-minouche-shafik-2022-01.

2. Ashley Eneriz, "What Will Social Security Look Like When You Retire?" investopedia .com, updated December 21, 2022. https://www.investopedia.com/articles/personal -finance/022516/what-will-social-security-look-when-you-retire.asp.

3. Cameron Huddleston, "When Social Security Runs Out: What the Program Will Look Like in 2035," yahoo.com, November 6, 2021. https://www.yahoo.com/now/ social-security-runs-program-look-230016678.html.

4. Berkeley.edu, "Life Expectancy in the USA, 1900–1998," u.demog.berkeley.edu, retrieved January 27, 2022. https://u.demog.berkeley.edu/~andrew/1918/figure2.html.

5. Berkeley.edu, "Life Expectancy."

6. Gretchen Jacobson, Aimee Cicchiello et al., "When Costs Are a Barrier to Getting Health Care: Reports from Older Adults in the United States and Other High -Income Countries," commonwealthfund.org, October 1, 2021. https://www .commonwealthfund.org/publications/surveys/2021/oct/when-costs-are-barrier -getting-health-care-older-adults-survey.

7. Jacobson, Cicchiello et al., "When Costs Are a Barrier."

8. Michelle Fox, "Americans Are Behind on Saving for Retirement. Here's How to Get on Track," cnbc.com, September 22, 2021. https://www.cnbc.com/2021/09/01/ americans-are-behind-on-retirement-savings-heres-how-to-get-on-track.html.

9. Rob Portman, "People Still Aren't Saving Enough for Retirement. Congress Can Help," fortune.com, June 11, 2021. https://fortune.com/2021/06/11/rob-portman-retirement-savings-congress-bill/.

10. Nikki Carvajal, "Biden Signs $1.7 Trillion Government Spending Bill into Law," cnn.com, December 29, 2022. https://www.cnn.com/2022/12/29/politics/joe-biden-omnibus/index.html.

INTRODUCTION

1. Caleb Silver, "The Push to Require Financial Literacy Education," investopedia.com, updated August 21, 2022. https://www.investopedia.com/the-push-to-make-financial-literacy-into-law-4628372.

2. Silver, "Push to Require."

3. Carmen Reinicke, "56% of Americans Can't Cover a $1,000 Emergency Expense with Savings," cnbc.com, January 19, 2022. https://www.cnbc.com/2022/01/19/56percent-of-americans-cant-cover-a-1000-emergency-expense-with-savings.html.

4. Robert Frank, "The Wealthiest 10% of Americans Own a Record 89% of All U.S. Stocks," cnbc.com, October 18, 2021. https://www.cnbc.com/2021/10/18/the-wealthiest-10percent-of-americans-own-a-record-89percent-of-all-us-stocks.html.

5. Jordan Rosenfeld, "10 Jaw-Dropping Stats about the State of Retirement in America," gobankingrates.com, February 1, 2022. https://www.gobankingrates.com/retirement/planning/jaw-dropping-stats-state-retirement-america/.

6. Silver, "Push to Require."

7. Carmen Reinicke, "25 States Have Introduced Personal Finance Education Legislation So Far This Year," cnbc.com, June 3, 2021. https://www.cnbc.com/2021/06/03/25-states-have-introduced-personal-finance-education-bills-this-year.html.

8. The Investopedia Team, "Microeconomics vs. Macroeconomics: What's the Difference?" investopedia.com, updated November 30, 2021. https://www.investopedia.com/ask/answers/difference-between-microeconomics-and-macroeconomics/.

9. Jason Fernando, "Gross Domestic Product (GDP): Formula and How to Use It," investopedia.com, updated September 29, 2022. https://www.investopedia.com/terms/g/gdp.asp.

10. Futurescholar.com, "Financial Literacy Program," futurescholar.com, retrieved February 21, 2022. https://futurescholar.com/news-events/financial-literacy-program/.

11. Carly Urban Olivia Valdes, "Why is Measured Financial Literacy Declining and What Does it Mean? Maybe we Just Don't Know," finrafoundation.org, August, 2022. https://finrafoundation.org/sites/finrafoundation/files/Insights-Why-is-Measured -Financial-Literacy-Declining.pdf

12. Oscar Contreras and Joseph Bendix, "Financial Literacy in the United States," milkeninstitute.org, July 6, 2021. https://milkeninstitute.org/sites/default/ files/2021-08/Financial%20Literacy%20in%20the%20United%20States.pdf.

13. Contreras and Bendix, "Financial Literacy."

14. Jason Fernando, "What Is Financial Literacy, and Why Is It So Important?" investopedia.com, updated August 15, 2022. https://www.investopedia.com/terms/f/ financial-literacy.asp.

15. Poonkulali Thangavelu, "Capitalist vs. Socialist Economies: What's the Difference," investopedia.com, updated March 12, 2022. https://www.investopedia.com/articles/ personal-finance/082415/pros-and-cons-capitalist-vs-socialist-economies.asp.

16. Habib Ur Rehman, "15 Socialist Countries That Have Succeeded," yahoo .com, July 22, 2021. https://www.yahoo.com/video/15-socialist-countries -succeeded-130731664.html.

17. Kurt Andersen, *Evil Geniuses: The Unmaking of America* (New York, Random House, 2020), p. 18.

18. Anand Giridharadas, "Kurt Andersen Asks: What Is the Future of America?" nytimes .com, April 11, 2020. https://www.nytimes.com/2020/08/11/books/review/kurt -andersen-evil-geniuses.html.

19. Milton Friedman, "A Friedman Doctrine—The Social Responsibility of Business Is to Increase Its Profits," nytimes.com, September 13, 1970. https://www.nytimes .com/1970/09/13/archives/a-friedman-doctrine-the-social-responsibility-of-business -is-to.html.

20. Robert Longley, "What Is Neoliberalism? Definitions and Examples," thoughtco.com, July 28, 2021. https://www.thoughtco.com/what-is-neoliberalism-definition-and -examples-5072548.

21. The White House, "Remarks by President Biden before Meeting with the White House Competition Council," whitehouse.gov, January 24, 2022. https://www .whitehouse.gov/briefing-room/speeches-remarks/2022/01/24/remarks-by-president -biden-before-meeting-with-the-white-house-competition-council/.

22. Jason Fernando, "Market Capitalization: How Is It Calculated and What Does It Tell Investors?" investopedia.com, updated August 10, 2022. https://www.investopedia .com/terms/m/marketcapitalization.asp.

23. Omri Wallach, "The World's Tech Giants, Compared to the Size of Economies," visualcapitalist.com, July 7, 2021. https://www.visualcapitalist.com/the-tech-giants -worth-compared-economies-countries/.

24. Richard Holden, "Vital Signs: 50 Years Ago Milton Friedman Told Us Greed Was Good. He Was Half Right," theconversation.com, September 17, 2020. https:// theconversation.com/vital-signs-50-years-ago-milton-friedman-told-us-greed-was -good-he-was-half-right-146294.

25. James B. Stewart, "I Became a Disciplined Investor Over 40 Years. The Virus Broke Me in 40 Days," nytimes.com, March 27, 2020. https://www.nytimes .com/2020/03/27/business/stock-market-pandemic-coronavirus.html.

26. Adam Barone, "What Is the American Dream? Examples and How to Measure It," investopedia.com, updated August 1, 2022. https://www.investopedia.com/terms/a/ american-dream.asp.

27. Leslie Cook, "Homeownership Drifts Further Out of Reach as Mortgage Rates Climb," sfgate.com, February 15, 2022. https://www.sfgate.com/shopping/article/ Homeownership-Drifts-Further-Out-of-Reach-as-16920619.php.

28. U.S. Bureau of Statistics, "Economic News Release: Real Earnings Summary," bls.gov, retrieved January 17, 2023. https://www.bls.gov/news.release/realer.nr0.htm.

CHAPTER 1

1. Vocabulary.com, "Protestant," vocabulary.com, retrieved February 23, 2022. https:// www.vocabulary.com/dictionary/protestant.

2. Robert Wilde, "Indulgences and Their Role in the Reformation," thoughtco.com, April 28, 2020. https://www.thoughtco.com/indulgences-their-role-in-the -reformation-1221776.

3. National Geographic, "The Protestant Reformation," nationalgeographic.org, April 7, 2021. https://www.nationalgeographic.org/article/protestant-reformation/.

4. National Geographic, "Protestant Reformation."

5. Korcula.net, "Martin Luther and Reformation—Catholic and Other Religions in Europe 1500–1600s," korcula.net, retrieved February 24, 2022. https://korcula.net/martin-luther-reformation/.

6. Korcula.net, "Martin Luther."

7. National Geographic, "Protestant Reformation."

8. Korcula.net, "Martin Luther."

9. Karl Thompson, "Max Weber: The Protestant Ethic and the Spirit of Capitalism (Revision Notes)," revisesociology.com, August 17, 2018. https://revisesociology.com/2018/08/17/max-weber-religion-society-change/.

10. Max Weber, *The Protestant Ethic and the Spirit of Capitalism* (London: Routledge Classics, 1992), pp. 10–11.

11. Yonatan Reshef, "The Protestant Ethic and the Spirit of Capitalism," sites.ualberta.ca, retrieved February 28, 2022. https://sites.ualberta.ca/~yreshef/orga432/weber.htm.

12. Weber, *The Protestant Ethic*, p. 56.

13. Weber, *The Protestant Ethic,* p. 124.

14. Daniel T. Rodgers, "'Was America Born Capitalist?': On John Winthrop's 'A Model of Christian Charity,'" lareviewofbooks.org, November 26, 2018. https://lareviewofbooks.org/article/was-america-born-capitalist-on-john-winthrops-a-model-of-christian-charity/.

15. Rodgers, "Was America Born Capitalist?"

16. Vivienne Brown, "'Mere Inventions of the Imagination': A Survey of Recent Literature on Adam Smith," cambridge.org, December 5, 2008. https://www.cambridge.org/core/journals/economics-and-philosophy/article/abs/mere-inventions-of-the-imagination-a-survey-of-recent-literature-on-adam-smith/E82D64B07E411991C03510FC1BD3E040.

17. Editors of Encyclopaedia Britannica, "Protestant Ethic," britannica.com, retrieved March 2, 2022. https://www.britannica.com/topic/Protestant-ethic.

18. Jack Russell Weinstein, "Adam Smith," Internet Encyclopedia of Philosophy, iep.utm .edu, retrieved March 2, 2022. https://iep.utm.edu/smith/.

19. The Investopedia Team, "What is a Laissez-Faire Economy, and How Does It Work?" investopedia.com, updated January 26, 2022. https://www.investopedia.com/terms/l/ laissezfaire.asp.

20. Charley Dewberry, "Adam Smith Was No Laissez-Faire Ideologue," gutenberg.edu, March 3, 2013. https://gutenberg.edu/2013/03/adam-smith-was-no-laissez-faire -ideologue/.

21. Richard Gunderman, "The Beef with Greed: Leo Tolstoy and Adam Smith," econlib.org, January 3, 2022. https://www.econlib.org/library/columns/y2022/ gundermangreed.html.

22. Gunderman, "Beef with Greed."

23. Eamonn Butler, *The Condensed Wealth of Nations and the Incredibly Condensed Theory of Moral Sentiments* (London: Adam Smith Research Institute, 2011), p. 79.

24. Marcelo Gleiser, "What the 'God of the Gaps' Teaches Us About Science," npr.org, April 8, 2015. https://www.npr.org/sections/13.7/2015/04/08/398227737/what-the -god-of-the-gaps-teaches-us-about-science.

25. The Investopedia Team, "Marxism: What It Is and Comparison to Communism, Socialism and Capitalism," investopedia.com, updated December 18, 2022. https:// www.investopedia.com/terms/m/marxism.asp.

26. Paul Zacharia, "What Did Karl Marx Say about Religion," newindianexpress.com, December 17, 2020. https://www.newindianexpress.com/opinions/2020/dec/17/ what-did-karlmarx-say-about-religion-2237307.html.

27. Martin Evan Jay, "Religion, Civilization, and Discontents," britannica.com, retrieved March 5, 2022. https://www.britannica.com/biography/Sigmund-Freud/Religion -civilization-and-discontents.

28. Bernd Magnus, "Friedrich Nietzsche," britannica.com, retrieved March 5, 2022. https://www.britannica.com/biography/Friedrich-Nietzsche.

CHAPTER 2

1. David Tulloch, "Isaac Newton's Principia Mathematica Greatly Influences the Scientific World and the Society Beyond It," encyclopedia.com, retrieved March 10, 2022. https://www.encyclopedia.com/science/encyclopedias-almanacs-transcripts-and -maps/isaac-newtons-principia-mathematica-greatly-influences-scientific-world-and -society-beyond-it.

2. Merchants and Mechanics: Exploring the History of Economic Growth, "The Scientific Revolution, the Enlightenment, and the Industrial Revolution," merchantsandmechanics.com, retrieved March 10, 2022. https:// merchantsandmechanics.com/2017/12/25/two-revolutions-and-an-enlightenment/.

3. Merchants and Mechanics, "The Scientific Revolution."

4. Rebecca Beatrice Brooks, "Inventions of the Industrial Revolution," historyofmassachusetts.org, September 13, 2020. https://historyofmassachusetts.org/ inventions-industrial-revolution/.

5. Stanford Encyclopedia of Philosophy, "Progress," plato.stanford.edu, retrieved March 19, 2022. https://plato.stanford.edu/entries/progress/.

6. Britannica.com Editors, "The Gilded Age," britannica.com, retrieved March 20, 2022. https://www.britannica.com/topic/The-Gilded-Age.

7. Love Money Editors, "The Incredible Lives of the Real Gilded Age Billionaires," lovemoney.com, February 21, 2022. https://www.lovemoney.com/gallerylist/128652/ the-incredible-lives-of-the-real-gilded-age-billionaires.

8. Sam Dangremond, "What Exactly Was the Gilded Age?" townandcountrymag.com, January 23, 2022. https://www.townandcountrymag.com/society/a38651973/gilded -age-history-meaning/.

9. Digital History Editors, "Overview of the Gilded Age," digitalhistory.uh.edu, retrieved March 20, 2022. http://www.digitalhistory.uh.edu/era.cfm?eraid=9.

10. Digital History Editors, "Overview."

11. Library of Congress, "Immigration to the United States, 1851–1900," loc.gov, retrieved March 21, 2022. https://www.loc.gov/classroom-materials/united-states -history-primary-source-timeline/rise-of-industrial-america-1876-1900/immigration -to-united-states-1851-1900/.

12. Charles W. Calhoun, *The Gilded Age: Essays on the Origins of Modern America* (Lanham, MD: Rowman & Littlefield, 1995), pp. 53–70.

13. Khan Academy Editors, "Laissez-Faire Policies in the Gilded Age," khanacademy.org, retrieved March 22, 2022. https://www.khanacademy.org/humanities/us-history/the -gilded-age/gilded-age/a/laissez-faire-policies-in-the-gilded-age.

14. History.com Editors, "'Origin of Species' Is Published," history.com, retrieved March 23, 2022. https://www.history.com/this-day-in-history/origin-of-species-is -published-2.

15. Ker Than, Tom Garner, and Ashley P. Taylor, "What Is Darwin's Theory of Evolution?" livescience.com, updated October 14, 2022. https://www.livescience .com/474-controversy-evolution-works.html.

16. Psychology Wiki, "Survival of the Fittest," psychology.fandom.com, retrieved March 23, 2022. https://psychology.fandom.com/wiki/Survival_of_the_fittest.

17. Science Daily Editors, "Belief in Social Darwinism Linked to Dysfunctional Psychological Characteristics, Study Finds," sciencedaily.com, August 11, 2021. https://www.sciencedaily.com/releases/2021/08/210811162808.htm.

18. Harry Burrows Acton, "Herbert Spencer: British Philosopher," britannica.com, retrieved March 23, 2022. https://www.britannica.com/biography/Herbert-Spencer/ The-synthetic-philosophy-in-outline.

19. U.S. History Editors, "The Gilded Age," ushistory.org, retrieved March 23, 2022. https://www.ushistory.org/us/36e.asp.

20. Study.com, "Child Labor in the Progressive Era," study.com, retrieved March 23, 2022. https://study.com/learn/lesson/child-labor-progressive-era-history-opposition -reform.html.

21. U.S. History Editors, "The Gilded Age."

22. Christopher Klein, "How Gilded Age Corruption Led to the Progressive Era," history .com, February 4, 2021. https://www.history.com/news/gilded-age-progressive-era -reforms.

23. Klein, "Gilded Age Corruption."

CHAPTER 3

1. Adrian Eaton, "The Club That Changed the World," medium.com, July 15, 2021. https://medium.com/share-the-wealth/the-club-that-changed-the-world-2d78d9f34b22.

2. Eaton, "Club That Changed."

3. Stuart Mills, "Ghosts of Mont Pelerin," medium.com, July 25, 2019. https://medium.com/swlh/ghosts-of-mont-pelerin-b1db91c3a63c.

4. Mills, "Ghosts."

5. Mills, "Ghosts."

6. The Investopedia Team, "Keynesian vs. Neo-Keynesian Economics: What's the Difference?" investopedia.com, updated August 31, 2021. https://www.investopedia.com/ask/answers/012615/what-difference-between-keynesian-and-neokeynesian-economics.asp.

7. Eva Vergara, "Lucía Hiriart, Widow of Chilean Dictator Pinochet, Dies at 99," washingtonpost.com, December 17, 2021. https://www.washingtonpost.com/obituaries/2021/12/17/pinochet-widow-hiriart-dead/.

8. Daniel Matamala, "The Complicated Legacy of the 'Chicago Boys' in Chile," promarket.org, September 12, 2021. https://www.promarket.org/2021/09/12/chicago-boys-chile-friedman-neoliberalism/.

9. Michael A. Peters, "The Early Origins of Neoliberalism: Colloque Walter Lippman (1938) and the Mt Perelin [sic] Society (1947)," tandfonline.com, July 25, 2021. https://www.tandfonline.com/doi/pdf/10.1080/00131857.2021.1951704.

10. Matamala, "Complicated Legacy."

11. Matamala, "Complicated Legacy."

12. Binyamin Appelbaum, "Blame Economists for the Mess We're In," nytimes.com, August 24, 2019. https://www.nytimes.com/2019/08/24/opinion/sunday/economics-milton-friedman.html.

13. Appelbaum, "Blame Economists."

14. David R. Henderson, "Milton Friedman: 1912–2006," econlib.org, retrieved April 12, 2022. https://www.econlib.org/library/Enc/bios/Friedman.html.

15. Milton Friedman, "A Friedman Doctrine—The Social Responsibility of Business Is to Increase Its Profits," nytimes.com, September 13, 1970. https://www.nytimes.com/1970/09/13/archives/a-friedman-doctrine-the-social-responsibility-of-business-is-to.html.

16. David Rosen, "When the Sh*t Hit the Fan: Recalling the 1970s," counterpunch.org, July 21. 2021. https://www.counterpunch.org/2021/07/21/when-the-sht-hit-the-fan-recalling-the-1970s/.

17. ACLU, "ACLU Opposes Nomination of Judge Alito," web.archive.org, retrieved April 12, 2022. https://web.archive.org/web/20070406173742/http://www.aclu.org/scotus/alito/.

18. Sandeep Vaheesan, "How Robert Bork Fathered the New Gilded Age," promarket.com, September 5, 2019. https://promarket.org/2019/09/05/how-robert-bork-fathered-the-new-gilded-age/.

19. Vaheesan, "Robert Bork."

20. Joe Hagan, "The Hive Interview: Can We Undo the GOP's Decimation of America?" *Vanity Fair*, August 10, 2020. https://www.vanityfair.com/news/2020/08/the-hive-interview-can-we-undo-the-gops-decimation-of-america.

21. Mark W. Johnson, "Do the U.S.'s Big Four Tech Companies Have a Vision for the Future?" *Harvard Business Review*, July 24, 2020. https://hbr.org/2020/07/do-the-u-s-s-big-four-tech-companies-have-a-vision-for-the-future.

22. Andersen, *Evil Geniuses*, p.12.

23. Andersen, *Evil Geniuses*, p.15.

24. Andersen, *Evil Geniuses*, p.7.

25. Merriam-Webster Dictionary, "Greed noun," merriam-webster.com, 3/15/2023. https://www.merriam-webster.com/dictionary/greed.

CHAPTER 4

1. Matthew Wilburn King, "Why the Next Stage of Capitalism Is Coming," bbc.com, May 26, 2021. https://www.bbc.com/future/article/20210525-why-the-next-stage-of-capitalism-is-coming.

2. Lydia Saad and Jeffrey M. Jones, "What Percentage of Americans Own Stock?" news

.gallup.com, August 13, 2021, updated May 12, 2022. https://news.gallup.com/poll/266807/percentage-americans-owns-stock.aspx.

3. Ryan Boykin, "Reason to Invest in Real Estate vs. Stocks," investopedia.com, updated June 29, 2021. https://www.investopedia.com/investing/reasons-invest-real-estate-vs-stock-market/.

4. John Bromels, "What Are Stock Market Corrections?" fool.com, March 23, 2022, updated February 27, 2023. https://www.fool.com/investing/how-to-invest/stocks/stock-market-corrections/.

5. Matthew DiLallo, "The Biggest Stock Market Crashes in History," fool.com, May 2, 2022, updated January 18, 2023. https://www.fool.com/investing/stock-market/basics/crashes/.

6. Bromels, "What Are Stock Market Corrections?"

7. Historical Society of Pennsylvania Editors, "Progressive Era and Economics," portal .hsp.org, retrieved April 19, 2022. https://www.portal.hsp.org/unit-plan-items/unit-plan-22.

8. Chris Seabury, "The Cost of Free Markets," investopedia.com, updated June 23, 2021. https://www.investopedia.com/articles/economics/08/free-market-regulation.asp.

9. Adam Hayes, "Irrational Exuberance: Definition, Origin, Example," investopedia .com, April 5, 2022, updated April 8, 2022. https://www.investopedia.com/terms/i/irrationalexuberance.asp.

10. Hayes, "Irrational Exuberance."

11. Adam Richards, "The Great Depression: The Wall Street Crash of 1929 and Other Causes," study.com, retrieved April 25, 2022. https://study.com/academy/lesson/the-great-depression-the-wall-street-crash-of-1929-and-other-causes.html.

12. Kimberly Amadeo, "1920s Economy," thebalance.com, February 17, 2022, updated March 28, 2022. https://www.thebalance.com/roaring-twenties-4060511.

13. Reem Heakal, "What Is the Glass-Steagall Act of 1933? Purpose and Effect," investopedia.com, April 10, 2022, updated September 25, 2022. https://www .investopedia.com/articles/03/071603.asp.

14. FDIC, "Trust/Fiduciary Activities," fdic.gov, retrieved April 25, 2022. https://www .fdic.gov/resources/bankers/trust-fiduciary-activities/.

15. The Avalon Project, "First Inaugural Address of Franklin D. Roosevelt," avalon.law.yale .edu, retrieved April 24, 2022. https://avalon.law.yale.edu/20th_century/froos1.asp.

16. Heakal, "Glass-Steagall Act."

17. Adam Hayes, "The New Deal," investopedia.com, updated October 18, 2021. https:// www.investopedia.com/terms/n/new-deal.asp.

18. Book Vea Editors, "What Was Fordism and How Did Workers Respond to It?" bookvea.com, January 30, 2022. https://bookvea.com/what-was-fordism-and-how -did-workers-respond-to-it/.

19. Rose Heichelbech, "The Changing Landscape of Buying a Home (1920–Now)," dustyoldthing.com, May 19, 2021. https://dustyoldthing.com/home-ownership-cost -changed/.

20. Pbs.org, "Mr. Weill Goes to Washington," pbs.org, retrieved April 27, 2022. https:// www.pbs.org/wgbh/pages/frontline/shows/wallstreet/weill/.

21. Simpson Thacher & Bartlett LLP, "Federal Reserve Approves Merger of Travelers and Citicorp," stblaw.com, retrieved April 22, 2022. https://www.stblaw.com/docs/ default-source/cold-fusion-existing-content/publications/pub410.pdf?sfvrsn=2.

22. Wayne Duggan, "This Day in Market History: The Priceline IPO," benzinga.com, March 30, 2022. https://www.benzinga.com/general/education/21/03/20402600/ this-day-in-market-history-the-priceline-ipo.

23. Betsy George, "Fraudulent Accounting and the Downfall of WorldCom," sc.edu, August 11, 2021. https://www.sc.edu/about/offices_and_divisions/audit_and_ advisory_services/about/news/2021/worldcom_scandal.php.

24. Paul Nolan, "What Is a Hedge Fund," thebalancemoney.com, September 14, 2022. https://www.thebalancemoney.com/what-is-a-hedge-fund-357524.

25. Kimberly Amadeo, "The Great Recession of 2008: A Timeline and Its Effects," thebalancemoney.com, April 24, 2022. https://www.thebalancemoney.com/the-great -recession-of-2008-explanation-with-dates-4056832.

26. Amadeo, "Great Recession."

27. Shira Ovide, "Big Tech Has Outgrown This Planet," economictimes.indiatimes.com, July 30, 2021. https://economictimes.indiatimes.com/tech/technology/big-tech-has -outgrown-this-planet/articleshow/84879979.cms.

28. Aimee Picchi, "The New Gilded Age: 2,750 People Have More Wealth Than Half the Planet," cbsnews.com, December 7, 2021. https://www.cbsnews.com/news/wealth-inequality-billionaires-piketty-report/.

29. Edwin J. Feulner, "Preventing 'The Tyranny of the Majority,'" heritage.org, March 7, 2018. https://www.heritage.org/conservatism/commentary/preventing-the-tyranny-the-majority.

30. Anna Massoglia, "Unprecedented $1 Billion First Quarter Lobbying Haul Puts 2022 on Track for Record Year," opensecrets.org, May 5, 2022. https://www.opensecrets.org/news/2022/05/unprecedented-1-billion-first-quarter-lobbying-haul-puts-2022-on-track-for-record-year/.

31. Jake Frankenfield, "Which Industry Spends the Most on Lobbying?" investopedia.com, June 2, 2022, updated September 29, 2022. https://www.investopedia.com/investing/which-industry-spends-most-lobbying-antm-so/.

32. Frankenfield, "Which Industry Spends?"

33. Frankenfield, "Which Industry Spends?"

34. Frankenfield, "Which Industry Spends?"

35. Frankenfield, "Which Industry Spends?"

36. Frankenfield, "Which Industry Spends?"

37. Frankenfield, "Which Industry Spends?"

38. Frankenfield, "Which Industry Spends?"

39. Frankenfield, "Which Industry Spends?"

40. Troy Segal, "Bribery vs. Lobbying: What's the Difference?" investopedia.com, September 11, 2021, updated July 20, 2022. https://www.investopedia.com/financial-edge/0912/the-differences-between-bribery-and-lobbying.aspx.

41. Angie Mohr, "The Biggest Bribery Cases in Modern Business History," investopedia.com, February 6, 2022, updated July 20, 2022. https://www.investopedia.com/financial-edge/0512/the-biggest-bribe-cases-in-business-history.aspx.

42. Mohr, "Biggest Bribery Cases."

43. Mohr, "Biggest Bribery Cases."

44. The Federal Election Commission, "Citizens United v. FEC," fec.gov, retrieved June 5, 2022. https://www.fec.gov/legal-resources/court-cases/citizens-united-v-fec/.

45. Dorothy S. Lund and Leo E. Strine Jr., "Corporate Political Spending Is Bad Business," hbr.org, January–February 2022. https://hbr.org/2022/01/corporate-political-spending-is-bad-business.

46. Open Secrets, "More Money, Less Transparency: A Decade Under Citizens United," opensecrets.org, retrieved June 5, 2022. https://www.opensecrets.org/news/reports/a-decade-under-citizens-united.

47. Open Secrets, "More Money."

48. Alan Rappeport and Margot Sanger-Katz, "Social Security Is Projected to Be Insolvent a Year Earlier Than Previously Forecast," nytimes.com, September 24, 2021. https://www.nytimes.com/2021/08/31/business/economy/social-security-funding.html.

CHAPTER 5

1. James Chen, "Risk: What It Means in Investing, How to Measure and Manage It," investopedia.com, September 20, 2020. https://www.investopedia.com/terms/r/risk.asp.

2. Market Business News, "What Is Economic Risk? Definition and Example," marketbusinessnews.com, retrieved May 15, 2022. https://marketbusinessnews.com/financial-glossary/economic-risk/.

3. Markus Brunnermeier, Simon Rother, and Isabel Schnabel, "Asset Price Bubbles and Systemic Risk," scholar.princeton.edu, April 1, 2019. https://scholar.princeton.edu/sites/default/files/markus/files/brs_bubbles.pdf.

4. Kimberly Amadeo, "Financial Regulations," thebalancemoney.com, April 25, 2022. https://www.thebalancemoney.com/financial-regulations-3306234.

5. Will Kenton, "Deregulation: Definition, History, Effects, and Purpose," investopedia.com, updated April 6, 2022. https://www.investopedia.com/terms/d/deregulate.asp.

6. Sam Peltzman, "The Economic Theory of Regulation after a Decade of Deregulation," brookings.edu, retrieved May 18, 2022. https://www.brookings.edu/wp-content/uploads/1989/01/1989_bpeamicro_peltzman.pdf.

7. William Kleinknecht, *The Man Who Sold the World: Ronald Reagan and the Betrayal of Main Street America* (New York: Nation Press, 2009), p. 107.

8. James Chen, "High-Yield Bond: Definition, Types, and How to Invest," investopedia .com, October 23, 2020, updated August 23, 2022. https://www.investopedia.com/ terms/h/high_yield_bond.asp.

9. Kenton, "Deregulation."

10. James Chen, "Volcker Rule: Definition, Purpose, How It Works, and Criticism," investopedia.com, February 3, 2022, updated June 22, 2022. https://www .investopedia.com/terms/v/volcker-rule.asp.

11. Cory Janssen, "Stock Buybacks: Benefits of Share Repurchases," investopedia .com, May 24, 2021, updated February 7, 2023. https://www.investopedia.com/ articles/02/041702.asp.

12. Derek Silva, "How Do Employee Stock Options Work," smartasset.com, December 29, 2022. https://smartasset.com/investing/how-do-stock-options-work.

13. Elvis Picardo, "Employee Stock Options (ESOs): A Complete Guide," investopedia .com, April 23, 2022, updated October 12, 2022. https://www.investopedia.com/ terms/e/eso.asp.

14. Andersen, *Evil Geniuses*, p. 184.

15. Sarah Williamson, Ariel Babcock, and Allen He, "The Dangers of Buybacks: Mitigating Common Pitfalls," corp.law.harvard.edu, October 23, 2020. https:// corpgov.law.harvard.edu/2020/10/23/the-dangers-of-buybacks-mitigating-common -pitfalls/

16. Adam Barone, "Rule 10b-18 Definition and How Compliance Works," investopedia .com, January 10, 2021. https://www.investopedia.com/terms/r/rule10b18.asp.

17. Andersen, *Evil Geniuses*, p. 185.

18. Andersen, *Evil Geniuses,* p. 185.

19. Ray Williams, "How Executives Use Stock Market Manipulation for Personal Gain," raywilliams.medium.com, September 30, 2021. https://raybwilliams.medium.com/ how-executives-use-stock-market-manipulation-for-personal-gain-28459280e95f.

20. Lance Roberts, "Bailouts and the Demise of Capitalism and Free Markets," realinvestmentadvice.com, March 28, 2022. https://realinvestmentadvice.com/ bailouts-and-the-demise-of-capitalism-and-free-markets/.

21. Pronita Naidu and David Brennan, "Boeing, Airlines, Under Fire for $90 Billion

in Share Buybacks, Stoke Controversy with Bailout Pleas for at Least $110 Billion," newsweek.com, March 24, 2020. https://www.newsweek.com/boeing-airlines-under -fire-90-billion-share-buybacks-stoke-controversy-bailout-pleas-least-1493934.

22. Public Citizen, "Corporations That Received Billions During the Pandemic Cut Thousands of Jobs and Gave CEOs Millions," citizen.org, April 26, 2021. https:// www.citizen.org/news/corporations-that-received-billions-during-the-pandemic-laid -off-thousands-of-workers-and-gave-ceos-millions/.

23. Naidu and Brennan, "Boeing, Airlines, Under Fire."

24. Public Citizen, "Corporations that Received Billions."

25. Public Citizen, "Corporations that Received Billions."

26. Public Citizen, "Corporations that Received Billions."

27. James Chen, "Corruption: Its Meaning, Type, and Real-World Example," investopedia .com, updated June 1, 2022. https://www.investopedia.com/terms/c/corruption.asp/.

28. Mohr, "Biggest Bribery Cases."

29. Will Kenton, "What Is a Shell Corporation? How It's Used, Examples and Legality," investopedia.com, August 25, 2021, updated July 17, 2022. https://www .investopedia.com/terms/s/shellcorporation.asp.

30. Tricia Christensen, "What Is Cooking the Books?" smartcapitalmind.com, June 2, 2022, updated March 4, 2023. https://www.smartcapitalmind.com/what-is-cooking -the-books.htm.

31. Christensen, "What Is Cooking?"

32. Christensen, "What Is Cooking?"

33. Christensen, "What Is Cooking?"

34. Christensen, "What Is Cooking?"

35. Jeff Schmidt, "Top Accounting Scandals," corporatefinanceinstitute.com, January 30, 2022, updated March 4, 2023. https://corporatefinanceinstitute.com/resources/ knowledge/other/top-accounting-scandals/.

36. Vance Cariaga, "Thanks to Inflation, 64% of Americans Now Live Paycheck to Paycheck," yahoo.com, March 9, 2022. https://www.yahoo.com/video/thanks -inflation-64-americans-now-140102090.html.

37. Jesse Eisinger, Jeff Ernsthausen, and Paul Kiel, "The Secret IRS Files: Trove of Never

-Before-Seen Records Reveal How the Wealthiest Avoid Income Tax," propublica.org, June 8, 2021. https://www.propublica.org/article/the-secret-irs-files-trove-of-never -before-seen-records-reveal-how-the-wealthiest-avoid-income-tax.

38. Catherine Thorbecke, "How Our Tax Codes Let the Rich Get Richer: 'We Need Better Tax Laws,'" abcnews.com, June 14, 2021. https://abcnews.go.com/Business/ tax-codes-rich-richer-tax-laws/story?id=78182056.

39. Thorbecke, "How Our Tax Codes."

40. Thorbecke, "How Our Tax Codes."

41. Kate Dore, "The Wealthy May Avoid $163 Billion in Taxes Every Year. Here's How They Do It," cnbc.com, September 20, 2021. https://www.cnbc.com/2021/09/20/ the-wealthy-may-avoid-163-billion-in-annual-taxes-how-they-do-it-.html.

42. Will Kenton, "Board of Governors Definition," investopedia.com, updated February 27, 2023. https://www.investopedia.com/terms/b/board-of-governors.asp.

43. Kenton, "Board of Governors."

44. Kenton, "Board of Governors."

45. Kenton, "Board of Governors."

46. Andrew Beattie, "How the Federal Reserve Was Formed," investopedia.com, updated October 21, 2021. https://www.investopedia.com/articles/economics/08/federal -reserve.asp.

47. Sean Ross, "How Quantitative Easing (QE) Affects the Stock Market," investopedia .com, updated July 25, 2021. https://www.investopedia.com/ask/answers/021015/ how-does-quantitative-easing-us-affect-stock-market.asp.

48. The Investopedia Team, "Fed Balance Sheet: The Federal Reserve's Assets and Liabilities," investopedia.com, updated April 7, 2022. https://www.investopedia.com/ terms/f/fed-balance-sheet.asp.

49. Bram Berkowitz, "Will the Fed's Shrinking Balance Sheet Continue to Roil Markets?" fool.com, April 12, 2022. https://www.fool.com/investing/2022/04/12/will-the-feds -shrinking-balance-sheet-continue-to/.

50. Gary Gerstle, "America's Culture Wars Distract from What's Happening Beneath Them," theguardian.com, April 5, 2022. https://www.theguardian.com/ commentisfree/2022/apr/05/america-politics-culture-wars-republicans-democrats.

51. Andersen, *Evil Geniuses*, p. 148.

52. Gerstle, "America's Culture Wars."

53. Principal Financial Group, "What's Investment Risk and Why Does It Matter?" principal.com, retrieved May 25, 2022. https://www.principal.com/individuals/build-your-knowledge/what-is-investment-risk-and-why-does-it-matter.

54. Brian Perry, "Evaluating Country Risk for International Investing," investopedia.com, March 18, 2022, updated June 22, 2022. https://www.investopedia.com/articles/stocks/08/country-risk-for-international-investing.asp.

55. James Chen, "Political Risk," investopedia.com, updated March 24, 2020. https://www.investopedia.com/terms/p/politicalrisk.asp.

56. Gordon Scott, "Bubble Theory," investopedia.com, August 30, 2021, updated February 27, 2023. https://www.investopedia.com/terms/b/bubble-theory.asp.

CHAPTER 6

1. Weston Blasi, "1 in 3 Americans Earning $250,000 or More Say they Live Paycheck to Paycheck—Are They Really?" marketwatch.com, June 11, 2022, updated August 15, 2022. https://www.marketwatch.com/story/1-in-3-americans-earning-250-000-or-more-say-they-live-paycheck-to-paycheck-are-they-really-11654271836.

2. Kelly Anne Smith, "These States Now Require Students to Learn About Personal Finance," forbes.com, updated April 1, 2022. https://www.forbes.com/advisor/personal-finance/states-mandating-personal-finance-in-school/.

3. Goldman Sachs, "Is the 60/40 Dead?" gsam.com, October 15, 2021. https://www.gsam.com/content/gsam/us/en/institutions/market-insights/gsam-connect/2021/is-the-60-40-dead.html.

4. Goldman Sachs, "Is the 60/40 Dead?"

5. Mallika Mitra, "Even the Classic 60/40 Investment Portfolio Is Getting Clobbered This Year," money.com, June 17, 2022. https://money.com/60-40-stocks-bonds-investment-portfolio-clobbered/.

6. Sigrid Forberg, "The 60/40 Investing Rule Is Dead, Experts Say—Time to Be More Creative," moneywise.com, March 1, 2023. https://moneywise.com/investing/investing-basics/60-40-investing-rule-dead.

7. Antti Ilmanen and Thomas Maloney, "Viewpoint: Where Now for the Stock/Bond Correlation?" ipe.com, June 24, 2022. https://www.ipe.com/viewpoint-where-now-for-the-stock/bond-correlation/10060488.article.

8. Jeff Cox, "This Was the Worst First Half for the Market in 50 Years and It's All Because of One Thing—Inflation," cnbc.com, June 30, 2022. https://www.cnbc .com/2022/06/30/the-markets-worst-first-half-in-50-years-has-all-come-down-to-one -thing.html.

9. Chris Seabury, "How Interest Rates Affect the U.S. Markets," investopedia.com, updated June 17, 2022. https://www.investopedia.com/articles/stocks/09/how -interest-rates-affect-markets.asp.

10. Claire Boyte-White, "What Is the Best Measure of Stock Price Volatility?" investopedia.com, June 3, 2022, updated July 12, 2022. https://www.investopedia .com/ask/answers/021015/what-best-measure-given-stocks-volatility.asp.

11. Financial Samurai Editors, "Sequence of Returns Risk and How It Affects Your Retirement," financialsamurai.com, March 26, 2022. https://www.financialsamurai .com/sequence-of-returns-risk/.

12. Jane Wollman Rusoff, "Father of 4% Rule Urges Caution, Cash as Market Risk Rises," thinkadvisor.com, May 9, 2022. https://www.thinkadvisor.com/2022/05/09/ bill-bengen-revises-4-rule-says-to-cut-stock-and-bond-holdings/.

13. Reshma Kapadia, "Forget the 4% Rule. Why Retirees Need to Rethink Their Withdrawal Strategy," barrons.com, December 21, 2021. https://www.barrons.com/ articles/retirement-withdrawal-strategy-4-percent-rule-51639177201.

14. Trina Paul, "Will Social Security Run Out of Money? Here's What Could Happen to Your Benefits If Congress Doesn't Act," cnbc.com, July 8, 2022, updated October 13, 2022. https://www.cnbc.com/select/will-social-security-run-out-heres-what-you-need -to-know/.

15. Mitra, "Even the Classic 60/40."

16. Rachel Christian, "Running Out of Money in Retirement: What's the Risk?" annuity .org, March 15, 2022, updated February 10, 2023. https://www.annuity.org/running -out-of-money-in-retirement/.

CHAPTER 7

1. Geraldine Fabrikant, "David Swensen, Who Revolutionized Endowment Investing, Dies at 67," nytimes.com, May 7, 2021. https://www.nytimes.com/2021/05/06/ business/david-swensen-dead.html.

2. Chris Arnold, "David Swensen, The Greatest Investor You Maybe Never

Heard of, Leaves Powerful Legacy," npr.org, May 8, 2021. https://www.npr
.org/2021/05/08/994794562/david-swensen-the-greatest-investor-you-maybe-never
-heard-of-leaves-powerful-leg.

3. David Swensen, *Pioneering Portfolio Management: An Unconventional Approach to
Institutional Investment* (New York: Free Press, 2000, 2009), p. 3.

4. Randy Brown, "How to Invest Like a Legend," forbes.com, June 2, 2021.
https://www.forbes.com/sites/randybrown/2021/06/02/how-to-invest-like-a
-legend/?sh=64d5aae93dd2.

5. Yale News, "David Swensen's Coda," news.yale.edu, October 22, 2021. https://news
.yale.edu/2021/10/22/david-swensens-coda.

6. Drake Bennett, Michael McDonald, and Janet Lorin, "How David Swensen Made
Yale Fabulously Rich," bloomberg.com, retrieved July 27, 2022. https://www
.bloomberg.com/news/features/2019-09-11/david-swensen-made-yale-fabulously
-rich-and-changed-endowments#xj4y7vzkg.

7. The Library of Economics and Liberty, "James Tobin: 1918–2002," retrieved August
27, 2022. https://www.econlib.org/library/Enc/bios/Tobin.html.

8. David Lautaret, "The Swensen Portfolio: How You Can Copy the Yale Model
At Home," listenmoneymatters.com, updated April 5, 2022. https://www
.listenmoneymatters.com/swensen-portfolio/.

9. David Swensen, *Unconventional Success* (Florence, MA: Free Press, 2005).

10. Robert McIlhatton, "Unconventional Success Analysis: Asset Allocation after the
Financial Crisis," stat.berkeley.edu, retrieved July 29, 2022. https://www.stat.berkeley
.edu/~aldous/157/Old_Projects/Robert_McIlhatton.pdf

11. McIlhatton, "Unconventional Success Analysis."

12. National Bureau of Economic Research, "The Endowment Model and Modern
Portfolio Theory," nber.org, retrieved July 28, 2022. https://www.nber.org/lecture/
endowment-model-and-modern-portfolio-theory-ltam-2018.

13. Wiley.com Editors, "Constructing Your Ivy Portfolio. Chapter 1: The Super
Endowments," catalogimages.wiley.com, retrieved July 29, 2022. https://
catalogimages.wiley.com/images/db/pdf/9780470284896.excerpt.pdf.

14. Josh Lerner, Antoinette Schoar, and Jialan Wang, "Secrets of the Academy: The
Drivers of University Endowment Success," hbs.edu, retrieved July 29, 2022. https://
www.hbs.edu/ris/Publication%20Files/09-024.pdf.

15. Lerner, Schoar, and Wang, "Secrets of the Academy."

16. Lerner, Schoar, and Wang, "Secrets of the Academy."

17. Financial Samurai, "How the Rich Invest: A Look Inside Yale Endowment's Asset Allocation," financialsamurai.com, April 7, 2022. https://www.financialsamurai .com/a-look-inside-investment-asset-allocation-of-massive-university-endowments/.

CHAPTER 8

1. James Chen, "What Are Alternative Investments? Definition and Examples," investopedia.com, updated February 26, 2022. https://www.investopedia.com/ terms/a/alternative_investment.asp.

2. Fabrikant, "David Swensen . . . Dies at 67."

3. Artem Milinchuk, "The Evolution of Alternative Investments," entrepreneur.com, November 8, 2021. https://www.entrepreneur.com/article/390027.

4. World Economic Forum, "Alternative Investments 2020: An Introduction to Alternative Investments," weforum.org, retrieved August 5, 2022. https://www3 .weforum.org/docs/WEF_Alternative_Investments_2020_An_Introduction_to_ AI.pdf.

5. World Economic Forum, "Alternative Investments 2020."

6. Ari Rastegar, "Understanding the Upsurge of Alternative Investments," forbes.com, December 15, 2021. https://www.forbes.com/sites/ forbesbusinesscouncil/2021/12/15/understanding-the-upsurge-of-alternative -investments/?sh=611b33714b0e.

7. U.S. Department of Labor, "Employee Retirement Income Security Act (ERISA)," dol.gov, retrieved August 6, 2022. https://www.dol.gov/general/topic/retirement/erisa.

8. World Economic Forum, "Alternative Investments 2020."

9. The DI Wire, "Blackstone REIT Registers $30 Billion Follow-on Offering," thediwire .com, October 11, 2021. https://thediwire.com/blackstone-reit-registers-30-billion -follow-on-offering/.

10. E. Napoletano and John Schmidt, "What ERISA Means for Your Retirement Plan," forbes.com, December 3, 2021. https://www.forbes.com/advisor/retirement/erisa -employee-retirement-income-security-act/.

11. New York Times Archive, "Hoffa Convicted on Use of Funds; He and 6 Others Are

Guilty of Fraud and Conspiracy with Teamster Pensions," originally published July 27, 1964, retrieved August 8, 2022. https://www.nytimes.com/1964/07/27/archives/ hoffa-convicted-on-use-of-funds-faces-20-years-he-and-6-others-are.html.

12. Rebecca J. Miller, Robert A. Lavenberg, and Ian A. Mackay, "ERISA: 40 Years Later," journalofaccountancy.com, retrieved August 11, 2022. https://www .journalofaccountancy.com/issues/2014/sep/erisa-20149881.html.

13. Miller, Lavenberg, and Mackay, "ERISA."

14. Miller, Lavenberg, and Mackay, "ERISA."

15. Nathan Bomey, "'It's Really Over': Corporate Pensions Head for Extinction as Nature of Retirement Plans Changes," usatoday.com, December 31, 2019. https://www .usatoday.com/story/money/2019/12/10/corporate-pensions-defined-benefit-mercer -report/2618501001/.

16. Bomey, "It's Really Over."

17. Chris Myers, "The New 'Rules of the Game': Balancing Profits and Social Responsibility in the 21st Century," forbes.com, retrieved August 10, 2022. https:// www.forbes.com/sites/chrismyers/2016/08/30/the-new-rules-of-the-game-balancing -profits-and-social-responsibility-in-the-21st-century/?sh=2b4c69a13afb.

18. Christine Williamson, "Cliffwater: U.S. State Pension Fund Returns 'Badly Trail' Aggregate Assumed Rate of Return," pionline.com, retrieved August 11, 2022. https://www.pionline.com/article/20190315/ONLINE/190319897/cliffwater-u-s -state-pension-fund-returns-badly-trail-aggregate-assumed-rate-of-return.

19. Williamson, "Cliffwater."

20. National Financial Educators Council, "Financial Illiteracy Cost Americans $1,819 in 2022," financialeducationcouncil.org, retrieved March 8, 2023. https://www .financialeducatorscouncil.org/financial-illiteracy-costs/.

CHAPTER 9

1. Jake Frankenfield, "Cryptocurrency Explained with Pros and Cons for Investment," investopedia.com, May 28, 2022, updated February 4, 2023. https://www .investopedia.com/terms/c/cryptocurrency.asp.

2. Kaspersky.com Editors, "Cryptography Definition," kaspersky.com, retrieved August 16, 2022. https://www.kaspersky.com/resource-center/definitions/what-is -cryptography.

3. Adam Hayes, "Blockchain Facts: What It Is, How It Works, and How It Can Be Used," investopedia.com, June 24, 2022, updated September 27, 2022. https://www .investopedia.com/terms/b/blockchain.asp.

4. Tim Fisher, "What Is a Node in a Computer Network?" lifewire.com, updated September 27, 2021. https://www.lifewire.com/what-is-a-node-4155598.

5. Saifedean Ammous, *The Bitcoin Standard: The Decentralized Central Banking* (Hoboken, NJ: Wiley, 1st Edition).

6. Rakhi Shah, "Bitcoin Pizza Day: Hanyecz's Pizzas Are Now Worth $300 Million," alexblockchain.com, May 22, 2022. https://alexablockchain.com/bitcoin-pizza-day -hanyeczs-pizzas-are-now-worth-300-million/.

7. Mara Calvello, "What Is a CAPTCHA? How Does It Protect You From Spam?" g2.com, February 7, 2022. https://www.g2.com/articles/captcha.

8. Euny Hong, "How Does Bitcoin Mining Work?" investopedia.com, updated May 5, 2022. https://www.investopedia.com/tech/how-does-bitcoin-mining-work/.

9. Luke Conway, "What Is Bitcoin Halving? Definition, How It Works, Why It Matters," investopedia.com, November 29, 2021, updated October 4, 2022. https:// www.investopedia.com/bitcoin-halving-4843769.

10. Alex Lielacher, "What Is the Bitcoin Halving and How Does It Affect It's [sic] Price?" axi.com, February 14, 2022. https://www.axi.com/int/blog/education/blockchain/ bitcoin-halving.

11. Lielacher, "Bitcoin Halving."

12. Lielacher, "Bitcoin Halving."

13. Conway, "What Is Bitcoin Halving?"

14. Aakanksha Chaturvedi, "Is Bitcoin Replacing Gold, Oil to Become 'Store of Value' of the Digital Age?" businesstoday.in, updated March 3, 2022. https://www .businesstoday.in/crypto/story/is-bitcoin-replacing-gold-oil-to-become-store-of-value -of-the-digital-age-324657-2022-03-03.

15. James Chen, "Fiat Money: What It Is, How It Works, Example, Pros & Cons," investopedia.com, updated April 19, 2022. https://www.investopedia.com/terms/f/ fiatmoney.asp.

16. CPI Inflation Calculator, "Value of $1,000 from 1980 to 2023," in2013dollars .com, retrieved August 27, 2022. https://www.in2013dollars.com/us/ inflation/1980?amount=1000.

17. Chaturvedi, "Is Bitcoin Replacing Gold?"

18. Ana C. Rold, "Bitcoin's Meteoric Rise and the Future of All Industries," digital
.thecatcompanyinc.com, retrieved August 26, 2022. https://digital.thecatcompanyinc
.com/g7magazine/june-2018/bitcoins-meteoric-rise-future-industries/.

19. Chaturvedi, "Is Bitcoin Replacing Gold?"

20. Todd Crosland, "How Close Is Crypto to Institutional Adoption?" tradersmagazine
.com, May 23, 2022. https://www.tradersmagazine.com/am/how-close-is-crypto-to
-institutional-adoption/.

21. Shannon Williams, "More Countries to Adopt Bitcoin as Legal Tender in 2022—
Expert," itbrief.co.nz, January 6, 2022. https://itbrief.co.nz/story/more-countries-to
-adopt-bitcoin-as-legal-tender-in-2022-expert.

22. Ian Allison, "Harvard, Yale, Brown Endowments Have Been Buying Bitcoin for at
Least a Year: Sources," coindesk.com, January 25, 2021, updated September 14, 2021.
https://www.coindesk.com/business/2021/01/25/harvard-yale-brown-endowments
-have-been-buying-bitcoin-for-at-least-a-year-sources/.

23. Crosland, "How Close Is Crypto?"

24. Sam Bourgi, "Despite Bearish Trend, Hedge Funds Are Dipping Their Toes in
Crypto: PwC," cointelegraph.com, June 8, 2022. https://cointelegraph.com/news/
despite-bearish-trend-hedge-funds-are-dipping-their-toes-in-crypto-pwc.

25. Jorge Suarez, Amneet Singh, and Sam Pittman, "Cryptocurrency and Investor
Portfolios: Is an Allocation Warranted?" russellinvestments.com, February 22, 2022.
https://russellinvestments.com/us/blog/cryptocurrency-investor-portfolios.

26. Suarez, Singh, Pittman, "Cryptocurrency and Investor Portfolios."

27. Keith Black, "What Happens If You Add Crypto to a 60/40 Portfolio?" caia.org,
September 30, 2021. https://caia.org/blog/2021/09/30/what-happens-if-you-add
-crypto-6040-portfolio.

28. Bloomberg, "Harvard, Yale and Brown University Endowments Among Those
Reportedly Buying Cryptocurrency," tech.hindustantimes.com, August 21, 2022.
https://tech.hindustantimes.com/tech/news/harvard-yale-and-brown-university
-endowments-reportedly-buying-cryptocurrency-71611643930133.html.

29. Bloomberg, "Harvard, Yale and Brown."

30. Mark Drozdowski, "Crypto Philanthropy Becoming Mainstream in Higher
Education," bestcolleges.com, December 13, 2021. https://www.bestcolleges

.com/news/analysis/2021/12/13/crypto-philanthropy-higher-education-bitcoin-ethereum/.

31. Cheyenne DeVon, "Crypto Prices Are Down, But It's Not Scaring Away Investors—Here's Why," cnbc.com, September 2, 2022. https://www.cnbc.com/2022/09/02/crypto-winter-isnt-scaring-away-investors-heres-why.html.

32. James Chen, "Exchange-Traded Fund (ETF) with Explanation and Pros and Cons" investopedia.com, February 26, 2022, updated October 17, 2022. https://www.investopedia.com/terms/e/etf.asp.

33. Chen, "Exchange-Traded Fund"

34. Charles Schwab, "Understanding Mutual Funds," schwab.com, retrieved September 3, 2022. https://www.schwab.com/mutual-funds/understand-mutual-funds.

35. Adam Hayes, "Futures Contract Definition: Types, Mechanics, and Uses in Trading," investopedia.com, updated October 30, 2021. https://www.investopedia.com/terms/f/futurescontract.asp.

36. Rakesh Sharma, "First Bitcoin ETF Begins Trading," investopedia.com, October 19, 2021. https://www.investopedia.com/first-bitcoin-etf-begins-trading-5206196.

37. Tom Wilson, Anna Irrera, and Jessica DiNapoli, "Explainer: Bitcoin on Your Balance Sheet? Here's What You Need to Know," reuters.com, March 8, 2021. https://www.reuters.com/article/us-crypto-currency-bitcoin-treasury-expl/explainer-bitcoin-on-your-balance-sheet-heres-what-you-need-to-know-idUSKBN2B00FP.

38. Wilson, Irrera, and DiNapoli, "Explainer."

39. Tom Gerken, "Elon Musk's Tesla Lost $140m on Bitcoin in 2022," bbc.com, February 1, 2023. https://www.bbc.com/news/technology-64428257.

40. Hugh Son, "Grayscale Tells SEC That Turning Biggest Bitcoin Fund into ETF Will Unlock $8 Billion for Investors," cnbc.com, May 11, 2022. https://www.cnbc.com/2022/05/11/grayscale-tells-sec-that-turning-biggest-bitcoin-fund-into-etf-willunlock-8-billion-for-investors.html.

CHAPTER 10

1. Harry Markowitz, "Portfolio Selection," math.hkust.edu.hk, March, Vol. 7, No. 1 (March 1952), pp.77–91. https://www.math.hkust.edu.hk/~maykwok/courses/ma362/07F/markowitz_JF.pdf.

2. Georgina Tzanetos, "The 60/40 Rule Is Long Dead—Modern Times Call for New

Investment Strategies," gobankingrates.com, June 17, 2021. https://www
.gobankingrates.com/investing/strategy/60-40-rule-long-dead-modern-times-call-for
-new-investment-strategies/.

3. The Investopedia Team, "Modern Portfolio Theory (MPT): What MPT Is and How
    Investors Use It," investopedia.com, updated September 10, 2021. https://www
    .investopedia.com/terms/m/modernportfoliotheory.asp.

4. Investopedia Team, "Modern Portfolio Theory."

5. Liz Aldrich, "Diversifying Outside of Stock: The Most Correlated and Non-
    Correlated Assets," moneymade.io, updated February 28, 2023. https://moneymade
    .io/learn/article/asset-correlation-study.

6. James Chen, "Business Development Company (BDC): Definition and How to
    Invest," investopedia.com, updated August 11, 2022. https://www.investopedia.com/
    terms/b/bdc.asp.

7. James Chen, "How a Closed-End Fund Definition Works and Differs From an Open-
    End Fund," investopedia.com, updated July 14, 2022. https://www.investopedia.com/
    terms/c/closed-endinvestment.asp.

8. Jim Probasco, "What Is an Interval Fund? Definition, Buying & Selling, Risks,"
    investopedia.com, updated July 14, 2022. https://www.investopedia.com/articles/
    investing/120516/what-interval-fund.asp.

9. James Chen, "What Is Asset Allocation and Why Is It Important? With Example,"
    investopedia.com, updated March 1, 2022. https://www.investopedia.com/terms/a/
    assetallocation.asp.

10. Adam Hayes, "Understanding Liquidity and How to Measure It," investopedia.com,
    March 9, 2022, updated March 3, 2023. https://www.investopedia.com/terms/l/
    liquidity.asp.

11. James Chen, "Passive Investing," investopedia.com, updated December 29, 2020.
    https://www.investopedia.com/terms/p/passiveinvesting.asp.

12. Adam Hayes, "Absolute Return: Definition, Example, vs. Relative Return,"
    investopedia.com, updated April 26, 2021. https://www.investopedia.com/terms/a/
    absolutereturn.asp.

13. CME, "Compelling Reasons to Allocate to Managed Futures," cmegroup.com,

retrieved September 18, 2022. https://www.cmegroup.com/education/courses/
managed-futures/compelling-reasons-to-allocate-to-managed-futures.html.

14. Jason Fernando, "Managed Futures Account," investopedia.com, updated May 26,
2022. https://www.investopedia.com/terms/m/managedfuturesaccount.asp.

15. John Summa, "Managed Futures: A Beginner's Guide," investopedia.com, May
25, 2022, updated October 31, 2022. https://www.investopedia.com/articles/
optioninvestor/05/070605.asp.

16. Summa, "Managed Futures."

17. Alexandra Hudson, "Happy Birthday to Montesquieu! Lessons on Human Nature
from America's Unofficial Founding Father, Born 333 Years Ago Today," civic
-renaissance.com, January 18, 2022. https://www.civic-renaissance.com/p/happy
-birthday-to-montesquieu-lessons.

18. Shu-Min Wu, Hao-Sheng Zeng, "Genuine Tripartite Nonlocality and Entanglement
in Curved Spacetime," arxiv.org, January 7, 2022. https://arxiv.org/abs/2201.02333.

CHAPTER 11

1. Financial Industry Regulatory Authority, "Investing Basics: Risk," finra.org, retrieved
November 11, 2022. https://www.finra.org/investors/investing/investing-basics/risk.

2. Chen, "Risk."

3. Adam Hayes, "Volatility: Meaning in Finance and How it Works with Stocks,"
investopedia.com, updated August 23, 2022. https://www.investopedia.com/terms/v/
volatility.asp

4. Marshall Hargrave, "Standard Deviation Formula and Uses vs. Variance,"
investopedia.com, updated July 5, 2022. https://www.investopedia.com/terms/s/
standarddeviation.asp.

5. Hargrave, "Standard Deviation Formula."

6. Hargrave, "Standard Deviation Formula."

7. James Chen, "Risk Averse: What It Means, Investment Choices and Strategies,"
investopedia.com, updated September 6, 2022. https://www.investopedia.com/
terms/r/riskaverse.asp.

8. Meeyeon Park, "Risk Tolerance," corporatefinanceinstitute.com, October 24, 2022, updated February 24, 2023. https://corporatefinanceinstitute.com/resources/wealth -management/risk-tolerance/.

9. Nick Lioudis, "The Importance of Diversification," investopedia.com, updated June 15, 2022. https://www.investopedia.com/investing/importance-diversification/.

10. Lioudis, "Importance of Diversification."

11. Google's English Dictionary as provided by Oxford Languages Dictionary, "Structure," google.com, retrieved September 21, 2022. https://tinyurl.com/55kejsse

12. Cambridge Dictionary, "Function," dictionary.cambridge.org, retrieved September 21, 2022. https://dictionary.cambridge.org/us/dictionary/english/function.

13. PublicDomainPictures.net. https://www.publicdomainpictures.net/en/view-image .php?image=42719&picture=cell

14. James Chen, "Dynamic Asset Allocation," investopedia.com, updated July 12, 2022. https://www.investopedia.com/terms/d/dynamic-asset-allocation.asp.

15. Sam Swenson, "The 10 Best Low-Cost Index Funds," fool.com, July 1, 2022, updated March 2, 2023. https://www.fool.com/investing/how-to-invest/index-funds/low-cost -index-funds/.

16. Adam Hayes, "What Is a Bond Fund? How It Works, Benefits, Taxes, and Types," investopedia.com, updated April 18, 2022. https://www.investopedia.com/terms/b/ bondfund.asp.

17. Kate Stalter, "Does Market Uncertainty Mean It's Time for a Tactical Investing Approach?" money.usnews.com, May 9, 2022. https://money.usnews.com/financial -advisors/articles/does-market-uncertainty-mean-its-time-for-a-tactical-investing -approach

18. Stalter, "Does Market Uncertainty?"

19. James Chen, "Liquid Alternatives: Definition, Purposes, Risks, and Examples," investopedia.com, updated September 13, 2022. https://www.investopedia.com/ terms/l/liquid-alternatives.asp.

20. Investor.gov, "Net Asset Value," investor.gov, retrieved September 26, 2022. https:// www.investor.gov/introduction-investing/investing-basics/glossary/net-asset-value.

21. Investor.gov, "Net Asset Value."

22. James Chen, "Net Asset Value (NAV): Definition Formula, Examples, and Uses," investopedia.com, updated July 22, 2022. https://www.investopedia.com/terms/n/nav.asp.

23. Chen, "Net Asset Value."

24. Akhilesh Ganti, "Preferred Stock," investopedia.com, updated January 26, 2023. https://www.investopedia.com/terms/p/preferredstock.asp.

25. Ganti, "Preferred Stock."

26. Akhilesh Ganti, "Preferred Stock," investopedia.com, January 26, 2023. https://www.investopedia.com/terms/p/preferredstock.asp#:~:text=What%20Are%20the%20Advantages%20of,in%20the%20event%20of%20liquidation.

27. Jim Probasco, "What is an Interval Fund? Definition, Buying & Selling, Risks," investopedia.com, July 14, 2022. https://www.investopedia.com/articles/investing/120516/what-interval-fund.asp

28. Probasco, "What Is an Interval Fund?"

29. James Chen, "Non-Traded REIT: Explanation, How They Work, Characteristics," investopedia.com, updated August 18, 2022. https://www.investopedia.com/terms/n/non-traded-reit.asp.

30. Kevin Vandenboss, "Best Non-Traded REITS," benzinga.com, updated May 16, 2022. https://www.benzinga.com/money/best-non-traded-reits.

31. James Chen, "Real Estate Investment Trust (REIT): How They Work and How to Invest," investopedia.com, updated April 4, 2022. https://www.investopedia.com/terms/r/reit.asp.

32. Daniel Kurt, "What are Non-Traded Business Development Companies (BDCs)?" investopedia.com, September 20, 2022. https://www.investopedia.com/articles/retirement/051616/what-are-nontraded-bdcs-and-should-you-stay-away-them.asp

33. Dan Moskowitz, "What are the Risks of Real Estate Investment Trusts (REITs)?" investopedia.com, April 11, 2022. https://www.investopedia.com/articles/investing/031915/what-are-risks-reits.asp#toc-risks-of-non-traded-reits.

34. Moskowitz, "What are the Risks?"

35. Wendy Connett, "REITs vs. Real Estate Mutual Funds: An Overview," investopedia.com, July 8, 2022. https://www.investopedia.com/articles/investing/040315/reits-versus-real-estate-mutual-funds.asp

36. Daniel Kurt, "WhaT Are Non-Traded Business Development Companies (BDCs)? investopedia.com, September 20, 2022. https://www.investopedia.com/articles/retirement/051616/what-are-nontraded-bdcs-and-should-you-stay-away-them.asp

37. Monroe Capital, "What Is Private Credit?" monroecap.com, retrieved September 27, 2022. https://www.monroecap.com/investment-products/private-credit-funds-overview/. This source should be added to the endnotes.

38. James Chen, "Bond Rating Agencies," investopedia.com, July 1, 2022. https://www.investopedia.com/terms/b/bond-rating-agencies.asp

39. Pamela Espinosa, "Private Credit," moonfare.com, June 20, 2023. https://www.moonfare.com/pe-masterclass/private-credit.

40. Jason Fernandez, "What Are Index Funds," investopedia.com, March 24, 2023. https://www.investopedia.com/terms/i/indexfund.asp

41. Titan.com, "Hedge Funds vs. Index Funds: Key Differences," titan.com, September 9, 2022. https://www.titan.com/articles/hedge-fund-vs-index-fund#.

42. Titan.com, "Hedge Funds vs. Index Funds: Key Differences," titan.com, September 9, 2022. https://www.titan.com/articles/hedge-fund-vs-index-fund#.

43. Jason Fernandez, "What Are Index Funds," investopedia.com, March 24, 2023. https://www.investopedia.com/terms/i/indexfund.asp

44. Akhilesh Ganti, "Private Placements: Definition, Example, Pros and Cons," investopedia.com, March 29, 2022. https://www.investopedia.com/terms/p/privateplacement.asp#:~:text=A%20private%20placement%20is%20a,to%20raise%20capital%20for%20expansion.

45. Akhilesh Ganti, "Private Placements: Definition, Example, Pros and Cons," investopedia.com, March 29, 2022. https://www.investopedia.com/terms/p/privateplacement.asp#:~:text=A%20private%20placement%20is%20a,to%20raise%20capital%20for%20expansion.

46. Financial Samurai, "The Return of the 60/40 Portfolio Plus Alternative Investments," financialsamurai.com, updated February 6, 2022. https://www.financialsamurai.com/the-60-40-portfolio/.

CHAPTER 12

1. Let's Make a Plan, "Risk Management," letsmakeaplan.org, retrieved October 6, 2022. https://www.letsmakeaplan.org/financial-topics/topics-a-z/risk-management.

2. Daniel Holbrook, "Existentialism Lecture," public.wsu.org, retrieved October 10, 2022. https://public.wsu.edu/~holbrodm/Existentialism.html.

3. Julia Kagan, "Insurance: Definition, How it Works, and Main Types of Policies," investopedia.com, updated July 18, 2022. https://www.investopedia.com/terms/i/insurance.asp.

4. Amy Fontinelle, "Life Insurance: What It Is, How It Works, and How to Buy a Policy," investopedia.com, May 25, 2022, updated December 22, 2022. https://www.investopedia.com/terms/l/lifeinsurance.asp.

5. Fontinelle, "Life Insurance."

6. Fontinelle, "Life Insurance."

7. Fontinelle, "Life Insurance."

8. Fontinelle, "Life Insurance."

9. Fontinelle, "Life Insurance."

10. Fontinelle, "Life Insurance."

11. Fontinelle, "Life Insurance."

12. Fontinelle, "Life Insurance."

13. Justin Kuepper, "Indexed Universal Life Insurance (IUL) Meaning and Pros and Cons," investopedia.com, March 2, 2022, updated March 3, 2023. https://www.investopedia.com/articles/personal-finance/012416/pros-and-cons-indexed-universal-life-insurance.asp.

14. Kat Tretina, "5 Top Benefits of Life Insurance," investopedia.com, updated February 26, 2022. https://www.investopedia.com/5-top-benefits-of-life-insurance-5105062.

15. Tretina, "5 Top Benefits."

16. Tretina, "5 Top Benefits."

17. Tretina, "5 Top Benefits."

18. Tretina, "5 Top Benefits."

19. Lindsay Modglin, "Long-Term Care Statistics 2022," singlecare.com, February 15, 2022. https://www.singlecare.com/blog/news/long-term-care-statistics/.

20. Modglin, "Long-Term Care."

21. James McWhinney, "Medicare vs. Medicaid: What's the Difference?" investopedia .com, updated June 30, 2022. https://www.investopedia.com/articles/pf/07/medicare -vs-medicaid.asp.

22. Elder Law Answers, "Can Medicaid Take Your Home?" elderlawanswers.com, January 7, 2022. https://www.elderlawanswers.com/medicaids-treatment-of-the-home-12140.

23. Elder Law Answers, "Medicaid's Power to Recoup Benefits Paid: Estate Recovery and Liens," elderlawanswers.com, July 19, 2021. https://www.elderlawanswers.com/ medicaids-power-to-recoup-benefits-paid-estate-recovery-and-liens-12018.

24. Julia Kagan, "Long-Term Care (LTC) Insurance: Definition, Costs, Alternatives," investopedia.com, updated September 15, 2021. https://www.investopedia.com/ terms/l/ltcinsurance.asp.

25. Pooja Dave, "8 Common Life Insurance Riders," investopedia.com, updated May 23, 2022. https://www.investopedia.com/articles/pf/07/life_insurance_rider.asp.

26. Progressive Insurance, "Should You Buy Life Insurance with a Long-Term Care Rider?" progressive.com, retrieved November 14, 2022. https://www.progressive.com/ answers/life-insurance-long-term-care-rider/.

27. Julia Kagan, "Umbrella Personal Liability Policy," investopedia.com, updated May 25, 2022. https://www.investopedia.com/terms/u/umbrella-personal-liability-policy.asp.

28. Ashley Kilroy, "How an Umbrella Policy Works and What It Covers," forbes.com, updated October 5, 2022. https://www.forbes.com/advisor/car-insurance/umbrella -insurance/.

29. Amy Fontinelle, "A Brief History of Taxes in the U.S.," investopedia.com, updated January 24, 2023. https://www.investopedia.com/articles/tax/10/history-taxes.asp.

30. Alicia Tuovila, "Marginal Tax Rate: What It Is, and How to Calculate it, with Examples," investopedia.com, September 6, 2021, updated October 24, 2022. https://www.investopedia.com/terms/m/marginaltaxrate.asp.

31. Bradford Tax Institute, "History of Federal Income Tax Rates: 1913–2023," bradfordtaxinstitute.com, retrieved March 8, 2023. https://bradfordtaxinstitute.com/ free_resources/federal-income-tax-rates.aspx.

32. Jean Folger, "Tax-Efficient Investing: A Beginner's Guide," investopedia.com, October 17, 2022, updated February 13, 2023. https://www.investopedia.com/articles/stocks/11/intro-tax-efficient-investing.asp.

33. Jean Folger, "Minimize Taxes and Maximize Your Bottom Line," investopedia.com, October 17, 2022, updated February 13, 2023. https://www.investopedia.com/articles/stocks/11/intro-tax-efficient-investing.asp.

34. Folger, "Minimize Taxes."

35. Charles Schwab, "Tax-Efficient Investing: Why Is It Important?" schwab.com, May 12, 2022. https://www.schwab.com/learn/story/tax-efficient-investing-why-is-it-important.

36. Sean Ross, "How Is a Savings Account Taxed?" investopedia.com, updated November 3, 2021. https://www.investopedia.com/ask/answers/052515/how-savings-account-taxed.asp.

37. Mark Henricks, "How Savings Accounts Are Taxed," smartasset.com, August 25, 2022. https://smartasset.com/taxes/how-savings-accounts-are-taxed.

38. David Dierking, "Benefits of Holding Stocks for the Long-Term," investopedia.com, updated May 3, 2022. https://www.investopedia.com/articles/investing/052216/4-benefits-holding-stocks-long-term.asp.

39. Claire Boyte-White, "The Basics of Determining Taxes on Mutual Funds," investopedia.com, updated June 3, 2022. https://www.investopedia.com/articles/investing/091715/basics-income-tax-mutual-funds.asp.

40. Julia Kagan, "Tax Deferred: Earnings with Taxes Delayed until Liquidation," investopedia.com, December 10, 2021, updated November 20, 2022. https://www.investopedia.com/terms/t/taxdeferred.asp.

41. Ameritas, "Tax Deferred Growth Example," ameritasdirect.com, October 17, 2022. https://www.ameritasdirect.com/annuities/tax-deferred-growth-example/.

42. U.S. Securities and Exchange Commission, "Traditional and Roth 401(k) Plans," investor.gov, retrieved October 17, 2022. https://www.investor.gov/additional-resources/retirement-toolkit/employer-sponsored-plans/traditional-and-roth-401k-plans.

43. The Investopedia Team, "403(b) Plan: What It Is, How It Works, 2 Main Types," investopedia.com, updated January 23, 2023. https://www.investopedia.com/terms/1/403bplan.asp.

44. Daniel Liberto, "457 Plan," investopedia.com, updated January 23, 2023. https://www.investopedia.com/terms/1/457plan.asp.

45. Adam Hayes, "Understanding a Traditional IRA vs. Other Retirement Accounts," investopedia.com, August 4, 2022, updated February 21, 2023. https://www.investopedia.com/terms/t/traditionalira.asp.

46. IRS, "Retirement Plan and IRA Required Minimum Distributions FAQs," irs.gov, March 19, 2023. https://www.irs.gov/retirement-plans/retirement-plan-and-ira-required-minimum-distributions-faqs.

47. Adam Hayes, "An Overview of Annuities," investopedia.com, April 28, 2022. https://www.investopedia.com/investing/overview-of-annuities/.

48. Hayes, "Overview of Annuities."

49. Hayes, "Overview of Annuities."

50. Hayes, "Overview of Annuities."

51. Troy Segal, "Roth IRA: What It Is and How to Open One," investopedia.com, July 26, 2022, updated March 8, 2023, https://www.investopedia.com/terms/r/rothira.asp.

52. Charles Schwab, "Should You Consider a Roth 401(k)?" schwab.com, July 20, 2022. https://www.schwab.com/learn/story/should-you-consider-roth-401k.

53. Amy Danise, "Is Life Insurance Taxable?" forbes.com, September 21, 2022, updated January 4, 2023. https://www.forbes.com/advisor/life-insurance/is-life-insurance-taxable/.

54. Thom Tracy, "Think Twice Before Buying Tax-Free Municipal Bonds," investopedia.com, updated July 10, 2022. https://www.investopedia.com/articles/investing-strategy/090116/think-twice-buying-taxfree-municipal-bonds.asp.

CHAPTER 13

1. Bryan Borzykowski, "The Ultimate Retirement Planning Guide for 2022," cnbc.com, September 20, 2022. https://www.cnbc.com/guide/retirement-planning/.

2. Fidelity Viewpoints, "Ready to Retire? You Still Need a Budget," fidelity.com, August 2, 2022. https://www.fidelity.com/viewpoints/retirement/retirement-and-budgeting.

3. Fidelity Viewpoints, "Ready to Retire?"

4. Frank Diamond, "U.S. Employers Brace for Healthcare Costs to Rise Next 3 Years," fiercehealthcare.com, September 16, 2022. https://www.fiercehealthcare.com/payers/employers-expect-healthcare-costs-rise-next-3-years.

5. Fidelity Viewpoints, "Ready to Retire?"

6. NerdWallet, "The 8 Best Budget Apps for 2023," nerdwallet.com, July 29, 2022, updated December 15, 2022. https://www.nerdwallet.com/article/finance/best-budget-apps.

7. Fidelity Viewpoints, "How Much Should I Save for Retirement?" fidelity.com, January 31, 2023. https://www.fidelity.com/viewpoints/retirement/how-much-money-should-I-save.

8. Reshma Kapadia, "Forget the 4% Rule. Why Retirees Need to Rethink Their Withdrawal Strategy," barrons.com, December 10, 2021, updated December 14, 2021. https://www.barrons.com/articles/retirement-withdrawal-strategy-4-percent-rule-51639177201.

9. Jeff Berman, "10 Things Advisors Should Know About Sequence of Returns Risk in Retirement," thinkadvisor.com, March 14, 2022. https://www.thinkadvisor.com/2022/03/14/10-things-advisors-should-know-about-sequence-of-returns-risk-in-retirement/.

10. RetireOne, "What Is Sequence of Returns Risk?" retireone.com, retrieved November 15, 2022. https://retireone.com/sequence-of-returns-risk/.

11. The Investopedia Team, "What Is a Pension? How It Works, Taxation, and Types of Plans," investopedia.com, updated September 3, 2022. https://www.investopedia.com/terms/p/pensionplan.asp

12. The Investopedia Team, "What Is a Pension?"

13. The Investopedia Team, "What Is a Pension?"

14. The Investopedia Team, "What Is a Pension?"

15. The Investopedia Team, "What Is a Pension?"

16. The Investopedia Team, "What Is a Pension?"

17. Miranda Marquit, "Guide to 401(k) Rollovers," forbes.com, October 24, 2022. https://www.forbes.com/advisor/retirement/what-is-401k-rollover/.

18. Brian Dobbis, "Secure Act 2.0: RMD Changes for 2023 and Beyond," lordabbett
.com, February 6, 2023. https://www.lordabbett.com/en-us/financial-advisor/insights/
retirement-planning/secure-act-2-0--rmd-changes-for-2023-and-beyond.html.

19. Mike Winters, "Over 20% of 401(k) Plan Funds Are Lost or Forgotten—Here's How
to Reclaim Yours," cnbc.com, June 3, 2022. https://www.cnbc.com/2022/06/03/over
-20percent-of-401k-plan-funds-are-missingheres-how-to-reclaim-yours.html.

20. Marquit, "Guide to 401(k) Rollovers."

21. Marquit, "Guide to 401(k) Rollovers."

22. Marquit, "Guide to 401(k) Rollovers."

23. Social Security Administration, "How You Become Eligible for Benefits," ssa.gov, June
2022. https://www.ssa.gov/myaccount/assets/materials/eligibility-for-benefits.pdf.

24. Julia Kagan, "Average Indexed Monthly Earnings (AIME)," investopedia.com,
October 23, 2022. https://www.investopedia.com/terms/a/aime.asp.

25. Amy Fontinelle, "When to Take Social Security: The Complete Guide," investopedia
.com, April 25, 2022, updated February 19, 2023. https://www.investopedia.com/
retirement/when-take-social-security-complete-guide/.

26. Fontinelle, "When to Take Social Security."

27. Fontinelle, "When to Take Social Security."

28. Julia Kagan, "What Is Medicare? How It Works, Who Qualifies, and How to Enroll,"
investopedia.com, updated November 10, 2022. https://www.investopedia.com/
terms/m/medicare.asp.

29. Kagan, "What Is Medicare?"

30. Medicare.gov, "Avoid Late Enrollment Penalties," medicare.gov, retrieved November
14, 2022. https://www.medicare.gov/basics/costs/medicare-costs/avoid-penalties.

31. E. Napoletano, "Fixed vs. Variable Annuity: Which Is Best?" forbes.com, April 4,
2022. https://www.forbes.com/advisor/retirement/fixed-vs-variable-annuity/.

32. Adam Hayes, "An Overview of Annuities," investopedia.com, updated April 28, 2022.
https://www.investopedia.com/investing/overview-of-annuities/.

33. Julia Kagan, "What Is a Fixed Annuity? Uses in Investing, Pros, and Cons,"
investopedia.com, updated April 25, 2021. https://www.investopedia.com/terms/f/
fixedannuity.asp.

34. Napoletano, "Fixed vs. Variable Annuity."

35. The Investopedia Team, "Variable Annuities with Living Benefits: Worth the Fees?" investopedia.com, updated October 30, 2021. https://www.investopedia.com/articles/retirement/08/variable-annuity.asp.

36. Investopedia Team, "Variable Annuities."

37. Fidelity Viewpoints, "Indexed Annuities: Look Before You Leap," fidelity.com, June 24, 2022. https://www.fidelity.com/viewpoints/retirement/considering-indexed-annuities.

38. Liz Brumer-Smith, "Why Owning Rental Property is 1 of the Best Retirement Moves," fool.com, January 15, 2022. https://www.fool.com/investing/2022/01/15/why-owning-rental-property-is-one-of-the-best-reti/.

39. Andrew Dunn, "What is the Average Home Value Increase Per Year?" creditkarma.com, August 30, 2022. https://www.creditkarma.com/home-loans/i/average-home-value-increase-per-year#:~:text=Since%201991%2C%20the%20average%20annual,significantly%20from%20state%20to%20state.

40. Andrew Dehan, "Everything You Need to Know About Home Equity Loans for Debt Consolidation," rocketmortgage.com, August 22, 2022, updated March 3, 2023. https://www.rocketmortgage.com/learn/home-equity-loan-for-debt-consolidation/

41. Carla Tardi, "Rental Properties: Pros and Cons," investopedia.com, September 8, 2021. https://www.investopedia.com/articles/investing/051515/pros-cons-owning-rental-property.asp#:~:text=The%20drawbacks%20of%20having%20rental,the%20neighborhood%27s%20appeal%20to%20decline

42. Carla Tardi, "Rental Properties."

43. Brumer-Smith, "Owning Rental Property."

44. Andrew Dehan, "Everything You Need to Know About Home Equity Loans for Debt Consolidation," rocketmortgage.com, August 22, 2022, updated March 3, 2023. https://www.rocketmortgage.com/learn/home-equity-loan-for-debt-consolidation/

45. Dehan, "Everything You Need to Know."

46. Adam Barone, "Home Equity Loans: What You Need to Know," investopedia.com, updated June 28, 2022. https://www.investopedia.com/personal-finance/home-equity-loans-what-to-know/.

47. Casey Bond, Mike Cetera, "5 Reverse Mortgage Pros and Cons," forbes.com, November 11, 2022. https://www.forbes.com/advisor/mortgages/reverse-mortgage-pros-cons/.

48. Bond, Cetera, "5 Reverse Mortgage Pros and Cons."

49. Bond, Cetera, "5 Reverse Mortgage Pros and Cons."

50. Bond, Cetera, "5 Reverse Mortgage Pros and Cons."

51. Barone, "Home Equity Loans."

52. Barone, "Home Equity Loans."

53. Amy Fontinelle, "Reverse Mortgage: The Pros and Cons," investopedia.com, updated June 22, 2022. https://www.investopedia.com/reverse-mortgage-pros-and-cons-5209641.

54. Bond, Cetera, "5 Reverse Mortgage Pros and Cons."

55. Fontinelle, "Reverse Mortgage."

CHAPTER 14

1. Glenn Curtis, "6 Estate Planning Must-Haves," investopedia.com, updated February 27, 2022. https://www.investopedia.com/articles/pf/07/estate_plan_checklist.asp.

2. Janet Berry-Johnson, "Estate Planning Is an Important Strategy for Arranging Financial Affairs and Protecting Heirs—Here Are 5 Reasons Why Everyone Needs an Estate Plan," businessinsider.com, updated August 12, 2022. https://www.businessinsider.com/personal-finance/why-is-estate-planning-important.

3. Berry-Johnson, "Estate Planning."

4. Berry-Johnson, "Estate Planning."

5. Berry-Johnson, "Estate Planning."

6. Berry-Johnson, "Estate Planning."

7. Julie Garber, "Differences Between the Estate Tax and Inheritance Tax," thebalancemoney.com, June 30, 2022, updated January 19, 2023. https://www.thebalancemoney.com/difference-between-estate-and-inheritance-tax-3505472.

8. Garber, "Differences Between."

9. Berry-Johnson, "Estate Planning."

10. Rachel Dupont, "When a Health Care Proxy and Power of Attorney Disagree," aplaceformom.com, updated April 22, 2022. https://www.aplaceformom.com/caregiver-resources/articles/proxy-and-power-of-attorney-disagree.

11. Dupont, "When a Health Care Proxy."

12. Dupont, "When a Health Care Proxy."

13. Matthew Jarrell, "Will vs. Trust: What's the Difference?" investopedia.com, July 25, 2022, updated January 5, 2023. https://www.investopedia.com/articles/personal-finance/051315/will-vs-trust-difference-between-two.asp.

14. Jarrell, "Will vs. Trust."

15. Jarrell, "Will vs. Trust."

16. Jarrell, "Will vs. Trust."

17. Julia Kagan, "Revocable Trust Definition," investopedia.com, updated October 6, 2022. https://www.investopedia.com/terms/r/revocabletrust.asp.

18. Barclay Palmer, "Should You Set Up a Revocable Living Trust?" investopedia.com, June 15, 2022, updated January 9, 2023. https://www.investopedia.com/articles/pf/06/revocablelivingtrust.asp.

19. Palmer, "Should You Set Up?"

20. Palmer, "Should You Set Up?"

21. Fidelity, "Credit Shelter Trusts and Estate Taxes," fidelity.com, March 16, 2022. https://www.fidelity.com/viewpoints/wealth-management/insights/credit-shelter-trusts.

22. Jean Folger, "Tips for Successful Retirement Investing," investopedia.com, August 3, 2022, updated December 10, 2022. https://www.investopedia.com/articles/personal-finance/111313/six-critical-rules-successful-retirement-investing.asp.

CHAPTER 15

1. Tom Hale, "Why Idiots Think They're Smart: Dunning on the Dunning-Kruger Effect," iflscience.com, June 14, 2022. https://www.iflscience.com/why-idiots-think-theyre-smart-dunning-on-the-dunningkruger-effect-64057.

2. Jonathan Jarry, "The Dunning-Kruger Effect Is Probably Not Real," mcgill.ca, December 17, 2020. https://www.mcgill.ca/oss/article/critical-thinking/dunning -kruger-effect-probably-not-real.

3. Kate Whiting, "Edelman Trust Barometer: Cycle of Distrust Threatens Action on Global Challenges," weforum.org, January 18, 2022. https://www.weforum.org/ agenda/2022/01/edelman-trust-barometer-2022-report/.

4. Money Crashers, "Men vs. Women—How the Sexes Differ in Their Psychology of Investing (Survey)," moneycrashers.com, September 14, 2021. https://www .moneycrashers.com/men-vs-women-psychology-investing/.

5. Money Crashers, "Men vs. Women."

6. Money Crashers, "Men vs. Women."

7. Money Crashers, "Men vs. Women."

8. Peter Hodson, "Five Reasons Women Are Better Investors Than Men," financialpost .com, updated February 14, 2022. https://financialpost.com/investing/five-reasons -women-are-better-investors-than-men.

9. G. Brian Davis, "Why Emotion Is the Enemy of Investing—How to Avoid Herd Psychology," moneycrashers.com, May 4, 2022. https://www.moneycrashers.com/ emotion-enemy-investing/.

10. Adam Hayes, "Irrational Exuberance: Definition, Origin, Example," investopedia .com, April 5, 2022, updated April 8, 2022. https://www.investopedia.com/terms/i/ irrationalexuberance.asp.

11. Olivia Guy-Evans, "How to Deal with FOMO in Your Life," simplypsychology.org, updated February 8, 2023. https://www.simplypsychology.org/how-to-cope-with -fomo.html.

12. Fernando Diaz-Diaz, Maxi San Miguel, and Sandro Meloni, "Echo Chambers and Information Transmission Biases in Homophilic and Heterophilic Networks," nature .com, June 7, 2022. https://www.nature.com/articles/s41598-022-13343-6.

13. Katherine Reynolds Lewis, "The Psychology Behind Your Worst Investment Decisions," kiplinger.com, updated July 22, 2021. https://www.kiplinger.com/ investing/603153/the-psychology-behind-your-worst-investment-decisions.

14. The American Yawp Reader, "John Winthrop Dreams of a City on Hill, 1630," americanyawp.com, retrieved November 20, 2022. https://www.americanyawp.com/reader/colliding-cultures/john-winthrop-dreams-of-a-city-on-a-hill-1630/.

15. John F. Kennedy Library, "Address of President-Elect John F. Kennedy Delivered to a Joint Convention of the General Court of the Commonwealth of Massachusetts, January 9, 1961," jfklibrary.org, retrieved November 21, 2022. https://www.jfklibrary.org/archives/other-resources/john-f-kennedy-speeches/massachusetts-general-court-19610109.

16. David Frum, "Is America Still the 'Shining City on a Hill'?" theatlantic.com, January 1, 2021. https://www.theatlantic.com/ideas/archive/2021/01/is-america-still-the-shining-city-on-a-hill/617474/.

17. Sam Lipscomb, "This Mistake Is Costing You $1,400: But You Can Fix It," aol.com, January 18, 2022. https://www.aol.com/news/mistake-costing-1-400-fix-220836119.html.

INDEX

alternative investments and, 106–8
consequences of poor financial literacy,
219–20
defined, 5
role of education in, 1–5
three-legged stool metaphor and, 83–84
FINRA. *See* Financial Industry Regulatory
Authority
fixed annuities, 173, 192
fixed-rate second mortgage, 195
FOMO (Fear of Missing Out), 122, 215
food, budgeting for, 179
Ford, Henry, 28
Fordism, 55–56
Foreign Corrupt Practices Act of 1977
(FCPA), 63
401(k) plan
rollovers, 187–88
taxes and, 172
403(b) plan, 172–73
457 plan, 173
four-legged chair metaphor, 89–90, 213–17
FRA (full retirement age), 189
Franklin, Benjamin, 139
Freud, Sigmund, 21
Friedman, Milton, 6, 38–40, 42, 44, 47,
60, 105
Friedman, Thomas, 13
FS Investments, 132–33
full retirement age (FRA), 189
function
of REALM model, 146–47
structure and, 143–44
Future Scholar Financial Literacy Program,
3
futures contract, 123

G

Galilei, Galileo, 20, 25, 27
Gates, Bill, 60, 74
Gaussian copula theorems, 101
genuine tripartite entanglement (GTE),
137
genuine tripartite nonlocality (GTN), 137
geopolitical risk, 77–78
Georgy, R. F., 110

Gilded Age
"Bosses of the Senate" cartoon, 35
corporate monopolies, 34–35
defined, 29
laissez-faire capitalism, 29–30
liberalism, 30
origin of term, 28–29
patronage system, 35–36
Social Darwinism, 30, 32, 34
transportation system, 29
Gilded Age 2.0
Amazon, 60–61
Apple, 60–61
Bill Gates, 60
corporate lobbying and political contri-
butions, 61–63
Elon Musk, 60
Facebook (Meta), 60–61
Google, 60–61
Jeff Bezos, 60–61
Mark Zuckerberg, 60
Microsoft, 60–61
parallels to first Gilded Age, 60–61
Steve Jobs, 60
wealth gap, 61
Gilded Age, The (Twain and Warner), 28
Glass-Steagall Act of 1933, 55, 56–57, 68
God, exclusion from public life
effect on moral values, 21–22
Friedrich Nietzsche, 21–22
Karl Marx, 20–21
methodical doubt, 20
Scientific Revolution, 20–21
Sigmund Freud, 21
gold, 119
Goodbudget app, 180
Google, 47, 60–61
Google Effect, 211
Google Mind phenomenon, xix
Dunning-Kruger Effect, 210–11
Edelman Trust Barometer, 211–12
Google Effect, 211
memory and, 210–11
overview, 209–10
value of financial advisor, 213–17
Why Bother Effect, 212
government bailouts, 40, 70–71
Gramm-Leach-Bliley Act of 1999, 68

ABOUT THE AUTHOR

CINDY COUYOUMJIAN is the founder of Cinergy Financial. It is her fervent belief that financial literacy is a moral imperative. She has dedicated her professional life to helping people understand the constantly evolving political, economic, and financial landscape that can potentially impact their capacity for achieving wealth, prosperity, and retirement security.

With 37 years of industry experience, she holds eight securities licenses (a series 63, 6, 65, 7, 22, 24, 31, and 26) and a California Insurance License, #0719038.

In 2021 she authored her first book, *Redefining Financial Literacy*, and it achieved the coveted national best-seller list on *The Wall Street Journal*. The following year she released her second book, *The Rise of Women and Wealth*, which landed her on the prestigious *USA Today* national best-seller list, as well as *The Wall Street Journal* and Amazon best-seller lists for the financial services industry.

In her third book, *The Silent Retirement Crisis*, Cindy explores how our broken economic system impacts millions of Americans who feel an acute sense of retirement uncertainty. This book, which represents years of rigorous study and research, is a clarion call to action. Americans need to understand there is a paradigm shift in how we plan and prepare for our retirement.

Cindy's next book will examine the seminal concept of prosperity and how we as Americans have moved away from our moral obligation to engage in the kind of collective prosperity that has set us apart from every other nation on earth.

Cindy has become not only a leader in the financial industry but also an innovator of an investment methodology whose aim is to keep up with the ever-changing times. She manages more than $300,000,000 in assets. Cindy ranked number two among her peers within her broker dealer Independent Financial Group in 2022.

In 2022 Cindy won the Bronze "Stevie Awards" in two categories: Woman of the Year in Accounting and Finance, and Female Thought Leader of the Year in Business. She was also a finalist for the Women of Inspiration Award in The Universal Women's Network. Also in 2022 Cindy was recognized as a nominee in *The Orange County Business Journal* in two categories: The Distinguished Leaders of Influence in Wealth Management and Women in Business. In 2023, Cindy received the *Los Angeles Times* Business to Business Visionary of the Year Award.

Her dedication and mission to empower with facts, not fear, has been promoted and heard through her appearances on NBC, CBS, and FOX 40, as a brand contributor with a *Forbes* article in 2020, and through talk radio AM870 and 790 KABC. Beginning in 2023, Cindy will have her own bi-monthly television program in Los Angeles on NBC, CBS, and ABC.

Her dedication and commitment are unwavering as she continues to educate and guide her clients toward their tailored financial goals and objectives.

*There is no assurance that any strategy will achieve its objectives.
The Financial Advisors at Cinergy Financial offer securities and advisory services through Independent Financial Group, LLC (IFG), a Registered Investment Advisor. Member FINRA/SIPC. Cinergy Financial and IFG are unaffiliated entities. Content provided for information & education only.*